Books By Tahir Shah

Travel
Trail of Feathers
Travels With Myself
Beyond the Devil's Teeth
In Search of King Solomon's Mines
House of the Tiger King
In Arabian Nights
The Caliph's House
Sorcerer's Apprentice
Journey Through Namibia

Novels
Jinn Hunter: Book One – The Prism
Jinn Hunter: Book Two – The Jinnslayer
Jinn Hunter: Book Three – The Perplexity
Hannibal Fogg and the Supreme Secret of Man
Casablanca Blues
Eye Spy
Godman
Paris Syndrome
Timbuctoo

Nasrudin
Travels With Nasrudin
The Misadventures of the Mystifying Nasrudin
The Peregrinations of the Perplexing Nasrudin
The Voyages and Vicissitudes of Nasrudin
Nasrudin in the Land of Fools

Teaching Stories
The Arabian Nights Adventures
Scorpion Soup
Tales Told to a Melon
The Afghan Notebook
Daydreams of an Octopus & Other Stories
The Caravanserai Stories
Ghoul Brothers
Hourglass
Imaginist
Jinn's Treasure
Jinnlore
Mellified Man
Skeleton Island
Wellspring
When the Sun Forgot to Rise
Outrunning the Reaper
The Cap of Invisibility
On Backgammon Time
The Wondrous Seed
The Paradise Tree
Mouse House
The Hoopoe's Flight
The Old Wind
A Treasury of Tales
The Tale of Double Six
The Forgotten Game
King of the Jinns
The Destiny Ring
Changing the World

Cat, Mouse
Frogland
Mittle-Mittle
Capilongo
The Princess of Zilzilam
The Singing Serpents
The Tale of the Rusty Nail
The Unicorn's Tear
The Clockmaker Who Travelled Through Time
The Fish's Dream
The Man Whose Arms Grew Branches
The Most Foolish of Men
The Shop That Sold Truth
Qwerty
Renaissance
The Man With the Tiger's Head
The Kingdom of Blink
The Wisdom of Celestine
Dream Soup
The Skeleton Factory
An Unexpected Gift
The Problem Exchange
The Pharaoh Code
The Monkey Puzzle Club
Liquid Time
Cat Dog, Dog Cat
Princess Pickle's Laugh

Miscellaneous
The Reason to Write
The Reason to Write Workbook: Comprehensive
The Reason to Write Workbook: Fantasy
The Reason to Write Workbook: Features
The Reason to Write Workbook: Fiction
The Reason to Write Workbook: Historical Fiction
The Reason to Write Workbook: Teaching Stories
The Reason to Write Workbook: Travel
The Reason to Write Workbook: Travel Writing
Zigzag Think
Being Myself

Research
Cultural Research
The Middle East Bedside Book
Three Essays

Anthologies
The Anthologies: Africa
The Anthologies: Ceremony
The Anthologies: Childhood
The Anthologies: City
The Anthologies: Danger
The Anthologies: East
The Anthologies: Expedition
The Anthologies: Frontier
The Anthologies: Hinterland
The Anthologies: India
The Anthologies: Jinns

The Anthologies: Jungle
The Anthologies: Magic
The Anthologies: Morocco
The Anthologies: Nasrudin
The Anthologies: People
The Anthologies: Quest
The Anthologies: South
The Anthologies: Taboo
The Anthologies: Teaching Stories
The Clockmaker's Box
The Tahir Shah Fiction Reader
The Tahir Shah Travel Reader

Edited by
Congress With a Crocodile
A Son of a Son, Volume I
A Son of a Son, Volume II

Screenplays
Casablanca Blues: The Screenplay
Timbuctoo: The Screenplay

THE REASON TO WRITE

An Author's Masterclass

TAHIR SHAH

THE REASON TO WRITE

An Author's Masterclass

TAHIR SHAH

SECRETUM MUNDI PUBLISHING
MMXX

Secretum Mundi Publishing Ltd
124 City Road
London
England
EC1V 2NX
United Kingdom

www.secretum-mundi.com
info@secretum-mundi.com

First published by Secretum Mundi Publishing Ltd, 2020

THE REASON TO WRITE

© TAHIR SHAH

Tahir Shah asserts the right to be identified as the Author of the Work in accordance with the Copyright, Designs and Patents Act 1988.
A CIP catalogue record for this title is available from the British Library.

Visit the author's website at: www.tahirshah.com

VERSION 25042023

ISBN 978-1-912383-52-8

All rights reserved. No part of this publication may be reproduced, stored in a retrieval system, or transmitted, in any form or by any means, electronic, mechanical, photocopying, recording or otherwise, without the prior written permission of the publisher.

This book is sold subject to the condition that it shall not, by way of trade or otherwise, be lent, re-sold, hired out or otherwise circulated without the publisher's prior consent in any form of binding or cover other than that in which it is published and without a similar condition including this condition being imposed on the subsequent purchaser.

*This book is for all the people who have ever
held me back or pushed me down.
You thought you were weakening me,
but you only made me stronger.
I owe you everything.*

*And it is for the one person who has believed in me –
My dear friend Agustin.*

As a writer, I am a dreamer.
And as a dreamer, I view the world differently
from those around me.
Some people say I'm blinkered to reality,
to which I reply:
It's dreamers like me whose eyes
are open widest of all.

And it does no harm to repeat, as often as you can, 'Without me the literary industry would not exist: the publishers, the agents, the sub-agents, the sub-sub-agents, the accountants, the libel lawyers, the departments of literature, the professors, the theses, the books of criticism, the reviewers, the book pages – all this vast and proliferating edifice is because of this small, patronized, put-down and underpaid person.'

Doris Lessing

Contents

PART I – SALINGER BRIGADE

The Magic Zone	3
Back to Front	5
The Quiet American	10
True-to-Oneself Creativity	14
First Things First	20
The Way of the Writer	24
The Teaching People	30
Foraging	35
The Bookcase	41
Not For Dummies	43
The Mind Game	47
Cloud Faces	52
Bricklaying	57
The Originality Matrix	60
Inked In	69

PART II – JOURNEY

Announcement I	87
Shoebox	88
Doris	96
The Wowing	112
Mo	123
Extermination	136
Way of the Crossbow	140
Weaving Cloth	156
The Wooing	164
William Watkins	174
The Food Chain	178
Trojan Horse	191
Roast Suckling Pig	199
The Curse of Sloth	209

Jinn	214
Internal Wiring	219
Sizzle	229
Samplers	238
Literary Leper	243
Burton	258
Perfection	275
Miracles	281
Hannibal Fogg	285
The Shelf of Wretched Reads	288
Gone Insane	301
Jinn Hunter	305
Full Circle	310

PART III – DETAILS

Announcement II	317
Beginnings	318
Samples	318
Fights	319
Dialogue	319
Description	321
Historical	322
Inspiration	323
Humour	323
Harnessing	324
Lists	326
Brown Water	327
First Sentences	327
Belief	329
Word Counts	330
Backups	332
Momentum	333
Introductions	333
Appendices	334

Glossaries	335
Collecting Words	335
Kubrick	336
Taking Notes	337
Anthologies	338
Wikipedia Vortex	339
Editing	340
Correcting	340
Daily Read	341
Listening	341
eBooks	342
Americanization	342
Motivation	343
Chair	343
Confidence	344
When You Know	344
Open Sesame!	345
Obelix Syndrome	346
Literary Identity	347
Doing What Works	349
In Character	349
Collaborations	350
Ongoing Tweaks	351
Originality	351
Payoffs	352
Alternation	353
Descriptive Detail	353
Peanuts	354
Brain Freeze	355
Sleep	355
Peaks, Troughs	357
The Ordinary	357
Dyslexia	358
Spell Check	359

Grammar Check	359
Dry Stone Wall	360
Work in Progress	361
Real Readers	362
Publicity Quotes	363
Writing Routines	365
Procrastination	366
Gaps	367
Typing	368
Breaking the Back	369
Questioning	370
Experimenting	371
Writer's Block	371
All Talk	372
First Book	372
Starting Afresh	373
Vocabulary Variety	374
Ticking Over	375
The Tingle	376
Thinking Big	376
Reading Aloud	377
Dedications	378
Whispering	378
Book Launches	379
Signings	379
Festivals	380
Pipeline	380
Beating Oneself Up	381
Letters	381
Gut-think	382
Clatter	383
Gunpoint	383
Steenbeck	385
Parking a Project	386

Commitment	387
Dialogue	388
Learning the Ropes	388
Priming	389
Loving Writing	390
Literary Seeds	391
Contracts	391
Foreign Rights	393
Film Rights and Options	394
Reviews	394
Dictating	395
Agents	396
Blithering Idiots	397
Literary Prizes	398
Secret of Writing	399
Cologne	400
Grammar	401
Chess	402
No Clones	402
Value of Words	403
Reading, Writing	403
Publishing Runes	404
Tweaking	405
Finishing Up	407

PART IV – DIRECT PUBLISHING

Promised Land	411
The New Model	415
First Draft	417
Cleaning	420
Editing	424
Proofreading	428
Typesetting	430
Typeset Proofing	435

Covers	437
Print-on-Demand	439
Pricing	440
Bound Proofs	441
Crowdfunding	443
Special Editions	447
Ultimate Control	449
Direct Publishing Resources	455
Tribal Publishing	456

PART V – WRITERS ON WRITING

Announcement III	461
Three Tips	462
Sir Michael Palin	462
Esther Freud	462
Paul Theroux	463
Justin Marozzi	463
Barnaby Rogerson	464
Dame Marina Warner	465
Nigel Cawthorne	466
Steven Nightingale	466
Nigel Hinton	467
Tim Mackintosh-Smith	468
Jane Johnson	470
Pico Iyer	471
Jason Webster	473
Simon Singh	473
Mark Salzman	473
Lisa Alther	477
Hugh Thomson	479
Robert Twigger	479
Jason Elliot	480
Rory MacLean	481
Kevin Crossley-Holland	482

Beatrix Mannel	482
John-Paul Flintoff	485
Dr James Lovelock	486
Tony Hiss	487
The Great and the Good	489
A Doris Lessing Afterword	493

PART VI – SAMPLES

Announcement IV	503
The Entrance	504
Desperation	516
A Meeting	519
Light vs Dark	526
Interleaving	533
Listing	545
Short, Sharp	548
The Unexpected	550
Grandeur	552
Stories Within Stories	562
Descriptions	574
Letters	581
Dialogue	584
Depth	586
Reusing Material	591
Endings	603
Book Proposals	607
Notes	640
Hannibal Fogg and the Supreme Secret of Man	641
Godman	676

PART I

SALINGER BRIGADE

The Magic Zone

I WAS BORN into a family of writers.

My father, aunt, both grandfathers, grandmother, sisters, and me – each one of us has walked the same path. A path that has at times reduced us to madness, just as it's sustained us with triumphant success.

Since the earliest days of childhood, I was introduced to the world through an author's eyes. Almost everything ever explained to me was explained from a writer's point of view – as if I were pitted against those who were not in the know.

Dozens of my parents' friends were writers, too – some the most successful literary names of their age – among them J. D. Salinger, Doris Lessing, and Robert Graves. Convening at our home in the lush English countryside, they would listen to my father, the author and thinker Idries Shah, taking more than what was merely spoken.

Looking back, it was as though they were members of a secret fellowship, one that I myself was eventually destined to join.

When I close my eyes and think back to my childhood, the overriding memory is not a sight, a smell, or even a taste.

But a sound.

The sound of a manual typewriter clattering away downstairs in my father's study.

Clack! Clack! Clack! Clack!

Like a knight in shining armour doing battle with a dragon, it was a tumultuous and intoxicating riot of noise. The clatter of typewriter keys was far more than the sound of an author tapping out books.

It was the musical score to my youth.

On the rare occasions the clatter stopped, I'd freeze, swallow hard with fear, and tiptoe downstairs to see what was wrong. My father would be hunched over his old Triumph machine, a fist of pages held up to his face.

Wincing, wheezing, his head framed in cigar smoke curls, he'd be lost in an enchanted realm – a state of mind.

I've come to know it as 'The Magic Zone'.

Back to Front

My father once gave a lecture at an Ivy League university in New England.

Listening to a recording of it, I can picture the scene perfectly. When he'd been introduced, he informed the students he was going to talk for an hour, just as he'd been asked to do. Then, smiling wryly, he said:

'But first I am going to let you into a little secret. I'm probably not supposed to tell you this, but I will anyway, because it's an example of the way I regard the world and everything in it.'

The students glanced up in genuine interest.

'Now that I have your attention,' my father went on, 'I'll tell you the secret... Although I'm scheduled to talk to you for an hour, I could do the talk in three and a half minutes. I could even do it in two minutes, if you listened hard. But I'm not going to – even though I'd probably be the most popular visiting professor ever to lecture here. The reason is because the Occidental society in which we live confuses container with content. If I were to say everything I had to deliver in three and a half minutes, the faculty which is covering my fee would regard me as a fraudster.'

As promised, my father went on to deliver the entire lecture, and was applauded long and hard at the end. The central theme – of 'Container and Content' – shaped the university lectures he delivered all over the world, as well as many of his books, most notably *The Book of the Book*.

'Container and Content' is an idea on which I myself was weaned.

In all my time hunting for examples of back-to-front thinking, one looms larger to me than any other. Indeed, in the same way my father might have delivered his lecture in a couple of minutes, I could pass on the entire meat of this book in a single line.

But I'm not going to, even though it would save on paper, and would give you more time to lavish on eating ice cream, lying on the beach, or provide extra hours to spend on your own writing.

Rather than condensing my material to a line, I'll shorten it to the bare bones of what it's all about:

There are all kinds of writers out there, writing all kinds of work.

My key point centres around the way things are, and the way things ought to be.

They're quite different – like two paths that once ran as one, before forking sharply away in different directions. My mission is to get the paths back to how they were supposed to be – running together like a lovely towpath following the twists and turns of a river... a towpath that did service to the writers first, and to everyone else second.

To understand what I'm saying, I must take you back to how the great scheme of things were shaped before they went off-kilter. So please bear with me and allow me a little poetic licence.

In 'the olden times' (as my kids used to call anything that happened a long time ago), there weren't many publishers as we know them today. Most of the time an author would write a book, then give it to a printer who would typeset it by hand, print it, and knock it back to the writer, who would go out and sell it to his chums.

Little by little the system took off.

The authors realized they could write a lot more if they didn't have to spend so much time selling their work. So they gave it to guys hanging around on street corners to sell on their behalf.

Time passed, and the street hawkers made money from peddling the writers' fresh work. They got themselves kiosks, and eventually fully fledged bookshops. Even though back then books weren't books as we know them. You see, until the 1830s a book was sold in its raw state – without covers as we have them today. The posh people (who were buying most of the books) didn't want covers anyway. They would send anything they bought to their binder to have it bound in the uniform livery of their private library.

Years dragged on.

The writers wrote, the booksellers sold, and all was generally good. By now some booksellers were doing so well that they branched out. Instead of just selling printed work given to them by writers, they started representing them, too. Note: it was the booksellers who did the branching out and not the printers – which surely would have made more sense.

A little further along, the bookseller-publishers were doing so well from the arrangement, they started to look for gaps in the market so they could clean up all the more. They grabbed hold of writers whose work was well received, and offered them cold hard cash in return for being locked into publishing contracts.

If I could go back to any time in history, it would be that moment.

The moment the first greedy, self-important publisher got an ingenuous author to sign away his or her rights and – more importantly – to sign away their control.

As you can imagine from my tone, my wish to time-travel was so I could break up the meeting, rip the contract into confetti, and hightail it out of there with the writer.

But I can't travel back in time, so we're stuck with a reality path that became a normality path – the path on which writers are told what to write by publishers, or at least how to write it. I know there are exceptions, and not all publishers are ghouls, but the vast majority of them are and always have been.

Of course they are.

Why?

Because the existing model of publishing is like the

standard red-light districts I've seen throughout my travels. A sordid underworld of brothels, hustlers, and pimps. I've seen pimps wearing some very flash outfits and sporting plenty of gold, but they're still pimps, just as the brothels are always brothels, despite what the sign says.

In the same way, I've known publishers who have crème de la crème offices, and who lay on lavish lunches with foie gras and champagne, but that doesn't make them any less pimpy than they are.

The bad news: Things are back to front, because they got flipped way back when.

The good news: Everything's going to be just fine.

'*Really?*' I hear you asking.

YES! YES! YES!

I can see you hovering over the page, eager to know how I can be so sure. The answer is a single word:

TECHNOLOGY

In the same way technology got authors into a bind in the first place, it's going to free them from the shackles of bondage.

Stay with me and I'll explain how and why.

The Quiet American

I HAVE A lot to say about writers and writing, about agents and publishers, about the way it is, and the way it could and should be.

As anyone who's had the misfortune of sitting next to me at a dinner party will know, I can rant on for hours, venting strong views like scalding jets shot out from a geyser. I suspect my fellow dinner guests imagine my opinions were dreamt up that very day. But they weren't. Like a baton passed on from one generation to the next, the way I understand authorship was laid down over an entire century.

One of my earliest memories is being six years old, sent from the playroom down to one of the formal salons at our home in the English countryside, Langton House. The Durbar was the former billiard room, dating to the time when Robert Baden-Powell – founder of the Boy Scouts – grew up there just like I did.

Sweeping in, dressed in a flowing 1970s kaftan, my mother ordered me to be on 'Best Behaviour', a phrase that meant sitting up ramrod straight and speaking only when spoken to. To me, Best Behaviour meant being trussed up in a tight Oriental costume and having my hair brushed very roughly.

But most of all, it meant someone important was about to arrive.

On that day when I was six, an American gentleman

strolled in through the front door.

I remember him more for what he was not than what he was. He was not loud, brash, or ostentatious, like the other Best Behaviour guests. Rather, he was exceedingly soft-spoken, gentle, and kind. When he left, my father exclaimed he was 'a truly great man'.

I asked who he was.

'He's a writer.'

'What is his name?'

'Mr Salinger.'

'Does he write children's books?' I asked.

'He writes for everyone,' my father replied. 'At the same time, he writes for himself.'

'Why does he write?'

My father considered the question, his brow furrowing as he did so.

'Mr Salinger writes because he *must* write,' he said. 'He can't help it... he can't stop.'

'Baba, what would happen if Mr Salinger stopped writing?' I asked.

'If J. D. Salinger stopped writing, he'd turn to stone,' my father said.

Years passed, and I often thought back to the Best Behaviour day when J. D. Salinger dropped in.

I remembered his politeness and the way he made me laugh. But most of all I remembered my father's observation – that Salinger was a writer who had to write, otherwise he'd turn to stone.

A child's mind approaches ideas in a back-to-front way.

In my estimation, it's the default setting in us all – the way we are preset to perceive information and ideas. On that day in the Durbar room, I latched onto the notion of someone writing because they had no choice. The idea of writing through a kind of self-induced therapeutic mania, a mindset that can't be changed because it's pre-programmed. Framed in the mind of a six-year-old I thought my father had meant what he had said – that Salinger would actually turn to stone if he stopped writing.

But the details of my understanding were unimportant, so much as what Salinger stood for in my world.

Whenever encountering other writers – either as a child or in adult life – I've tried to evaluate if they are cut from the same cloth as Salinger. Are they writing because they must write, or for other reasons?

This book has been written for the Salinger Brigade, and *not* for the faux, would-be, or wannabe writers who are curiously amused by the notion of writing. They're the ones who tell you dreamily, 'Would so love to write a book one day.' Most especially though, it's not written for the droves of people who think writing is a way to get themselves attention. Quite the opposite. I am searching for the secret army of manic, restless, roaming, roving souls who want nothing more than to be alone with a blank page and their thoughts.

There are hundreds of books available devoted to the business of authorship, specific genres, and areas of interest. Many of them are excellent in the information they pass on. But as far as I know, none are addressed to those of us who regard writing as nothing short of an obsession – something in the bone marrow, in the heart, and in every single cell.

Salinger Brigade writers tend to exhibit unifying traits:
- They regard the production of written work with reverence.
- They write because they MUST.
- They're less interested in what they have created as in the creation process itself.
- They don't write for the glory, so much as to satisfy an inner need.
- They are uninterested in discussing writing for the sake of it.

If this list proves you are in the Salinger Brigade, please read on. But if you don't recognize yourself from the description, please close this book and pass it on to someone else – even if you have to leave it on a park bench for a random stranger to find.

True-to-Oneself Creativity

As a paid-up member of the Salinger Brigade myself, I write because I have to, and for no other reason except to please myself through the art of creativity.

Sure, I'd love to make zillions and retire to a mansion in the Hollywood Hills, or the Côte d'Azur. Likewise, it would be amusing to win a Nobel Prize in Literature, and to be slapped on the back by the great and the good of the literati set.

But all that stuff – the money and the fame – is foam on the ocean.

Getting work down as I want it to be, then released in the same state as I created and shaped it, is my main interest. The last thing I want is for some schmuck publisher in a fancy office to chop my work around so they can sell more copies.

This next thing I'm about to say isn't going to go down well. It never does. I say it because I mean it in a deep-down way:

I don't care about selling books. I care about writing the books the way I want them to be.

If the work I put out sells – Hoorah! If it doesn't, I feel proud that on my gravestone they can inscribe the following epitaph:

HERE LIES A MAN TRUE TO HIS CRAFT

Before the path of the writer got side-tracked by

publishers, creative people spent their time working on projects that pleased them. If you're yelling out, 'Yeah, but all kinds of people, including the likes of Leonardo da Vinci and Shakespeare, had patrons!' – you'd be right.

But patrons aren't publishers.

Back in the day, before creatives were hijacked, they'd sweat and toil over work that fulfilled them, and then they'd try and sell it. It was the model I've already described. Musicians, painters and writers were all in the same boat in this regard. They composed, painted, and wrote – because, if they didn't, they'd turn to stone.

The model was important for a couple of key reasons.

First, it got creative people pushing the boundaries of their own creativity. They experimented – whether it be with musical notes, with colours, or words. Even more importantly, they had control over the individual parameters of their work.

On nights when I cannot sleep, I flip open my laptop and trawl Wikipedia for the lives of those who were celebrated only after their departure – people like Bach, Van Gogh, and Emily Dickinson. What strikes me about them is that we celebrate their achievements because they're untainted.

Their work stayed on the track of their choosing, because they didn't succumb to the pressure of meddlers. At the time people may have thought they were rotten, but the fact they didn't sell out means what they left behind is all the more remarkable.

My view on all this is that the 'Land of True-to-Oneself Creativity' is a realm we need to steer back to. Only then will writers, artists, musicians, and other creative people out there be able to produce the work they want to produce with pride.

In order to get there, key things must change. Creative people must:
- Remember they are free.
- Believe in themselves.
- Shun dying models of convention.
- Move briskly forward to the horizon.

It's at this point I have to come clean.

I'm as guilty as anyone else for selling out.

I've allowed books to be chopped up by editors who didn't know diddly about how to write or tell a story. The one book of mine that was hacked about to the point of no return was *In Search of King Solomon's Mines* – a travel book about my zigzagging journey through Ethiopia, on the trail of the biblical land of 'Ophir'.

I remember the day the edited manuscript came back to me. It was covered – and I mean COVERED – in the editor's red ink. The feeling was like having had a teacher scrawl all over your work, with those dreaded words 'See Me' at the end of it.

Looking back, I should have dug in my heels and refused to make changes that turned it from my book into my editor's one. But, being a relatively young writer, and one frequently reminded that I'd signed a contract, I didn't dare speak out.

The reason I'm admitting my own shortcomings in staying on course is to make a point: in writing – as in almost everything else – it's never too late to change tack. I signed with the publisher of my Ethiopian book because I was lured by a wall of love they sent my way. A wall of love which included a massive bouquet of flowers when my daughter was born, and a couple of especially heavy lunches in Mayfair.

The existing model – the one that's on its way out – is constructed on one thing and one thing alone:

Cold hard cash.

Namely, how much cold hard cash the agent and the publisher can make from your work. That's all they're interested in, although I swear I can hear at least a dozen publishers bawling: 'You're oh-so-wrong!'

I wish I were.

But I'm not.

Believe me, I enjoy the thrill of money as much as the next guy. That said, the money model leads to distortions. It's rather like (apologies in advance for seeding this in your head) one of those factory-bred chickens destined for fast food chains with no beaks or chins... or however they are. Books written for the guys in sharp suits and slicked-down hair are like chickens raised for the fast-food trade.

They're knocked about, or shaped from the ground

up, so as to sell as many as possible. The prevailing model is the one in which the big book business is like the fast food industry. Just as fast food chains don't give a damn how unhealthy their burgers are, publishers package books alluringly, pile them high, and sell them cheap.

Modern publishing is about marketing and about numbers. It's not about authors, and is certainly not about good writing or love.

I closed my eyes for a moment just now and was transported back to a hillside in Burgundy, near the little village there, where my mother spent the last years of her life.

The region is celebrated for its wine.

One of the most beautiful things I've ever seen, arriving on a snowbound night, were the hillsides glowing with lanterns – placed by the farmers so as to stop their beloved vines from freezing.

Closing my eyes as I just did, I see a grizzled old vintner called Monsieur Rollec tending his vines. Pausing, he weighs a bunch of plump grapes in his hand and says:

'I've just been offered a fortune to sell my vineyards to a foreign buyer with wine estates all over the world.'

'Are you going to sell?'

Monsieur Rollec shakes his head angrily.

'Of course not!'

'Why not?'

'I make wine because it fulfils me rather than to make money.'

The elderly Burgundian vintner, whose skin is as gnarled as his vines, loves his grapes in the same way I love words. His appreciation for the wine he makes is the same as the admiration I hold for creating written work.

For Monsieur Rollec, making wine is a passion – the same passion that any member of the Salinger Brigade has for their craft.

First Things First

THE FIRST THING to understand is that writing is a craft – just as much as being a cabinet-maker or a portrait painter... or even a wine-maker like Monsieur Rollec.

In my opinion, you can teach someone good grammar, passable delivery, and all kinds of other elements, but it's impossible to transplant the gland that produces magic dust if it's not there at the start. If you read the previous pages, and have kept on going, I'm assuming you're a member of the 'Salinger Brigade', and that you know what it feels like when you write something with a sprinkling of magic dust.

Magic dust doesn't have to be held in reserve for books and highbrow work. You can sprinkle it in emails, blogs, even in a quick text message to a friend. The point is that you know when you've scattered it, because you get a warm glow in your back – like the intoxicating sensation of true love.

The first thing is to sit down with a blank sheet of paper, or a white screen, close your eyes tight, and slip into an enchanted realm of fantasy, or wherever you draw your inspiration. Conjure your senses to create, like a sorcerer preparing to transmute lead into gold.

Write a single line of prose about anything: a knight in shining armour, a windswept landscape, a woman sitting in the window of a diner, her mind awash with dreams.

Look at the line.
Tweak it.
Tweak it more.
Drink it in.
Gargle with it.
Read it twenty times from different angles. Tweak some more. Then, if you've fashioned something from nothing, you should get the sprinkling of magic dust and the warm glow in your back – the sense of ultimate creation, like the rush of endorphins in the gym.
Appreciate the euphoria.
Cherish it.
Enthuse about it.
Remember, you created it from nothing.
Being an author is a rollercoaster ride, but you already know that if you're in the Salinger Brigade. The highs are spectacular, just as the lows are monstrous. The hardest thing of all is getting on track and staying on track.
Self-doubt is the scourge of anyone with real talent.
I frequently observe how people with no talent at all have no self-doubt either – which leads me to conclude that talent and doubt go hand in hand.
Writing is about rituals – more on those later.
Whenever I doubt myself, I have a ritual ready to click me back on track. It's not always the same one – different moods and circumstances call for different strategies.
Sometimes I'll find myself sitting at my desk, gloomy

as hell. Re-reading a sentence, I'll plunge my head in my hands, moaning like a wounded animal on the savannah. Or, I'll read something by another author and consider packing it all in because their work is so tantalizing.

On occasions when I'm downcast and self-doubting, I'll indulge myself in writing a mind-blowing opening sentence or paragraph – the kind of thing that reminds you that you're King (or Queen) of the World. If I am feeling chatty, I'll write a letter or email – or a clutch of them. I hate to admit it, but I tend to write the same message over and over, sending different drafts to friends and acquaintances, the most polished version going to someone I cherish very greatly indeed.

Sometimes I'm not downbeat because of self-doubt, but because life has kicked me in the head for other reasons. When that happens, I have a special series of rituals. My favourite may sound nuts, but try it if you doubt me...

Go into the bathroom and turn on the lights so that it's as bright as possible. Clear everything from the washbasin, get a cleaning spray and a roll of kitchen paper. Observe the basin from different angles – not in a passing way, but as though your life depends on it. Make note of the grime lurking in the overflow, or around the plug-hole. Look at the taps, and the limescale that may well be caking them.

Summoning every iota of anticipated delight, clean the washbasin like you've never cleaned it before. If done properly it ought to take about five minutes and should leave you glowing, and with a fabulously clean basin.

With your state of mind buoyed and bolstered, make a beeline for your desk and get back into the groove.

The Way of the Writer

As I SAID, writing is a craft, and as such it's something that needs to be honed.

The Salinger Brigade is born with an innate skill, but it's often not the skill outsiders imagine it to be. Equally, a successful writer has to overcome barriers, develop specific sub-skills, and perfect their narrative voice. These are all immense subjects, and what's right for one author will be wrong for another.

When I look back at books I published at the start of the journey, I blush beetroot red. I made every imaginable mistake. The greatest one of all was trying too hard to:

- Impress readers with my grand vocabulary and a knowledge of rare subjects.
- Give characters layers which weren't necessary.
- Frame the story in a way that was too complicated.

The result was uneven work – like a suit that fitted well in some places but not in others. With time, I have learned to tell the story in the simplest way possible, resisting the urge to heap on layers of complexity.

It reminds me of something I witnessed thirty years ago last summer.

I was living in Bombay, later rechristened Mumbai, and had befriended an American musician called Wood. While the others from his generation were all copying the Rolling Stones, Wood travelled to India, by way of

West Africa, and studied sitar music under the greatest Indian musician alive.

One evening, he invited me to hear his teacher play.

Getting my hands on an invitation was a very big deal as the master was so highly regarded. I sat in the front row of the auditorium, old-fashioned ceiling fans whirring listlessly round. Wood's teacher came on, performed a series of elementary pieces to rapturous applause, and walked off.

When he'd left the stage, I asked Wood why the maestro hadn't thought to challenge himself with more complex displays of his skill. The American turned to me. Emerald-green eyes glinting, he replied:

'When you're a true master there's no need to prove yourself. Instead, he demonstrated perfection in simplicity.'

I've always remembered that lesson, and have used it in my writing journey. With experience, an author learns that it's about what they leave out as much as what they put in.

Likewise, Picasso's *Dove of Peace* was supposedly drawn on a restaurant napkin for a wag who wanted to buy a masterpiece. When the client pointed out the sketch had been executed in seconds, the artist explained how in actual fact it had taken him forty years.

Appreciating simplicity is the Way of the Writer.

Avoid developing an overly convoluted style and

you'll be able to hone the craft faster, and set yourself on a path to publishing all the sooner. By pursuing that route you can make forays into other genres and styles, and begin amassing a body of work in next to no time.

Those born with the prerequisites of the Salinger Brigade are rather like foals yearning to be racehorses. Fast, elegant, and enthusiastic, they have the predisposing characteristics regarded as requirements. But years of training will be needed at the stud before they can win medals.

Learning how to write is similar, but not the same.

I'm outspoken on honing the craft, and so am likely to offend at least half the people reading this. I've never studied writing, although I've known all kinds of people who have. Looking back at my own journey, five elements honed my work, and I will consider them in the pages that follow:

- Surrounding myself with mentors and soaking myself in their advice.
- Writing a lot of work so part of my style honed itself.
- Doing masses of journalism, which taught me technicalities.
- Striving to be original.
- Writing for myself.

Almost everyone I encounter, or who contacts me on social media at any rate, gushes at how they've been taking courses in creative writing. When I hear this, I tend to recoil. This is where I am sure to offend. The reason for my displeasure is complicated but, for now, I'll answer like this:

In my life-long preoccupation with originality, the thing that scores highly on my TCS (Toe-Curling Scale) is when potential authors take courses and get shaped as nice little clones of one another. Don't get me wrong – creative writing courses have uses. In my opinion they are not for the Salinger Brigade – but rather for recreational writers who aren't driven by a wellspring of natural mania.

The other day, while giving a lecture in Boston, I met a clean-cut young man from Wisconsin. He revealed he'd spent a fortune on creative writing courses. When I asked what he'd learnt, he listed a long inventory of material, such as:

- What publishers' editors want and don't want.
- What words to never use and which ones to rely on.
- How to structure a novel and what to avoid.
- Plots to keep away from and those to use.

The clean-cut young writer stuck out from the crowd because he was apparently touched with the mania – the kind producing magic dust. I saw the glint in his eyes when he approached the table where I was signing books. His raw need to write impressed me as greatly as the creative writing nonsense he'd spewed had irritated me.

It's at this point I feel I have to stand on an upturned

soapbox, grab a megaphone, and yell something really loud.

Here goes, and apologies in advance for deafening you:

BE ORIGINAL!

This is a point I'll come back to repeatedly, so there'll be no hope of forgetting it. Originality is the reason every celebrated writer in human history is fêted. Hell, it's the reason why anyone you've ever heard of who's done anything BIG has been both remembered and championed.

William Shakespeare, Robert Byron and Virginia Woolf, J. K. Rowling, Victor Hugo and Cervantes; James Joyce, Charles Dickens, Doris Lessing, and J. D. Salinger – we go on and on about them all because of what they did to break the mould as much as the quality of their work.

Human society celebrates those who come up with something first, while it encourages the rest of us to follow the flow. This is a key point – one I've never understood. The way I see it, the sure-fire route to inspired genius and creativity is to reward people for thinking differently, and not for thinking the same.

The rank-and-file society is supposed to adore, and be delighted by, a creative elite... an elite chosen by a tiny discerning minority of king-makers. Everyone else has to conform to creative standards, otherwise they'll be blackballed for being 'off-piste'.

When the clean-cut young writer in Boston waxed lyrical about how he'd learned in a writing course what editors want and what they don't want, I reeled. It's true there are toe-curling clichés to avoid, but almost everything has a value – even doing the opposite of everything I've suggested so far. I assume something would be off-limits because an editor might consider such a style as being non-commercial. If that's the case, it suggests only overtly commercially viable books have a chance of seeing the light. The Harry Potter series was famously rejected by lots of publishers before being snapped up by Bloomsbury. The rest is history.

As this book will attempt to explain, there's a brave new world out there in which Salinger Brigade authors will rule supreme.

The model is changing, and it's changing fast.

The Teaching People

OVER THE YEARS I've written and published a great deal about my childhood.

In adolescence I tended to believe my early years were a jumbled mishmash of happenstance that made no sense – a span of years unlikely to be of any use in later life. But as I've zigzagged through adulthood, I've found myself drawing long and hard on the events, and the encounters with 'Teaching People'.

Observing them with hindsight, I've come to appreciate how certain people were positioned like clues on a treasure trail. The realm of Teaching People is like one of those expensive Christmas Advent calendars containing chocolates all wrapped up in foil. But unlike the calendars, none of the windows are labelled.

From the time I could walk, I was encouraged to learn from Teaching People – the droves of miraculous oddballs I'd met in the flesh, and those presented at arm's length in stories and books. As time has passed, and as I've made use of Teaching People, I have learned to see it all from the far end of the tunnel.

Some Teaching People passed on one or two choice fragments of information, while others provided a kaleidoscope of wonder. Most of them fell somewhere in the middle.

A few of the Teaching People – the ones I value most greatly – are like a ball of brightly coloured ribbon in a box. The more I tug at the end, the more ribbon comes out for me to use.

My favourite Teaching People are all kept together in my head. They're different coloured ribbons in the same box, the ends poking out. Over the years I got to know them very well indeed – from things they said to me, things they wrote, or a mixture of both. As with anything that boasts a timeline of its own, a relationship with Teaching People is as much about you as a pupil as it is about them.

By that, I mean you have a responsibility to knead the material amassed in the particular mental file, as though it were dough. It's for you to draw out the information useful to your situation and circumstances, break off a chunk, and shape it.

Some of the information I received from Teaching People was in the form of general life lessons. Other bits and pieces were fragments of insight and detail. Yet more were specifically targeted to the business of writing and publishing.

All together the knowhow formed a matrix: the matrix I've come to live and work by.

I sprinkle life lessons here and there as they bubble up, using them as and when they're needed.

For now, here's a taste of something which just flashed into my mind:

One Saturday night forty years ago, an Australian family arrived at Langton House. There were the mother and father, and three small children – each one a younger version of the last, like Russian Matryoshka dolls. Deeply affected by my father's work and desperate to meet him, they had come overland from Australia – an adventure which took them three years.

Five years after the dark autumn night of their arrival, the father, Rob, was giving me a ride up to London in his van. He described the journey from Down Under, up through Indonesia, westwards to India, across Central Asia, Turkey, and Europe.

When he was finished, I asked him what he'd learned on the trip.

By the time the question was posed, we were zigzagging through the labyrinth of south London suburbs. Rob jammed his foot down on the brakes and the battered old van jolted to an uncomfortable stop. Turning to me, he paused for an eternity.

Then, while I wondered if he'd gone mad, he said:

'Never, ever listen to anyone who holds you back.'

Teaching People don't have to be alive to inspire. In fact, there are clear advantages of tapping into their lessons when they're long departed.

One of my greatest mentors, whom I reluctantly share with millions of others, is Sir Richard Francis Burton. The life of the Victorian explorer, writer, and polymath is one of those monumental extravaganzas of impossibility – the kind of thing that made him both a pariah and a hero in his own time. If anyone lived the life lesson passed to me by our overland Australian friend, it was Burton.

An explorer, linguist, swordsman, connoisseur of the remarkable, and delighter in shocking the establishment, he published scores of books on every conceivable theme. The main reason for my admiration for Burton was that he worked on a thousand projects all at once. His biographers describe how he had nine desks in his study, works in progress on each one. Moving from desk to desk, he would add to whichever manuscript took his fancy.

Another reason for my life-long fascination with Burton is that he embarked on a clear path right from the start. It wasn't the path his family or friends would have wished for him. Rather, it was one he mapped out for himself. The path was shaped by an absolute preoccupation with having an interesting life.

At this point, I imagine some people who've read this far will be grinding their back teeth, irritated they're not getting their money's worth on the secrets of writing. If that's the case, please understand something:

WRITING ISN'T JUST ABOUT WRITING
– IT'S ABOUT **EVERYTHING**

The droves of would-be writers (the ones who'll never, ever be members of the Salinger Brigade) who take pointless creative writing classes assume writing is a prim and perfect distillation of the literary arts.

Nothing could be further from the truth.

Writing is about looking and listening, touching, tasting and smelling, about testing and experimenting, researching, and doing the hard grind.

But most of all, writing is about making connections.

Foraging

I WAS LUCKY enough to have a spectrum of Teaching People planted for me by my parents, with others ready and waiting along the way.

Like a pig snuffling out truffles in the forests of Provence, I've spent much of my life ranging through libraries, bookshops, and the Internet, in search of what my children's generation would call 'Inspirators'.

Imagine you've got a nice wicker basket and you're in the same forest in which the pigs are seeking truffles in the magnificent Provençal hinterland. Find yourself a clutch of mentors – the more the merrier. You can collect some you have known personally, and others who – like Sir Richard Burton – are celebrated and long since dead.

A favourite pastime of mine is searching out historical Teaching People who've long been forgotten. So special is my collection of forgotten mentors to me that I almost never speak of them. In doing so now, I'm breaking a spell that's endured for decades.

So here goes...

When I was living in Tokyo almost thirty years ago, half-starving and camped out under the dining table of my friend and fellow author Robert Twigger, I would occasionally visit a private library in the suburbs. The reason for going there was to research my obsession with the native Ainu people of Japan, and the 'wise fool' of their folklore. I adored the library because many of the books were in English, and the stacks were open – which meant I could browse through them all day long.

One afternoon, I was scuttling along a stack, looking for a volume on the Ainu's bear festival, when a pair of books with blood-red spines caught my attention. Written by the mysterious aristocratic adventurer Lewis Strange Wingfield, they were entitled *Wanderings of a Globe-trotter in the Far East*.

From the moment I opened the first volume and began to read, I found myself in a lost realm of wonder. Wingfield dedicated his life to following strands of mystery and intrigue.

As with others in my shrine of Teaching People, he'd completed a frantic cornucopia of exploits that pleased him, and him alone.

Born into a landed Irish family in 1842, Wingfield was fantastically original and equally camp. He was a war correspondent, painter, theatrical set designer, impresario and actor, a surgeon and soldier, an explorer, and the author of more than a dozen astounding works of both fiction and non-fiction.

For thirty years, I've researched Wingfield's life, collected his books, read his private letters, and generally marvelled at him – drawing inspiration from all he accomplished. It seemed we shared obsession with travel, friendship, and with our hatred for publishers.

A favourite letter of Wingfield's includes this:

Forgive my not replying sooner – but I was in the last throes (with accompanied teeth gnashing and outpullings of best hair by handfuls) of my new book, which I have this day duly delivered to [my publisher] the omnivorous but cheating Bentley who will of course rob me as usual. However, that is in the day's work and part and parcel of a wicked world.

Scathing in tone, his entry in *The Dictionary of National Biography* contains a sentence that's often in my mind:

In everything but his friendships Wingfield was capricious and unstable, turning from one pursuit to another, and wearying of everything, except writing, so soon as he had mastered its difficulties.

Laid down layer on layer, the lives of the Teaching People I've known first-hand, and the others I've appreciated distantly through a circuitous route, have formed a kind of soil into which I've planted thoughts and ideas.

Real writers need heroes because the business of literary creation is mirrored by a dark side, a 'psycho zone'.

All the most creative writers I've come across – either knowing them personally or as a reader of their work – have been on the borderline. No surprise in that. In our upside-down configuration of the world, which has strayed far from the default setting of how we ought to be, mania is regarded as BAD, and an even keel is considered to be GOOD.

I'm likely to come over as a nutcase here, and possibly one who's imparting misleading or even dangerous advice. But I don't care. Or, rather, I care so much that I'm going to reel out my thinking full force.

In my opinion, real writers have to descend into the darkness if they want to reach the Magic Zone. The most successful authors I've known personally – especially those with an overtly developed sense of imagination – occupy the Magic Zone ninety-five per cent of the time. They only snap out of it occasionally. They love wallowing there, in a literary equivalent of a muddy hollow for hippos. And, importantly, they know full well leaving the Magic Zone – even for a moment – means they'll have to be calibrated again once they wish to return.

Particular Teaching People don't have to hold all the answers. They can be championed for certain reasons. For instance, I cherish the Argentine writer Jorge Luis Borges for his sense of magic realism, and Bruce Chatwin for fusing fact with fantasy. Our family friend Doris Lessing is special to me for all sorts of reasons, but most of all for a blend of doing whatever she wanted, and for producing a breathtaking amount of work.

Like Doris, my father and grandfather were driven by an insatiable need to create. All three of them worked as though the Devil were on their backs. The more they wrote, the more they wanted to write – like a turbo engine fuelling itself.

Doris once told me you have to write twenty books before you get 'to the higher ground'. By that, I think she meant the plateau above the cliffs, the one most authors never quite reach. My father would talk about the need to have a million words in print before anyone takes you seriously.

My view is that the number of words or books is pretty much insignificant. After all, a book can be a few dozen pages or stretch to many hundreds. Hearing about the methods of other writers is useful, if only because it helps you establish methods of own.

I am naturally drawn to Teaching People with a vast and dizzying back catalogue of work. I find myself reading biographies about them, and poring over their Wikipedia pages – glowing with delight at feats of bone-numbing diligence.

Likewise, I'm enthused by authors who cross genres and break boundaries – testing themselves and their readership as they go.

For anyone with an itching desperation to rush to

Wikipedia for a quick bout of Teaching People Research (don't stress, I know what the craving is like), a handful of names follow.

No apologies are offered that they're all from the Victorian age:

1. Isabella Bird
2. Richard Francis Burton
3. Arthur Conan Doyle
4. George Eliot
5. Elizabeth Gaskell
6. Charles Hamilton
7. Rudyard Kipling
8. Guy de Maupassant
9. Mark Twain
10. Constance Fenimore Woolson

The Bookcase

SIT AT YOUR desk, get comfortable, and close your eyes.

Imagine a really lovely bookcase. The one I see is antique oak, hand-tooled with ornamental acorns and oak leaves. The shelves are empty... utterly bare. But they're clean, and they are ready.

Slowly, conjure your imagination to fill the shelves, inch by inch and foot by foot with books.

Rows and rows of them.

Hardbacks and paperbacks.

Thick books and slim ones.

Rare editions and mass market ones.

Books in English and French, Italian, Japanese, and in every other imaginable language.

The detail is up to you.

What's important are the spines, or rather, what's written on them.

This bookcase is your publishing career. Every single book has *your* name on the spine. This is the point at which I urge you to THINK BIG.

Why?

Because thinking big is so much more fun than thinking small.

My bookcase contains three hundred and twenty-two shelves. I know because I just counted them. Each shelf is ten feet long. That's more than three thousand feet of shelving.

Don't roll your eyes and dismiss it. You see, my imagination features anything I like.

The bookshelf is currently empty, but it can be filled... by you.

Set your mind to it, and you can get the shelves packed tight with books much faster than you'd ever know. The way to do it is simple...

Apply yourself, and don't listen to anyone who tries to hold you back.

Not For Dummies

THIS MORNING I spent almost half an hour trawling the Internet for books on writing, and found exactly what I expected:

A mass of volumes on writing fantasy, general fiction, travelogues, and every other conceivable genre. Each of them was packed with secrets revealed, lists of bullet points for aspiring writers in a rush, and a zillion ideas aimed at idiots, dummies, and numbskulls.

Most were written by people I'd never heard of. There were two notable exceptions. The first was *Why I Write*, an essay by George Orwell. The other, in class of its own, was *On Writing* by Stephen King. It's different because it leads the reader down into the twilight zone of King's own magical brand of genius.

Having browsed the online bookshelves for books on writing, I checked out what self-help guides there are for the other creative arts. As you'd imagine, there's no shortage at all – with the major franchises covering all the bases. What surprised me was that – in most cases – the people writing these books are not experts in the fields in which they're dishing out advice.

Writing that line just dredged up a flash of memory:

Ten years ago a well-known American publisher messaged me to ask if I'd come up with a new line of self-help books based on a traveller's life.

Replying with thanks, I declined.

A terse email shot back, which read:

'Fear not. Learn on the job! Key thing is that the series can take in everything from button-making to Bengali.'

Mainstream publishers design their 'How to Write' books for wannabes – for the droves of non-creatives who buy the gear to compensate for the fact they can't do the work.

When I was a child my parents had a friend called Remi Lacoux. One of the most genteel and elegant gentlemen I've ever had the good fortune to know, he must have been born at the turn of the last century. A celebrated chef, he worked at the restaurant in Fortnum & Mason on London's Piccadilly. He could take a couple of old potatoes, a sprig of mint, and half an onion, and conjure a feast fit for a king.

I was once invited to his home on the outskirts of London, and remember the sense of anticipation – my longing to see the maestro's kitchen. I imagined it packed with every culinary contrivance.

How wrong I was.

He owned a few old knives, a strainer, two or three pots and pans, and a cutting board so worn out it would have been discarded by anyone else.

The great chef must have read my thoughts.

'Never confuse ability with equipment,' he said softly.

Fifteen years ago I bought a haunted mansion in the middle of a Casablanca shantytown. During the long renovation, I used to watch the craftsmen laying the magnificent terracotta floors.

Their tools were no more than a sharp-edged hammer, a cheap wooden mallet, a metal sieve, and a U-tube half-filled with water – to make sure the tiles were laid flat. As I watched them work, I would think to myself how the Western world replaces genuine skill with its fixation on cutting corners.

Just like Monsieur Lacoux and the Moroccan craftsmen, real writers don't need fancy gear. Think about it. Almost every great book in human history was written by hand.

My own grandfather – The Sirdar Ikbal Ali Shah – wrote and edited seventy-four books, almost all with a dipper pen. His son, my father, accomplished the bulk of his writing with a manual typewriter as I've already described.

And, to the delight of my children, the first computer I owned – a wretched model of Amstrad without a hard drive – is displayed as an antique at London's Science Museum.

The tool you write with is meaningless, along with all the crap that many budding writers fuss over.

You don't need any of it.

You need something quite different to be a real writer:
SPACE!

Not physical space to move about in, so much as mental space:
- Space to collect your thoughts.
- Space to seed and then develop ideas.
- Space in which to run from bouts of mania.
- Space to fantasize and dream.
- And, most importantly of all, space to know yourself.

The Mind Game

WRITING IS A mind game, plain and simple.

Get your head around it and you can and will work wonders. Surpassing your wildest dreams is within relatively easy reach. As I've said already, you have to be original and be faithful to your trade. Add to that a certain level of diligence, as well as an obsessive love of the craft, and you'll be set up to win.

Describing mental head-space is challenging. It's an area I rarely talk about even to my close writer friends.

So if what I say sounds weird, cut me some slack.

I believe great writers must be freed from the confinement of standard social norms. By this I don't mean they should be stripping naked and running through the streets, so much as allowing themselves the indulgence of cerebral nonconformity.

An actor needs a stage, and a writer needs one too.

It may not be fashioned from wooden boards, but it's just as real – at least as real for the purposes of creation. The way I imagine it is the darkness that preceded the Big Bang.

A dark, empty void.

One that can be filled with absolutely anything of your choosing – from the tiniest seed of an idea to the greatest visualization of fantastic scale and scope.

Over the last few years I have turned my hand to a number of fictional works, which have honed the imagination process I work with. My exact method depends partly on what I'm writing, or planning, and my mood. But the basics are usually the same:

Sitting at my desk, I calm myself, and train my line of sight on a tree out of the window. While looking at it, I'm not taking in the details. Instead, I tilt my head slightly downwards while keeping sight of the tree – as though I were looking over the top of reading glasses. This sense of looking up and out has a profound effect on me. I probably would never have mentioned it but I recently saw a documentary on mindreading in which it was explained that the brain is stimulated in a certain way by looking up and to the side. Apparently it's the reason why, when asked a question or to do a mental calculation they need to think about, people sometimes break eye contact and glance to the side.

When in that zone my brain makes links between one thought and the next in a surprising way. Rather than being linear, the connections are routed in slaloming lines of thought.

So, peering out of the window obliquely, I'll introduce an idea. Or, one will slip onto the stage of my mind, amid the blurred green foliage of the tree that's the backdrop to my session. Before I know it, one thought has connected to another and another, has blended with memories and colours, with sensations, digressions, layers and sub-layers.

The result is something curiously different from the

elements of the process which created it. It's almost like willing something into existence. Work away on it, and suddenly it's there in three-dimensional form.

Although of course it's a thought, and it doesn't have any mass.

It's then I'll close my eyes, and continue the imagining.

My vision trained up and to the right, I start with the nucleus of the idea that's been imagined into existence. I'll subject the newly born idea to a hailstorm of attack, like a planet being bombarded by a meteor shower. Nothing will break through – not at first. But then, quite suddenly, a dazzling connection will be made.

Then another, and another.

That's the point at which the treasure trail begins.

I used to think everyone was creative.

It was a mindset supported by seeing bookshop shelves overflowing with work aimed at aspiring writers. The books were written by authors who insisted that anyone can learn to master an instrument, paint, or write. But the point I'd missed was that the thousands of self-help titles on writing, and everything else, were commissioned by publishers who knew full well that a dream come true sells books like nothing else.

If I wasn't speaking directly to the Salinger Brigade – to writers who had to write or else they'd turn to stone – I might be less harsh. But since my audience has been vetted, I tell it how it is...

The ability to create written text in a profound way is a gift, one real writers possess in abundance. The way I see it, throughout human history creatives were never the norm. They were needed to jolt a society or clan onto the right path, or to solve problems, but they were far too unstructured to fulfil rank-and-file roles. This surely explains why creative people are always in the minority.

Reflecting on the established order of things, I'm happy for the non-creatives. They don't have the anguish of a life beset with angst and self-doubt. Instead, they can enjoy orderly lives without pendulum swings of raw emotion, mania, and frantic psychotic urges to conjure the miraculous.

Those of us who are creative – whether our disposition is for writing or another equally worthy field – know who we are. We recognize, too, the distress the gift brings, just as we acknowledge the pain of the responsibility. As a result, all of us have hidden behind the mask of the ordinary at one time or another.

When I was twenty-one I got a job as a busboy in a restaurant in California. After that, I drove cars for a rental firm in London – dead-end jobs which taught me all kinds of valuable life skills. Recollecting those jobs now, I see they were a way of shutting off – because I was so fearful of the journey of creativity ahead.

THE REASON TO WRITE

My message to others who understand what I mean, is to feel great about the road connecting with the far horizon. Being the creative you, the productive you, the inspired you, will breathe life into the version of yourself you've always dreamt of being.

But in order to be that person you have to step out from the shadows and stop hiding. Step into the creation zone and get ready for the dizzying sense of fulfilment... the wild rush of literary endorphins that shape the writer's mind.

Cloud Faces

HAVE YOU EVER seen what looks like a heart in the middle of a bread roll?

Or the outline of a dog running full tilt in the lengthening shadows of late afternoon?

Or what looks like the face of an old woman high above you in the clouds?

Of course you have.

This is what psychologists call 'apophenia', and what the rest of us might call 'making meaningful sense of random patterns in whatever's around us'.

I mention it here because to creative people like you and me, it's mesmerizingly important. Seeing layers invisible to others – whether they're actually there or not – is central to our creative perceptions.

I'm not a psychologist, but there's nothing stopping anyone running tests of their own.

So I did.

Over the last months I've shown a set of ten images to a wide spectrum of folk – ranging from a circus clown to business people, and from professional authors to electricians, and even to psychologists.

Some of the pictures were far more apophenic than others – with what most would class as a central image, such as a face. But most of them were far more ambiguous.

As you might imagine, the people who made sense of

the underlying scenes came from the creative end of the spectrum.

Out of a group of thirty-five, only one person managed to miss all of the apophenic patterns. The most impressive reading came from an abstract painter. The most unremarkable was made by a retired airline pilot. As for the three psychologists tested, they all came in the lowest third on my homespun apophenic scale.

Since I had an audience ready and willing to answer questions, I went a stage further, and asked my participants to tell me about the people or things they saw in the pictures.

Again, as predicted, the creatives revealed far more than those on the other end of the spectrum. One lady, who'd made a career for herself as a theatrical costume designer, invented a magical story, all from looking at a cluster of soap bubbles on a dish.

But the details or the stories weren't what interested me, so much as something else:

When asked to elaborate on an apophenic slice of life, the creative participants tended to do so without the need for further encouragement. In almost every case, however, the non-creatives were stumped.

It was as if they needed my permission to turn their imagination on.

The way I see society is I suppose characteristically imaginative. Everyone's going around in their daily lives, some happy, others sad. On the side of their heads there's a dial, about the size of a bottle-top. Invisible to everyone else but me (well, it's my imagination so I can make up the rules), it's located just above the left ear.

The dial relates to a person's imagination quotient.

Writers, painters, actors, and many others within the arts have the dial turned way up. And, those who are generally regarded as being 'left-brained' have their dials on a much lower setting.

As creative people, real writers rely on their imagination. It's what drives us, enthuses us, and fulfils us in ways those outside our realm can rarely understand.

Readers of my books will know I rant on at any available opportunity about how the Occidental world has become separated from the default setting of our ancestors. They may not have had bread rolls, but they had cloudscapes, shadows, and mottled moss-strewn bark on the trees around them. Mixing these with their sensory perceptions – sounds, sights, smells, tastes, and the sense of touch – they created folklore, religions, and order in the natural world.

I used to think that as creative people it was our mission to get non-creatives to tweak up the dials on the side of their heads. As a child, I was singled out for slipping into the imagination zone as frequently and as effortlessly as I did, and lampooned for being different. I thought that if creatives could get everyone else to see life as we did, then the entire world would be flipped the right way up.

But my thinking changed on a winter afternoon twelve years ago.

An anthropologist friend rented a screening room in London's Soho and showed the same film to different groups of people. As I was at a loose end, he invited me to one of the screenings. Rather than watch the movies from the cinema, or even from the projection room, we watched the audience through a viewing window mounted above the screen.

The film my anthropologist friend had chosen was *Jurassic Park*, and the people selected to view it were all briefcase-carrying executives. That audience was possibly the most creatively sterile group of individuals ever assembled in one room. Part of the study was to interview them en masse before the show, then ask a series of questions about their likes, dislikes, and their lives.

As they leaned back and enjoyed the movie, we watched them warm, then open up.

They all knew that dinosaurs hadn't come back to life, but went along with the convention of suspending disbelief. They laughed at the jokes, recoiled where we expected them to, and one or two even sobbed at the end.

As the credits faded, and the house lights came on, we asked the same questions again. To my surprise, that room full of hard-nosed corporate types had been profoundly affected, as though melted from the inside out. This time round they answered the questions sensitively, undeterred by what they imagined their colleagues thought of them.

Bricklaying

MY WRITER HEROES have typically turned their hand to all kinds of genres – whether they be fantasy, poetry, historical fiction, short stories, non-fiction, or anything else.

Real writers are like bricklayers.

They can make walls with their bricks, and houses from the walls. Or they can make office buildings, or hospitals, apartment blocks, or anything else they care to choose. Of course, some bricklayers stick to one style of building because it's what they have grown to love.

There's nothing wrong with that at all.

As I have sauntered along the path, I've come to appreciate the delight in turning my skill as a wordsmith from one genre to another.

My first publications were so-called 'travel books' – quests through some of the most challenging landscapes on earth. I started off with a book called *Beyond the Devil's Teeth*, which I wrote when I was twenty-two. At the time I wrote it, I was sure it was a work of unrestrained genius. Alas it was not. But it was important – to me at any rate – because it broke the spell and showed me I could write a full-length book.

I went on to write about a dozen non-fiction works of travel, published by a range of firms – including John Murray, who represented Jane Austen, and Random House, who regard themselves as one of the most powerful publishers of all.

One of my first forays into fiction was an historical novel called *Timbuctoo*, based on the true-life story of the first white man ever to visit the legendary African outpost in the Sahara.

I remember telling my agent and my publisher how I wanted to write the historical novel. Damning the idea with faint praise, they both suggested I go to Timbuktu (to use the current spelling) and write a first-person travel book on my adventure.

Needless to say, I didn't follow their advice.

I wrote *Timbuctoo*, having agonized about making the transition from first-person travel narrative to third-person fiction. Through weeks, and then months, I'd worked myself up into a florid state of worry – wondering aloud to anyone and everyone how I'd ever be able to write in the third person.

A clutch of self-important agents and editors all opined it would be far too challenging a transition, and that I ought to pack my nonsensical notions right away and stick to what I knew.

I was about to give up before I'd even started, when I went to visit Elizabeth, the widow of the writer Bruce Chatwin.

I've known Elizabeth a long time – from the days when we used to spend the afternoons in conversation at the fabulously run-down Royal Bombay Yacht Club. Her late husband has been a guiding light to me for all kinds of reasons – as much as for who he was than for his writing.

Elizabeth was padding through the ramshackle rooms of Homer End, and I padding after her. She was talking about sheep, and I was thinking about changing from the first person to the third.

Making her way into the kitchen, Elizabeth went over to the Aga cooker and put on some water for tea.

'Bruce didn't care,' she said out of the blue.

'Didn't care about what?'

'About the kind of things others cared about.'

'I'm not with you,' I said.

'Well, think about it. He wrote travel books and novels, and he had all kinds of friends – it was a life without restraints.'

At that moment I saw the future in sharp focus, or at least one facet of the future. I vowed never again to limit myself to one style or type of performance.

I was a bricklayer with ambition...

A bricklayer destined to build little cottages on mountainsides and great hulking tower blocks. But that would only be the start. I'd be a bricklayer who'd invent new kinds of buildings, and even new kinds of bricks.

The Originality Matrix

As I've ALREADY said, members of the Salinger Brigade don't write because they want to – but because they have to.

Life would be so much easier if we didn't have that insatiable urge. We'd be free, or at least freer from the tumultuous peaks and troughs. I know my friends would regard me as far more 'normal' if I wasn't a fully loaded member of Salinger's Army. 'Normal' is a word rarely spoken in a sentence along with my name.

Believe me – I've tried to be normal!

But it never works. I can't hold down a job with fixed goals, because my thoughts are bouncing all over the place like a rubber ball. For me, and those like me, life is an off-piste existence, dedicated to creation, and devoted to experimentation. Like all real writers, I'm thrilled by the process of mixing ideas, genres, and artistic styles, in the same way a great chef pushes the boundaries of cuisine.

Please understand something deeply important:

A real writer isn't a copier.

A real writer is original.

Forgive me for circling back again and again to the same central points – it's something I do when I'm absolutely obsessed with an idea. And nothing is so central to being a writer – or any other creative – as being original. The only other thing as important is creating for oneself.

Through my school days we were forced to learn great long passages of text by heart. One by one we'd have to stand in front of the class and spew out memorized lines, while the teacher evaluated our performances.

As you might have guessed, doing anything by rote was something I found inordinately challenging. My entire outlook has always been off-piste – even back then. In the grim classes at prep school, the master would leap from his chair, clenched fists shaking, as I did my level best to please him.

On one occasion I remember him yelling so loudly the veins on his throat swelled up, and we all thought he was about to have a heart attack.

'Damn you, Shah!' he wailed. 'Why can't you mug up a few bloody lines without always trying to reinvent them?!'

Delivered in the faintest whisper for fear of being beaten, I answered:

'Because, sir, I am an *originalist*!'

Bringing up my children, Ariane and Timur, I have always rewarded them for feats of originality. When they were small, I adored watching them solve problems with thinking that was naturally deep inside them – rather than learned.

Given the standard education system it's amazing the Western world has any creative people at all. By nailing children down to a grid of 'right' and 'wrong' they're held back by at least a decade – maybe even more. As a result, adolescents emerge from childhood with a stunted sense of creativity – so much so it usually takes until one's thirties until people are ready to break free.

That was certainly the case with me.

Even though I'd grown up in an intensely creative household, I was chronically fearful of putting a foot out of line. Profound dyslexia was mixed up in my own creative stew. It meant that I was – and still am – terribly messy. My handwriting was and is appalling, and I've never had any hope of being able to spell even the simplest words. So, anything I wrote at a young age was immediately critiqued, lampooned, ripped up, and binned.

A secondary bloodstream flows to every cell and organ, the need to create gushes inside me from morning to night, streaming ideas and thoughts. The duty of a creative person is to harness the slipstream and make use of it.

I would normally rail against our society round about now, the one which champions the culture of copying. The way everyone wants to be 'just like' Madonna, J. K Rowling, or Kim Kardashian leaves me bereft – because copying is the absolute opposite of what it is to be creative.

Before buckling down to write, it's important to get your originality matrix working as it's supposed to work. The danger is that you'll grab hold of something seen on social media, so you have to tread with care. To avoid copying you have to reach deep into yourself and sense the raw magma of your inner originality.

Feel it, appreciate it, and draw it up from the depths of darkness onto the stage of your mind, like some twisting serpent of raw originality.

Never doubt that a wellspring of creativity is in you.

It may be asleep, waiting, but it's there. The only way to know it's there is to call out to it, to believe in it, and to get down to business.

If you were four years old you could start immediately. But I'm guessing you're more seasoned than that – which means your sense of originality has probably been bashed about, shunned, and ridiculed. Or, at least, it'll have been dumbed down.

Like a lump of dough left in the fridge overnight, you've got to knead it. Only when it's warmed up will you be able to get it churning out the kind of ideas non-creatives could only dream of originating.

They say if you want to be a great dancer you have to dance like no one's watching. The same is true about creating. Silence the growling-howling voice in your head – the one which constantly chides and critiques. For years it's forbidden you from generating original work for fear of being knocked down. That growling-howling voice has no place in the new you – the *real* you.

Promise yourself something:

From now on you'll never listen to the growling-howling voice again.

If you want to write in a particular way, you're free to, just as you're allowed to hop to work on one foot, or wear fluorescent green clothes. After all, it's not hurting anyone else.

To be original is to be a rule-breaker.

Most of the rules shaping our lives are nonsensical, and have to be shredded if you want to move briskly ahead.

When she was about five years old I took my daughter, Ariane, to a posh restaurant in Paris. She asked what I was going to order for her.

'Anything you like,' I replied.

Ariane's face lit up.

'I'll have ice cream to start, then ice cream for my main course, and ice cream for dessert.'

And that's exactly what she had.

Children are who they are because their lives are all about harnessing the originality matrix they're born with. There's a geyser gushing originality inside them from morning till night, which is how and why they create differently to adults. They create in the *real* way – the way we writers spend years relearning.

From time to time I sense my own originality matrix being pushed down deep into the underside of my creative soul. It's usually when I've been forced to do my accounts, or think in a grown-up way for too long. Yes, I said, 'in a grown-up way' – which to me is a truly horrific thing. The originality matrix is silly and fun, because silly and fun are what being original is all about. Silly and fun are the stew from which creativity comes, and they are the default ingredients of all humanity.

We're taught that childish ways have to be rooted out, exchanged for moderation and self-control. And we're reminded 'play' is for children and certainly not fit for adults.

That's absolute tripe, of course.

Play is the secret to developing the originality matrix, and it's why children and their ideas should be at the heart of a creative, forward-thinking culture. Anyone doubting me should see how children learn best – through playing. Remember the facts: video games outsell Hollywood movies and books combined.

When I get the feeling my originality geyser isn't gushing quite as it ought to be, I don't just sit in a chair and wait for it to fire up – because it won't.

Instead, I galvanize it into action by having fun.

The easiest way to spark your originality into life is to chit-chat to children under the age of about seven. They're in the zone already. You can say to them: 'Imagine I've got tentacles coming out the top of my head.' They won't even blink. If you haven't got small children, you can get the same effect by reading a few pages of a sci-fi novel, or watching ten minutes of *Men in Black*. It doesn't have to be sci-fi – but the genre is good at recalibrating the boundaries, albeit in a conventional, adult-centred way.

Originality is tethered to the part of our consciousness which creates dreams and yearns for stories. The nocturnal dreamscapes to which we escape each night are surely proof of our ability to originate. The joy of dreams is that they are preposterous, 'childish', and progress along a sequence of unrelated thoughts.

Everyone's originality matrix works differently.

My sense is that real writers have a well-honed ability to originate, part of their overall yearning to create. My own originality matrix seems to work on making connections. To spark it up I prefer to be alone. If I'm with other people I can sometimes feed off their creativity. But the originality stream isn't as pure as when I descend into the zone by myself.

To get there I slow my thinking so that vents open up in my mind. I'll focus on something on my desk, using it as a seed – then on something else.

Gradually, a tapestry emerges... it's like a collage shrouded in mist.

One thing links to the next and, soon, I start getting flashes.

Flashes of memory.

Flashes of random detail.

Flashes of oddity.

THE REASON TO WRITE

Whether the flashes continue, or die away, is up to you. Don't try too hard, because if you do, everything's lost – like a soap bubble bursting in sunshine. A daydream only happens because your thinking mind is diverted, just like you only slip into sleep when you're expecting it least.

Twenty years ago I spent many months in the Upper Amazon in Peru, a vast green wilderness of life. I was staying with a tribe called the Shuar, who once shrank human heads to the size of grapefruits. Anthropologists regard them as a primitive tribe but to me they – and other indigenous peoples the world over – are a remaining hope. They're still programmed with the default settings, just as our ancestors were until a handful of centuries ago.

The Shuar believe we live in an illusionary world. When faced with a huge problem there's no choice, they say, but to fly into the real world in order to receive a solution. In order to reach reality they drink a hallucinogenic tea made with ayahuasca, the so-called 'Vine of the Dead'.

Since taking that hallucinogen with the Shuar, I have developed techniques of entering the world of glorious reality – without the need of ayahuasca.

Sitting here at my polished wooden desk, I take in the pens and the post-it notes, the USB cables, the keyboard, and the mouse pad. My mind maps them, picking out the way a cable is looped back on itself, and how the wood's grain is like a kingdom, or an inland sea.

All of a sudden the grim reality of the illusionary world in which we reside melts away, as a seed has been planted.

I imagine a boy... he's called Robbie... and he lives with his family on the shore of an ocean. One night he goes to sleep and awakes to find something extraordinary has occurred in the night.

The land has turned to ocean, and the ocean to land.

Robbie's the only person who's noticed the change. His parents, brothers, sisters, and everyone else assume the world is as it's always been. Rushing to the globe in his bedroom, Robbie sees that what was blue is now brown, and what was brown is blue.

A minute passes while I sit stock still, imagining.

My mind fills in the gaps, and finds a story:

Robbie is the only person alive who can turn things back to how they were. He can do it because he knows a secret – a secret passed down from every father to son in his family...

...a secret that's a door into another world.

Inked In

ONE DAY, WHEN I was nine years old, my father called me down to his study.

'Want to show you something,' he said.

'What, Baba?'

'Come with me and you'll see.'

I followed him into the drawing room, a realm usually reserved for Best Behaviour tea parties with the great and the good. Once we were inside, my father shut the door. Until that moment I'd hardly ever been alone with him before.

As one of the twins, I was only half of a whole. No one ever divided us.

'Shall I go and get Safia?' I asked perkily. 'She's upstairs.'

'No,' my father said softly. 'Because what I have to show is for you.'

Sensing butterflies in my stomach, I wished it were over – whatever it was.

Before I could shoot out a volley of questions, as I tended to do, my father touched a fingertip to his lips.

'What I am going to show you is for you to know about,' he said. 'And for you alone.'

'But I can tell Safia, can't I?'

'Best not to. Best not to tell anyone. This isn't something for Tahir Shah the Information Officer.'

'Is it a secret?' I asked, scandalized.

'Yes, in a way it is.'

While I held a hand to my mouth, my father went over to the cupboards which spanned the entire end wall. Among them were recesses in which exquisite Oriental objects were displayed.

With both hands he lifted a magnificent brass candlestick – a legacy of ancient Al-Andalus, standing as tall as a man.

Then, with force, he punched the back wall of the niche in which the candlestick had stood.

A door swung inwards, revealing a secret cubbyhole.

About a metre in width, it rose floor to ceiling, and was packed with all kinds of wonders: sacks and tea-crates labelled in Arabic script, ancestral swords wrapped in waxed cloth, dozens of Eastlight-brand box files, reels of 16-mm film, and numerous cardboard boxes overflowing with trophies and awards.

'Didn't know this was here,' I whispered fearfully.

'No one knows, except for me... and now you.'

'Is this the secret, Baba?'

'Yes it is. It's *our* secret.'

Again, I felt butterflies, stronger than before. Safia didn't like me having secrets. Twins were supposed to tell each other everything.

Reaching up, my father pulled out a file, dustier and much older than all the rest. Leading me into the pool of light streaming in, he opened it.

Inside was a document.

With great care he turned it so that I could make sense of it.

'Do you see what it is?' he asked.

'No, Baba.'

'It's our family tree – stretching back centuries.'

'How many centuries, Baba?'

'More than twenty... that's more than two thousand years.'

The tip of my father's finger roamed down through the forest of names, each one written neatly in Arabic.

'That's your name there,' he said.

I read the words in Arabic, mouthing the letters as I'd been taught to do. As I did so, two things struck me:

First: my name was written in pencil.

Second: all over the family tree there were gaps, where names were missing.

I asked why.

My father turned to me. His gaze catching the shaft of light, his eyes were coal black and stern.

'This is very serious,' he said.

'What is, Baba?'

'This document... the reason your name is in pencil... the gaps where names should be. I will explain why, and I want you always to remember it. Do you understand?'

I nodded as I always did, even though I never understood.

'We are not like other families,' he went on. 'You see,

in our family we are bound by duty. It's a solemn duty that's gone back thousands of years.'

'Two thousand years?'

'Yes, two thousand years, and even longer than that.'

'But why is my name written in pencil, and why are there gaps where a lot of the names should be?' I asked again.

'Because, in our family, when a boy is born his name is written in pencil, just as yours is now. And then, by about the age of twenty-five we review what he's achieved. If he hasn't achieved anything, or been a good person, his name is rubbed out. And that is why there are so many spaces, where the names should be.'

Sitting on the floor of that cubbyhole in the pool of light, my bottom lip quivered as though I might burst into tears.

'Am I going to be rubbed out, Baba?' I asked.

He didn't answer for what seemed like an eternity.

Then he said:

'Not if you make something of yourself.'

A day doesn't go by without me thinking of that secret.

Over the years I've asked myself ten thousand questions about it. I've questioned why such pressure needs to be laden onto the shoulders of anyone; and I've wondered why little girls never had their names recorded on our family tree. On the rare occasions I plucked up the courage to ask my father, he simply said it was the way things were, and had always been.

When Ariane and Timur were born, the first thing I did after we'd brought them back from hospital was to write their names on the family tree in thick black ink.

At the same time, I have watched myself, as if from a great height – desperately trying to achieve for fear of being erased.

Since I am sharing secrets, I'll tell another:

Having learned the secret of the family tree, I would make a pilgrimage to the secret cubbyhole at least once a month. In the beam of a torch, I'd stand on a tea-crate, open up the file, unfold the document and check…

…whether my name was in ink or still in pencil.

Slipping in behind the ancient mosque lamp became second nature, and I could be in and out in a couple of minutes. As the years passed I no longer needed to stand on a crate to get up high, although after a while I had to move the candlestick aside.

It sounds crazy, but I became obsessed as to whether my name had been inked in – or, rather, that I hadn't been rubbed out. I've never spoken of it, let alone written of it, but it was as if I were a shadow of myself, a spectre hanging by a thread.

In the incongruous landscape of my fantastical mind, being deleted on paper would have been tantamount to being erased from life.

I was jealous of my sisters, and of my school friends, because they were fully rounded, as all other people were. I was the only person I'd ever heard of who was only part of who they were supposed to be.

For this reason I latched on to a story my father wrote for us as children, called *Neem the Half-Boy*. I was certain he'd written it to remind me of my duty, and the fact that his eraser was always within arm's reach.

The last day I spent at Langton House was desperately sad.

Safia and I were almost twenty-four, and had lived there since we were born. The order of our childhood had now become the disorder of relocation.

Boxes, boxes, and yet more boxes.

The curtains had been taken down. Cosy reception rooms in which prim visitors were once entertained were now cavernous, cold, and filled with echoes.

Slipping into the drawing room I shut the door, sneaked into the cubbyhole, and opened up the file.

But I couldn't find my name.

The tip of my finger searched for the looped letters of pencil.

I felt as though I would collapse.

Then I saw it – my name...

In jet-black ink.

I wasn't going to write this chapter, which may be the reason I've left it so late in the section. The last thing I want is for it to seem as though I am fishing for compliments, or trying to show that our family is any different, or better than it is.

But there's a point I want to make.

And it's because of that point I lifted the veil on the secret of pencil and ink.

The point is this:

Although I am firmly against pressuring anyone with the threat of being expunged, I have come to see something remarkable – that a literary family such as mine has a chain of transmission.

Since my grandfather published *Eastern Moonbeams* in Edinburgh just over a century ago, he, my father, and I, have published scores of books. Each one of us has written differently, and thought differently, too. But, at the same time it's as though we've all be working at the same mine.

We are storytellers.

Or, at least, we tell stories as a way of enabling our audience to absorb ideas, the kind which will change the way they see the world around them.

Through a century of writing we've forged a body of work that is cumulative – just as all the stories and adventures of our ancestors have made each one of us who we are.

I may be what my father called 'the soup of the soup', but I suppose we all are, just as we are more.

I want to end this section with a list of the books the three of us have written and under pseudonyms as well:

THE SIRDAR IKBAL ALI SHAH

A Briton In India
Afghanistan of the Afghans
Afridi Gold
Allah Cries For Blood
Alone in Arabian Nights
Bahadur Khan Warrior
Best Indian Chutney
Black And White Magic
Brothers In Arms
Eastern Moonbeams
Eastward To Persia
Escape From Central Asia
Exploits of Asaf Khan
Extracts From the Koran
Fifty Enthralling Stories From the Mysterious East
Fighting Through
Fuad: King of Egypt
I Spied For the Empire
Islamic Sufism
Kemal: Maker of Modern Turkey
Lights of Asia
Lion of the Frontier
Mohammed: The Prophet
My Life From Brigand to King
Nepal: Home of the Gods

Occultism: Its Theory and Practice
Pakistan: A Plan For India
Peeps At Many Lands: Arabia
Peeps At Many Lands: Turkey
The Book of Oriental Literature
The Diary of a Slave
The Golden East
The Golden Treasury of Indian Literature
The Lion of the Frontier
The Prince Aga Khan
The Spirit of the East
The Tragedy of Amanullah
The Wanderings of Asaf
The White Terror of the Khyber
Through the Garden of Allah
Vietnam
Westward To Mecca

IDRIES SHAH

A Perfumed Scorpion
A Veiled Gazelle
After a Swim
Caravan of Dreams
Darkest England
Destination Mecca

Evenings with Idries Shah
Fatima the Spinner and the Tent
Kara Kush
Learning How to Learn
Knowing How to Know
Letters and Lectures of Idries Shah
Neem the Half-Boy
Neglected Aspects of Sufi Study
Observations
Oriental Magic
Reflections
A History of Secret Societies
Seeker After Truth
Speak First and Lose
Special Illumination
Special Problems in the Study of Sufi Ideas
Sufi Thought and Action
Tales of the Dervishes
The Ants and the Pen
The Book of the Book
The Boy Without a Name
The Clever Boy and the Terrible Dangerous Animal
The Commanding Self
The Dermis Probe
The Elephant in the Dark
The Englishman's Handbook
The Exploits of the Incomparable Mulla Nasrudin
The Farmer's Wife

The Horrible Dib Dib
The Hundred Tales of Wisdom
The Idries Shah Anthology
The Lion Who Saw Himself in the Water
The Magic Horse
The Magic Monastery
The Man and the Fox
The Man With Bad Manners
The Natives Are Restless
The Old Woman and the Eagle
The Onion
The Pleasantries of the Incredible Mulla Nasrudin
The Secret Lore of Magic
The Silly Chicken
The Subtleties of the Inimitable Mulla Nasrudin
The Sufis
The Tale of the Sands
The Way of the Sufi
The World of Nasrudin
Thinkers of the East
Wisdom of the Idiots
Witches and Sorcerers
World Tales

TAHIR SHAH

A Son of a Son, Volume I
A Son of a Son, Volume II
A Treasury of Tales
An Unexpected Gift
Being Myself
Beyond the Devil's Teeth
Capilongo
Casablanca Blues
Casablanca Blues: The Screenplay
Cat Dog, Dog Cat
Cat, Mouse
Changing the World
Congress With a Crocodile
Cultural Research
Daydreams of an Octopus & Other Stories
Dream Soup
Eye Spy
Frogland
Ghoul Brothers
Godman
Hannibal Fogg and the Supreme Secret of Man
Hourglass
House of the Tiger King
Imaginist
In Arabian Nights
In Search of King Solomon's Mines

Jinn Hunter: Book One – The Prism
Jinn Hunter: Book Three – The Perplexity
Jinn Hunter: Book Two – The Jinnslayer
Jinn's Treasure
Jinnlore
Journey Through Namibia
King of the Jinns
Liquid Time
Mellified Man
Mittle-Mittle
Mouse House
Nasrudin in the Land of Fools
On Backgammon Time
Outrunning the Reaper
Paris Syndrome
Princess Pickle's Laugh
Qwerty
Renaissance
Scorpion Soup
Skeleton Island
Sorcerer's Apprentice
Tales Told to a Melon
The Afghan Notebook
The Anthologies: Africa
The Anthologies: Ceremony
The Anthologies: Childhood
The Anthologies: City
The Anthologies: Danger

The Anthologies: East
The Anthologies: Expedition
The Anthologies: Frontier
The Anthologies: Hinterland
The Anthologies: India
The Anthologies: Jinns
The Anthologies: Jungle
The Anthologies: Magic
The Anthologies: Morocco
The Anthologies: Nasrudin
The Anthologies: People
The Anthologies: Quest
The Anthologies: South
The Anthologies: Taboo
The Anthologies: Teaching Stories
The Arabian Nights Adventures
The Caliph's House
The Cap of Invisibility
The Caravanserai Stories
The Clockmaker Who Travelled Through Time
The Clockmaker's Box
The Destiny Ring
The Fish's Dream
The Forgotten Game
The Hoopoe's Flight
The Kingdom of Blink
The Man Whose Arms Grew Branches
The Man With the Tiger's Head

The Middle East Bedside Book
The Misadventures of the Mystifying Nasrudin
The Monkey Puzzle Club
The Most Foolish of Men
The Old Wind
The Paradise Tree
The Peregrinations of the Perplexing Nasrudin
The Pharaoh Code
The Princess of Zilzilam
The Problem Exchange
The Reason to Write
The Reason to Write Workbook: Comprehensive
The Reason to Write Workbook: Fantasy
The Reason to Write Workbook: Features
The Reason to Write Workbook: Fiction
The Reason to Write Workbook: Historical Fiction
The Reason to Write Workbook: Teaching Stories
The Reason to Write Workbook: Travel
The Reason to Write Workbook: Travel Writing
The Shop That Sold Truth
The Singing Serpents
The Skeleton Factory
The Tahir Shah Fiction Reader
The Tahir Shah Travel Reader
The Tale of Double Six
The Tale of the Rusty Nail
The Unicorn's Tear
The Voyages and Vicissitudes of Nasrudin

The Wisdom of Celestine
The Wondrous Seed
Three Essays
Timbuctoo
Timbuctoo: The Screenplay
Trail of Feathers
Travels With Myself
Travels With Nasrudin
Wellspring
When the Sun Forgot to Rise
Zigzag Think

PART II

JOURNEY

Announcement I

IN CASE I'VE snagged anyone in my net of readers who hasn't grasped this isn't a conventional book about writing – one a mainstream publisher would release to fill their coffers with cash – I'm going to spell something out here:

THIS BOOK FOR REAL WRITERS
HAS BEEN CRAFTED ORGANICALLY

As such, it's not going to bore you to death, providing must-do rules and regulations of the writing business. Instead, it's going to pass on what I've found to work, as well as lifting the veil on what has most definitely failed.

The only way I know how to achieve any of this is by revealing it in a kind of story, the story of my own journey...

Shoebox

WHEN I WAS nineteen years old I remarked at breakfast one morning how I was interested in African dictatorships.

By the end of the week I was enrolled in a little American university in Nairobi, Kenya – itself a dictatorship under President Moi. My father had enthused at the breakfast table that not to follow such an interest would be a crime. Looking back, I wonder whether he realized it was exactly what I needed. I like to think he'd planted the interest in my mind as a way of setting me on a life path which was well and truly off-piste.

Until then, I'd jumped through the usual hoops of conventional study – beating and scolding at the hands of tyrannical masters, exams, and yet more exams. Had anyone taken the time to investigate it, they'd have realized I was creative. It was blindingly obvious – although for the wrong reasons.

You see, most of the time I was zoned out, lost in 'Tahirland' – a realm of my own creation where I was both happy and safe.

That magical dreamscape had been conjured into existence as a way of surviving the trauma of a wretched and authoritarian prep school.

Thank God for it, because without Tahirland I'd never have become a writer.

THE REASON TO WRITE

In some ways the first footsteps on my life path were taken in Kenya. Until then I had been sheltered, travelling with my family, or living in the bubble of Langton House. I'd not understood the true immensity of the world until Kenya.

On weekends my friends sat by the pool, while I took local buses all over East Africa. Little by little I hitch-hiked through Tanzania and Uganda, and on through Central and then West Africa. Travelling on the cheap ensured a wild rollicking time of unspeakable adventure. I was robbed more times than I remember, given shelter by witchdoctors and mercenaries, and introduced to bone-numbing reality in a big, wide way.

After university I returned to Africa time and again, and went on to Asia and Latin America, too. Every few months I'd retreat to London where I had a dead-end job driving cars for a plush rental company. I drove so much that I had calluses on my palms. Whenever I'd amassed enough money for a trip, I'd buy a flight somewhere off all tourist routes and stay away for as long as my funds held out.

Within two years, I'd criss-crossed three continents, and had dozens of notebooks packed with spidery black script. I'm not sure why I felt it necessary to keep notes as I did – but something inside me willed me on. Each night I would spend hours detailing where I'd been and whom I'd met, listing stray ideas and fragments of information. Although many travellers make such notes, mine were written for me, and me alone.

The journals were kept in a shoebox under my bed back home in London. Between adventures, I would pore through them, marvelling at the close scrapes and the hardship I'd endured.

Two years after crossing the equator for the first time in my quest to learn about dictators, the shoebox was full. I was proud of my achievement, although I wasn't quite sure what the achievement actually was. Sitting on my bed, the notebooks laid out in a grid, I was certain I'd reached the first step on a ladder.

The only problem was I didn't know where the ladder went, or indeed how to scale it. So the journals were returned to the box, which was stowed back beneath my bed.

Then a series of unrelated events took place:

First, while waiting for a friend, I dropped in at Daunt Books on Marylebone Road. Thirty years ago Daunt's was still very much the preserve of off-beat travellers and connoisseurs of adventure. I liked the way it was arranged by continent and country – and how out-of-print editions were mixed in with new ones. Having recently visited West Africa, I checked what travel writing there was on that region. Over an hour or two I dipped in and out of a dozen books – some old, others new, all of them featuring a realm I'd got to know from the inside out.

The best thing about Daunt's was the armchairs.

THE REASON TO WRITE

Sitting in one, books piled up on the floor all around, I had a Eureka moment.

Every single book I'd flipped through was dull as dishwater.

The classic texts which had been in print for decades were toe-curlingly monotonous, as were most of the new books, too. The only gem in the entire section was *The Innocent Anthropologist* by Nigel Barley – it was different because it was funny.

Everything else sucked.

Grabbing a pen and paper from my satchel, I made a list:

1. India & Pakistan
2. West, Central & East Africa
3. Latin America

Unfurling a map in the bookshop's cartography section, I realized I'd travelled a zigzagging route through much of the world – a journey fashioned on a preoccupation with oddity. The journals under my bed were packed with anecdotes, details, and distillations of characters – every page a hymn to the bizarre curiosities of the lands through which I'd travelled.

The shoebox under my bed contained everything I needed for a travel book of my own – a travel book certain to be anything but dull. The only thing I didn't have was a central theme with which to sew the tapestry together.

Over the next month I got my notes in order, and

made plans for the book. Writing it was all I could think about. But still I couldn't come up with a theme which would enable me to convert the raw ingredients into a meal.

I took inspiration from *Destination Mecca*, my father's one and only travel book, published in the 1950s when he was in his early thirties. A rattling read, it is at times disjointed and even awkward – but it works. As a device to link up his travels through an Arab world in flux, my father had placed seven stones on a map of the region and vowed not to return until he had visited each one.

Appropriating his idea was tempting, and I might have done it had I not come up with something else during a low-life dinner party in high-life Kensington. I was only invited because someone had dropped out, and because – having just returned from the Amazon – my stock value was moderately high.

The host knew she could count on me to entertain the other guests with a few tall tales.

I was wondering how I would ever get through the evening when a dish of potato gratin was pushed down the table, a crust of thick grilled cheese on the top. Without being able to prevent it, I got a flash of geography class when I was eleven. The sulphurous master who'd picked on me for years was standing at the blackboard, an outline of the world sketched over it. But it wasn't the world as we know it – rather as it was once thought to be.

A world that resembled the baked cheese on the gratin.

Africa, South America, and the Indian subcontinent were originally all joined together in a vast landmass called Gondwanaland. The name had stuck in my mind because it sounded mysterious and magical, like something from *The Arabian Nights*.

When I least expected the name to appear it did so, projected on gratin.

Next day I read up on Gondwanaland, learning how the supercontinent was christened after a region of central India, called Gondwana, and how it in turn was named after an aboriginal tribe, the Gonds.

Over yet another month, I ran all the material I'd amassed through the matrix of Gondwanaland and continental drift. Rather than using the theory in a geological way, I invented a cultural offshoot of continental drift. Beginning with the little-known tribe of the Gonds, my travel narrative would snake east and west, as it followed the course of my adventures.

I wanted to start writing – I was desperate to, but had worked myself up into a state of terrible dread.

Universally regarded as being thick by those around me, I was condemned even before I began. Everyone said I would fail because my handwriting was bad, and my spelling was worse. They suggested I got a proper job and put a lid on my fantasies.

My mistake was to listen to the opinions of others.

Agonizing over how to keep going, I covered hundreds of blank pages with text while I beat myself up in every imaginable way. I might have shelved the entire project but, one evening, I went to see my aunt – the traveller, storyteller, and writer, Amina Shah.

In the summer of 1937, when she was eighteen, my grandfather presented her with two parcels wrapped up in brown paper and string. The first was a portable typewriter, and the second was a ream of paper. Within six weeks she had finished the first draft of a novel – *Tiger of the Frontier*. The following year it was published by Sampson, Low & Co., my grandfather's publishers at the time.

Aunt Amina and I were pressed from the same mould. She loved travelling, despised silence, never stopped talking or moving, and was drawn to the curious underbelly of far-off lands. As she filled her lungs with air with which to begin a new story, I spat out the word 'Gondwanaland'.

'What is it?' she asked, intrigued.

'A landmass.'

'In the Americas?'

'No, well, yes... well, yes and no.'

I explained what Gondwanaland was and how I hoped to trace it, at least in a cultural way. Aunt Amina listened, her hands crocheting a cap from unwanted scraps of wool.

'Write every day and do not stop until you've

finished,' she said, her voice unusually cold and firm. 'Do you understand?'

'Yes.'

'And on no account tell anyone about it until the entire first draft is done – especially your father!'

When working on a book I write every day without exception. In the few cases where I've been forced to put a project aside, it's never easy to get back on track.

My aunt's advice, to keep the book to myself, was something I follow faithfully. In my experience, it's the deciding factor on whether a project is easy or arduous, a failure or a success. By talking about it you lose momentum orally – momentum which ought to be channelled through written words.

As for my father, my aunt's advice was shrewd.

A prolific author, the son of another prolific author, he could be intimidating and even jealous when asked for guidance in what was his chosen profession. There's nothing he liked less than talking about the craft.

In his opinion, writing was something best done rather than discussed, proof if it were ever needed that he was a member of the Salinger Brigade.

Doris

THE DAY AFTER visiting my aunt, I bumped into a family friend at a café in West Hampstead.

He was reading the last page of a little paperback with a red cover.

It was called *Iron & Silk*.

'Wow!' he said as he closed the book. 'That was incredible!'

He handed it me.

'Take it,' he said.

So I did.

Over the years I've been given many hundreds of books – books on travel and adventure, on folklore, literature, and on philosophical themes. I'm grateful to anyone who gives me the books they love, because it's a way of getting to know the donor as much as it is a pleasure to read work that's new to me.

Out of all the books I've been given, *Iron & Silk* stands out above all the rest for two reasons.

First, it's written more elegantly than almost anything else I've ever read.

Second, it was exactly what I needed.

Written by Mark Salzman, a young American martial artist, it describes living in China in the early eighties. While studying under a tyrannical *wushu* master, Salzman taught English to a group of adult students.

I can hear you thinking: 'Yeah, there are loads of

books out there like that – what's so special about this one?'

The answer is simplicity.

While everyone else who's churned out similar books has suffocated the narrative with unnecessary layers, Salzman related his tale with the elegance of a ballerina pirouetting across the stage... or rather of a martial artist performing sword-play.

Although intricate, the book is composed of a series of short episodes, each of which ends on a tiny yet tantalizing denouement.

Whenever I hear of someone planning to take a creative writing course, I direct them to *Iron & Silk*. It's a fully formed blueprint – a masterclass in creative writing.

The book taught me that being an author is as much about what you don't say as what you do. Through Salzman's example, I learned that a story could be created with little episodes, which link up to provide an extraordinary feast – in which every single ingredient can be tasted.

But most of all it taught me that the holy grail is simplicity.

Iron & Silk was the last piece of my puzzle.

I combined it with the notebooks in the shoebox under my bed, with the theme of Gondwanaland, and with my Aunt Amina's advice – to keep writing at all costs.

Fearful, angst-ridden, and top to toe with self-doubt, I typed out a first pair of sentences:

'The waiter poured me a glass of straw-coloured tea. He turned and went to lie in the shade, removing his artificial right leg and using it as a pillow.'

This quirky, jerky start was far more than the beginning of my first book – it was the dawn of my entire writing career. With the two lines typed out, I congratulated myself.

An imaginary voice whispered to me:

'Well done, you've just conquered the hardest writing of your life.'

In the late eighties computers were expensive, and I was broke because everything I earned was spent on travel.

A friend took pity on me. He gave me a key to his office and said I could use his computer if I came in after midnight and was out by six a.m. That's how my nocturnal lifestyle as a writer began, and how things stayed for years.

Mine was the life of Cinderella in reverse.

As the clocks struck twelve, I'd emerge from my hole. Tapping away, I wove a story from my unrelated travels, anecdotes, and from characters linked together by the curiously neglected theme of Gondwanaland.

Being limited to six hours a night gave me a ready-made structure. Six hours is plenty of time to churn out a pleasingly thick wad of pages. And pages were what I knew – that and the writer's dependable pseudo-science of counting words.

Every two or three days I'd print out what I had written, stuff it into my satchel, and take it home long before dawn had broken over London. From the moment the manuscript was a single page, I regarded it as a seed. With the right care and attention it was destined to grow.

And it did.

The centre of my life, I put it in the middle of the sitting-room floor, in a little house I was sharing with my twin sister, Safia. I was so often away on my travels that she'd taken me in. Each night when I came back from writing, I'd place the fresh pages on the pile, as though I were building a monument.

During the course of the day, Safia would pick the pages up, tidying them away to a shelf. We rarely met, because I was out all night and asleep most of the day, or at the British Library trying to learn more about Gondwanaland.

Safia never once mentioned the pages.

Following my aunt's orders, neither did I.

Gradually, the seed grew into a sapling and, night by night, the sapling transformed into the beginnings of a tree. Until then, I'd never written more than a few pages on any one project – samplers that were always abandoned before they were complete.

For the first time I was working on a full tapestry. I could feel it in my bones, because things were linking up. Anyone who's written a big chunk of pages will know what I mean when I say it felt like magic.

Seasoned writers are sometimes blasé about creating text. It's what they do, despite hitting bouts of fear and angst throughout their career. But I'm certain they all remember the first fleeting moment of wonder – the sense the tree's growing, and all you have to do is to keep typing.

After three weeks of night journeys through my travels, the double-spaced manuscript was an inch and a half thick. Squaring it perfectly, I'd put the pages on the sitting-room floor and walk around them, marvelling.

A month after that, my pages had become a fully fledged tree – a tree three inches thick. I'd worked my way through India and Africa, and was now recounting tales of the Amazon. The more I wrote, the easier and faster it became, like a muscle strengthened by exercise.

Each night, when I sat down in my friend's office, I would put out a few pages of handwritten notes, my rough plan, and the slim red paperback which had so inspired me – Mark Salzman's masterpiece, *Iron & Silk*.

Although I had the plan, the story sloshed around anywhere and everywhere. I went off on spectacular tangents before trying awkwardly to rein myself in. The theme of Gondwanaland may have been inspired, but there was a reason no one had used it in a cultural context before. Much of the time, the book – which I called *In Gondwanaland* – was like a square peg stuffed into a round hole, bashed down with the heel of a shoe.

Whether or not the book worked didn't matter.

What mattered was that it broke the spell – the universal spell holding most would-be authors back from ever writing at all. It proved to me, and to those around me, that I was capable of keeping at a project long enough to finish it.

One snowbound night seven weeks after planting the seed, the tree was ready. At least I thought it was. By this time the manuscript was five inches thick and stretched to 120,000 words. Beginning in central India, it ended on a frozen glacier in Patagonia.

Made in six-hour sessions under the cover of darkness, the journey had changed me. Nothing in my life had ever provided the same intoxicating sense of satisfaction, and almost nothing has since.

Even though the book wasn't edited, I assumed it was all A-OK and ready to go. Having followed my aunt's advice, I'd kept it under wraps. Now that it was finished I wanted everyone to know of my achievement. Desperate for attention and praise, I proclaimed it from the rooftops.

Wherever I went, the manuscript went with me.

If I met friends in a café, it would come – on display at all times, as it was when I went to dinner parties and museums, and even to the cinema. Gloating when anyone asked me about it, I waxed lyrical on the challenges I'd overcome on becoming what I thought was a writer.

By the summer, word of my triumph had spread far and wide.

My father had heard I'd written a book, but I was far too scared to give it to him to read, and he was far too guarded to ask.

So I showed it to Doris Lessing instead.

Out of all our family writer friends, Doris was the person with the most experience and literary clout. When it came to real writers – members of my Salinger Brigade – none was so real as Doris. The very best thing about her was she didn't mince her words.

It was the very worst thing about her as well.

Since I was ten Doris and I had exchanged regular letters and postcards. The correspondence began on the afternoon my parents had a special meeting together in my father's study. I knew it was a special meeting because otherwise they never closed the door except when important guests arrived – people like Salinger.

My twin sister and I sat at the top of the stairs, peering down through the banisters.

'What d'you think they're talking about?' I asked.

'About you!' Safia cackled with certainty.

'What?!'

'You came bottom of the class again, and they're not happy about that.'

'Churchill always came bottom of the class,' I said. 'And he did pretty well later on.'

'Did you tell them that?'

I nodded. 'Yup.'

Before Safia could reply, the study door opened, and my parents called me down. Standing to attention in front of them, like a prisoner before the firing squad, I was reminded how school was important, and that Churchill had been not only literate but prolific. In my parents' estimations anyone who'd written books in abundance was a success.

'Every night you're to write a letter at the desk in the drawing room,' my father said, his voice stern.

'Who to?'

'To anyone you like. To your aunts and uncles, and to the weekenders.'

'But I don't have their addresses.'

My father strode over to a filing cabinet behind the door and tapped a fingertip to the top.

'Every evening when you've written a letter you're to put it up here,' he said, 'and I'll see that it gets posted – do you understand?'

I nodded.

'In your best handwriting, darling,' my mother urged. 'Make sure it's always your best.'

From then on, I became Tahir the letter-writer.

I wrote letters to everyone I could think of...

Letters to my aunts and uncles, and letters to the members of my father's institute who came down at the weekends. Letters to the gardener, to the handyman, the cleaner, and letters to Greville Hayat – the storytelling carpenter who was camped out in what was the old village school. Letters to dozens of rank-and-file family friends, and to the well-known ones, too. Letters to Robert Graves and his wife, Beryl, to the celebrated gardener Russell Page, to Walter Gotell, who played villains in James Bond movies.

But most importantly, letters to Doris.

I took to letter-writing like a duck to water. Observing it in hindsight, it was proof the need to write was inside me, buried down deep under a blanket of communal disbelief.

Within a week or two I got into my stride.

Instead of writing a single letter each evening, I wrote a dozen. Each one was filled with anecdotes and random details of our curious lives at Langton House. Straining to write legibly in fountain pen, I was inquisitive and polite. Just as my letters went out, replies came in – finding their way to the top of the same filing cabinet where my outgoing communications were left each night.

Many of the incoming letters were rushed. Some were patronizing, or thin on detail. Over the weeks, I culled my list, concentrating on those who traded quality with quality.

Of all the people with whom I corresponded, none was quite so accomplished a letter-writer as Doris Lessing. She understood something fundamental, something I myself had grasped hold of early on. It was this:

Fine letter-writing isn't about running through the banal ins and outs of daily life.

Rather, it's about description.

In her letters, Doris's descriptions were things of wonder, just as they were in her published prose. When she wrote to me, she gushed effusively – as if plugged into a bewildering slipstream of imagination. On writing back, other children may have been reserved in their replies. But, as Tahir the letter-writer, I returned the gushing with gushing of my own.

Throughout my travels I wrote to Doris, as usual. I'd send endless aerogrammes and postcards, with an address of the next poste restante. My plans changed constantly, so I imagine there are still unclaimed letters and postcards from Doris still waiting for me in all kinds of places. I found one last year at the poste restante in Nagpur, India. It had been ready for me to collect since the summer of 1989.

Letters were one thing; manuscripts were another.

I'd always known Doris as the funny old lady who stayed at weekends and dried leaves in the herb garden.

Doris the letter-writer.

Doris, the woman who loved cats almost as much as my mother did.

Doris, who gave us each a fifty-pound note at Christmas.

Doris, who said whatever she felt.

Until then I'd not encountered Doris the professional writer, the woman who was to go on to win the Nobel Prize in the last decade of her life. I'd heard about that Doris, or at least had caught glimpses of her – railing against injustice, or defending my father in the press. I assumed Doris the professional was the same as the kindly letter-writing Doris who'd written to me since I was ten.

So, I wrote a letter explaining how I'd written a book, and asking whether she would read it. My sneaky plan – or rather my hope – was that Doris would read it, give a thumbs-up, and the rest would be history.

All I wanted was an easy ride.

After all, having written the damn book I was ready for praise.

The day after I wrote to her, Doris wrote back, her postcard featuring a miniature from Bidpai's *Khalila and Dimna*. In her famously small, spidery script opposite my name and address was an equally small, spidery line:

'Bring it over. I'll read it.'

The next day I arrived at 24 Gondar Gardens in West Hampstead, where Doris lived with her son, Peter. The house was filled with books, with cats, and with clutter, all of it on a mesmerizing scale.

Clambering over unopened parcels, books, and cats, I made my way to the sitting room, on the first floor.

When mugs of treacle-black builder's tea had been brewed up, we sat down in the kitchen.

I made small talk about cats for a good long while, then whipped the manuscript from my satchel.

'Here it is,' I said, as if expecting a round of applause.

Doris swallowed hard.

'Why did you write it?' she asked.

'I'd been on lots of travels,' I said.

'I remember.'

'So I thought I'd craft them into a book.'

'How did you feel when you were writing?'

It was an unexpected question.

'Happy,' I said.

'Good.'

'Is it?'

'Yes. Writing should always make you happy.'

'What if it doesn't?'

'Then it means you're not a writer.'

Retracing the route back through the books, parcels, and cats, I went home, leaving Doris to read *In Gondwanaland*.

Two days later, a letter arrived – small, spidery writing on the front.

I sat on my bed, the envelope in my hands. Gripped with fear and anticipation, I knew it would be make or break.

Doris Lessing may have been a genius, but she had no halfway setting – she either loved or despised.

Tearing the envelope open, I read the contents.

Right from the start I could tell it wasn't the kind of letter I was used to getting from Doris. Gone was the lyrical description of life at home with the cats, or of her childhood in Africa. Gone, too, was the seductive frivolity of one traveller writing to another. In their place was the brutal yet dazzling advice from an author at the top of her game to a would-be nobody...

A would-be nobody who expected success to be dished up right away on a plate.

For thirty years I've kept Doris's letter in the drawer beside my bed, along with a clutch of other papers and mementos, the kind which root me to reality. In all that time I've only ever read it once – on the morning it arrived. On occasion I've taken it out and tried to read it, but I've never managed to. There's no need to re-read it, because its message is seared into my mind.

In unmasked language it confirmed that my story was energized and enthusiastic – that was good. But it was careless and needed editing – bad.

A line towards the end summarized Doris's thinking. As I remember, it went something like:

'I think you are capable of writing something very extraordinary. My advice would be to put this book down and start work on something else. Throw yourself into it as though your life depended on it.'

The letter made for a sour-tasting tonic – one I wasn't ready to understand. It put an immediate end to my high-spirited gloating. I threw the manuscript under the bed with the shoebox full of journals and forced myself to forget about it.

Secretly, I cursed Doris.

Cursed her for not clapping and whooping with delight.

Cursed her for not packaging her advice in warm, slushy love.

But most of all, I cursed Doris for not giving me a helping hand up onto the top table.

Years later, I received a message from a close friend.

She said her ex-boyfriend had written a novel and, as I knew about books, she wondered whether I would give him some advice.

Ever happy to help, I asked for the manuscript to be sent over. It arrived a week later, furled up in sheets of tissue, and printed on some of the finest typing paper I've ever seen.

'Gosh,' I thought, 'this guy thinks highly of himself.'

It reminded me of myself.

Intrigued, I dropped the book I was working on, retreated to the sofa, and read the manuscript from beginning to end. A long, twisting tale of adventure, tribulation, and unrequited love, it spanned three centuries and three-quarters of the globe.

As I reached the last page, I got a flash of myself sitting with Doris in her kitchen, cats mewing at my heels, *In*

Gondwanaland clutched to my chest.

Picking up my laptop, I wrote two messages.

The first said this:

'You've written the most incredibly exciting and wonderful novel, and I congratulate you for writing it. Your power of observation is incomparable, and your ability to tell a tale in an original way is sublime. The very best luck, Tahir Shah.'

Leaving a few lines blank, I typed a second message:

'Thank you for sending me your manuscript, which I read with interest. From the first page onwards, I realized it was dull, laboured, badly written and – in places – tedious in the extreme. But on page 326, I found a nugget of genius – the likes of which I cannot ever remember experiencing. My advice to you is to put this book on a high shelf and start a new one. Make sure to take out page 326, and tape it above your desk. Study it. Believe in it. Make that page the seed for your writing career, learn from it, and you will be destined for unknown success.'

Then I wrote a covering note to my friend, whose ex-boyfriend had sent me the manuscript.

It read:

'Having not met your ex-boyfriend, I'm not sure whether he wants praise or serious guidance. For this reason, I leave it to you to judge. You will find two letters attached. If you think he's in need of praise, please give him the first letter. But, if you think he has what it takes

THE REASON TO WRITE

to be a real writer, make sure to delete the first, and give him the second instead.'

I never heard which letter she gave him.

Alas, I expect it was the first.

The Wowing

MALCOLM GLADWELL GOT a tidal wave of attention when he came up with the concept of needing ten thousand hours' experience, and quite rightly so.

But in my opinion, he could have doubled it to twenty thousand hours.

Most writers don't churn out A-grade work after such a short amount of time. Writing eight hours a day for three and a half years or so gets you to the magic figure of ten thousand hours.

Agreed, three and a half years isn't insignificant, but it's not enough to get into the maestro zone. You may say some people are naturally brilliant, and you'd be right. Even then, I'd say mastery takes longer.

What I've learned is that a real writer – who writes because if he doesn't he'll turn to stone – begins as a feeble little stream heading down a mountain. You can drop a boulder in the stream to dam the flow. It'll work, at least for a while. Then the water will well up, flow around the rock, and carry on down the mountain.

Boulders dropped into the stream are a good thing.

Good, because they force the wannabe member of the Salinger Brigade to take stock, redouble their efforts, and set off again.

Doris Lessing's letter – the one I've never re-read out of my own shamefaced sense of wretchedness – got me thinking. If I wanted to break in, I'd have to take writing seriously, and treat it like a job.

While reeling from Doris's knockout blow between the eyes, I flew down to Kenya to stay with my friend, the seasoned explorer Sir Wilfred Thesiger. He was living near Maralal with the nomadic Samburu tribe, in a shack perched halfway up a mountainside. We'd spend the days eating overcooked goat stew and sipping sweet tea. Between the long bouts of silence, Thesiger would recount his adventures in Africa and Arabia fifty years before.

One afternoon, we were drinking hot, sweet tea in the shade of a thorn tree as usual. It was forty-three degrees outside. Dressed in a patched tweed jacket, Thesiger was telling me about the time he attended Emperor Haile Selassie's coronation back in 1930. I'd heard it dozens of times before – but the best stories improve with repetition, and that one certainly did.

Sir Wilfred was about to describe the Imperial procession. I knew exactly what line he would utter next, and awaited it with anticipation.

The veteran explorer gazed into the middle distance as he relived the pomp and circumstance. His lips parting, he was about to deliver the next line, when a little boy charged into the shack and yelled something loudly in Swahili.

'Be quiet, little horror!' Thesiger yelled. 'I'm telling a story!'

Shaking his fists and stamping his feet, the boy cried

the same thing over and over.

'What's he saying?'

Thesiger listened, then raised his eyebrows.

'Oh,' he said.

'What?'

'The little horror says there's a man in Maralal with an electric arm.'

Curious by nature, I left Thesiger to his memories and slipped down to the Green Bar – at the time Maralal's one and only watering hole. Almost lost in the shadows was a short, stout Indian man. Around his neck were dangling three Nikon cameras and, strapped to his left shoulder, was what looked like a bionic arm.

'Nice bit of kit,' I said, pointing at the device.

'It is when it works – which is none of the time.'

'What's the trouble?'

'The heat and the dust.'

'Sorry to hear it.'

The man with the bionic arm glanced at me sideways.

'Here for the circumcision, are you?'

'Excuse me?'

'The circumcision.'

'*Circumcision?*'

'Yeah. The Samburu one. Supposed to be any day now.'

'I'm staying with Thesiger,' I said. 'Thesiger the explorer.'

'I know who he is. He usually comes to it – enjoys a

circumcision, Thesiger does.'

'Does he?'

'Course he does.'

Maralal is a small town by any standards, or at least it was back then. So small that strangers get chatting in ways which might be unnatural elsewhere. In such outposts, strangers are thrust together because if they weren't, they'd go insane.

The Indian removed his arm, laid it on the table, and invited me to sit.

Without quite knowing why, I blurted out:

'Just wrote a travel book. It started with a waiter taking off his leg and using it as a pillow.'

'A writer, are you?'

'Yes.'

'What've you written?'

'A travel book. It's called *In Gondwanaland*.'

'Is it published?'

'Going to be soon,' I lied.

The man with the bionic arm stretched out a hand.

'I'm Mohamed Amin,' he said.

I believe sequences of unrelated events determine our future, and that you have to cling hold of opportunities when they come along.

Despondency at Doris's letter had led me to lie low in Samburuland with Thesiger. And being there in the time of the circumcisions had led me to Mohamed

Amin. Just as I'm a believer in key sequences of events, I've come to value the big characters life throws one's way.

Most of the time they pass you by, like fallen leaves carried down the river. They're usually moving too fast to catch, or they're obviously meant for someone else. But sometimes they head for you in a way which signals you're supposed to grab them.

Mohamed Amin was destined to influence me in an unlikely and particular way. Sitting in the cool shadows of the Green Bar, I had no idea how he would shape the course of my writing life. At the time of our first meeting, I assumed he was a nutcase with an unhealthy preoccupation with circumcisions.

A few weeks later I mentioned meeting a man with a bionic arm to Dirk, my Dutch war-junkie journalist pal in Nairobi.

Dirk rolled his eyes.

'D'you know him?'

'Sure I do. Everyone knows Mo.'

'Really?'

'He's a one-man publicity machine. I swear he had his arm blown off just for the attention.'

'How did he lose it?'

'In the fall of Mengistu.'

'Addis Ababa?'

'Yup. 'Ninety-one. An ammunition dump went up. Mo was filming right near it. God knows how he survived. A shell zipped past the soundman's head. Didn't even touch him, but the speed was enough to cave his head in. Imagine that. The same shell took off Mo's left arm.'

'Who does he work for?'

'Viznews, the BBC, anyone who pays. Mo's a gun-for-hire. He's got his own outfit in the Press Centre – Camerapix. He's still dining out on the famine.'

'Which one?'

'The big one. Korem 'eighty-four.'

'The one that kickstarted Live Aid?'

'Yup.'

'Mo was there?'

My journalist friend grinned.

'It was only because of Mo the story got out.'

'Thought it was Michael Buerk and the BBC.'

'Buerk was the face on camera, but it was Mo who got access, filmed it, and broke the story.'

'Then he's a frigging legend!'

'A legend and a shameless self-publicist.'

'I want to meet him again,' I said.

'Why?'

'To hear his stories.'

Dirk groaned.

'He's gonna gobble you up,' he said.

An hour later, I was in Mo's office at the Press Centre, the walls hung with oversized shots of him posing with celebrities and heads of state. Mo with Idi Amin, with Mother Teresa, with Mandela, Qaddafi, Clinton, George Bush Sr, and the Queen of England.

Laid along one wall were stacks of equipment – TV cameras, tripods, cables, and battered aluminium cases marked 'PRESS'. Across from them, beside a tower of coffee-table volumes, was the bionic arm sitting in its open case.

I was admiring it when Mo walked in.

'That's a fucking useless piece of shit!' he said angrily.

'How was the circumcision?'

Mo Amin scowled.

'The fucking Samburu cancelled it. Can't rely on them for anything.'

'Probably best for it to stay private,' I said.

Mo scoffed.

'They called it off because there weren't enough press.'

'You mean they want attention?!'

'Of course they do! The Samburu are sick of being outdone by the Maasai tribe.'

I sat down on the frail fold-out chair reserved for visitors, while Mo sashayed round to the far side of his voluminous desk. In his own time he lowered himself onto a plush leather throne – the kind of thing usually reserved for African dictators.

Through my own insecurity, I spewed out a random anecdote featuring a well-known actor friend. It was supposed to help me make a point about the power of the press, but it nose-dived in the most spectacular way.

Mo Amin's smile soured ferociously.

Inhaling deeply, he launched into the mother of all anecdotes that cemented his position as the most famous cameraman and news operator in the known world. It featured presidents and royalty, actors, dictators, Nobel Laureates and Live Aid, Bob Geldof, and the Rolling Stones.

When it was over, I was pinned rigid to the rickety old chair. It was as though every cell in my body had been realigned from the full force of the most impressive extravaganza in name-dropping.

'Wow,' I whispered. 'That was incredible.'

'That's nothing!' Mo growled. 'One day I'll tell you about the time I first met Idi Amin.'

Having been raised in England, a realm in which self-promotion is frowned upon, I would usually have dismissed the hype as nonsense. But there was something irresistible about it. The only other person I'd ever seen get away with laying it on so fabulously thick was when the boxer Muhammad Ali appeared on talk shows. Conceited and egotistical to the point of caricature, the legendary boxer had earned his fame through sustaining pain in the ring – just as Mo had earned it by having his left arm blown off in the fall of Addis Ababa.

For three hours I sat there as the fusillade of anecdotes was fired at me full force. In all that time I wasn't asked for my opinion once, or whether I had any stories of my own. The bombardment was the kind of thing the US military has called 'Shock and Awe', and what I came to know as 'The Wowing'.

As Mo's stock-in-trade, it was like the strutting of a peacock with his tail out for all to see, combined with the head-thrown-back howling of an Alaskan wolf. I didn't realize it, but there was a purpose to The Wowing – a purpose far more than merely making Mo feel good about himself.

I was being wowed for a reason.

That first day at the Camerapix office was a kind of interview, part of an elaborate set-up. Only later did I realize Mo had picked me out back at the Green Bar in Maralal. He'd chosen me to write for him because I possessed the one thing he regarded as supremely important – the quality that could not be bought or indeed sold:

Enthusiasm.

In the big wide world there are plenty of enthusiastic people out there – and some of them are extremely enthusiastic indeed. But I like to think my enthusiasm is in an entirely different league. That's because somehow – and I'm not sure how – I managed to maintain the enthusiasm levels of a six-year-old who's desperate to eat ice cream down at the beach.

For that reason I can 'out-enthusiasm' almost anyone I meet.

THE REASON TO WRITE

As soon as he'd experienced my enthusiasm in the fly-infested shadows of the Green Bar, Mo had wanted to fish me from the river. He knew full well that were he to catch me and wow me, I would work like a maniac... because I was running on High Octane Enthusiasm.

By the early nineties, Mo Amin was the most famous cameraman ever to have lived – thanks to the Ethiopian famine and the global Live Aid concert that followed. Long before the break onto the world stage, he'd been a news cameraman and photographer – having begun honing his craft in the sixties, in the Tanzanian capital, Dar-es-Salaam.

As a sideline to the news business, Mo had started producing guides and coffee-table books, most of them relating to Africa. By the time we crossed paths in Maralal, he had a well-developed pipeline, with glossy new titles being churned out all the time.

Mo took the pictures himself. The texts tended to be written by Brian Tetley, an affable old Fleet Street hack who'd moved to Nairobi, lured by the prospect of cheap beer, cigarettes, and plenty of sun.

Added into the mix were a handful of submissive editorial assistants, most of them living on crumbs. Reigning over the empire that was Camerapix Publishing was Mohamed Amin: enforcer, chairman, and editor-in-chief.

The only thing lacking was an endangered species – enthusiastic young writers who'd write books under impossible conditions, and never ask questions. The problem was that writers with experience elsewhere would never work for Mo. The conditions of his employment were tantamount to slavery, and his bouts of indiscriminate rage were almost as remarkable as the intensity of The Wowing.

I can't think of any writers who stuck it out at Camerapix, except for Tetley. He was different from the keen young writers in that he'd been broken by Mo years before, like a tamed elephant toiling in the forest of the Indian hinterland. The enthusiastic new arrivals became ensnared for two or three books, before legging it.

But each of them left with the same gift as me:
The gift of belief in one's own productivity.

Mo

A COUPLE OF weeks after The Wowing, I was dangling from the open door of a Jordanian Air Force Super Puma above the ancient rock-hewn city of Petra.

Beside me, bionic arm strapped in place, was Mo.

I'd been conscripted to write a guidebook to Jordan, having signed the contract with no questions asked. I'd never signed a literary agreement before, and so had no reason to think the terms were odd.

On offer was:
- A luxurious two-week jaunt around Jordan
- £400 cash
- Three economy tickets on any Ethiopian Airlines flight
- A Somali passport

In return, I agreed to hammer out the full text of the guide – all 140,000 words of it – in no more than a month.

The Jordan trip had been arranged by the kingdom's royal family, and all the stops were pulled out. Having been flown in first class, I was given my own private guard and chauffeur, and permitted access to anything I liked.

During the two weeks I spent in Jordan, Mo appeared for a few days, then jetted off to pose with a line-up of African dictators at a conference somewhere far away.

Following the jaunt, I regrouped in my digs in London, trying to work out how I'd come up with a massive wordage in such a remarkably short amount of time. These were the days before the Internet, when research material had to be tracked down on foot.

That first morning, I made a list of everything which had to be covered, as well as a daily writing list. If I was to get the manuscript handed in on time I'd have to write 6,000 words a day for just over three weeks. That would give me five days to read through and correct, and a day to tie up loose ends.

Thankfully, my friend with the office let me write there again. He stretched my hours, allowing me to work there from eight p.m. until seven a.m. I later repaid him with a flight to Beijing on Ethiopian – spoils of my hard grind.

Night after night, I described the Jordanian kingdom in a way that I hoped sounded fresh and seamless. I did my level best to paper over the glaring shortcomings in my knowledge, because there'd simply been no time to do all the research. Each evening, I'd type like a maniac whose family would be put to death if he didn't complete the task.

I wrote about Jordan's history from Neolithic times right up to the current date, about the kingdom's towns and cities, the Crusader castles and the pleasure palaces of the eastern desert. I wrote about the festivals and the folklore, about the carpet-weaving, the jewellery, the minorities, and pages and pages about the royal family – who'd funded the project.

By the end of a month I was shell-shocked. I'd forgotten how to speak, was half-blind, and my fingertips were numb. All I could think of were words and the white spaces between them. On the last night, having typed my way through the hotel listings, I'd fallen asleep at the keyboard.

My friend whose office I was using found me snoozing when he came in.

'Jesus Christ!' he yelled. 'You look like death warmed up!'

'Feel like it,' I said limply. 'But at least I'm done.'

'Hope you've learned your lesson.'

I nodded.

'I'll never work for that bastard again,' I said.

Three months later, I was back with Mo – this time in Namibia.

Having cut my teeth on the guidebook – surely the most wretched writing task in the history of wretched writing tasks – I was upgraded to produce a coffee-table book. The route from London to Windhoek, the Namibian capital, was anything but direct. Calling it 'zigzag' would have been a kindness.

It was way more indirect than that.

In addition to his book-publishing business, Mohamed Amin produced a slew of in-flight magazines as well – including for Ethiopian Airlines and Air Seychelles. In a publishing empire built on barter rather than currency, he was provided with fistfuls of tickets in return for handling the magazines.

Although there was a direct flight from London to Windhoek, I was cajoled into making the trip via Frankfurt, Addis Ababa, Mumbai, and Johannesburg.

At the time of our arrival, Namibia was the newest country in the world.

A few days before the Queen of England had come and gone, having attended a ceremony that provided a glorious chunk of Africa with full independence. Samuel Njoma had been sworn in as president – a good thing because he was Mo's closest pal. No surprise in that, of course. As Mo used to say, 'You've gotta back the winning side in Africa or else you'll never make it out alive, and your pictures won't ever see the light of day.'

As well as being skilled in identifying enthusiastic young writers to labour in his salt mines, the veteran newsman instinctively knew who'd rise to the top – in Africa at least. For thirty years he'd befriended dictators and despots – including presidential serial killers, psychopaths, and at least two cannibals. For someone like me, who'd studied African dictatorships, his stories were irresistible. Drawn in deep, I allowed myself to be enslaved in Mo's own tyrannical regime.

With only two weeks on the ground, there wasn't a hope in hell of seeing more than a fraction of Namibia. While I was sent to the north, another fledgling writer, who'd been drafted in to do the guidebook, was sent to the south. Mo gave strict instructions for us to meet in the middle and to tell each other about what we'd seen.

The highlight of my Namibian journey was being flown up to the Skeleton Coast, on the border with Angola, in a Cessna. The brutal Benguela current has wrecked ships there for more than a century, and has washed up whale carcasses throughout history. I was deeply affected by that secret corner of wilderness, and during the journey my love for Africa was made complete.

If the Skeleton Coast was the highlight, the lowlight was Etosha National Park.

I am by nature a lone traveller, and can't bear tourism in any shape or form. It repulses me – disgusts me in the most primeval way. The reason is that tourists don't have a reason – they're there just because they're there. So it was a terrible shock to be drafted in to an organized tour of Etosha, which bills itself as Africa's most sensational game park.

I found myself in the rear of a Mercedes tour bus packed with retired workers from a ball-bearings factory in Düsseldorf. From the moment I clambered aboard, they could smell I wasn't one of them.

As the bus traversed the desert on its way to Etosha, towering termite mounds peppering the landscape from horizon to horizon, I vowed to escape.

That's exactly what I did.

A few miles from Etosha we pulled in at a service

station in the middle of nowhere. An announcement was made in German, saying we had ten minutes to use the facilities. To me, it meant I had ten minutes to come up with a plan.

The only other vehicle there was a ramshackle jalopy which looked like it had gasped its last gasp. The bonnet was open, and clouds of smoke were billowing from the engine. A pair of spindly legs were poking out from underneath, ending in worn-out boots.

I tapped one of the feet.

Shuffling and struggling, the man extricated himself, spat hard at the dirt, and greeted me with an ear-to-ear grin.

He had an ample beard – the kind Islamist suicide squads tend to sport – and big blue eyes hinting of real kindness.

'Can you take me with you?' I asked.

'Take you where?'

'Anywhere.'

'Running away from something are you?'

'How did you guess?'

'The look in your eyes. You look frightened.'

'It's the Germans,' I said, 'I'm running from the Germans. They don't like me, and I don't like them.'

The man with the jalopy held out a hand. It was callused and worn like the barnacled hull of a ship.

'I'm Hennie,' he said. 'Hennie van Wyk.'

Hennie and I spent a week together zigzagging through Namibia.

He was a scrap metal dealer on a mission, and I was a wannabe writer hiding from the Germans from Düsseldorf, and from Mohamed Amin. As Hennie explained again and again in his lyrical voice, times were bad – and in bad times you couldn't sit on your ass. That was because in the bad times you had to remind people you were their friend, so they'd be your friend when the good times finally rolled around again.

Hennie was one of the most naturally friendly people I'd ever met. His friendliness was overwhelming and bona fide – unlike Mo's friendliness, which was laid on in a frightening way as a means to an end.

When we finally rumbled into Windhoek, Hennie and I were dear friends. Hugging each other, we promised to stay in touch, and to write letters every week.

Standing on the forecourt of the hotel, I watched as Hennie's dilapidated pickup trundled away, the back brimming with twisted scrap metal, exhaust fumes streaming behind like a vapour trail.

Keeping my promise, I sent dozens of letters and postcards.

But Hennie never wrote back.

As instructed, the other writer – who was working on the guidebook – told me about the south, and I told him about the north. Or, rather, I told him about Hennie van Wyk. I recounted every tale he'd told me – about the boom years in scrap metal, and about the dark times as well.

'Wish you could have met him,' I said with a sigh. 'Hennie was a king among men.'

'Not sure how much scrap metal talk I can squeeze into the guide,' the other writer said.

'Pity. We should all have the gift of Hennie van Wyk. His stories have a way of opening up your mind.'

'You gonna write about him?'.

'You bet I am – an entire chapter. I'll call it "Travels With Hennie". Come to think of it, I'll dedicate the book to him.'

The other writer's face froze.

'Mo's not gonna like that,' he said.

'Why not? He's doing the pictures. The text is up to me.'

The return trip to London took me via South Africa, the Seychelles, Ethiopia, India, and Germany.

For reasons I never understood, it was necessary to fly from Addis Ababa to Mumbai twice – like a tennis ball being knocked back and forth over a net.

Mo had saved the one direct ticket to London for himself, and was waiting for me at Heathrow when I landed.

'I'll need the text in two weeks,' he snarled.

'Not sure if that's possible. I've got a week booked in the country with my family.'

'No you don't! You've got two weeks with your nose down, writing.'

'But I don't even have a computer. I have to sneak into my friend's office and work through the night.'

'Then you have two weeks of night-sneaking.'

'OK,' I said mournfully.

Mo scratched a thumbnail to his bald head as if remembering something.

'And I'll need a speech about Namibia as well. A good long one gushing with love for Namibia.'

'Where are you going to deliver it?'

'It's not for me,' Mo said. 'It's for Sam Njoma, the president.'

Falling back into my pattern of nocturnal writing, I knocked out the manuscript for *Journey Through Namibia* in under two weeks. Compared to the trial and tribulation of the guidebook, it was a cakewalk. Besides, I delighted in describing my friend, Hennie van Wyk – and wrote an effusive dedication to him at the front.

I put the typescript on a floppy disk and it was taken down to Nairobi in a diplomatic pouch. Mo Amin was all about calling in favours – and the diplomatic corps of African dictatorships was a linchpin in his favour network.

A month later, an edited, typeset version of my manuscript arrived. Eagerly, I opened it up, and turned to my florid dedication to Hennie van Wyk. It was missing – deleted, as was every mention of my dear scrap-metal-dealer chum.

Slowly, I flipped through the printout.

Almost every word had been rewritten by Tetley, the Fleet Street hack.

I sent Mo a message ordering him to remove my name from the book, saying I wanted to distance myself from him and his wretched firm.

He didn't reply, but went ahead and published under my name.

Three years passed.

Throwing myself into journalism, I felt empowered by the knowledge I could produce massive wordage with nothing to go on. From time to time I'd get an urge to reach out to Mo. Like one half of an estranged couple who'd once shared intensity, I despised him – but I missed him all the same.

One Sunday afternoon I found myself in Nairobi. I'd been up in Samburuland again – on the trail of an English woman called Cheryl, who'd married a Samburu warrior.

With a few hours to spare before my flight home, I picked up the phone and called Mo on his hotline – the one he reserved for heads of state.

Ten minutes later I was sitting on the dining chair in his office once again.

'What was all that fucking crap about scrap fucking metal?!' Mo thundered. 'Tetley had to chop it all out!'

'He rewrote every line, the bastard.'

'Course he did. That's what he gets paid to do.'
'Paid in Somali passports and zigzag flights?'
'Some people would kill for a Somali passport!' Mo growled.
'Would they?'
'Yes, they would!'
'I'll bear that in mind.'
Mohamed Amin leaned back on his tinpot dictator's chair.
'So what's next?' he asked.
'I'm going up to London to file my story.'
'Not that.'
'Then what?'
'What's next for us – for you and me?'
I let out a high-pitched giggle crossed with a scream.
'There is no *next*.'
'Got a problem with the colour of my money?'
'Your money doesn't have a colour because it's invisible.'
'Want to go to Mecca with me – full access?'
The Holy City had been at the top of my wish list ever since I'd read my father's classic travel book *Destination Mecca*.
I narrowed my eyes.
'What are you offering?'
'Flights on Ethiopian and Air Seychelles.'
'What else?'
'A diplomatic Somali passport...'

'And...?'
'And a tour of Swaziland.'
'I hate tours,' I said.
'All right,' Mo bristled, bringing out the big guns. 'I'll give you breakfast with Idi Amin.'

For me, as a former student of African dictatorships, the holy grail was meeting the deposed cannibalistic ruler of Uganda and self-styled King of Scotland.

Mo's family may have been originally from the Indian subcontinent, but the fact he shared a last name with the dictator had enabled him to acquire rare and unparalleled access – access Mo exploited shamelessly.

We shook hands, and I forgave him for expunging Hennie van Wyk from literary history, and for allowing Brian Tetley to butcher my work.

The Mecca trip was scheduled for the next month, followed by breakfast with Idi Amin, who was enjoying sanctuary in Jeddah.

Returning to London, I got on with my journalism.

Three weeks later I was woken early on a Saturday morning by my sister, Saira.

Our father was dead.

It was a phone call that pressed 'pause' on my life, and an event I've never quite recovered from.

That afternoon something prompted me to turn on the TV news.

An Ethiopian Airlines flight ET961 from Addis

Ababa to Nairobi had been hijacked. As fate would have it, Mohamed Amin and his sidekick Brian Tetley were on board. Mo was up front in first class, while Tetley was at the back of economy. Apparently drunk and armed with grenades, the hijackers had ordered the pilot to fly them to Australia. They'd selected the destination from the map in the in-flight magazine, *Selamta* – of which Mo was the publisher.

The hijackers had ordered the pilot to stop following the African coastline and to cross the Indian Ocean. As the plane neared the pristine beaches of the Comoro Islands, it ran out of fuel.

A wingtip brushed the water, and flight ET961 disintegrated.

Amazingly, a few passengers at the back of the aircraft survived.

Brian Tetley, the Fleet Street hack, was not one of them.

As for Mo Amin, he'd been desperately negotiating with the hijackers. Until the moment the plane hit the water, he had once again been on top of the biggest news story in the world.

On that bewitched day in late 1996, I lost my father, Mo, and all hope of ever having breakfast with Idi Amin.

Extermination

THIRTY-FIVE YEARS before that late November day took its unspeakably heavy toll, my father had established a publishing company, called The Octagon Press.

Octagon published classic Oriental texts on folklore and philosophy, storytelling, wisdom, and what my father termed 'practical psychology'. The firm was based on a concept I myself have championed – no doubt a result of my living in its shadow all my life.

The concept was that conventional publishers are in search of one thing, and one thing alone – work which will sell in its millions and make them richer than rich.

Along with a handful of small independent publishers, Octagon followed another model. Rather than trying to sell zillions of books in the hope of literary bonanza, it was established to release work my father regarded as being important to a select group. He recognized that, as things stood, there was no chance the material he was launching would be welcomed by the mainstream.

At least, not in his lifetime.

His thinking went that if one person read something he had written, and then applied it, a change would occur on a micro level. That change would enable another change to take place, and then another, and another.

In the final year of his life I questioned why he didn't release everything through more established publishers.

'For three reasons,' he said. 'First, publishers are idiots. They're only in publishing because they're too stupid to get proper jobs. Second, because through Octagon Press I can present work in the purest and most perfect state with no danger of it being hacked about. And, third, because this method enables us to release a great deal of interrelated work. When it's all put together, it'll form a kind of course in its own right.'

At that moment my father looked at me hard, as though what he was about to explain was of vital importance.

'The work I've released so far isn't even half of my total corpus,' he said. 'There's a mountain of material left to be launched in the decades after my death. I'm leaving it to you and your sisters to publish it when the right time comes.'

'But why don't you publish it all now, Baba?' I asked.

'Simple: because people aren't ready. I've spent thirty years preparing the ground, planting the seeds, and watching them grow into saplings. The last thing we need to do is to rush. So be patient and bide your time. It's going to be a long while before the saplings have matured into young trees.'

'*Years?*'

'*Decades.*'

'But everyone will be begging us to publish it.'

'Naturally they're all crying out for new books. They want *new, new, new*, when they should really be asking for *old, old, old!*'

'So...?'

'So don't tell them about this other work. Keep it secret, or else they'll stop studying the material I've published so far. And without the first steps they won't get anywhere at all.'

'How will we know when the time's come to release the other work?'

My father stared at me without speaking.

Of all the time we ever shared, it was burnt into my memory more powerfully than any other. It was as though he was thinking of three things: the work he was leaving, the audience for whom it was destined, and me.

'You will know when the time is right,' he said.

In the years before my father's death, I helped out with Octagon Press.

As a result, I got a well-rounded idea of the publishing business – albeit on a micro scale. I learned about editing and typesetting, how books were proofed, printed, and warehoused, the ins and outs of distribution, bookselling, and publicity.

The most valuable thing of all was when I took queries to my father – whether they concerned foreign rights, ongoing projects, or plans to reprint. It was valuable because he always answered my questions in the most fantastically clear way. He never contradicted himself, and almost every decision was supported by a concise line of explanation, as if he wanted me to learn.

A month or so before he died, he held up the morning newspaper, in which he'd circled an item in the business section. The piece included a photo of a printing machine which looked like an overgrown photocopier, and a caption: 'The way of things to come.'

'Publishing's going to change,' my father said studiously. 'And about time too.'

'What d'you think will happen?'

'Just as the newspaper says, people are going to be able to read books on electronic screens – like laptops, only smaller. You'll be able to order a book on the Internet, and have it printed just for you.'

'What does that mean for publishers?' I asked.

'Extermination,' my father said approvingly. 'But for writers it means freedom!'

Way of the Crossbow

IN THE YEARS since Doris imparted her unpalatable blend of wisdom and truth, I'd carved out a life for myself in journalism.

Unlike my sister, Saira, who was a proper news journalist from the get-go, I recognized my calling was different. This was due largely to the fact that, as a dreamer, I was unable to keep to the facts. As I saw it, facts were dull and ought only to be used when human-interest material was unavailable.

The first article I ever wrote was for *High Life*, the British Airways in-flight magazine. I'd been pestering the editor about something. Out of the blue she asked if I'd write a piece about a tiger reserve in India.

'We'll need it by tomorrow night,' she said. 'So, of course you'll have to invent it. Best if you can give us the sense you were actually there.'

Hanging up the call, I closed my eyes and imagined myself on the back of an elephant, tramping through dawn mist on the trail of tigers. A couple of hours later I'd conjured the text. To my surprise, it was received with giddy delight.

'That was easy,' I thought to myself. 'I've become a journalist.'

For three years I did nothing but write articles – most of them on subjects proper journalists would have considered horrific or bizarre.

THE REASON TO WRITE

A writer I knew had written an inspiring piece about Emma McCune, an Englishwoman who'd fallen in love with a Sudanese rebel commander and gone to live with him. He'd sold British rights to the *Daily Mail*, then syndicated it internationally to women's magazines all over the world – making a small fortune in the process.

Over egg and chips at a greasy spoon in Kilburn he revealed the secrets of feature writing he'd picked up so far:

- Concentrate on key people. Give masses of detail so readers feel as though they know them. Tell them how they look, sound, and smell. Start with the main character and end with them, too. Pepper the piece with a few facts to make it look like you know what you're going on about, but don't overdo it, because in feature writing detail and description are the key currency, not facts.
- Take the pictures as well. Make sure you get a wide range – big wide shots, close-ups, and everything in between. The golden rule is to look for colour – anything with colour, even if it's not related to the subject matter... you can weave it in later.
- The article has to be tight and have a clear message. It's not about you – it's about the person, or people, you're writing about. Keep to the length you've been asked for. Make sure every paragraph earns its place.
- Freelance journalism is about selling – not writing.

It doesn't have to be prize-winning literature, but it has to work – both on its own and with the pictures.
- Never sell world rights as a whole. Split them down. You make far more money that way. Supply the photos as well, and never let a magazine send a photographer if you can avoid it, because you'll end up splitting the budget.
- Most important of all: if you manage to sell a feature, hit the editor right away with another and then another – prove you're a safe, reliable pair of hands.

As with creative writing, I often hear of courses teaching journalism – courses aspiring writers swear by.

I realize there's journalism and there's journalism.

First, there's journalism that assembles the facts, examining them from every angle; and then there's the other kind of journalism – the journalism which is more like an enchanted treasure trail twisting through people's lives.

I'm against studying journalism for all sorts of reasons. The main one is that it's too observational and not sufficiently hands on. Some things have to be studied – like brain surgery or mathematics. But more abstract fields are far more about intuition.

In my opinion, the best way to learn how to write is to sell your work; and the best way to get started on selling your work – and to learn to write at the same time – is to follow the journalist path. Nothing teaches a budding member of the Salinger Brigade the nuts and bolts of the craft in such a systematic and intensive way.

You may be reading this and thinking to yourself – 'Yeah, well that's what he thinks because it's the way he did it. I've done the courses and learnt so much.'

If that's the case, I'm happy for you.

But trust me.

Try writing something short and selling it.

When we were kids, we were given almost no money at all. It didn't really matter, because the only thing we wanted to buy was chocolate. I have described somewhere else how our father showed us how to make money by selling seeds gathered from the garden. Our meagre pocket money was bolstered by seed-selling, and by the crisp fifty-pound bonanza which usually arrived from Doris Lessing at Christmas.

All in all, it wasn't a bad livelihood for a kid.

Except for selling seeds, the only other time I learned how to make money was the summer I made crossbows.

Throughout my childhood, I used to go up to the old village school-house on the edge of our land, where I'd find Greville, the carpenter, who built all the furniture for Langton House. He was a gifted storyteller, and I loved listening to the tales he conjured while he worked.

I always got the feeling Greville wanted me to learn carpentry, so that I could be a proper craftsman like him. He must have seen that my skill set lay in another area, because my motor coordination was wretched.

One summer, Greville told me that the secret of creating was to look at what materials were on hand, and to use them as best you could. A valuable life lesson, it was the reason I learned to make crossbows.

Greville urged me to look in the pile of old wood, to find a few good bits, and bring them to him. Doing as he'd asked, I fished out a couple of long batons.

'What d'you think we could make from those?' he asked.

'Crossbows,' I said.

'Why d'you say that?'

'Because I've always wanted a crossbow.'

Nodding, Greville told me a story about an archer who fell down a tunnel in the forest and emerged in a magical kingdom.

Then, little by little, he showed me how to make a crossbow from two short lengths of wood, a couple of hooped nails, and a long strand of elastic cut from the curtains. For arrows, I used a finer grade of baton, which I notched at one end, and sharpened at the other.

The crossbow was an immediate sensation.

The next afternoon, my father emerged from his study to walk around the garden, where he found me with my crossbow. A line of younger children were following me, like rats behind the Pied Piper – each one desperate to have a go with my precious weapon.

Calling me aside, my father whispered in my ear:

'Why don't you knock up some more of those and

sell them to your friends?'

Slinking back to the workshop, I began a crossbow-making production line. There was plenty of wood, hooped nails, and miles of elastic in the curtains. Applauding my sense of industry, Greville helped me get to the higher strands of elastic, once the lower-hanging fruit had been harvested.

Next day I had twelve crossbows, which I sold for 25p each.

My father found me on the lawn counting my coins.

'Selling what you've made feels good, doesn't it?' he asked.

I nodded.

'Feels amazing.'

My father frowned.

'Where's your own crossbow, the first one?'

'Sold it.'

'Didn't want to keep it?'

'Nope.'

'Why not?'

'Because I can make myself another crossbow any time I like.'

The crossbow extravaganza had brought joy to everyone, except for the poor person who had to repair the curtains. It taught me the joy of being paid for something I'd created. The feeling is different from re-selling an object you already own. What was important was making something from scratch which had an intrinsic value of its own – a value others would be willing to pay good money for.

Selling the first article I ever wrote – the one about watching tigers from elephant back – was my first taste of the Promised Land. Later, I got the same feeling from chipping away in Mohamed Amin's salt mines, but it wasn't nearly so intense.

I've reflected why not, and have concluded that knocking out that initial article, and banking the cheque, was magical because it was so immediate. It must have been how Picasso felt when he sketched the *Dove of Peace* on the restaurant table and sold it to his fan for a small fortune.

The joy for me was how the process had been stripped down to its bare moving parts. I'd been asked for sixteen hundred words, thought about it, knocked it out, sent it in, and *boom*! – I got paid, just like that.

'Wow!' I thought to myself. 'This is fabulous... all I need to do is churn out pieces, and I'll be rich.'

So I churned and I churned, and I churned and I churned.

I wrote articles about the taste of coffee in my favourite café up in Hampstead, and pieces about London's obscure blue plaques. I wrote pieces about abandoned cinemas, and historic tram routes, endangered species, home-made lemonade, Oriental carpets, and a long, rambling treatise about London's canals.

But almost none of the work sold.

'I'm being productive, but the editors won't bite,' I told a journalist pal despondently at one of our regular greasy spoon sessions.

'That's because you're giving them stuff anyone else could serve up.'

'Don't get you.'

My pal jabbed a hand at the list.

'Any staffer could have knocked that stuff out.'

'So?'

'So they don't need it from you.'

'So what *do* they want?'

'The unusual,' my pal said.

More than once in my life the same journalist friend has given me just what I needed at exactly the right moment – usually delivered in the form of a throwaway line.

The idea of providing editors with the abnormal was a masterstroke, largely because abnormality is what I've always been about. On the rare occasions I have written about the ordinary, I've flopped. It's not that I'm against the ordinary, but rather my ability to describe it is limited.

Following the valuable advice, I changed tack.

Combing the papers for inch-long mentions of oddity, I developed them into full journalistic extravaganzas. First, I wrote a piece about hunting for rare Islamic antiques in London's nocturnal markets, and then about a retired lion-tamer who lived with his cats in a tunnel under Holborn. I wrote pieces about eccentrics and contortionists, about blindfolded cemetery tours, registered witches and warlocks, scorpion soup, and about couture clothing made from cured fish-skin.

Unlike before, every single article sold.

The next time I met the same pal for egg and chips I moaned how I was sick of being stranded in London, because England was thin on the top-notch bizarre.

'To hit the big time you're gonna have to get out,' he said.

'Get out where?'

'Out of Europe.'

'But I'm skint.'

'Course you are, because living in London's sucking you dry.'

'How do I get out into the wacky world if I can't afford a ticket?'

My pal, a hardbitten hack in his own right, sucked his upper lip.

'Be creative,' he said.

That evening, while thumbing my way through the newspapers on the trail of odd ideas, I noticed a tiny piece about a village in rural India where a witch had been blamed for starting a plague. She had apparently been trapped in a cage, and kept prisoner there for weeks.

It was one of those two-inch stories which had come over the wires – the kind which didn't have any real meat because it was too much hassle for anyone to get a correspondent over to cover it.

Tearing out the clipping, I put it on my desk and stared at it. It was the sort of story I dreamed of covering – a story filled with full-spectrum possibility... a human-interest story the likes of which England could never provide... not even the retired homeless lion-tamer and his cats.

I believe certain moments in life are made for decision, just as I believe in there being a sequence of key events.

That was such a moment.

Granted, there were problems. For a start, I wasn't in India, nor did I have any more than the most basic details. But through primitive pre-Internet triangulation, I was confident I'd be able to get to the place if need be.

It was then I remembered something a family friend had once said. Having spent a lifetime on Fleet Street, she drip-fed me fragments of information throughout my childhood. 'Switchboard operators at all the newspapers have orders to take reverse-charge calls,' she said. 'The way they see it, if you call collect from far away you must have a story worth their while.' Another thing she told me which had rooted itself deep in my mind was that editors had special reserves for amazing stories, and plenty of extra cash to cover expenses.

I had one of those nineties cordless phones, the kind with a telescopic aerial you had to pull up to get a signal. I'd bought it one night in Bermondsey's nocturnal junk market, and it was complete crap. No matter how close you were to the base unit, there was no way of getting a clear signal.

As I glanced at the two-inch press clipping about the witch, then at the pitiful cordless phone, the seed of an idea hit me.

Although it was late evening, I remembered our Fleet Street friend once explaining how hard-nosed hacks worked all night – none more than the news teams, because they had masses of copy to get into shape.

Grabbing the cordless phone, I jerked up the aerial and dialled the operator. When she came on, I asked to be put through to the *Daily Mail* on a reverse-charge call.

The line was crackly as I'd hoped, but it could've been cracklier still. Opening the back door, I strode down to the end of the garden. As I reached the shed, the news editor was put through.

The line crackling wildly, and my voice stuttering, I blurted out:

'This is Tahir Shah. I'm a freelancer, calling you from rural Bihar – where a witch has been thrown in a cage, blamed for failed crops and plague!'

The editor's voice was calm, like that of a trained negotiator talking someone off a window ledge.

'Have you offered it to anyone else?' he asked, as

though checking out the ground.

'No, but I'd like to offer the *Mail* first refusal.'

'Written for us before?'

'My background is on the wires,' I said, pleased at how crackly the line was sounding.

'Have you met the witch?'

'Not yet. Plan to get over as soon as I can. It'll be a couple of days at least before I can file – and I'll be off-grid.'

The editor put his hand over the receiver and had a quick, muffled exchange with his colleague.

'Can you get pictures as well?'

'Yes. Transparencies or black and white?'

'Transparencies, always transparencies!'

'Got it.'

'Give me two thousand words and pictures, I'll give you four hundred quid.'

The line was so crackly by now we could barely hear each other. As sometimes happens, I saw myself from a great height, struggling to bluff my way through what was a hand of high-stakes poker.

'I'll need expenses,' I yelled. 'Got to get transport, a translator, and pay off the guards.'

'All right. The same again for expenses. When can you file?'

'Give me five days.'

Again, the editor confirmed with his colleague.

'Five days it is. But don't you dare let me down!'

First thing next morning I got an Indian visa, then bought a last-minute ticket, malaria tablets, and masses of slide film.

That evening, before boarding the night flight to Delhi, I splurged on an expensive Sony shortwave radio in duty free. Like everything else, I charged it on my credit card.

Having reached the Indian capital in the peak of the summer heat, I caught a terrifying connecting local flight to Patna. I had never taken a domestic flight in India before, because the trains were so much more affordable. But as the newest member of Fleet Street's finest, I was in a rush – a rush to the captured witch drop zone.

My worst-case scenario was that another journalist had got to the witch before me. The second-worst case was that the story had been invented by a reporter with nothing else to file.

Landing at Patna, I made a beeline for the offices of the *Bihar Times*. I didn't have any press credentials, but I was the man who'd bluffed my way to a commission in far-away London. So, marching into the chief editor's office, I said I'd been sent to cover the story about the witch.

Time froze as I waited for him to reply, 'What witch?'

To my delight, he did not.

Greeting me warmly, he asked how things were on Fleet Street. Then he said:

'Our star reporter's heading down there at dawn. Go

with him if you like.'

After seven hours of jolting in an ivory-white Ambassador, we reached the village – or rather, as close to the village as a vehicle could get. The last few miles were covered on foot, the *Bihar Times*' star reporter leading the way as though he knew exactly where to go.

As we stumbled over the dry riverbed and into the village, a crowd gathered. They were far more interested at having outsiders visit than having a witch in a cage.

We were given cool water, tea, and presented with gifts – straw hats and boxes made from tree bark for keeping our tobacco dry. Having given abundant thanks, we asked the village elders whether we could see the witch.

'She's bad,' the village's head man replied. 'We do not like her.'

'What's she done?'

'She cursed our crops and made all the children sick.'

'I heard she brought plague.'

The chief scowled.

'Worse than plague.'

'What's worse than plague?'

'Whispering.'

'*Whispering*?'

'Yes.'

'What kind of whispering?'

'The kind which makes ordinary people mad.'

Thanking the chief, I filled an entire roll of film

with photos of him and his family. I may have been new to journalism, but life had already taught me that a little attention goes a long way – especially in a quiet backwater of Bihar.

After more tea, gifts, and impromptu speeches, we were taken to the witch. She was languishing in a rickety wooden cage no bigger than a fridge. As expected, she was exceptionally irritated.

Speaking to the witch – or, rather, the poor woman who'd been accused of being a witch – was the first time I interviewed a victim of incarceration. The theme has followed me through my writing career, and is one in which I have developed a special interest.

I once heard a Pulitzer prize-winning journalist being interviewed. He was asked for the most important thing about being a journalist. He answered with three words: 'Not getting involved.'

It's because of those three words I know I was never destined to be a journalist, but rather a writer.

I *always* get involved.

Just can't help it.

The seasoned Pulitzer-clutching reporter would have recorded the witch's situation, photographed her, and then retreated, leaving her to fester in her cage.

Unlike him, I was incapable of not allowing reason to win the day.

By the time we trudged back to the Ambassador car, the old woman had been freed, fed, and sent back to her home. The villagers had agreed to let her go in return for a bribe...

A shiny new Sony radio, with extra batteries thrown in.

By nightfall next day, I was back in Patna. A few hours after that, having massaged the story into gloriously heart-rending shape, I'd faxed my article to London – where it was received with jubilation. The photos were dispatched by courier, and the fee and expenses were wired into my account.

My journalist chum's advice to 'be creative' had stood me in good stead. It's advice I've passed on to hundreds of others, but which I fear few, if any, have ever heeded.

Creativity is at the heart of a real writer's life.

Nothing else can seduce the writer's senses with the same delicious feeling of achievement, pride, or hope.

Weaving Cloth

HAVING WRITTEN AND filed the feature about the witch, I'd learned to think on my feet and make the most of what I had to work with.

More importantly, it taught me the basics of shaping a text – something I was to learn through journalism, and through journalism alone. Writing for newspapers and magazines trained me in the thrill of creating something and then selling it – like making the crossbows when I was a kid. But it's far better than that – because writing is about assembling individual letters into words, words into sentences, and sentences into pages of text.

The crossbows took hooped nails, wooden batons, and elastic stripped from the curtains. But writing takes even less. You could argue that you need an expensive tool – a computer – to type it out, but you don't.

Almost all the most important books in human history were written by hand. Until 1878, and the invention of the mechanical typewriter, everything was written manually. Even when the technology was out there, many writers – my grandfather included – continued to write with a pen. The repetitive act of dipping a nib into ink then touching the page transports a writer's mind into the realm of creation.

My journalistic career may have been short-lived, but for me it was a masterclass in technicalities. The medium taught me what was important and what was not. This may sound crazy, but through it I learned the value of words.

Newspaper and magazine editors are in the bulk business. To be honest, they're trying to fill space around the adverts. I don't expect anyone but the most veteran old hacks would ever admit it.

As far as editors are concerned, incoming text is the raw material from which the publication is put together. Just like cloth being woven in a sweatshop, it's brought to the cutting room and cut up around a pattern. As with making a jacket, you need material of a particular size and shape for the collar, arms, shoulders, pockets, and for the lining too.

Seasoned journalists are masters of gauging what's needed, in the same way a Savile Row tailor can cut a suit without a pattern. They don't need one – because it's in their head. An experienced editor can draw the best out of the work, and a journalist who's done his time can rehash text on cue.

When producing my early journalism I made a common mistake. It was to think what I wrote was right, and that anyone who wanted to make changes was wrong. The point I hadn't grasped was that the free-flow of book writing is very much at odds with the rigidity of a daily newspaper or a monthly magazine.

A features editor has an entire floor of people to please – from superior editors, to layout people, and the marketing team. In the way a film script is hacked about endlessly until finally the actor utters their line of dialogue, so magazine or newspaper text is chopped about before it ultimately gets set in stone.

Grasping hold of the bandwagon of the bizarre – the journalistic genre in which I so enjoyed creating – I learned fast that to get published I'd have to give editors what they wanted, rather than what I hoped they'd like.

My journalist friend was right: a freelancer's life is about selling far more than it is about finding stories and actually writing them. The easiest way to sell is to deliver work which hits the nail on the head.

Do that, and selling isn't a chore but a delight.

Putting in my twenty thousand hours, I perfected how to do emergency open-heart surgery on a text. Give me half an hour and I can take a two-thousand-word article and rewrite it from any angle an editor chooses. I can grab the beginning and put it at the end, suck out the guts and smear them around the edges, or swap the leading character for an insignificant understudy waiting in the wings.

By learning the value of words, I honed a strange inside-out skill which all successful journalists master, even though I doubt whether they ever speak of it: the skill is appreciating the innate worth of a particular word.

But it's more complicated than that.

You have to know what's packed inside a word – like the contents of an atom – and the relation between the word in question and the others around it. You've got to ask: is the word I've chosen pulling its weight? Could I use a shorter one that will allow me to strip away the elongated adjective? Or, can I delete paragraph three because it's misconstrued gobbledygook?

Every word printed in a newspaper or magazine is there because it's earned its place, just as every line of dialogue in a screenplay is there because it's needed.

Books are different, and we'll come to them. You can embed thirty pages of irrelevant fluff in the middle of a four-hundred-page tome and no one will ever notice. Try slipping in five lines of waffle in a well-edited newspaper, and they'll hang, draw, and quarter you.

Having dived in at the deep end, I churned out bizarre human-interest features on an epic scale.

For about three years I wrote hundreds of pieces, filing them from all corners of the earth and under all kinds of pseudonyms. I concentrated on the kind of gritty real-life stories to be found in women's magazines at the time. The media explosion hadn't quite happened, and the lives and suffering of a great many women hadn't been thrust into the public eye.

The most successful pieces I wrote involved the kind of subjects that got everyone – both women and men – debating. They included in-depth features about women on Death Row in the United States, the women running the Ku Klux Klan, and widows in Cambodia who were clearing landmines for a living.

I filed plenty of less hard-hitting pieces, too – on subjects such as the Bible-based weight-loss programme in Tennessee, the ceremony in India at which people swallowed live fish as an asthma cure, and the cryonic suspension centre in Arizona, where men and women had their heads frozen in the hope of being brought back to life.

Following my pal's lead, I sold rights country by country, making a healthy income. The workload was colossal as I did everything myself.

I found the seed of each story and researched it, travelled to the drop zone, wrote the piece, took the photos, copied and mounted the transparencies, called editors, sent out texts, shipped out pictures, invoiced, chased up late-payers, and all the rest.

In the last throes of the pre-Internet age – when photos weren't shared digitally in the blink of an eye – magazines and newspapers needed the originals. That was the saving grace. It meant no one would dare rip off work, as they tend to do now.

As I saw it, the ultimate thrill was being able to get on a midnight flight to anywhere I liked, and to travel there on a mission. Just as I despise tourism, I adore being on a trail – whether it be on a mission for bonded labourers in India, or an Amazonian quest for shrunken heads.

Later I compiled a book from my journalism called *Travels With Myself*. Those years were exactly that.

Lone travels in search of a story which consumes your life for a while, but which gets replaced by another soon enough.

Last week I had some time to spare, so I indulged myself. I spent three days trawling through the archives at the London Library, and others online. My mission was to unearth the journalism my father had written, and the pieces published by his father in the wake of the Great War – under their own names, and under pseudonyms as well.

The trawling paid off.

I unearthed hundreds of articles each of them had written for newspapers, journals, and magazines when in their twenties – as I was at the time of my journalistic career.

They began with a piece published in 1918 by my grandfather – a medical student at the time – entitled 'Leechcraft in Afghanistan'. Much of their combined journalism relates to travel and culture, while much more touches on lesser-known aspects of what makes us human.

Although of interest, the content of their early journalism isn't quite as important as something else: the way the medium was formative for them – just as it was for me. Reading the pieces they wrote for a wide range of publications, you get the sense they were learning on the job.

Their earliest articles were clunky and over-written,

just as mine were. But, with time and experience, their style became honed and polished.

I once saw Charles Schultz interviewed on a chat show. He was talking about *Peanuts*, the cartoon strip he'd originated decades before. The interviewer asked him what he valued most about Snoopy and the other characters. He replied: 'I like them because I've reached the stage at which I can describe anything through them. They're a lens to my thoughts and my mind.'

I often think of that wise observation, especially with reference to journalism. As writers, we all want to learn the skill so we can put it to work. Some people don't realize there's a skill to learn – they tend to flounder early on and fall off the map. Those who put in the hard grind get rewarded with a lens – the kind of lens Charles Schultz described.

The joy of a writer is being able to hold the lens you've earned up to something, and observe it in an extraordinary way.

Like Schultz, my father and grandfather put in the time and effort to learn their craft. The creator of *Peanuts* acquired his lens from sketching thousands of strip cartoons, just as writers get one from hammering out and editing hundreds of thousands of words.

Or, as I like to think of it, weaving miles and miles of cloth.

The dreadful day I've already mentioned – the one on which both my father and Mohamed Amin departed

– occurred exactly a week after my thirtieth birthday.

That day was a line drawn in the sand of my life.

A line marking two distinct halves: what had been, and what was to come.

The far side of the line was the world of the professional author – a realm my father and grandfather had stepped into at my age. Both had harnessed the skills they'd learned, and gone on to write scores of books which had a significant impact on other people's lives.

Bracing myself, I looked back at where I'd come from, pondering for a moment on all the outlandish adventures, each one of which had been a teacher.

Then, swallowing hard in anticipation, I stepped over the line and closed the door to journalism.

The path of the book-writer lay ahead.

The Wooing

IN GONDWANALAND HAD been under my bed for years, keeping company with the shoebox filled with travel journals and assorted files of notes and junk.

Whenever I thought of the unpublished manuscript, I thought of Doris Lessing's letter, the one I kept in the bedside drawer which I was too fearful ever to read a second time.

Doris had been right – the book desperately needed editing. Since I had done the self-imposed nightshifts at my pal's office, I'd become a seasoned features writer.

A features writer who knew not only how to edit, but who understood the value of words.

Best of all though, I'd earned enough money to buy a laptop of my own.

Loading *In Gondwanaland* onto it, I went through the manuscript line by line – weighing up the value of the words in the way journalism had taught me to do. Ripping out entire sections, I swapped others around, developed new sub-themes, and deleted others.

A month after I'd started on my crusade, the book was clean.

Or, rather, it was cleaner.

I paid a professional editor to tidy up the grammar. She was proficient but so ruthless I wished I'd never asked her to do the job. The experience was like getting your teeth drilled and being slapped with a huge bill for good measure.

Five years on, *In Gondwanaland* wasn't the book I would have written were I to have sat down and shaped the same material again. I was a different person, and capable of better. Although gushing with rip-roaring enthusiasm, it was uneven and clunky. In places the quality of the writing was embarrassing, and the anecdotes were weak.

But it was all I had to go with. And, as any writer will tell you, there's something deep-down wretched about having an unpublished manuscript on a shelf or under your bed.

Wretched, not because your ego isn't being fanned as you'd like, but because an unpublished book is a door that's still very much ajar.

A new door can only open when one has closed.

Besides, not having my first book published would have allowed the nay-sayers to have the last laugh. So, I decided to get *In Gondwanaland* published.

On the back of an envelope I listed seventeen contacts and targeted them one by one. Some worked in publishing, others were authors, or friends who knew agents.

As when I first wrote to Doris about the book, I expected to be ushered up to the chairman's office in a mainstream publisher, being given a cigar, a brandy, and a celebratory pat on the back.

No hope of it.

All seventeen of the back-of-the-envelope contacts flopped.

One or two of them read the manuscript. A few arranged meetings. Eager to get rid of me, a handful passed me on to friends of friends. Right away I got a sense I was asking the impossible.

Selling my journalism had got me used to rejection – especially when my early work was turned down. Journalistic rejection is like being shot at with a Gatling gun – no-nonsense, high-velocity hellfire. Publishing rejection is a quite different thing altogether. Kind and measured, it was apologetic rather than offensive – but it hurt all the more.

Newspaper and magazine editors lay their cards on the table right from the start. There's no time to beat around the bush, because the next issue's got to be put to bed. So, even though you're slapped in the face, or annihilated by their machine-gun fire, you know where you stand. An editor at a daily newspaper once sat through my pitch over the phone and yelled:

'We're not interested because we're not in the business of taking putrid fucking crap!'

Book publishers were far more consoling in their rebuffs. Unlike the Fleet Street editors I'd got to know, they tended to write letters, typed out neatly by secretaries. Again, this was the mid-nineties, when publishers mailed their rejections on fine bonded writing paper, signed in fountain pen.

Even if there was no corporate logo stamped onto the envelope, you could always tell when a letter was from a publisher.

It was a thing of wonder.

The stationery was the same grade as used by royalty, the name and address were always impeccably typed, and a franking mark was in place of a stamp.

Having had no luck with my seventeen contacts, I got my hands on a copy of the *Writers' & Artists' Yearbook*, made a list of the top publishers, and sent a précis of *In Gondwanaland* to each one.

A flurry of letters arrived by return post.

The wording was always the same – so much so I wondered whether a standard text was dished out to them all at publishing school. After cursory thanks, there'd be a line or two of effusive appreciation, before the neat clincher – 'We are sorry to say, it's not for us.' Fantastically polite, the line was the direct reverse of the kind of response you'd get from a news editor, in suggesting the rejection was not your fault, but theirs.

The introduction to the *Writers' & Artists' Yearbook* explained no publishers worth their salt would accept anything which hadn't been sent through an agent. They were overwhelmed, it said – overwhelmed with a tidal wave of manuscripts by old aunts who had nothing to say.

The introduction maintained that the invention of the word processor was responsible. Because of it, and it alone, everyone was suddenly writing a book. A culling process was needed – and it came in the form of literary agents. Of course there'd been agents for decades, but it wasn't until then – according to the *Yearbook* at least – that agents became mini-potentates in their own right.

Following the advice, I wrote to every literary agent listed in Great Britain, and to more than a dozen in New York. They all replied in the negative, their stationery not nearly as swish as that of the publishers.

Dejected, I crawled into bed, pulled the duvet over me, and lay there like a wounded zebra lying on the savannah waiting for death.

Then, out of the blue, an elderly gentleman friend invited me to tea at his home near Marble Arch.

I've always had a thing for being in the presence of such people, because of their excellent stories and their exquisite manners.

The elderly gentleman in question was Hugh Carless, a traveller and retired diplomat for whom I held a great affection. He'd been British ambassador in Venezuela at one time, and we often spoke of visiting the Angel Falls, reached by crossing a ring of rocks, the so-called 'Devil's Teeth'.

Like all fellows of the elderly gentleman race, he was supremely skilled in apologizing. The species is long gone now, alas. But when I was a child, apologizing gentlemen of retirement age were in plentiful supply – it was as if the grasslands of the savannah were awash with them.

Carless served tea with slices of lemon and extra hot water on the side. He'd apologized when I'd been late – taking blame that his building was hard to reach, which it was not. He'd apologized for the weather being inclement, and that the cakes were not the best of the best.

As I gorged myself on the most delicious pastry my mouth had ever had the good fortune to taste, Carless whispered he had heard I'd written a book.

I swallowed hard.

'No one wants to publish it, though,' I said.

'Might I ask its name?'

'*In Gondwanaland.*'

'A curious title.'

'I've used the theory of continental drift in a cultural way. I've covered my travels through India, Africa and Latin America – even wrote about the Angel Falls.'

'How intriguing,' Carless replied. 'Have you sent it out on the rounds?'

'Yes, to agents and publishers.'

'Any bites?'

'None.'

'"*Not for us*"?'

'Exactly... every one of them.'

Carless poured me a second cup of tea, Darjeeling leaves caught on the strainer.

'It's a game,' he said.

'What is?'

'Publishing.'

'Well, I wish someone would tell me the rules.'

'I will.'

'But, respectfully, you're not a publisher, agent, or a writer.'

'A fish in the sea could never hope to explain water,' Carless said.

As I sipped my tea, he explained the ins and outs of a business he had not been involved in directly, but knew from intense observation.

'The first thing you have to recognize,' Carless said, 'is that publishers are frightened of making mistakes. They may appear all self-important in their offices, with those nice leather chairs, but don't be deceived. They have to answer to the shareholders, and that means they have to be wooed.'

'*Wooed?*'

'Yes, wooed.'

'How?'

'With the kind of sizzle that's utterly irresistible.'

'Like what?'

Hugh Carless smiled vacantly in a way that's a challenge to accurately describe – the smile of a man whose thinking has reached a higher plane.

'I am certain your book is sublime,' he said, 'but unfortunately that's not enough. If you want to sell it, you must be less Tahir Shah, and more Coca-Cola.'

'Not sure I follow,' I said.

'How does Coke manage to sell a brown, sweet, carbonated drink?'

'By marketing the hell out of it.'

'Yes. And how do they do that?'

'By advertising.'

'Advertising it how?'

'By showing happy people swilling their brown fizzy drink.'

'What kind of happy people?'

'Beautiful happy people?'

'There's something even better.'

'Rich happy people?'

'Even better still.'

'Famous happy people?'

'Precisely,' Carless said.

We spent the remainder of the afternoon making the mother of all lists – a list of the world's great and the good.

It featured presidents and kings, politicians, artists and actors, movie directors, spiritual leaders, opera singers, and writers...

...dozens and dozens of writers.

While I sat at the desk overlooking Bryanston Square, Carless flicked through *Who's Who*, calling out addresses. By early evening we had an entire dossier filled with names and contact details.

'They're the perfume,' Carless said. 'The perfume you're going to woo with.'

'You mean I have to woo the people on the list, then woo the publishers with them?'

'That's right.'

'What about the agents? Surely they need wooing as well.'

'We'll come to them in a minute.'

Standing at the mantelpiece, his back always characteristically ramrod straight, my favourite elderly gentleman dictated a list:

'One: send a gushing letter to everyone on the list, rave about how they've inspired you, and ask for a publicity quote for your book, a sample of which you'll enclose. The letters must be works of art in their own right – the kind of thing which would move a pillar of society to tears as it reminds them of when they were struggling to break in.

'Two: have the best quotes printed in huge lettering on sheets of brown paper.

'Three: make copies of the manuscript and wrap them in the brown paper sheets, tied up with parcel string.'

'Do I mail them out to agents?'

Carless held up an index finger and shook it side to side.

'No need,' he said.

'Why not?'
'Because you're your own agent.'
'Am I?'
'Yes, you are.'
'What's my name?'
'Who'd you like to be?'
'Worldwide Media,' I said. 'It sounds important.'
Carless pushed back his shoulders.
'Four: while you're waiting for the publicity quotes to come in, make a beeline to the most exclusive printers you can find, and have a letter-heading knocked up for Worldwide Media. The paper must reek of expense, and the artwork printed on a Heidelberg Platen Press.'
'Then what?'
'Then, my dear Tahir, you send the wrapped-up manuscripts to every publisher you can think of. Attach to them a cover letter that's as glorious to read as it is to hold.'
'But dozens of publishers have already rejected it.'
'An insignificant triviality,' Hugh Carless said.
'Won't they recognize the name?'
'Change it.'
'What to?'
'Something mysterious and fantastic.'
I caught a flash of the Angel Falls in Venezuela, the singularly most mysterious place I'd ever been.
'I'll call it *Beyond the Devil's Teeth*,' I said.

William Watkins

FOLLOWING HUGH CARLESS'S instructions, I wrote to dozens of well-known people all over the world.

My letters were carefully crafted to achieve maximum impact, and they certainly caused a stir. To my great surprise, more than half the names on the hit-list wrote back with publicity quotes. They included a former American president, A-list actors, explorers, a *Who's Who* of royalty, and a galaxy of celebrated authors.

I had the cream of the quotes printed large on sheets of brown paper. These were used to wrap up sample chapters and an outline of the *In Gondwanaland* reincarnation, *Beyond the Devil's Teeth*.

Borrowing fifty pounds from my twin sister Safia, I had a letter-heading printed. The stationery was sublime. A friend said holding it was like making love to his fingers.

At last, I was ready to draft the cover letter to publishers. There was no question of writing it from myself, so I chose a pseudonym that was simple with a hint of alliteration:

William Watkins.

Loading my expedition backpack up with the packets, I clambered onto my bicycle and delivered them to publishers all over London. No one ever imagined the panting, sweating delivery boy was also the agent, and author as well.

A week passed.

Then another.

I cursed Carless for reducing me to total impoverishment, and myself for taking publishing tips from someone who'd never published anything at all.

Retreating to my bed – the one place I could rely on for solace – I hid under the duvet and hoped the world would be struck by a massive meteorite right there and then.

The meteorite didn't come.

The phone rang instead.

Pulling myself out of bed, I staggered over to the landline and picked it up.

'Yes?!' I snapped.

'Good afternoon,' said a prim voice – the kind you don't get in the pitiless companies touting carbonated brown water. 'May I speak to William Watkins, please?'

I screwed up my face.

'William *Who*?'

'Mr Watkins... is he available?'

I was about to yell an obscenity and slam down the phone when I remembered the name. The name of the agent – the one who'd taken on Tahir Shah, the greatest writer of the age.

Thinking fast, I replied in a cockney voice:

'This is the switchboard, miss. Putting you through now.'

My father used to say agents were failed publishers

who liked to throw their weight around. That tallied with what I'd learnt first-hand. A race unto themselves, the few agents I'd encountered were smarmy, greedy, uncouth, and wretched in the extreme. Most of all, I'd learnt they kept people waiting, because it made them seem important.

So, putting the receiver down on the floor, I shuffled through to the kitchen, made a quick mayonnaise sandwich, and strolled back to take the call.

'Hello, William Watkins here,' I oozed unctuously.

'Good afternoon,' the prim voice cooed. 'Calling from Weidenfeld & Nicolson. We received the chapters by Tahir Shah. They're absolutely wonderful. We're definitely interested.'

Having slipped into character – a cross between a used car salesman and a bookie – I did my best to talk the talk:

'Ah, yes, Tahir Shah – wonderful writer. Never had anyone like him on our books. Certain stardom ahead. A sure thing if ever there was one.'

'Are the paperback rights still available?' Little Miss Prim asked, a tone of anticipation in her voice.

'Available? Er, yes. But we're expecting them to go fast. At least a dozen firms have expressed interest.'

'I imagine they have. We'd like to see the rest. Could you have it biked down to us this afternoon?'

I rolled my eyes.

Biking it down meant me getting on my bicycle and

playing the part of the delivery guy again.

'Of course,' I said, taking down the details.

'Actually, as time is of the essence,' the editor said, pearls clattering, 'perhaps it's best if Mr Shah came in to meet us – say tomorrow morning at ten?'

At that moment I was ready to come clean, and explain that I was Tahir Shah the writer, and Tahir Shah the agent, just as I was Tahir Shah the switchboard operator, Tahir Shah AKA William Watkins, and Tahir Shah the cycle courier as well.

But I didn't have the guts.

'No problem,' I answered, a mayonnaise sandwich in one hand and the phone in the other. 'I'll see that he's there.'

'Would you like to check the time's convenient with him?'

'I happen to know he can make it,' I said firmly.

'Please do come along, too,' replied Little Miss Prim.

'Alas, madam, that would be distinctly impossible,' I said.

The Food Chain

BEYOND THE DEVIL'S *Teeth* was published to a muffled fanfare, the deal having been arranged with terrible difficulty by William Watkins of Worldwide Media.

The experience taught me to keep life simple, and to avoid situations in which an avatar would be expected to turn up in person. Thankfully, Tahir Shah was as well-rounded a character as William Watkins was not.

Whenever I was asked to come in for meetings at the towering glass-and-steel structure a stone's throw from Trafalgar Square, I gave everyone tremendous bang for their buck. After a while I dismissed Worldwide Media and moved on to a real agent – one who was more than a posh letter-heading printed on an antique Heidelberg, and a funny voice on the phone.

In those first months of as a bona fide author, I was a clone of every other writer who believed in the emperor's new clothes.

I may have succeeded in wooing the great and the good to get my publicity quotes, but I was myself wooed by the fabulousness of it all.

I was wooed by the atrium of the building and by the potted plants, by the thick-pile carpeting down the long corridors, and by the sense of intellectual understatement – as though great works of literary merit were being commissioned and shaped. Most of all, I was wooed by the fact Orion, which owned the publishing firm Weidenfeld & Nicolson, was also the name of the gleaming white tower in which its offices were found.

Much later, when I was cynical and seasoned, I realized the genius: a start-up publishing firm with no track record had rented a couple of floors in Orion House, thereby implying the building had been named after them.

Thinking about it, that nugget of information is magnificently impressive – the illusion of the prim and proper exterior almost as ingenious as William Watkins and Worldwide Media.

The best thing about being published by Weidenfeld & Nicolson was being inducted into the hallowed halls of accepted authorhood. The film director David Flamholc, with whom I have made documentaries and spent sixteen days with in a Pakistani torture prison one time, always talks about breaking a spell.

'If you want to pick up a girl,' he once told me, 'you need two things. The first is to make it look as though you know what you're doing. The other is having picked up a girl before.'

I always think of that second point.

If you haven't picked up a girl before, you have to give the impression you have. It's not easy. But with writing, keeping up pretences is even harder. Anyone can simply look online and see what you've published. While it really shouldn't matter whether you've been published or not, it does. It's nuts, of course, but somehow –

through an inexplicable literary death curse – everyone cares.

As soon as you're published, you're in the club. No one ever grills you again – just like when you have a university degree, it never has to be passed around.

For months after signing with Weidenfeld I was wooed and I was wowed.

Wooed by being part of the club, and wowed by the thrill of being accepted. *Beyond the Devil's Teeth* had been published, and my name was on the spine. I'd be featured on the radio, and was dishing out advice to everyone I met on how to be a published author just like me.

As time passed, I began to appreciate how – while being signed with a mainstream firm – I was pathetically low on the food chain. At one end there were killer whales, and at the other there were minnows – and I was definitely a minnow... a baby one at that.

Three things proved this point to me loud and clear:
- Orion's CEO never asked to meet me. He didn't even call me, or write me a note. However hard I tried not to mind, not being worthy to meet him got under my skin.
- When I was taken for lunch, it was to second- or even third-grade restaurants. On one occasion the editor cried out, 'Rather expensive here, so I think we'll dispense with starters!'
- My advance was way beyond pitiful.

Although it bothered me at the time that the head of Weidenfeld & Nicolson wouldn't meet me, I'm long since over it. And I've learned that if I want a good meal, I ought to take myself to lunch.

The matter of the advance was just about the single most important thing I learnt when my first book was published.

It's a key point, so I'll shout it out loud:
IF YOU WANT A PUBLISHER
TO PROMOTE YOUR BOOK
THEY'VE GOT TO HAVE SPENT LOADS
OF CASH IN BUYING IT
– CASH THEY WANT TO RECOUP!

Publishing is as simple as that.

If they've forked out next to nothing for your masterpiece, they're going to fork out next to nothing to get their next to nothing back.

Getting a big fat advance is fabulous because you can wine and dine your friends, but it's not the reason an author should ever want an advance. The one and only reason is so that money is spent on getting the publisher's money back.

In the conventional system, it's the single sure-fire way to rise up the food chain.

Floundering about on the forest floor, you get trampled on by everyone else. As I soon learned, entry-level writers are expected to be seen and not heard. No one listens to their ideas, and when they speak out of turn (i.e. anytime they utter anything) everyone recoils in horror...

As they did to me.

Other than turning me overnight into a published author, the best thing about Weidenfeld was that they wanted another book. This is an important point, one which a great many aspiring writers simply don't grasp:

There's hardly a publisher on the planet that ever wants one stand-alone work by an author. The model doesn't exist. If a first book bombs, Book No. 2 is commissioned in the hope it might be a hit, and be a lifeline to save Book No. 1. Of course you reach a point at which a publisher will cut their losses, but you can bet anything that if they've forked out cash on one book, they'll be ready and willing to double down to get their investment back.

Beyond the Devil's Teeth wasn't the publishing sensation of the century. Thinking about it now, I'm chuffed it was released at all. I may have been wiser to have followed Doris Lessing's advice and park it for good, and start with a fresh slate. The way I see it though, the tale that had begun as my beloved *In Gondwanaland* was the slipway down which I could launch a proper, well-constructed ship – one that hadn't been under my bed for years gathering dust.

When Little Miss Prim asked at a third-rate lunch if I had a first-rate book idea, I did a double take. I couldn't believe she believed in me. I now know it was more a case of needing to get the initial advance back.

'Oh yes, I've got an idea,' I said, lying. 'A big, amazing idea – an idea that'll make you fall right off your chair.'

'Sounds wonderful, what is it?'

My mind raced, just as it had when she'd called for the first time asking for my agent, William Watkins.

'Can't do it justice in a line or two of chat. I'll jot it down for you. Give me a couple of days.'

Outside the restaurant I punched the air with both fists. They loved me, and wanted more of me – YAY! Unclenching my fists, I froze with horror. What idea could be worthy of my big build-up and knock Little Miss Prim off her chair?

Back at my flat, I went into deep-thought mode, making lists of ideas, then dismissing them one by one. The obvious thing would have been to grab something on which I'd written a feature, and turn it into a travel book. Although sensational, the subjects didn't have the depth needed to fill five hundred pages of double-spaced manuscript.

Collapsing on my bed, I got under the duvet and hunkered down in the foetal position. I mentally scrolled through all the places I'd been and the people I'd met – like one of those split-flap display boards at an airport.

Hundreds of people and place names rolled by, as I rejected them one by one. The more I concentrated, the worse the ideas.

So I did something that seems to activate another part of the mind.

I stopped thinking.

I've never meditated, but I suppose that's what it's like. The thought-cascade was replaced instantly by blackness – a state of cerebral tumbleweed.

Then a face slipped onto the stage of my mind.

The face of my tormentor.

Hakim Feroze.

As a child at Langton House we had all manner of visitors, as I've already described. By any standards they were a varied bunch – with plentiful oddballs. By far the most adored – by me at least – was the ancestral guardian of my familial tomb.

Hafiz Jan was a colossal brute of a man, whose forefathers had followed my great-great-great-grandfather, Jan Fishan, from Afghanistan to India back in 1842. 'Jan Fishan' was a *nom de guerre* translating loosely as 'He Who Scatters Souls'. A warrior-savant, he helped save British women and children from slaughter at the end of the first Anglo–Afghan War, and was rewarded with a principality in India as a result.

Jan Fishan was interred in a grand mausoleum in Sardhana, near Meerut, in northern India. Having sworn an oath to protect their master in this life and the next, Hafiz Jan's line took on the responsibility of guarding the tomb.

Having come overland from India, Hafiz Jan

turned up unexpectedly at Langton House, his arrival coinciding with a freak summer hailstorm. His luggage, which consisted of a lone tea crate, was packed not with clothing but rather with chemicals – the kind for use in wildly hazardous magic tricks.

In the weeks he stayed, Hafiz Jan and I became inseparable friends. He regarded me not as a schoolboy but as a warrior in training. When he wasn't passing on vital information – like how to disembowel the enemy with a blunt bayonet – he was teaching me magic.

One afternoon, he put on a magic show in the drawing room, in which a fireball almost incinerated my parents, sisters, and me.

Hafiz Jan was dispatched back to India, leaving me bereft. I vowed that when I was old enough, I would go in search of him – to continue my training in stage magic.

That's exactly what I had done.

But Hafiz Jan refused to teach me. Instead he sent me to his own teacher, a sadistic conjuror in Calcutta...

Hakim Feroze.

It was his face that slipped onto the stage of my mind as I lay under the duvet, desperate for a fantastical idea. As soon as I saw Feroze grinning at me, I expunged him. The months I'd spent studying magic with him had been private – to write about them would have been to belittle the experience.

The harder I fought to rid myself of the idea, the more strongly it dominated. Worse still was that a title had linked up to the idea. Cemented together, they had formed a seed.

The seed for my next book – *Sorcerer's Apprentice*.

Little Miss Prim commissioned the idea on the spot. Waxing lyrical about it, she said she wanted it as soon as possible. The good news was I'd done most of the research already – research that was never intended for a book.

Travelling to India, I filled in the gaps. These included staying with the skeleton dealers in Calcutta, who supplied the world's medical skeleton trade. From them, I learned the secret of their business – to avoid cadavers ridden with syphilis. The disease corrodes bones like you'd never believe.

From Calcutta I travelled across to Mumbai by train, picking up details which could be woven into the story. Most of all, I considered India, reflecting how it was the perfect source of A-grade material for a rip-roaring travel book.

Five years had passed since I'd written *In Gondwanaland* in my friend's office. I'd done two books for Mohamed Amin, and a mass of journalism, but somehow they didn't count.

The thought of writing a new book from scratch terrified me. It terrified me because I'd talked it up – to Little Miss Prim and to myself as well. It terrified me, too, because it would force me to lift the lid on what was the ultimate in psychological thrillers.

THE REASON TO WRITE

But most of all it terrified me because I didn't feel up to the job.

So I phoned Hugh Carless to ask his thinking.

A life of diplomatic training had taught him to deliver clear, perfectly enunciated advice.

'It's a mountain to climb,' he said. 'A challenge of which you are more than worthy.'

'Don't know where to start,' I said.

'Preparation,' Carless affirmed. 'It works for the Boy Scouts, and it will work for you.'

For an entire month, I prepared.

I wrote seven hundred pages of notes – first by hand, then I typed them out. Next, I planned the book in extraordinary detail – in the way film directors storyboard a movie. After that, I wrote lists of extra information I could weave in if I dried up, lists of useful and intriguing words, more notes, and even notes on my notes.

Then I did something which I have done in one form or another ever since:

I typed numbers down the left-hand side of an A4 sheet – from 1 to 50, and a line of dots against each one on which I could record the day's wordage.

Writing is about doing what works for you, and not much else. Through time spent in the salt mines as Mo Amin's slave, and as a feature writer knocking out words against the clock, I'd learned the importance of wordage.

Every writer I've ever met works in a different way.

But nothing works for me more than striving towards a daily word count. Different kinds of book can be written at different speeds, just as writing when you're warmed up is faster and far easier than writing when you're cold.

I'm writing this current book at five thousand words, or about thirty pages, a day. On a good day the wordage takes between six and seven hours. On a not-so-good one, it can take twice that.

The secret is not to have bad writing days, only good ones – and to love the process of creation...

...but more about that in a bit.

Sorcerer's Apprentice was the wackiest book I've ever written – because I never intended my time studying magic to end up between the covers of a travel book.

When launched it got a lot of attention – partly because I'd cajoled Little Miss Prim into putting the mind-blowing picture by Roland Michaud of a Kali *sadhu* on the cover... and partly because the subject matter was so downright odd.

In Europe, numerous reviewers said they didn't believe a word – that I'd made the whole thing up. The host of one radio book programme claimed I was a fantasist. Another said I'd stretched the truth to breaking point on page one.

What nobody in the West understood was that, far from inventing the story or exaggerating, I was guilty of doing the opposite. India is a land where the improbable

– and even the impossible – are not only likely, but practically certain to occur.

The good news was that the book sold – not enough for me to be introduced to the head of Orion, or to be allowed to order a starter at lunch, but in sufficient quantities for me to get an increased advance for my next book.

When the subject of a third book came up, I wasn't caught unawares. Little Miss Prim's question was fully expected when it came, couched in the same publisher-speak which gave us that other gem, 'It's not for us.'

'Have you given thought to a new book?' she asked inquisitively.

'As a matter of fact I have,' I answered, pushing an inedible minute steak across my plate.

'Do tell,' the editor clucked.

'Flight,' I said.

'*Aeroplanes?*'

'No.'

'If not aeroplanes, then what?'

'Primitive flight.'

'Oh.'

Laying down my fork, I fished a scrap of paper from my inside pocket, and read aloud:

'Antonio Calancha, a conquistador priest, recorded that the Incas flew over the jungle like birds.'

'Oh,' Little Miss Prim said again.

'It'll take me to the jungles of Peru.'

'Sounds marvellous. Do you have a title in mind?'
'*Trail of Feathers*,' I said.

Trojan Horse

BY THE TIME I started my research, the Internet was firmly on stream.

Granted, for me it was via a deplorable dial-up connection with an ISP that's long since gone. But thank God for the Web. Before it, I'd have had no chance to link one thing to another as is now instantly possible.

After learning about Friar Calancha, I unearthed flight myths in dozens of other cultures, from Borneo to Botswana. It was proof ancient civilizations were thinking about flight, whether they were actually flying or not. My understanding was that the Incas may have been jumping off mountains, or towers constructed for ritual, with a canopy held out to break their fall. The same kind of thing had certainly been in use elsewhere, although the subject of primitive flight tended to be championed by the lunatic fringe.

There comes a point at which you have to leave the comfort of published material and get out into the field for hands-on research. I know plenty of authors who wouldn't dream of heading out until they'd nailed down a full academic study. I hate to admit this, because it'll make me sound capricious: I'm a deep-end-jumper. Research is all well and good but it's bloody boring when compared to being on the ground. Besides, do too much advance research and you snuff out the flame of spontaneity.

As well as being enthusiastic by nature, I'm excitable. I've always been excitable – not in a bad way, but in a good one. Unbridled excitement prevents me from reading instructions for electrical gadgets – they're just too damned dull. Moving briskly forward, I rip the thing out of its packaging and figure out how it works by trial and error.

A lack of preparation may be frowned upon by Boy Scout leaders, by seasoned explorers, and by the military as well. But as far as I'm concerned, not preparing properly is the only way of guaranteeing a slipstream of wonder.

Crouch down low like a bobsleigh rider in a skin-tight Lycra onesie, taking the twists and turns of the slalom super fast...

...and an invisible piste materializes.

Arriving in Lima, I made my way to the famous Nazca Lines on the coast, which can only be viewed from the air – first proof that the ancient peoples of Peru had a connection with flight in ancient times. This theory was borne out by the textiles shrouding mummy bundles at Paracas. A great many of them were adorned with stylized images of 'birdmen'.

As I travelled around Peru, piecing together the clues in my trail of feathers, I thanked Providence for not tying me down to a conventional job. Time and again, I was reminded that, by a mixture of chance and conditioning,

I was following a route mapped out by my father and his father, too.

I only have the most fleeting memory of my grandfather, The Sirdar Ikbal Ali Shah, whom we visited days before his death in Tangier when I was three. I've known him through the files he left behind – containing thousands of pages of papers and ephemera gathered on his expeditions, manuscript notes and photographs.

Most of all, though, I've known him through his genes – which live on inside me... the genes of a man devoted to travel and adventure.

During the 1920s he travelled by land from Europe to China, and back again – in an era still connected to an ancient time. The forty-thousand-mile journey was ample fodder for two of his first travelogues – *Westward to Mecca* and *Eastward to Persia*. They're rattling reads, which taught me a great deal about creating a book of observations and random meetings, sewing it together around a grand central theme.

The most glorious piece of self-publicity I've ever seen is a brochure printed in the late twenties, describing my grandfather as 'The World-Famous Oriental Lecturer'. Eager to promote his travel books, he embarked on a lecture tour, complete with magic lantern slides – to wow the potential readers of his bestselling travelogues.

Peru may have been quite different to the wilds of Central Asia, but I found myself facing the very same hardships my grandfather had experienced seven decades earlier. For me, the hardest thing of all was piecing together the story while bushwhacked by both desert and jungle.

The grave-robbers at Paracas, and the mummy bundles they exhumed on a nightly basis, led me on a zigzagging trail through Peru – eventually spewing me to the north of Puno. There, at a place called Sillustani on the western banks of Lake Titicaca, I came across a series of towers which, according to local folklore, were once used for ritual flight.

Next thing I knew, the trail was sending me eastwards deep into the Upper Amazon. I took a flight to Iquitos, a city founded a century or so before by the so-called 'Rubber Barons'. Fortunes had been made there overnight, leading to astonishing wealth – with the city's super-rich lighting their cigars with five-dollar notes.

Any other travel writer may have avoided the jungle and concentrated instead on Cusco, the charming capital of the Inca Empire. As far as I was concerned, the trail's secret lay not with the Incas, but rather with the Shuar. A former tribe of head-shrinkers, they wore macaw-feather crowns, and believed the world in which they lived was an illusion.

Although the Shuar no longer shrink heads, they continue to believe in the myth of illusion. It's the bedrock of their entire existence, and they only ever reach the real world when answers are needed to problems in their illusionary lives.

As soon as I heard the Shuar 'fly' into the real world by taking the hallucinogen ayahuasca, I recognized it was the single most important lead I'd get.

At Iquitos, I was accosted by a rough and ready Vietnam vet called Richard Fowler. He had fluorescent-green eyes and the swagger of a man living in the psycho zone.

Hire him and, he promised, he'd take me to the jungle to live with the Shuar and – more importantly – he'd bring me out alive.

Without giving it any thought, I rented *Pradera*, a spider-infested boat complete with its derelict crew, and spent what was left of my advance on supplies. For weeks we went upriver on a mission right out of *Apocalypse Now*.

Having lived with the tribe of former head-shrinkers, and taken ayahuasca – the so-called 'Vine of the Dead' – I returned to London to hear the news that Little Miss Prim had resigned.

In the same way publishers are polite in their rejection letters, so are they understated in describing the loss of one of their people. No one ever came out with it straight, but I knew my editor had left because she couldn't stand the phoniness of it all. I would have followed her, as authors often do, but Little Miss Prim got out of the rat race entirely, taking a position at the Centre for Alternative Energy in Wales.

Without delay a new editor was assigned to me. Although kindly, he was battered by his superiors and by life, and had no real interest in the head-shrinkers of the Upper Amazon.

Buckling down, I wrote up my notes, first by hand, then typing them out, as I had done with my previous book. The process gave me time to think about the birdmen in a deep-down way. The process was like spinning wool in preparation for knitting.

On the face of it, *Trail of Feathers* was an ordinary travel book – a quest with a beginning, a middle, and an end. But, for me, it was more than that. It was the first book I wrote which wasn't a book at all.

It was a horse...

A Trojan Horse.

Over the weeks spent on the *Pradera*, infested as she was with wolf spiders, I'd had plenty of time in which to think, swinging back and forth in my hammock.

I thought of my father and grandfather, and all the books they'd written. I thought of the way churning out a book is the ultimate therapy for the machinations of a writer's mind. And I thought about how a book is a device capable of concealment.

I kept getting flashes of my father pacing about Langton House, brandishing newspaper clippings about the Soviet invasion of Afghanistan. It was the early eighties and the conflict was at its height. My father was distraught because the Western world had no grasp of

THE REASON TO WRITE

Afghanistan's geography or culture.

Dropping everything, he decided to write a novel about the country which would essentially be a handbook to all things Afghan.

'It'll be a Trojan Horse,' he said, 'a book containing everything you'd ever need to know about Afghanistan. Not the kind of dead wood they give you in an encyclopaedia, but living material – the kind a people know about their country.'

Unlike me, my father was a master of precision.

He spent weeks gathering books about writing fiction, and dozens of novels as well. Having never written a novel, he was fearful of making the break from one genre to another – a difficulty I was later to appreciate myself.

Sitting down at his IBM electric, he typed solidly for two weeks – producing a manuscript of 180,000 words, over a thousand pages. When released, the book, *Kara Kush*, became an international bestseller. My father was thrilled it got so much attention – not because the adulation fanned his ego, but rather because it positioned the Trojan Horse where it needed to be.

In the aftermath of 9/11, the West got dug down in Afghanistan, which surprised us all. For decades, my family had been ranting on about that landlocked mountainous Central Asian stronghold, and had published dozens of books about its culture and traditions. As the war against Al-Qaeda dragged on,

I watched as my father's Trojan Horse continued to dispense its magic – showing facets of the country largely unknown in the West before *Kara Kush*.

Taking inspiration from that book, I crafted *Trail of Feathers* as a Trojan Horse as well. I embedded a mass of material about folklore and so-called 'primitive societies', presenting what I wrote in a good-humoured way. Shaping the container to suit the content is a technique I've used in every book I've written since.

Most of the time I get the feeling people don't notice. I hope they don't.

Because it means I succeeded in what I set out to do.

Roast Suckling Pig

IF, AS AN author, you lose the editor who brought you on, you're dead in the water.

It's as simple as that.

There's no chance of reviving things – especially if you've been downgraded from third-rate restaurants to a mug of warm Nescafé and a stale digestive.

I may have been wooed at the start, and wowed as well, but I knew my days with Weidenfeld & Nicolson were numbered.

Unfortunately for me, I inherited not only my family's enthusiasm for writing and adventure, but their gusto for making a stink as well. I'd been raised with my father reeling with bouts of rage, screaming about his publishers until his face turned the colour of sun-ripened plums.

Whereas my writer friends loved nothing better than hanging on their publishers' every word, I forbade myself to believe in a system run by imbeciles and held together by duct tape.

Days before *Trail of Feathers* was published, I signed with the legendary publisher John Murray.

Take a poll of every author in the world and you're unlikely to find any quite so disparaging about publishers as me. They're a truly rotten bunch who deserve the extinction they're about to get. But, although my revulsion for the species is extensive, it isn't exclusive.

There is, or at least there *was*, an exception...
John Murray.

A building may only be a container, but in the case of publishers it speaks volumes about what's going on inside.

Orion, which owned the imprint that published me under Little Miss Prim, was as I've said housed in the glass-and-steel tower. Orion House was all about creating an impression which might give a mediocre publishing empire an edge.

Less than a mile away as the crow flies, Murray's was a million miles from Orion in every other way. Founded in 1768, the firm represented just about everyone of any nineteenth-century literary significance – including Austen, Livingstone, Darwin, Byron, and even Conan Doyle.

The offices were nestled away in a discreet townhouse on Albemarle Street in London's Mayfair, an address where the company had been based for two hundred years.

From the first moment I stepped in through the door, I fell in love.

Weidenfeld & Nicolson may have wooed me with its spacious atrium and thick pile carpeting, but Murray's out-wooed them a million to one with understated charm.

Invited into the drawing room on the first floor, I was shown the fireplace at which Lord Byron had famously burned his diaries. The walls of that exquisite salon were hung with oils of legendary authors, and members of the Murray family. In a delightful eccentricity, the first male member in each generation had been named John – so the firm was always run by a John Murray.

On my introductory visit, I was invited to meet the current John Murray, the seventh. He was down in the basement stacking boxes of books against a wall.

Surprisingly down to earth, he wiped the sweat from his palms and shook my hand up and down hard.

'Welcome to our family,' he said cheerily.

And that's exactly what Murray's was – a family.

A family of indescribable delight that valued me as a member first and as a book-writing machine second. The extraordinary thing about Murray's was that they welcomed me in before we'd even discussed new projects. I was under their wing, and that's what mattered to them and to me. Unlike other publishers, there was a sense an author would be there for life – like an employee at an old-fashioned family firm.

In many ways John Murray was more like a gentleman's club than a publisher. No one ever spoke about sales figures, or about clawing back money forked out on advances. The only thing anyone seemed to care about was whether the authors were happy. At Murray's editors fussed over their authors like mother geese.

On my birthday I was sent flowers – not a mingy little posy, but a top-of-the-range bouquet. When I needed a place to write, I was given John Murray VI's study, which led on to the drawing room.

Best of all were the lunches.

A throwback to Georgian London, they were feats of unbridled gastronomic delight. Still reeling from being barred when it came to ordering a starter during my courtship with Weidenfeld & Nicolson, I pointed to the most modest dish on the menu – a lacklustre quiche Lorraine – when the waiter came around.

'I'd like that,' I said.

The editor regarded me with the kind of horror you'd experience in Afghanistan, where a family's honour goes hand-in-hand with honouring a guest.

'Nonsense!' she boomed. 'He'll have the roast suckling pig, and so will I – and we'll start with a bottle of the Château Latour '91.'

Once we'd clinked glasses and dug into the roast, my new editor began probing.

'Had any thoughts on what to write?'

As before, I had anticipated the question, and was ready.

'King Solomon's mines,' I said, my mouth full of pork.

'Like the sound of that!' the editor gushed. 'Any idea where it might take you?'

Swilling a good long glug of wine, I looked her in the

eye, and said:

'To the Highlands of Ethiopia.'

Searching for King Solomon's mines was a family obsession.

In the twenties, my grandfather had hunted for them in Yemen, narrowly avoiding being banged up in jail as a result. In the fifties, my father had scoured Sudan's Red Sea coast for the fabled mines. He'd eventually located a cave system which was said by locals to have been worked by King Solomon's enslaved legions of jinn.

My hunch was that they were both looking in the wrong place. After just enough basic research, I flew to the Ethiopian capital Addis Ababa, where I hoped to pick up the first clue.

Talking big over roast suckling pig was one thing, but being on the ground and wondering desperately where to start was another. Twenty years ago there were no tourists at all in Ethiopia, and anyone searching for ancient gold mines would probably have been locked up as a spy.

For an entire week I fumbled about, tiptoeing my way around museums and monuments, hoping the first clue would find me rather than me find it.

Remarkably, that's exactly what happened.

I leapt into a taxi, a decrepit old Lada, and asked the driver to take me to the tomb of Emperor Menelik II. Unusually chatty, the cabbie introduced himself as

Samson. When I descended into the crypt beneath the floor of the Saint Gabriel Cathedral where the legendary emperor and his empress were interred, he joined me.

The next thing I knew, I'd seconded Samson as my best friend. It wasn't because we had much in common or that I even liked him – but because of something he let slip as we stumbled through torrential rain back to the car.

'I used to be a gold miner,' he'd said.
'Where?'
'At Shakiso.'
'Where's that?'
'In the south.'
'Who owns the mine?'
'No one. They're illegal.'
'Sounds like something out of the Wild West.'
Samson shrugged.
'Wild West of what?'
'How far are the illegal gold mines?'
'Very far.'
'Damn.'
'I'll take you there if you like.'

Samson and I spent months criss-crossing Ethiopia on the trail of King Solomon's mines.

We visited the Afar desert in the east, where the testicle-hunting tribesmen had once tormented my friend Sir Wilfred Thesiger in his youth. We went up to Axum as well, where the Ark of the Covenant is supposedly housed. Then we trekked on mules to a sacred mountain in the west of the country, following leads left by a British explorer in the thirties. During the ramshackle journey we came upon colossal excavations from antiquity, which I felt sure had supplied King Solomon with gold.

The greatest scene of all was Shakiso, where Samson had been an illegal gold miner before he threw it in and became a taxi driver instead. Thousands of men, women, and children were digging with their hands, panning the clay down at the river, using a technique pioneered by the Ancient Egyptians millennia ago.

A zigzag approach to life throws out opportunities in an extraordinary way – the kind of opportunities well-planned explorers never find. I've always found that in order to pick up leads you have to tune your head to pick up a rare frequency.

The frequency of ultimate possibility.

Tune in, and amazing adventures take place, so long as you open your mind and give the waves the chance to emerge from the ether.

Even though my travel book *In Search of King Solomon's Mines* was eventually hacked up far more than I would have liked by my editor, the story seemed to hit the mark. Programme executives at Channel 4 commissioned it as a documentary for their flagship series *To the Ends of the Earth*. As presenter, I was cajoled to return to Ethiopia with a film crew in tow and do the entire zigzag journey again.

Many weeks later I reached Heathrow Airport on a Monday morning after the red-eye from Addis Ababa. My clothing was caked in blood and filth because we'd gone straight from the sacred mountain of Tulu Wallel to the airport. Dragging a pair of military kit bags behind me, I went down to the Underground for the ride into central London.

Waiting for the Tube, my festering luggage stacked beside me, I felt distinctly out of place. Strewn down the platform were impeccably dressed businessmen who'd come in on early flights from Europe.

As they regarded me with contempt, I remember thinking:

'Look at you all, you bastards! You may be clean and perfumed, but you've never lived! You wouldn't know what it's like to push yourself to the baseline – to scour Ethiopia for King Solomon's mines!'

A few days before my first book with Murray's was launched, a cheap envelope was posted through my front door – not the kind used by John Murray.

Inside was a hastily photocopied letter with urgent news:

John Murray and Company, owned by the Murray family since the eighteenth century, had been sold.

In what was possibly the greatest act of miscalculation

in British publishing, Murray ended up being torn to shreds. The editorial staff were turfed out of Albemarle Street and moved to a glass-and-steel monolith on the Euston Road, rivalled in its depravity only by Orion House.

The Murray family retained the building in Mayfair, with its magical drawing room.

But it didn't matter.

What mattered was that the magic was gone.

The loss of my beloved publisher John Murray is a subject I've deliberated upon a great deal over the years. On nights when I cannot sleep, I've cursed the Murray family for selling up, begging the spirits of the Underworld to exact a horrible revenge.

At the time John Murray was sold – to the newsagents W.H. Smith of all people – the authors were informed the firm was being sold because the numbers didn't add up.

While I'd been wolfing down an oversized plate of roast suckling pig, a financial officer was going through the firm's books. He must have been horrified to find that Murray's didn't make money in ways modern publishers were supposed to do.

The result was a slash and burn bonanza, in which staff were laid off, assets were stripped and sold off, and what was left became a third-rate imprint in a towering glass office block. My point is that once in a while in life you come across a group of people creating marvels,

marvels whose numbers don't add up. In such rare cases, the balance sheet is secondary to the heartbeat.

Murray's was one of the very last Georgian publishers, dragged off to the knacker's yard and ripped limb from limb for no good reason. Having defied the conventional model of twentieth-century publishing until the millennium, it was tripped up because a number cruncher couldn't make sense of its accounts.

Like my father's firm, The Octagon Press, Murray's operated on a system gloriously above convention. That was the most delicious thing about it. The books it published were unlikely to ever sell in their millions, and thank God for that. If they had, the firm would have been rocked on its foundations – which is what happened over at Bloomsbury. An editor there defied all reason and bought a book about a shy young wizard with wiry specs.

Before stepping forward for execution, John Murray gave me a final gift.

They commissioned a book about the second epic Peruvian journey I'd made, in search of Paititi, the greatest lost city in human history...

House of the Tiger King.

The Curse of Sloth

As WITH ALL my books, I wrote *House of the Tiger King* not to make money, but rather as a way of staving off the terrible curse hanging over my life like a death cloud...

The Curse of Sloth.

Having read *Trail of Feathers*, a Swedish film crew consisting of a father, Leon, and his son, David, made contact with me. Uproariously enthusiastic, they moved from Stockholm to London, where they stalked me. Insisting they were diehard fans, they pleaded with me to allow them to follow me on my next big journey.

Over egg and chips at my favourite North London greasy spoon, I told them the truth – I was broke and had no strings to pull in TV.

'No problem,' said David Flamholc, dabbing an extra-thick chip into a pool of egg yolk.

'Think you'll find you can't do anything without funding,' I replied curtly.

'We sold our flat,' David said.

'So we've got cash,' his father piped in.

'Wow.'

'So when do we leave?!' David exclaimed.

'For where?'

'Anywhere!'

'Expeditions take months of careful planning,' I explained.

'Do they?'

'Yes, months... or even years.'

'That's not what you said in the magazine article.'

'Huh?'

David Flamholc pulled a crumpled scrap of paper from his jeans and read it aloud:

'"I pride myself on never doing any research," Tahir Shah said, "because research gets in the way and kills the spirit of real adventure!"'

'So where shall we go?' Leon probed, his head lowering subversively.

'The jungle!' David cried. 'Let's go to the jungle!'

'I hate the jungle,' I said. 'It's frigging horrible.'

'Great!' the Flamholcs exclaimed in unison.

'*Why?*'

'Because hardship looks fantastic on film!' cried David.

I like to think that by commissioning *House of the Tiger King* my editor at John Murray was sticking a pair of fingers up to the company who'd bought them out.

There are two reasons.

First: The book was a gritty account of an equally gritty river journey deep into the Madre de Dios cloud forest.

Second: The very same editor had commissioned another book by a fellow explorer, searching for the very same lost city at the very same time.

No other publisher would have allowed two Paititi-

THE REASON TO WRITE

Lost-City books to be launched in the same decade, let alone the very same month.

My own version of Joseph Conrad's *Heart of Darkness*, *House of the Tiger King* was the tale of an insane expedition through my eyes, rather than through those of the film's director – the version which eventually made it to the screen.

The weeks I spent writing the book were the hottest in living memory. Stripping down to my boxer shorts, I typed away manically, sweating like a madman in the jungle.

Tiger King was about mania from beginning to end, and about allowing myself to descend through interwoven layers to a bedrock of unfettered lunacy. During the weeks of writing I felt powerful and strong – like Conrad's antihero Colonel Kurtz.

The book allowed me to become enveloped in strains of glorious mania – the kind non-fiction authors are rarely permitted to embrace.

I hardly dared admit it, but the mania felt good.

Better than good.

It felt as though I'd finally reached where I yearned to be.

Mania was a theme I would have continued to explore had the tectonic plates of my life not destined me for something else.

By the time *House of the Tiger King* was published,

Ariane was two, and Timur was a babe in arms. We were living in a cramped flat in the East End of London. All I could think of was how my own childhood had been played out in the comparatively lavish surroundings of Langton House, where Lord Baden-Powell, founder of the Boy Scouts, had been a child, too.

Every morning the apartment's walls seemed to move in a little closer, as I wondered how we'd ever make it through another day. Memories of Langton's abundant space and beauty flooded both my waking hours and my dreams. It was the only thing I could think about.

Well, almost the only thing.

A mesmerizing backdrop for a childhood, Langton House was countered by something else – something even more magical.

Morocco.

My earliest memories are of sitting in the garden at my grandfather's little villa on Tangier's rue de la Plage. Close my eyes and I can hear the birds tweeting in the trees, smell the delicate scent of orange blossom, and feel the warmth of sunshine on my young skin.

I longed to be back there – not a passing longing or a fleeting whim, but the longing of deepest love.

As though not in charge of my faculties, I stood up on a dining chair, the top of my head brushing the ceiling.

'We're moving!' I yelled loud and clear.

'Moving where?' my wife, Rachana, enquired.

'Moving to Morocco!'

The exclamation was met with delight.
'Can we afford it?'
'I'm sure we can.'
'*Really*?'
'Oh yes, Morocco's not very expensive at all.'
Rachana's face fell.
'Oh, *Morocco*.'
'Yes, Morocco!'
'Thought you meant *Monaco*,' Rachana said.

Jinn

SWEPT UP IN the moment, we set about searching for a house to buy in Marrakesh, Tangier, or in Morocco's spellbinding labyrinth, Fès.

Considering it in hindsight, I'm impressed I didn't want to test the waters by renting for a few months. Mine is an all-or-nothing character. The all-or-nothing approach to Morocco meant there was no choice except to move lock, stock, and barrel.

After various adventures we were offered the most extraordinary house I've ever known. Located on the edge of Casablanca, it was called Dar Khalifa, which translates as 'The Caliph's House'.

Hearing on the expatriate grapevine that we were in the market for adventure, the mother of an old school friend offered us her mansion for a knock-down price.

Sprawling over more than an acre, the walled gardens were a fragment of paradise. Set within them was the house itself – a vast, rambling pile, abundant with shaded courtyards, gardens, fountains, and birdsong.

The only apparent downside was that the property was encircled by a seething shantytown – a colossal rumpus of a thing.

Having sold our London apartment, we arrived prepared for challenges. Anything, that is, except the news which greeted us.

As though by some medieval right of sale, Dar Khalifa

was supplied with a fraternity of guardians They had apparently always worked at the house, just as their parents and grandparents had done. Firing them was out of the question.

The guardians were not the problem. The problem was what they told us:

The Caliph's House was filled from floor to ceiling with legions of invisible jinn – the parallel life-forms which Muslims believe inhabit the world along with mankind.

Over the first months we were introduced to facets of Morocco I'd never imagined existed. It wasn't the face of the kingdom you get shown in the glossy tourist brochures or sleek coffee-table books.

From the moment of our arrival I was struck by the beauty, the sense of freedom, and the stark contrasts. Most of all, however, I was affected by the belief in dark forces served up in the form of jinn.

The ancestral guardians were agitated beyond belief that we'd moved into the house itself. They claimed the jinn would swallow us up and spit out our bones. The only way to placate them was to hire an exorcist.

Had we moved to a haunted house in Europe or the United States, I wouldn't have known where to find someone to banish wayward spirits. But Morocco is different. In *The Arabian Nights* the kingdom is often referred to as the 'Land of the Sorcerers' for good reason.

Having hired a fixer who could fix the unfixable, I

travelled into the hinterland with him. We pitched up at Meknès, and started asking for exorcists. I had planned to recruit one or two. Having heard the details of the problem, an exorcist-supplying contact suggested a far larger contingent. To scrimp on exorcists was, he assured me, a perilous thing to do.

In the end, I hired twenty exorcists from the Aissawa Brotherhood. In the hope of keeping me sweet, the go-between threw in another four for free. My fixer and I returned to Casablanca, where Rachana yelled at me for paying in advance.

'You've just been had,' she said.

Days passed, and there was no sign of the exorcists. I sunk into a deep depression and got under the duvet – my place of comfort since childhood.

Then, one morning against the cries of the *muezzin* calling the faithful to prayer, I heard the sound of wheels grinding. I looked out and spied the exorcists coming down the lane on the back of a cement truck.

For days and nights the Aissawa wreaked their terrible work. They killed rams and chickens, nailed the internal organs to the window-frames, and splattered the walls of every room with milk and blood in a frantic rumpus of sorcery. Drums thundered through the house and *qarkabeb*, the great iron castanets from the Sahara, clattered until we all thought we'd go mad.

When they were not writhing about in a trance, or devouring the jinn, the exorcists were devouring platters of food, which they expected us to provide.

After three days Rachana ordered me to throw them out.

Tiptoeing up to their leader, I thanked him for his team's diligence, and said he and his men could leave.

'We will only go when all the jinn have been dispatched!' he cried.

'We're quite happy for you to call it a day,' I said.

The chief exorcist looked horrified.

'Leave a single jinn and they'll multiply overnight!'

Four days later, the Aissawa finally left, clambering back onto the cement truck, whooping and hollering as they went.

Rachana, the kids, and I sat in the small courtyard outside the kitchen like survivors of a forgotten war. The remains of a sacrificial ram had been strung up from the balcony above. Headless and dismembered, its entrails were spewing out, blood dripping down.

'Other people don't live like this,' Rachana said.

'I wonder why not,' I replied.

'Because it's horrid.'

'What is?'

'The shantytown, the exorcists, and *that*,' she said, pointing up at the dismembered carcass above.

'It's living,' I said. 'Living in a real way – lives which aren't phony and dull.'

Rachana balked.

'Give me phony and dull any day of the week.'

Standing up, I strolled out into the garden, bathed in the long shadows of dusk. My nostrils caught the scent of honeysuckle as the call to prayer wafted out over the shantytown's rusted tin roofs.

'This would make the most extraordinary book,' I thought to myself. 'A book called *The Caliph's House*.'

Internal Wiring

A FEW MONTHS before 11th September 2001, the date which changed all our lives, my sister Saira had made a documentary about women living under Afghanistan's dreaded Taliban regime.

The film, called *Beneath the Veil*, was an outright sensation. Saira was fêted by just about everyone you can imagine. Her face was plastered over the covers of magazines, and she was showered with awards. Quite rightly so. The film, which was extraordinary, was a window into another world.

As soon as *Beneath the Veil* aired, a literary agent with a nose for a story signed Saira, and asked for an outline for a book. Rather than simply write a straight version of the film, she chose instead to work on something far more profound.

As children, we were raised not to concern ourselves with the obvious. Our parents stressed that things of real consequence were hidden to others. Tease them out and, they told us, you find you can observe the invisible guy-ropes holding our world in place. Understand how the system is configured, they said, and one's experience is far deeper, and immeasurably more rewarding.

Saira wrote the outline for a book entitled *The Storyteller's Daughter*. A tale of our shared childhood, it explained how the magical realm in which we were raised set her on a particular path, just as it had done for me.

In Saira's case the path led from Langton House to the wilds of Soviet-occupied Afghanistan – the land of our ancestors, the one described in our father's novel, *Kara Kush*.

Represented by the savvy agent with a nose for a story, the book proposal kicked off a publishing feeding frenzy. On both sides of the Atlantic and all over the world, *The Storyteller's Daughter* was rewarded with eye-watering advances.

Now I had a Moroccan mansion to keep up, and droves of ancestral staff to pay each week, I yearned for a project which might bring in some cold hard cash.

In their memoirs, billionaires always seem to note the same point:

To make money you must do what you love.

Life has certainly taught me that, too. But it's also taught me something else: in order to make money you have to do what fascinates you. Loving something and being fascinated with it are similar, but not quite the same.

Enthusiasm may be a dominant force in my life, but it's never been a question of enthusiasm for the sake of enthusiasm. Rather, it's been enthusiasm for a reason – enthusiasm that allows me to plunge in the sacred pool of enthralment.

Almost nothing I've ever succeeded in has been done in a conventional way.

It's an important point, and one that's shaped what I

do and who I am. I refuse to follow the standard path of doing something because it's the recognized course of action. My entire life has been structured around being original, and creating in a way that I find stimulating.

Through my childhood and adolescence I was widely regarded as a weirdo, because my internal wiring is different from that of other people.

Those who believed it were right – I am wired differently.

But the way I see it, it's me who's wired up in the right way, and they who are misaligned.

When I started writing books, my work was frequently dismissed as being unbelievable or downright odd. Only now after I've published more than forty books do my original detractors leave me alone. All I can hope is they've understood what I was working towards all those years.

As a writer I'm always in search of a lens through which to observe. Self-important literary types rant on about themes being key. And they are. But in my opinion the lens through which the content of a book is considered by its author is even more important than any theme.

Standing in the garden at dusk on the night the exorcism ended, I grasped something which was to alter the path of my life:

Dar Khalifa was a way to show others the Morocco I myself was learning about.

At dawn next morning I went down to the kitchen, sat at the one and only table in the house, and knocked out the proposal for *The Caliph's House*.

Half-expecting him to dismiss the idea, I sent it to Saira's agent.

But he didn't dismiss it.

He loved it, as did his colleague in New York.

Book proposals are hooks with which to go fishing. The more elaborate the bait loaded on the hook, the fatter the fish you have a chance of catching.

In the hope of hooking myself a monumental beast of a deal, I expanded the proposal, piling on the description I'd learned to do back in my feature-writing days. I showcased a few choice anecdotes and pages of lovely description, conjuring the smells and sounds, the sights, and the feel of Morocco – from the inside out.

Only when the agents were completely satisfied with the hook and the bait did they drop it into the water.

Right at once fish began to bite.

From the get-go, the story of an impulsive writer relocating to a mansion in a Moroccan shantytown wooed publishers, as did the backdrop of mysterious Casablanca. But the aspect that the literary fraternity found irresistible was the house itself – the matrix through which I observed my tale.

Any writer who's blasé or dismissive about having

their book proposal go to a bidding war is lying. It's an almost unrivalled thrill – not because it means you'll make a ton of money, but rather because it signals you're in demand.

Publishing has changed since the feeding frenzy which secured my deal for *The Caliph's House*.

But, more to the point, I've changed.

Having signed with Random House on both sides of the Atlantic, I was left alone to get on with writing the book.

Through many months we renovated Dar Khalifa, restoring the house and outbuildings to their former glory, feeling our way forward an inch at a time.

Living in a place for the first time gives you 'fresh eyes' – the ability to witness what everyone else regards as the ordinary. Those fresh eyes stood me in good stead while researching *The Caliph's House*.

Better still, floundering in an ocean of house-related trial and tribulation as I was, provided fantastic material for my book.

For the first time I found myself delighting when things went terribly wrong – as they seemed to do all the time. Misadventures make for alarming anecdotes, which were woven through the manuscript.

The worse things got, the better the material was.

In describing our misfortunes, I sought to highlight our own naivety. More importantly, the book was to provide a platform on which to display the kingdom itself.

The Caliph's House is a treasury of information about Morocco and about 'Moroccan-ness' – shaped for the post 9/11 era, and for a world so mistrusting of Arab culture.

If proof were ever needed that a publisher shells out cold hard cash in order to regain the cold hard cash they've shelled out for an advance – I got it in spades. *The Caliph's House* was met with rave reviews – both by the publishing industry, and by the mainstream media as well. When *TIME* voted it as a 'Top Ten Book of the Year', I felt my feet rise up off the ground.

Luckily, Rachana and the kids were there to remind me I was definitely mortal.

Breathless and excitable, my editor in New York called me to gloat at the sales figures. My English teacher from prep school wrote to congratulate me. And Hugh Carless phoned unexpectedly from London to applaud me, too.

'It's an inspiring read!' he cried.

'I don't quite know why it's caught the public's imagination,' I beamed.

The elderly diplomat went silent as he thought how to answer.

'It works because the Morocco you have presented is the one no one has dared to show before now.'

Emails from readers came in thick and fast, as did letters, and packages as well. Sacks brimming with post arrived, many of the letters addressed simply:

THE REASON TO WRITE

Tahir Shah
The Caliph's House
Morocco

Hundreds of readers wrote to me with their memories of the kingdom. Some revealed their own associations with Dar Khalifa, and even sent me photographs of the house from decades before.

My best friend, who was living in Paris, called me to say he'd overheard a couple on the Métro discussing '*la maison du Calife*' as if it were some magical Shangri-La in the Himalayas.

Plenty of fans didn't stop merely at writing.

Beating a trail to Casablanca, they set about tracking the house down for themselves. I've never liked hearing stories of authors who keep their readers at a distance, so I invited everyone in when they came. Some afternoons there were thirty or forty people traipsing through the house, posing for selfies in our bedroom, or even rooting through my drawers.

Not wishing to be left out, dignitaries started to arrive, among them a stream of ambassadors. It was on one such occasion I had cause to witness a particularly fine example of diplomacy.

The American ambassador and his wife asked me if they could come and visit, and we set a date. By chance, the Swedish ambassador and his wife asked if they could come on the same day. 'Great, we'll get it all over at once!' I thought to myself.

The day before the Americans turned up, a security team appeared. The kind you always see in the movies, they had the dark glasses, the raincoats, and the standard look – as though everything you're telling them is an outright lie. As they poked through every nook and cranny, I reminded them it had been the ambassador who'd invited himself.

Next afternoon, a snaking cortège of armoured black SUVs rolled through the shantytown and down the narrow lane to Dar Khalifa. Even before the vehicles had halted, a slew of secret service agents leapt out, followed by a troop of towering uniformed Moroccans. I found out later they were the bodyguards to the King.

As we received our guests inside, the soft-spoken Swedish couple arrived on foot, having left their modest Volvo out in the shantytown. During the tour of the house, which the Americans had asked for, the Swedes remained in the sitting room.

At the end of the afternoon, the Americans thanked us, leapt back into their motorcade, and reversed back up the lane. The Swedish ambassador asked if he and his wife might stay a few minutes longer, on the pretext of waiting for a telephone call. As soon as his American counterpart had gone, he presented Rachana and me with a small gift.

Although I didn't give the matter a second thought at the time, the training of a career diplomat, as opposed to a political appointee, touched me later. In Morocco, it would be unthinkable to visit the home of anyone without bringing a token gift. Noticing the American delegation had come empty handed and not wishing to upstage them, the Swedes had waited until we were alone before making their presentation.

The Caliph's House kept on giving.

Making the most of a good thing, my literary agent got his team onto selling foreign rights. Before I knew it, the book was available in more than three dozen editions – published in everything from Arabic to Lithuanian, and from Hebrew to Mandarin.

Every new language brought yet more emails from fans and from the media in far-flung lands. More and more people wanted a piece of me virtually, or to come and experience Dar Khalifa for themselves.

It wasn't just the readers who'd bought and read the book who felt a close association – my publishers did, too. Their connection tended to be rather more mercenary and assertive. As far as they were concerned, the big fat advances had been paid not so much for a manuscript, but for a life.

My life.

I'd been bought pound for pound, and I was owned – in the way actors used to be in the glory days of Hollywood. Of course the sense of obligation to jump when told to do so was wrapped up in frivolity and joy, but it was there all the same.

My star sign is Scorpio.

I chalk my inability to forget a grudge down to the sting in my tail. Don't get me wrong – some of my best friends are Scorpios and they're wonderful people. But in my experience there's frequently an underlying sense of bitterness in Scorpios who've been crossed.

My editor at Random House in New York was a king of kings. He was the kind of man whose colleagues laughed when he told a joke, whether they found it funny or not. Mild-mannered most of the time, he didn't try and mask the power he wielded.

Only once did he bare his teeth at me. The details aren't important. What mattered was that it'd happened.

In a single Scorpio moment I vowed to get out – like Little Red Riding Hood desperate to flee her grandma's house. I was ready to run and never come back, big fat advance or no big fat advance.

But that's not what I did.

Sizzle

SUCCESSFUL FIRMS MAKING detergent cottoned on to something long ago: why make one kind of soap powder when you can make dozens of varieties?

Publishers may imagine they're in a more cerebral business than producing soap, but their model is essentially the same:

- Find a product that's not half bad.
- Launch it to great fanfare.
- Market the hell out of it.
- Develop an almost identical product and do it all again, and again.

As the heady glow of *The Caliph's House* began to die down, New York's king of kings probed politely:

'Just wondering if you've thought of an idea for another book?'

Naturally, having anticipated the question, I'd agonized over it in advance.

My book about a first year living in Casablanca hadn't been about a conventional quest. Even though much of the action took place at Dar Khalifa, it was very much a journey.

As we were living in Morocco, I wanted to continue with what I'd started, identifying the internal rhythm. Dar Khalifa and Casablanca were all well and good, but there was so much more to take in and explore throughout the kingdom as a whole.

Even though *The Caliph's House* wasn't a conventional travelogue, I wanted to write a book to build on the foundations I'd laid down... a book which allowed Morocco to reveal itself in a spectacular and unusual way.

Uncertain what to choose as my lens, I visited my elderly aunt, Amina, the next time I was in London.

In her eighties, Amina had an encyclopaedic knowledge of world folklore. She was a traveller, and a consummate storyteller. Like the Shuar tribe of the Upper Amazon, she resided in an illusionary world – having succeeded in never allowing herself to be stripped of her childlike sense of imagination.

Amina was sitting in the conservatory of the house where she lived, a half-knitted hat, yarn, and a crochet hook in her hands.

As soon as she saw me, she flustered about, showering the visitor with stories and gifts. Eventually, the gift-giving and the stories ceased like the last strains of a once-great wave rolling up the shore.

Returning to her crocheting, Aunt Amina looked at me hard, as if enquiring telepathically what was on my mind.

'The publishers want another book about Morocco,' I said.

'Of course they do,' she countered. 'After all, why would they want to change the recipe when the soup sells?'

THE REASON TO WRITE

'I'm looking for a way to let Morocco describe itself.' Aunt Amina's attention was focused on the hat she was crocheting. Assuming she hadn't heard my comment, I was about to repeat it.

Looking up, she said:

'*The Arabian Nights*. Show Morocco through *The Arabian Nights*.'

The idea went down well with my agent and my publishers.

Another healthy advance was handed over and I got down to researching the book, called simply *In Arabian Nights*.

A tribute to my aunt's suggestion, the title honoured my grandfather as well. In 1933 he'd published a travel book about the Arab world – taking in Iraq, Syria, Palestine, and the fledgling kingdom of Saudi Arabia.

It was titled *Alone in Arabian Nights*.

From the moment I started gathering material, I gleaned that Morocco was constructed on a bedrock of folklore more deeply than anywhere else I'd ever been. Stories and storytelling are ubiquitous in human culture, but in Morocco – the Land of Sorcerers – they form a kind of fourth dimension.

Writing the book while Ariane and Timur were young gave me the opportunity to perceive stories through their eyes. That sense of childhood wonder obsessed me, dragging me back through the folds of

231

time to when I was a child at Langton House.

After months of research, writing, and editing, I printed out the manuscript, placed it on my desk, and looked at it.

Rachana found me standing there, staring at the book.

'They're not going to get this one,' I said.

'Who aren't?'

'Random House.'

'Why d'you say that?'

'Because I've done something very subtle.'

'What?'

'I've woven a tapestry as subtle as Morocco's culture. It's not obvious, and that's going to be a problem.'

'Why would it be a problem?'

'Because publishers are in the business of dishing up the obvious.'

'To hell with them, then,' Rachana said.

Of my first two works on Morocco, *In Arabian Nights* is without doubt the better book in all sorts of ways.

Composed of interwoven layers of culture, it provides a story of considerable depth. I'm not a miracle-worker, but Morocco is. All I did was to hold a mirror up to what I saw, and to tune my ears to what I heard.

Writing is always an act of self-therapy, never more so for me than writing *In Arabian Nights*.

Having sent the manuscript off, I waited for the king of kings to respond. That initial silence is always a curious thing, a time of extraordinary anticipation. It's like the hush when a rocket loses contact from ground control as it breaks through the edge of the atmosphere into space.

Cold, dark silence.

All of a sudden, a signal came through from Random House. Communications were re-established, and a phone call was hastily arranged.

'Think it needs something,' my editor said intently.

'Something like what?'

'Like a sizzle at the start... a sizzle which ripples through the entire book.'

'*A sizzle?*'

'Yes, sizzle.'

'A sizzle... like bacon frying in a pan?'

'*Yes!*' the king of kings chuckled. 'Just like that.'

Hanging up the call, I struggled to dream up a sizzle worthy of Moroccan stories – a sizzle that would enable the sales teams at Random House to sell a subtle tale of tales.

For days I sulked around the house, irritated at having to tweak my creation which – in my opinion – needed no tweaking at all.

Eventually an idea came to me, and I ran with it, although in my opinion it was like spreading a thick layer of sweetened cream all over a chocolate cake.

I passed the idea on.

The king of kings was beside himself with joy. 'Can't believe it!' he yelled. 'It'll be perfect!'

The sizzle I chose was inspired by a series of disagreeable events that had recently taken place.

Having filmed our documentary in Peru, the Flamholcs wondered aloud what we could work on next. I ought to have said nothing – it would have saved us a great deal of misery.

But I didn't.

I said: 'Afghanistan.'

Eagerly, David and Leon repeated the name as a question.

'We'll go hunt for the lost treasure of Ahmed Shah Durrani,' I said, 'the one my father wrote about in *Kara Kush*!'

Months spent in the Peruvian cloud forest had been hard going and at times dangerous. But mounting an expedition through war-torn Afghanistan in search of a possibly fictitious treasure – said by some to be worth $500 billion – was tantamount to suicide.

That's what made it so appealing.

Before embarking on the main adventure, we decided to travel from India to Afghanistan overland to get a sense of the difficulties we might face when filming. Tracing the route the treasure itself was believed to have taken, we crossed the heavily fortified border at Wagah, dividing India and Pakistan. Then, with spirits high, we made our way west towards the Hindu Kush.

The night before we descended onto that fabled thoroughfare – the same one used by Alexander the Great many centuries before – we slept at Peshawar, legendary outpost of the North West Frontier. It was a week after the 2005 terrorist bombs in London, the effects of which had rippled throughout Central Asia.

David Flamholc was filming me strolling down a street, talking about the last time I'd been in Peshawar.

Without warning, an armed officer strode out of nowhere.

He ordered us to turn the camera off.

We were frogmarched to a military police checkpoint.

Our passports were confiscated.

Right away, things spiralled out of control.

We were blindfolded, chained, thrown in the back of a pickup truck, and taken to a torture prison known locally as 'The Farm'.

For the next sixteen days and nights we languished in a twilight zone of utter depravity – the kind few people, other than full-blown terrorists, ever get to see from the inside out.

I hadn't planned to write about my life and times in the Pakistani torture jail. The experience was still too raw. But the king of kings needed a sizzle, and solitary confinement and nightly interrogations sizzled very loudly indeed.

So, pandering to my master's orders, I gave them

the best sizzle I had – despite the fact it went against everything I believed to be right.

The only way I had been able to stay sane in solitary confinement was to retreat into the maze of my mind. I imagined a projector was set on the floor, beaming stories over the back wall of my cell.

Stories my father had told me as a child.

Stories I'd collected on my travels through Morocco.

Stories gleaned from a life-long obsession with *The Arabian Nights*.

The projections had been a life-saving mechanism, but they were now something else...

A sizzle by which a publisher could claw back an advance.

On the day *In Arabian Nights* was published I bought a bottle of warm Dom Pérignon from a street-seller in Casablanca's souq, assuming it had been pilfered from an upmarket villa.

Rachana clinked her glass with mine.

'Here's to your book.'

'I'm not drinking to that,' I said.

'Of course you are.'

'No, I'm not.'

'Then what are we drinking to?'

'To being free of the enslavement.'

'What do you mean?'

'I'm never going to allow myself to be usurped by a

publisher again.'

'You say that now, but when they're back with a crisp bundle of cash you'll change your tune.'

'I won't.'

'Why not?'

'Because I've learnt the hard way,' I said.

Samplers

WE SCORPIOS ARE not only grudge-bearing – we're obstinate as well.

When we make up our minds, we stick to it, even if a decision causes misery to everyone around us. Most other writers would have sold another Morocco book and gone on yet another spending spree with the advance. But I'd made up my mind never to allow my work to become a lump of meat again – a lump requiring a deafening sizzle for it to sell.

When *In Arabian Nights* was launched, I made a promise to myself. Through a solemn oath, I vowed thenceforth to write for myself and for no one else.

It may seem like a vacuous pledge made on the spur of the moment – but it was the most sacred vow of my professional life.

Writing for myself changed everything...

It changed the way I went about selecting book projects and researching them.

It changed the way I wrote books, and edited them.

Most of all, though, it changed the actual framework.

I no longer chased publishers, and I refused to allow them to chase me. Observing book-writing for the first time as something wholly creative, I regarded it in a way writers used to do, as I described right at the start.

In my late teens, a painter friend of my parents invited me to have lunch with him at his studio in South

Kensington.

His work was wonderfully expressive and he had a worldwide following. The studio was situated in what must have once been the drawing room of the grand townhouse, a giant south-facing window providing glorious light.

While our friend shuffled down to the kitchen to get the meal ready, he left me in the studio to look over his latest work.

For fifteen minutes I observed that room and its contents in almost forensic detail.

I looked at how the brushes were arranged, and how oil paints were blended together on a testing palette. I noticed the way the easel had been tilted slightly upwards to catch the light, and the pattern of paint-spatter over the floor.

But the thing which grabbed my attention more than anything else was a series of small canvases laid up along the back wall. No more than about twelve inches square, each one was different.

When the artist came back through, I asked him what they were.

'They're my samplers,' he said.

'You mean like the kind on which Victorian embroidery students practised their skill?'

'Precisely.'

'What do you learn from doing them?'

'Everything.'

The painter explained how sampling allowed him to experiment with diverse colours and techniques, demonstrating what was possible, and allowing him to push the boundaries of his skill.

Describing himself as an alchemist, he said painting was something he did for the purest love of creation, not to provide visual entertainment for others.

'No one ever understands,' he said gently as we stood there in the intoxicating stream of late summer light. 'They insist that just because a painter can create work with a perceived pecuniary value, that it's the reason he paints.'

'It's not?' I asked.

The artist shook his head.

'I paint to know myself, and to interact with the world around me,' he replied. 'I paint to feel fulfilled, to dream, to lust, to be complete.'

'What about the paintings you create?'

'The process of creating them is what matters to me, and that's all. When they're done, they're done.'

'But surely you're happy if they sell for a fortune.'

The artist shrugged.

'Not really,' he said. 'By the time I have finished a work, it's left my system, and I have left it – like a serpent sloughing its skin. We are no longer connected. For me, the great joy is to move on, and to experiment on something else.'

Before leaving the studio after lunch, I asked the

painter if he accepted commissions.

A look of absolute horror descended over his face.

'I cannot imagine anything worse,' he said. 'It's hard enough pleasing myself, but the idea of pleasing a total stranger as well is beyond the pale.'

My visit to the artist all those years ago has stayed with me, and it helped me to glimpse the light.

His samplers pop into my head often, lined up as they were against the back wall. Journalism was a medium of experimentation for me, one that taught me so much. It was fast, fun, and frivolous – but was the ultimate method of learning the craft.

Turning my pledge over in my mind, I thought of the artist, remembering how he sampled and how he painted not to produce, but to learn and to create.

Write books in the same way, and an author would most likely be banished from the self-important world of conventional publishing. But follow the artist's example, and I'd have a chance at creating in a way that fulfilled me right down to the marrow of my bones.

Surely that outweighed anything else.

Retreating to my little office, which doubled as my dressing room, I thought it over. I'd follow the artist's example and blaze a trail of my own.

A trail focused on learning, experimenting, creating, but not preoccupied with selling.

A trail fulfilling me in a sacred way.

A trail which would produce the body of work I wanted to be remembered for, rather than a sizzling mass of fodder publishers hoped to sell.

The question was where to start on this grand new scheme.

Casablanca...

The city on the other side of the shantytown.

Literary Leper

AN ASPIRING MOROCCAN actress from a wealthy family had appeared out of the blue, wining and dining Rachana and me over several months.

In a way that was curiously Oriental, she charmed me more expertly than I'd been charmed in a very long time. Once we had become friends, she enquired whether I might write a movie in which she would play the starring role. The film could be made without any need for outside funds, she said, because her father would pay for everything.

It sounded like a great plan.

Oddly, it came along at the same moment I'd decided to write a novel about Casablanca. The only hitch was that the story I had dreamt up was likely to be prickly for the actress and her family, but I brushed that small point aside.

An image had rooted itself in my mind.

The image of an ingenuous fresh-faced American arriving at Casablanca airport at the start of a mid-life crisis.

I could see him clearly.

He was dressed in a crumpled old Burberry raincoat and fedora – like Humphrey Bogart of Rick's Café Américain.

Each night before I drifted off to sleep, I allowed myself to imagine the adventures of the *Casablanca-*

obsessed visitor. Within a week or so I had an entire storyline planned out.

Drilling down into the dark side of Morocco's seething modern metropolis, it exposed the subculture of gangsters, corruption, and vice. The story would be played out against a backdrop of crumbling art deco architecture and speakeasies, and would highlight the gaping chasm between Morocco's haves and have-nots.

Wasting no time, I sat down and wrote *Casablanca Blues* as a movie.

Writing screenplays is the absolute opposite of creating novels. Book writing is all about lavishing one's readers with sumptuous descriptions, and developing a story that will captivate them through a good meaty text. Screen writing is a case of less being more. It's the *nouvelle cuisine* of the writing business. Use a single word more than is needed, and you're guilty of the most terrible crime.

Not long before, I'd been brought on to write several drafts of an Imax movie about Ibn Battuta's fourteenth-century journey to Mecca, and through that had learned the basics of writing for the screen. I'd made the mistake of thinking screen work was Book Writing Lite, when I ought to have seen it was a different animal altogether.

My friend, the American author Paul Theroux, has written scores of fiction and non-fiction books. He once told me he'd never undertaken screen work.

I asked why not.

THE REASON TO WRITE

'Because it's something I don't know about,' he said.

It was a good point, one I learnt with *Casablanca Blues*. My script was twice the length it ought to have been, largely because I insisted on developing both the male and female leads to the maximum. In fashioning it, I was a cobbler who was used to making riding boots doing my best to fashion a pair of ballet shoes.

While writing the story, I was influenced by the actress who'd asked for a movie. The tale was infused with her existence – the super-decadent lifestyle of Morocco's super-rich who have no comprehension of reality. For that reason I'm eternally grateful things panned out in the way – and in the order – they did.

We spend our lives agonizing over why things happen, and why other things *don't* happen. I've beaten myself up about it for decades now, and have at last understood a salient point:

Everything in the life of a creative person occurs as it does, and when it does, for a reason. Try to change what's meant to be and you get slammed in the face. Go with the flow – even if you question it – and you're swept downriver on a whitewater ride of pre-determined wonder.

As you might have imagined, *Casablanca Blues* didn't go down well with the actress. Three days after sending her the script, she messaged back to say it 'wasn't for her'. Rather than being disappointed, I was thrilled, because I had the material for my first novel.

It may be a challenge for a book writer to knock out a convincing screenplay, but turning a screenplay into a novel couldn't be simpler. A script contains the bare bones of storyline, description, sense of people and place.

Best of all, it contains all the dialogue.

Turning *Casablanca Blues* the screenplay into a novel of the same name was like opening a packet of dehydrated soup, tipping the desiccated contents into a mug, pouring in water, and stirring long and hard. The process was so easy-going I can't even remember writing it.

As with *House of the Tiger King*, the only reason not to have reworked the tale into another form would have been laziness. By reshaping the script into a book, I succeeded in creating something I'd feared until then:

A novel in the third person.

By knocking the book out I taught myself a valuable lesson – to counter self-doubt with self-action.

The thought of writing a novel was one which had obsessed me for years. But all the signs were pointing in a different direction – most of them held up by my publishers and agents, who wanted me as Tahir Shah the Travel Writer, rather than Tahir Shah the Novelist.

A couple of months before, I'd written a mammoth-sized proposal for a novel called *The House of Wisdom*. It had tapped into the subject of the science of the Arab world's so-called 'Golden Age'.

Random House rejected the idea point blank.

Fumbling for excuses, they said it was hard to know whether I'd be able to pull it off. I realize now that what they were actually saying was:

'Keep writing *The Caliph's House* again and again, because it's a goose that lays golden eggs.'

Just as the book proposal was rejected, my agent – who'd shaped the project and enthused about it no end – slipped off into temporary retirement, leaving me high and dry.

Depressed beyond belief, I shelved *The House of Wisdom*.

Having finished *Casablanca Blues*, I was an instant novelist.

A novelist who'd made a vow to himself not to allow his work to be hacked around by money-mad publishers ever again.

The only question now was how to release the book. In my enthusiasm to write the novel, I hadn't given any thought at all to how to publish it.

Shuffling through to the kitchen, I asked Rachana what she thought.

'Release it yourself,' she said.

'How would I ever do that?'

'You always say publishers are halfwits, so surely it can't be as hard as you think.'

'But who'll typeset it?'

'I will,' Rachana said.

I got a flash of my father pointing to the newspaper article a few days before he died – the one with a photo of an elaborate machine, and the title: 'The Way of Things to Come'.

There must have been progress on the technology front in the intervening years. Hurrying to the Internet, I googled 'self-publishing', and was greeted with a list of firms offering the service. Most of them supplied Amazon, and the other online stores, direct.

Among the sites Google had trawled up was the 'Espresso Printing Machine'. Rather like an upgraded photocopier, it could print and bind entire books right there and then. I learnt how the machines were being wheeled out in public libraries across the United States.

What was clear was that the technology had moved on in leaps and bounds. The brave new world was hanging over the conventional publishing model like a death cloud – the same one which had so recently decimated the music business.

Under the new model, an author is asked to choose the format, type of binding, and paper, before being given a unit price. You simply upload a typeset file and cover artwork, and then the platform kicks in.

When a copy of the book is ordered – on Amazon or wherever it is – the order gets forwarded straight to the platform.

Within minutes a single copy of the book is printed, bound, packaged up, and mailed out to the customer.

THE REASON TO WRITE

There's no need for printing thousands of copies, or to schlep them to a warehouse – where they depreciate from the moment they arrive.

That's only part of the fabulousness of it all.

In the print-on-demand system you can tweak the layouts whenever you like, and simply upload the revised design files at the drop of a hat. That means any annoying typos can be corrected with ease.

Best of all is the cost – or rather the lack of it.

You get your work out there without having to spend much at all.

At the time I first started investigating print-on-demand, I was still very much in touch with the publishers who handled my work around the world.

Messaging each one, I asked for their thoughts on authors who release books direct to the public.

I expected them to meet my enquiries with good-humoured banter.

What came back amazed me.

Every single publisher and agent responded with the most excoriating attack on 'self-publishing' – something they regarded as tantamount to treason. They spat the term over and over as though it represented the most wretched concept imaginable.

A seasoned editor at one of my publishers wrote:

'Any author sufficiently misguided to go down the path of self-publishing will find himself banished and untouchable. For all intents and purposes he'll be regarded as a leper. The self-published are tainted beyond reproach, and they'll never be permitted back into the realm of respectable authorship.'

So by going it alone I'd be a literary leper?

Wow, I thought, let's bring it on!

While I was a university student living in Kenya, I went on a safari to Maasai Mara – a vast tribal land on the sublime plateau lost on the floor of the Rift Valley.

Late one afternoon we went to a vantage point over a watering hole and waited as the animals came forward to drink.

A family of warthogs scurried forward from the bush, tails upright, thirst very great indeed.

As we watched them drinking, the other creatures around them doing the same, one of the hyenas raised its head subversively from the surface of the water, and froze.

'He's heard something,' Anthony, my guide, whispered.

'Heard what?'

'Wait and see.'

One at a time, the other animals picked up the sense of threat, paused, panicked, and fled.

The only creatures which didn't react were the little family of warthogs.

As they slaked their thirst, no doubt delighting in having the waterhole all to themselves, a lioness charged out of the tinder-dry undergrowth and pounced.

In the ensuing scuffle, a male warthog was slain. Even though he'd been terribly wounded, he flipped over and managed to attack the lioness with his miniature tusks.

That warthog was outgunned a thousand to one.

But still he had a frenzied, frantic go at winning, rather than yielding to the inevitable. After a short tussle, the lioness slunk back into the savannah, dragging the prey as she went.

I commented on the warthog's bravery – how he'd dared to make a stand against such a formidable foe.

'When an animal is faced with death,' Anthony responded, 'he becomes the bravest, meanest son-of-a-bitch you've ever seen. He can't help it. It's instinct.'

The publishers were just like that warthog at Maasai Mara.

With their backs up against the wall, they were preparing themselves to fight for their very survival.

From then on, I threw myself into understanding the ins and outs of the new world order and how it would ultimately be arranged.

If I was going to be the author I longed to be, the one who wrote for himself, I'd have to release my own work directly to my readers.

That was the only way of ensuring total control, and to make certain the volume and range of writing I had in mind would get released as I needed it to be.

Fortunately, I was married to a graphic designer who'd designed some of the most beautiful commercially produced art books around.

Design was one thing, but direct-publishing platforms were another.

Eight years or so ago, when I first dipped my toe in the waters of this enchanted pool, the technology was much more rudimentary than it is now. Every month new formats and bindings came on stream, along with new avenues of distribution.

I like to think that one day someone will pick up this book and gasp at the undeveloped nature of what I'm describing as the potential way of things to come. What's certain is that the emerging model will continue, and will develop month on month, year on year.

There's no reason for it not to.

At the beginning of this story I described how the publishing model we've always known emerged from the street-hawkers touting unbound folios two centuries ago. It was a system that came about as a consequence of necessity – one which worked quite well.

The chief defect is of course that the publishers got their hands on the overwhelming control, and made most of the money, rather than the writers.

You may be scratching your head, wondering aloud if you've heard any of this before.

Yes, you have.

It happened in the music business a few years ago, when companies started streaming songs for next to nothing. There are plenty of parallels between books and music, and plenty of differences, too.

The point which amazes me is that, with their swollen sense of self-worth, publishers didn't realize the climate was changing.

Nor, apparently, did mammoths.

At the core of publishing's existential crisis is a central question:

WHAT DO PUBLISHERS ACTUALLY DO?

Here's an honest, if unwelcome, assessment:
Q. Do publishers pre-select the work?
A. Rarely. Agents do that.

Q. Do publishers edit the manuscript?
A. Rarely. It's outsourced to freelance editors.

Q. Do publishers typeset the manuscript?
A. Rarely. It's outsourced to freelance typesetters.

Q. Do publishers proofread the typeset book?
A. Rarely. It's outsourced to freelance proofreaders.

Q. Do publishers print the book?
A. Never. It's printed by a printer.

Q. Do publishers store the books they've printed?
A. Never. That's done by a warehousing firm.

Q. Do publishers distribute the book to booksellers?
A. Rarely. Distribution companies do that.

So if publishers don't do any of the stuff above, what *do* they do?

Here's the answer to that question:
- Publishers lock authors into brutal contracts.
- Publishers block writers from producing anything except material they think will make the firm a fortune.
- Publishers stifle real creativity and suck up most of the profit when profits are made.
- Publishers seize control and never let go.
- Publishers assert they're needed in a central and irreplaceable way.

It's that last point which both amuses and disturbs me the most.

From time to time I stick my head above the parapet and discuss with publishers what on earth they do. These days the debates are never very affable, especially when I give voice to my point that all I ever see publishers actually doing is trying to impress everyone else with self-importance.

Each time the subject is publicly aired, mainstream publishers seem more ferocious and enraged. All I can think is that, like the poor, brave warthog on the savannah in Maasai Mara, they're fighting for their lives.

I've noticed that politicians who are about to be slaughtered in the polls tend to cling to a single catchphrase or policy. Publishers do the same thing.

Over and over they repeat how they're needed to filter all the rotten writing out there, and select the cream of the crop.

Publishers see themselves as the 'Men from Del Monte'.

Think about it.

They're telling us that we need them to make the choice, because without them we wouldn't have any way of telling what was good and what was bad.

When I bite into a piece of fruit – chosen by the Man from Del Monte or anyone else – I know instinctively if it's good or bad.

And, if I don't know, I work it out through my own sense of judgement.

When I hear a song on the radio, I know whether I love it or hate it. I don't need a producer at a swish record label to tell me whether it's great or not.

The same goes for writing:

When I read a book that has no identifiable publisher's name, I decide for myself – just like I do with the fruit, the music, or with anything else.

In a last desperate fight for their own existence, publishers bang on about how they're providing a quality standard, like a well-loved brand of soup. They claim that by publishing certain authors, they're giving them the stamp of kudos – the 'Man from Del Monte' saying *YES*!

Three questions spring to mind:
- When was the last time anyone chose a book by the publisher rather than by the author?
- Why do we need publishers to filter, when we have Goodreads and other book community sites?
- Why would a writer who believes in their work need a publisher to extend the comforting arm of kudos – the kind which reminds me yet again of the Emperor's New Clothes?

But hold on... I'm getting ahead of myself.

My plan was to release my first novel *Casablanca Blues* through one of the print-on-demand platforms that were springing up all over the place. Just to make sure it wasn't some suicidal route destined for death and destruction, I resolved to start with a trial run.

For someone propelled through life in the slipstream of spontaneous decision, it was distinctly out of character.

But I'm glad it was the route I chose to take.

I'd been beavering away for a few weeks at creating

a book called *Travels With Myself*, from my collected journalism and miscellaneous writings. Having compiled it solely for myself, I'd done so without any hope of commercial success.

Being so low key it was a perfect test of the print-on-demand system.

Rachana typeset the book, which turned out to be a respectable four-hundred-page tome. After quite a bit of tweaking, and wondering whether we were doing anything wrong, I clicked the 'SEND' button.

The book was accepted by the system, and we were green-lit to route it through to Amazon.

As I was in London giving a lecture, I ordered a copy to be sent to where I was staying.

Next day a brown cardboard packet arrived.

I opened it up, amazed that it'd arrived so fast.

A moment later I was holding the one and only copy in existence of *Travels With Myself*.

Burton

As I SAID earlier on, my life has been shaped by mentors – none more important to me than the Victorian polymath and explorer, Sir Richard Francis Burton.

I've drawn inspiration from his view of the world and of the ultra-conventional society in which he lived. A titan from a lost age, Burton has inspired me through his sense of adventure, and by his adamant refusal to go along with accepted logic.

His attitude towards publishing is almost more inspirational than anything else.

Had I not known Burton was born on 19th March, I'd have sworn he was a Scorpio just like me. In my opinion the best biography about his life was written by Mary S. Lovell, and is titled *A Rage to Live*. The book, which describes the lives of Sir Richard and his wife Lady Isabel, captures the sense of the great polymath's all-consuming need to create, and to release his work as he wished.

The frequent tirades against the leading publishers of the day were a thing of legend. Coupled with the outbursts was Burton's enthusiasm for material that shocked the delicate sensibilities of Victorian society. The unfortunate combination led to him seizing the reins of control and publishing his corpus privately.

One of the most important works in my life has been *The Arabian Nights*. I'm fascinated by all kinds of editions of the monumental treasury – from the ancient handwritten Arabic texts to the first European printed volumes, and the later ones too.

Thousands of editions of *The Nights* have been published, but none matches Burton's in terms of scale or scope.

Between 1885 and 1888 Sir Richard released a colossal sixteen-book limited edition, comprising both the main as well as supplementary volumes. His *Book of the Thousand Nights and a Night*, as it was titled, is a challenge to read on account of the florid and decidedly archaic turn of phrase. I know of few other triumphs of industriousness quite so remarkable, or at times quite so obscene. Even though Burton marketed it directly to subscribers through a fictitious private society, there was still danger from the long arm of the law.

In the hope of putting the censorship police off the scent, Burton's printers – a respectable firm located in London's Stoke Newington – talked the hot-tempered author into advertising the address of his imaginary 'Kama Shastra Society' as being in Benares, India.

My own reasons for publishing directly have been rather different from those of Sir Richard. I've never needed to release scandalous material as he did. However, I was stirred by the way he – and other authors of the time – launched limited editions.

On this subject I have strong feelings and am relatively outspoken – believing certain objects, especially books, should at times be made available to a restricted audience. For this reason I published an initial edition of *Casablanca Blues* for certain people, and for them alone. The fact that the wider public were unable to get their hands on my Morocco-based novel delighted me.

For the first time in my literary life, I was wresting back control.

As I have already said, I discovered a book propping up a water pipe in the back stacks of the London Library, and was overcome by its true-life tale of love and survival. The story of an illiterate American sailor, named Robert Adams, infatuated me. I vowed to base a novel on it, even if it was the last thing I ever managed to do.

Until writing *Casablanca Blues* I didn't believe I had it in me to make the switch from the first person of a travel writer to the third person of a novelist. Now the great fear was recounting a story which took place two hundred years before. I knew all about the period from reading accounts of the time but didn't have the guts to take the plunge.

So, even though it was a circuitous route, I did what I'd done before.

I wrote a screenplay first, and used it as my framework.

In the run-up to knocking out the script, I wrote notes... thousands of pages of notes.

Notes on Georgian London, where much of the action takes place.

Notes on the Sahara.
Notes on principal characters, and minor ones too.
Notes on miscellaneous detail.
Notes on the lens of my story and on the themes.
Notes on history, fashions, and on points of etiquette.
Notes on dozens of other things which were of no use in themselves, but which added to the overall taste, like a stock cube crushed into a stew.

I even wrote notes on my notes.

There's no question I overdid the notes, but it doesn't matter – because things happen when they are ready to happen... or, rather, when they are more than ready.

I once read a quote from Doris which helped me to understand how things are. I liked it so much I copied it out and taped it to the mirror in my bathroom so I'd see it first thing in the morning and last thing at night:

'In the writing process, the more the story cooks, the better. The brain works for you even when you are at rest. I find dreams particularly useful... you can only learn to be a better writer by actually writing.'

As a child I was slow to learn riding a bicycle because I feared falling off.

I kept the training wheels on my bike for ages, even though there was no need for them.

I just wanted to be safe.

One morning Greville the storytelling carpenter said he'd take me out. He promised that by the end of the afternoon I'd be riding without any help.

As I gazed on wide-eyed and fearful, he unscrewed the training wheels and ordered me to get on. I did as he said. On flat ground he pushed me while holding the back of my seat, while I pedalled super-fast.

At the far end of the driveway I braked and cried out, 'Thanks for holding on!'

But Greville didn't reply.

Turning around, I saw he was way back in the distance.

I'd cycled fine without him or the training wheels.

My point is that I was ready to cycle by myself, even though I refused to believe it at the time.

Mentors are there to teach through their example, and there to give support by coaxing us on, even if they died centuries before we were born.

Although I'd researched and written *Timbuctoo* the screenplay, I'd got into a big, sick, panicky state.

It was as though scaling the mountain was beyond me.

Rachana had gone to India with the children to stay with her family for a few weeks, leaving me home alone. Moping around Dar Khalifa, I spent the days in my pyjamas, living on breakfast cereal and the thin pickings found at the back of the fridge.

Except for the guardians and the housekeeper, the only people I ever met were the fresh crops of fans. Arriving regular as the tide, they'd all read my books on Morocco, and made a beeline from all corners of the earth.

I was ready for a change of scene.

One night I had an idea.

I'd fly up to London and write *Timbuctoo* on the very same desk at which Burton had supposedly translated his *Arabian Nights*.

The circular desk was located in the library of the Athenaeum Club on London's Pall Mall.

Secret, sublime, and quite unsurpassed in its magnificence, the club was described by an American diplomat friend of mine as being 'right out of *Harry Potter*'. Membership of the Athenaeum was proof in Victorian society of having made it in life. Darwin, Dickens, Trollope, Thackeray, and Burton were all members. The club, which was founded in 1824, has boasted dozens of Nobel Laureates, and all kinds of other luminaries from the sciences and the arts.

For much of his life my father was a member. He liked to work in the library – which is how I first got to hear of the fabled circular desk. When he died I feared there would be no hope of ever reaching that seat of ultimate inspiration. But, fortuitously, and through an unlikely chain of circumstances, I was invited to join twenty years ago. The fact lady members had recently been admitted made it all the more agreeable a place to be.

So it was I found myself sitting where Burton had sat, my gaze roaming the glorious library shelves as his must have done a century and a half before me.

Flying up from Casablanca, I went straight from the airport to the club. Once there, I installed myself in the library and began to write my historical novel, *Timbuctoo*.

For years I kept a note stuck to the wall above my desk. A note to remind me of something very important:

DO WORK YOU ARE IN THE MOOD FOR!

It sounds obvious, but it isn't.

I'd often been coerced to toil away at something I was most definitely *not* in the mood for, a project which someone else wanted me to produce for their benefit, and their benefit alone.

If I've ever been put in the mood for something in the right way, it was sitting at the desk where Burton translated his masterwork.

Without realizing it, I'd been ready to write *Timbuctoo* for months, just as I'd been able to ride the bicycle by myself without knowing.

As a result, the delivery was speedy, like a baby impatient to get out into the world. Having taken a room in the club's attic, I would enter the library by seven each morning, and would write until midnight.

Within three weeks I had the first draft – all thanks to my mentor, Richard Francis Burton.

The editing process took far longer.

My fear was that I'd be crucified by the haughty

literary set if there was a misplaced comma. So I hired six editors. Contradicting one another with their infernal suggestions, most of them meddled rather than edited. I'm used to having my work edited, but the process with *Timbuctoo* was different. For the first time I could decide which edits to use and which to chuck firmly in the bin.

In the end I resorted to using the edits of the main editor, while culling occasional suggestions from the others. As the manuscript was chopped into shape – the shape I wanted – I gave thought to the book's physical look.

Were a publisher to have taken *Timbuctoo* on, they'd have probably released a standard hardback and then a mass-market paperback, and eBook editions a few months later. Relatively few people buy hardbacks these days, but publishers still tend to use the format – for two reasons.

They believe hardbacks offer a certain gravitas, and claim the literary media will only review a book that's appeared in hardback form.

Generally speaking the idea is outdated. It's true that, at one time, stuck-up literary editors at pretentious publications were equally stuck-up and pretentious about anything arriving in soft covers. Likewise, new books had a short window in which they would be featured in the print media.

But, as with everything else, the Internet changed all that.

Having been hidden away for weeks in what is surely the most elegant library in London, I felt justice had to be done.

The Narrative of Robert Adams, the book which had begun my obsession with the quest for Timbuctoo, had been published by my former publisher, John Murray, in 1816.

Bound in a magnificent quarto-size, it was set in a type called Bulmer, and had been printed around the corner from my seat at the round table in the Athenaeum Club. From the moment you open a copy of the *Narrative*, you can't help but be struck by the lavishness, and by an overriding sense that no expense was spared.

Although my decision would have caused consternation to a publisher's number-crunching department, the way forward was obvious to me...

Timbuctoo would have to be released in an edition fitting for the story it told.

To work out how best to envisage the right format, I closed my eyes, clenched both fists tight, and imagined myself as Sir Richard.

Not the two-dimensional man featured on the pages of Wikipedia, or the one described in the scores of biographies. Nor the one you find by reading the books he wrote.

But the Burton you see only by studying the grouting between the tiles. Seemingly insignificant fragments that meant almost nothing alone. Yet, when collected altogether, they provided a dossier of overlooked information – the kind I'd need if *Timbuctoo* were to be the book worthy of the suffering of Robert Adams.

Slipping into Burton's body, exchanging my mind for his, I sensed the world open up in the most unpredictable and astonishing way. To think like the great Victorian polymath was to be freed from convention, and restriction – and was to live every moment as though it were the last hoorah.

Becoming Sir Richard – albeit in the limits of my imagination – the first thing to occur was that my jaw seized up. My teeth ground together, and I felt my features contort into a snarl. Not a snarl of anger, but of profound no-nonseneness.

Fists clenching all the more tightly, I saw the world – *my* world – through Burton's eyes, and I felt it in his bones.

Before I knew it, my focus had moved onto my novel *Timbuctoo*, and how best to release it. Until that moment I'd been fretting and flustering, anxious about overdoing it, or spending too much.

But all in an instant, the path forward became crystal clear.

I would do what Sir Richard would have done.

That meant finding the best printer available, and sparing no expense.

Above all, though, it meant releasing the novel myself.

In a recent book called *Travels With Nasrudin*, I wrote about the prep school I was sent to as a child, and where I was torn to shreds every day for six years.

Rather than recounting the time with animosity, I described my gratitude – for the school's abhorrent regime enabled me to lose myself in imagination. I mention it here because of a comment in one of my form master's reports. He wrote: 'Tahir Shah would be a far better student if he were far less enthusiastic!'

I've often turned that line around in my head, doing my best to see how enthusiasm could be the curse that brutal wretch of a man considered me to be afflicted by.

Enthusiasm has a lifeblood all of its own.

It is the reason Olympic athletes get up before dawn each morning and push themselves to the limits. It's why explorers have endured the unendurable, and is the magic dust enabling creative people to keep going at all costs.

As I sat there in Sir Richard Burton's body and bones, my jaw clenched tight and my eyes narrowed with cold, slow disapproval – I was overcome with a sense of the great man's enthusiasm.

An unbridled zest for a project was what launched him and kept him on trajectory.

In any work I have ever done, I've harnessed the power of enthusiasm. Not in a wishy-washy way – but as though my life depended upon it.

Never have I raged with raw enthusiasm more than

when I published *Timbuctoo*.

The first thing to do was to search for a printer to produce the finest edition of my novel imaginable, one worthy of Robert Adams and his tale.

What I had in mind was the kind of edition no commercial publisher would have allowed out of principle or because of expense. A thing of rare and unequalled wonder, it would be a book with embossed gold on the covers, marbled endpapers, a back pocket with curious inserts, the finest acid-free paper, bookmarks...

...and maps...

Numerous sheets of the most sublime and enormous maps.

Over weeks I corresponded with printers across Europe, United States, and India. Hundreds of examples arrived by courier. While most fell far below Burton's exacting standards, one or two were fabulous.

But none were quite so tantalizing as the samples which reached me from a printer in Hong Kong. So impressed was I that, the day after his samples arrived, I boarded a flight to meet him.

When I set about restoring Dar Khalifa, our beloved home in the middle of a Casablanca shantytown, I learnt that the best craftsmen said very little at all.

Rather than deluge you with a torrent of self-praise, they would sit there, sipping a glass of piping-hot sweet mint tea, lips tightly sealed. Whereas smug blustering types would rant on about their skill, a real *moualem*, a master, would allow his work to speak on his behalf.

The same was apparently true when it came to printers.

As subdued as he was precise, Maurice Kwan invited me into his office and listened rather than spoke. The owner of the impressively large Regal Printing Company, he might easily have palmed me off on one of his many staff.

But he didn't.

Once I had outlined exactly what I wanted, Mr Kwan scratched a thumbnail down his nose, blinking long and hard.

'We can do it,' he said.

'Yes, but don't you want to go over the details?'

Kwan blinked a second time – in the way that a tabby cat might do. A blink of understated self-assuredness.

'We can do it,' he said a second time.

And he did.

Although, as I've said, no publisher in existence would have agreed to print my elaborate 'Burtonian' edition of *Timbuctoo*. But even if they had, as the author I wouldn't have been allowed anywhere near the production zone.

Working with Mr Kwan and his team as I did, I felt like Alice slipping down the rabbit hole into a realm in which every detail was up for grabs. For the first time in my professional life, I was invited to select the paper from swatches, the thickness of the boards, the ribbon for the bookmark, the structure of the pocket at the end, and dozens of other details.

Timbuctoo segues back and forth from Regency London to the parched wilds of the Sahara, in which the illiterate American sailor, Robert Adams, was enslaved for many years. As a lover of all things cartographic, I wanted to use maps contemporary to the era to give a sense of life in Georgian London.

By chance I happened upon what is certainly one of the greatest works of cartography of the age – Richard Horwood's Plan of the English capital. Printed in thirty-two sheets, between 1792 and 1799, the map features almost every building in existence at the time. Despite his expertise as a leading cartographer, the work was not a financial success – Horwood died in poverty.

Selecting six maps over which many of my novel's scenes were set, I sent them to Maurice Kwan and asked for them to be reproduced full size. I had expected him to protest at there being too many maps. But he didn't. Instead, he devised a system by which the maps would be folded intricately by hand and then tipped into the book itself.

Inspired by Richard Burton and his 'Kama Shastra Society', I chose Secretum Mundi as the name of my publishing firm. Meaning 'the Secret of the World', it was linked to the chain of transmission which had released Burton's own self-published *opus magnum*. More importantly, it was the foundation stone in a wall I hoped would help in redefining publishing.

When the first copy of *Timbuctoo* arrived by courier, I was staying in a small family-owned hotel on Mount Olympus. A thing of wonder, it was wrapped in sheets of ivory tissue paper, having travelled straight from Hong Kong. Weighing in at almost two kilos, it was monumental and was absolutely perfect – all thanks to the soft-spoken Maurice Kwan.

The night the first copy reached me, I put it under my pillow and said a prayer to Zeus, King of the Gods... I was on Mount Olympus after all. I prayed circumstances would conspire to afford Robert Adams and his tale the publicity they deserved.

As so often happens in my life, my prayers were answered, but not for the reasons I may have wanted.

As the printed copies made their way westwards through Suez, I planned the media campaign. I hired a social media guru to get attention, had an elaborate website built, and wrote a slew of articles based on the story. And, inspired by the 1970s sensation by Kit Williams, *Masquerade*, I hid a gilded bronze head from the fabled city of gold in Timbuctoo, California. Yes, amazingly, there's another Timbuctoo. In fact, there are lots, with three of them at least in the United States.

But, alas, the treasure was never found.

Floods of messages came in from people who

thought they'd cracked the clues running through the book. The one adventurer who worked out the location put it all together from a thirty-second video I'd posted online. He'd managed to triangulate a range of details seen in the background. Triumphantly, he travelled to Timbuctoo with a shovel and GPS, only to find the designated spot had been dug up to build a new bridge. I often find myself wondering whether the contractors got their hands on the buried treasure, and what they made of it if they did.

Meanwhile, the printed copies of *Timbuctoo* finally arrived after their long voyage, and went on sale either side of the Atlantic. The hype had secured good publicity. But then, the day before the official launch, my prayers offered to Zeus on Mount Olympus were answered.

Under the flag of the so-called 'Islamic State', a Tuareg militia named Ansar Dine stormed into Timbuktu (to use the current German spelling) and began a reign of terror the likes of which the Dark Continent had not seen in centuries.

Schools and public buildings were torched, as were the ancient libraries of manuscripts from the Golden Age of Islam. Music, photography, and films were banned, women were ordered to be veiled top to toe in burqas, and anyone with a connection to the Occident was beheaded.

The morning of my launch, I woke to find the fabled

city of gold, to which Robert Adams had been taken as a white slave two centuries before, on the front of every newspaper in the Western world.

I cursed myself for having prayed for publicity at any cost.

Horrified at what was happening at the hands of fanatical Islamists, I used the launch to draw attention to what was going on. In media terms, the publicity surpassed the wildest dreams of any publisher. I was featured on the leading BBC TV and radio shows, published a lengthy article in *Newsweek*, and was the talk of the town.

Despite all the attention, my thoughts weren't on the book.

They'd moved on, and were searching for new material on which to feed.

Perfection

TIMBUCTOO WAS A magic spell freeing me once and for all from the inferior model that's locked mainstream publishing down for a century and more.

Exquisite beyond compare, the edition was proof that the path I had begun was better than any other. In the wake of what had become a sensation of its own, I vowed never to return to the old ways. Freedom was too sweet, and the aura of the horizon too dazzling to ever go back.

From that moment, I planned to write the books I wanted to write, and never again to be held to ransom by agents, editors, and lamebrain marketing men.

The vow had only just left my lips when I opened a newspaper, brought to Casablanca for me by a visiting guest. I had written somewhere of my fondness for the smell of the English newspapers. Having touched it to my nose, and been transported back to my father's study in Langton House, I opened the newspaper out.

Staring out from the third page was one of the most atrocious and yet enticing images I have ever seen.

A box of prosthetic glass eyes.

Orderly and neat, the eyes were arranged in rows – ten across and five high. Each one was a slightly different size and hue – ranging from chocolate brown to an almost emerald green.

I can only assume most people who picked up their

copy of the newspaper would have grimaced, winced, and turned the page.

But I couldn't.

I was transfixed.

Rachana found me in the sitting room at Dar Khalifa, the newspaper laid across my lap, my face pressed down close to the image of the glass eyes.

'Eek!' she squealed.

'I love them,' I whispered. 'And I loathe them, too.'

'They're revolting,' Rachana said sternly.

'I know they are, but I'm drawn to them like nothing I can remember ever being drawn to before.'

'Sounds as though you've just found the subject for your new novel.'

Frowning, I peered up at her, and then down at the eyeballs again.

She was right.

The glass eyes were the perfect first step on a treasure trail.

As we sat there, the picture spread out on the coffee table, Timur and Ariane blustered home from school. Dropping their satchels on the floor, they took in the picture, pointing and giggling.

Ariane asked a hundred questions in five seconds flat.

'Baba's going to write a book about the eyeballs,' Rachana responded firmly.

'Is he?' I said.

'Yes, he is!'

'What will you call it, Baba?' Ariane asked.
Timur held up a hand as though he were in class.
'*Eye Spy*,' he said.

As any creative person will tell you, the essence of creation is a love affair of being bewitched from the inside out.

It's not about the fame and the glory, or about the money you'll make, or won't make. Nor is it about a hundred other things which non-creatives assume to be true. In the way J. D. Salinger had to write because if he did not 'he would turn to stone', creating and creation are a self-therapy, a healing mechanism.

The way I see it, the process of writing is alchemy as much as it is anything else. You take the seed of an idea – in this case a box of glass eyes – and you shape it through your imagination, honing it this way and that. Then, after blending in assorted thoughts, characters, twists and turns, you spew it all out with paper and ink.

Eye Spy was a novel written out of a love-hate affair with a photograph... a photograph of prosthetic eyes. It would have been easier to have not written it at all. And were I to have been an author enslaved to a publisher, it would never have been written.

But the fact I was free, and writing for myself, meant it was not only written, but that it was written how I wanted to write it... and it was done without delay.

A month after first spotting the photograph in the

newspaper, I'd thrashed out the story, completed the first draft, and had it edited, too.

As my family and friends will attest, I am drawn to oddity.

I can't help myself. Few things delight me more than weaving a tapestry from layers of strangeness. And that was exactly what the story I came up with was devised to do.

The greatest eye surgeon of his age, Amadeus Kaine was fêted by celebrities, world leaders, and by despots as well. While treating a particularly odious Central Asian dictator in the presidential palace, he was served a little pie. Curious at its texture and taste, Kaine came to understand it was prepared from eyes gouged from the faces of prisoners in the dictator's opal mines.

Allowing my imagination to zigzag, I spun a tale taking in topics and places I have known. But, most of all, it allowed me to plant a seed and to nurture it.

First, into a seedling.

Then into a sapling.

After that, into a tree with leaves, twigs, branches, and a trunk.

Eye Spy was written for me, and me alone. It wasn't geared to getting attention, precious likes on social media, or fan mail. Rather, it was about satisfying a deep desire for creation. When ready, it was released with no fanfare at all. Rachana, the kids, and a handful of others knew about it, but no one else.

Birthing it into existence as it was, in a completely low-key way, allowed me to concentrate on what was important – the intense relationship between the author and his work.

In the decades Salinger visited us at Langton House and corresponded with my father, he was writing off and on.

But he wasn't publishing.

Having become resigned to write for himself, I can only imagine he reached the hallowed ground to which every real author aspires...

Perfection.

My belief is that to be truly perfect, a book must be the work of a single person, rather than a group effort that's been hacked around. You see, my own Salinger-esque viewpoint suggests a genuine masterpiece of perfection can only be so if it's been experienced solely by the mind which created it.

Far from claiming to be a master worthy of having created a masterpiece, I didn't lock *Eye Spy* away in a safe, but published it through Secretum Mundi, the Secret of the World.

Following close on its heels, I wrote another novel which bridged my love for France and for Japan. I happened to see a news report on the BBC website about so-called 'Paris Syndrome'. A real-life condition, the syndrome is an adverse reaction afflicting dozens of Japanese tourists flocking to the French capital each year.

Paris Syndrome is a state of mania visited upon numerous unfortunate tourists annually. They succumb to it after a long journey, too much rich food and wine, and having been ratcheted up to breaking point, in their bid to see and experience absolutely everything the French capital has to offer. The bizarre syndrome is regarded as untreatable. As the piece on the BBC website explained, 'The only known cure for Paris Syndrome is to leave the French capital, and never to return.'

Once again, I drew on people and places I have known, conjuring a tale which pleased me and allowed me to experiment.

When *Paris Syndrome* was published, I felt sorrow rather than joy. It was as though, by releasing the story into the wild, my one-on-oneness with it had come to an end.

Miracles

To ANYONE WHO'S known the ins and outs of conventional publishing, the new technology is little short of miraculous.

When ordered, a book is printed, put into an envelope, and mailed directly to the buyer. There's no longer the need to print a zillion copies, store them in warehouses, or to shunt them around. Best of all, the content can be updated in the blink of an eye any time you like.

But, however fantastic it is, print-on-demand doesn't satiate the cravings of a bibliophile like me. While thrilled to bits at having my new novels out there, I yearned for the titillation of electricity surging up and down my spine – the likes of which I'd felt with *Timbuctoo*.

So, without giving it much thought at all, I wrote a story.

Rather, a story in a story...

...in a story...

...in a story.

Inspired by the *Arabian Nights*, in which tales in tales are commonplace, and by my grandfather's book *The Golden Pilgrimage*, my story dug down deeper until it reached the point at which it had begun.

The book, entitled *Scorpion Soup*, was written as a daydream, or in the same way an artist doodles, hardly thinking at all. Throughout the writing process, I'd been preoccupied by a series of maps by the legendary eighteenth-century Dutch cartographer Joan Blaeu. The stories I had shaped had been born by allowing my imagination to be sucked down into the maps – themselves a hybrid of fact and fantasy.

For about ten seconds I thought of producing the book through print-on-demand. Shaking my head side to side, I sent a message to the one person who was tried and tested.

Maurice Kwan.

Through experience I have learned that, if something works, do it – or a variation on it – again.

Timbuctoo had worked.

Hell, it had done far more than work – it'd been a sensation.

So, *Scorpion Soup* was designed as another limited edition, once again packed with maps – the maps of Joan Blaeu. Unwilling to reduce the number of them, each one intricately folded, I coaxed Kwan to reproduce them all. The effect is that, like an old-fashioned Filofax brimming with inserts and pages, *Scorpion Soup* hardly closes at all.

Although some copies have found their way online, I have reserved most of the stock for myself. They tend to be presented randomly to people who have helped me. On occasion I have mailed copies anonymously to those in the news or in the public eye – people whom I believe could do with reading a story in a story.

My most private book, *Scorpion Soup* is about the essence of me as a writer, so much so that in a strange way I would prefer for it never to be sold. Unfortunately, in the online world everything lands up on eBay sooner or later.

A few weeks ago I got chatting to an author friend who's carved out a side business for himself in what many would regard as a shady practice. Although successful and relatively well known for his detective novels, the writer in question is always flat broke. Taking advantage of the fact that (a) he has a room full of first editions of his books, and (b) his fan-base are eager for editions with provenance, he produces collectable copies all the time – putting them for sale online.

His usual method is to keep an eye on the newspaper obituaries. Whenever he spots a high-profile candidate, he takes a first edition from his pile, inscribes it to the newly deceased, dates it with the year of original release, and gets a pal to advertise it on eBay.

Dealers, and the author's fans, assume the family of the newly departed A-lister must have disposed of their first edition. What interests me is not so much the ploy, but how the buyers of such editions are so ingenuous as to believe a book supposedly owned by a movie star, a Nobel Laureate, or a member of royalty, is especially valuable because it's inscribed with their name.

Last week I happened to bump into my writer friend

with the side business at a meeting of The Eccentric Club, of which we're both members. Although I come from a long line of eccentrics, I myself am more accurately a 'wannabe' eccentric, rather than the genuine article. In an effort to join the club (which was founded in 1781), candidates must list all their major eccentricities.

When called up against the panel, I claimed to dress only in yellow on Thursdays, and to hop everywhere every second Tuesday of the month.

Sipping our cocktails as we were at the Eccentric Club event – me head to toe in canary yellow, and my friend in a mohair suit embroidered with tarantulas – I asked him how the inscription scam was going.

'Never been better, old boy,' he said, his eyes glazing over with delight. 'Just sold an entire set of my backlist one by one, every book inscribed to a virtual god.'

'Care to say who it is?'

The friend's face erupted in a mile-wide grin.

'Nelson Mandela,' he said.

Hannibal Fogg

WORKING WITH MAURICE Kwan and his team in Hong Kong had proved to me that, however much I enjoyed the convenience of print-on-demand, nothing stirs my creative juices more than limited editions.

When ideas seed themselves in my life, they take shape best when a variety of factors are present. Unfortunately for my family and friends, I never stop. From the moment I wake up in the morning until the moment I lay my head on the pillow at night, I'm a taut clock-spring of thoughts, movement, and mania.

Those who have been driven crazy by 'me being me' make their judgement on my waking hours, and them alone. They have no idea that for me it's a whole lot worse – for I have to put up with my non-stop-ness in my dreams as well as my waking hours.

Twenty years ago I was lucky enough to have a windfall of cold hard cash. At the very same moment I'd seen a manuscript for sale at Maggs, the rare-book dealer, based at the time in London's Berkeley Square. Although remarkably short – no longer than about nine pages – the document had been handwritten by Sir Richard Burton. On his death, the grieving Lady Burton burned the bulk of her husband's papers in a monumental bonfire. By chance a steamer trunk of material in Sir Richard's hand was apparently discovered many years later, having avoided the inferno of literary destruction.

I assume the document put up for sale at Maggs came from that trunk. Commissioned by the Foreign Office, it was a handwritten draft of a secret report on the wealth of the Sultan of Zanzibar.

Blowing the windfall on the manuscript allowed me to be inspired by physical contact with an object that Burton had himself created. For years, I kept it on my desk, picking it up from time to time, pressing it to my nostrils, and being transported to another time and place.

As one of the great Victorian explorers who searched for the sources of the Nile, Burton sits in the panoply of luminaries at whose altar I worship. My fascination for their ideals and their eccentricities, too, ensnares my attention like almost nothing else. I have collected printed copies of every journal of exploration I can find – their pages spattered with blood and sweat, the covers worn smooth through trial and tribulation.

But the secret manuscript in Sir Richard's spidery hand was different. It was real.

Fondling it in my study one morning, I found myself wondering what it would be like to discover a steamer trunk packed with papers from a lost age. Papers and ephemera documenting the travails and the travels of a resounding polymath – a magnificent role model of a man, like Richard Francis Burton.

Closing my eyes, I allowed my imagination to wander. Almost at once I saw it laid out in my mind.

A magnificent camphor-wood chest with brass fittings and luggage labels from all corners of the known world – Siam, Rangoon, Buenos Aires, Cape Town, Cairo, Marseilles.

My nostrils flinched at the scent of dust and of adventure as I opened it up. Packed tight were a hundred bundles – each one sewn up in cloth, sealed with a monogram...

HF

As I sat there, my eyes twitching beneath their lids, I heard the name spoken by a voice... a voice in my head. Not the voice of my mind's eye, but rather that of the greatest explorer who ever lived.

Hannibal Fogg.

The Shelf of Wretched Reads

CHARGED WITH RAW enthusiasm, I cleared my desk and prepared myself for a treasure trail of wonder – the likes of which I had never before known.

As all authors know, developing a character can be an arduous task at times. It involves taking a seed and building the character layer upon layer – back story and emotions, secrets, superstitions, passions, and the rest.

Right from the start, Hannibal Fogg was different.

The moment I allowed my mind to conjure him, he swept in and *he* did all the work. When I was a teenager I saw a late night documentary on 'automatic writing'. Looking back, it was almost certainly nonsense from beginning to end. But it stuck in my head, along with all kinds of other detritus. For days and nights after imagining Fogg for the first time, I found myself scribbling notes in a frenzy, like the psychic I'd seen in the film.

Until that point, the protagonists from my novels were just characters... people whose stories amused me as they developed through my literary and imaginative incubation:

Robert Adams – enslaved Christian who reached Timbuctoo.

Amadeus Kaine – eye surgeon turned serial killer.

Miki Suzuki – sales girl who succumbed to Paris Syndrome.

Blaine Williams — romantic idealist obsessed with *Casablanca*.

Hannibal Fogg was different in every conceivable way. An amalgam of the titans of exploration I'd worshipped for decades, and of the destinations they — and I — had discovered. He was hard as nails but sophisticated, arrogant but kindly, a swordsman and adventurer, a scientist and inventor... and without doubt the most accomplished polymath ever to have lived.

Fogg was Sir Richard Burton, Percy Fawcett, Samuel White Baker, Charles Babbage, and Sir Joseph Banks — all rolled into one. Born into extraordinary wealth, he was a renegade and an outcast. Women swooned at the mere thought of him, and men longed to be like him.

Identical-twin writer friends in Hollywood happened to ask what I was working on a short time after first hearing the name whispered in my head. In a jumbled mishmash of description, I told them about Hannibal Fogg and his lost journals.

'Sounds like a project for Dick,' they both said at once.

'Who's Dick?'

'A media mogul with very deep pockets. He's looking for something big to turn into a movie and media franchise.'

The next thing I knew, Dick phoned. He was one of those sorts you meet from time to time who are so self-confident you wonder whether they're breathing different air to you. His conversation was peppered with garbled anecdotes of time spent with world leaders and A-listers. And, when I'd been deluged with stories and wooed until weak at the knees, Dick said he'd heard from the twins that I had 'something bigger than big'.

Right on cue I hit him with Hannibal Fogg.

'I like it,' Dick said.

'Thank you.'

'I see it as movies and video games, as mangas and merchandising.'

'Wow,' I said.

Dick grunted.

'We're gonna have to plan it from the ground up.'

'Great.'

'Own all the rights, do you?'

'Yes.'

Again, Dick grunted, deeper and harder than before.

'The lost journals are good, but they're not where we start,' he said. 'What we need is to go out with a novel which tells the audience who Fogg is and what he's about.'

'A novel – great!'

Dick grunted again.

'If I give you a massive advance can you write it fast?'

It was the moment starving authors living in ramshackle mansions with shantytowns all around dream of their entire lives.

A Promised Land.

'Faster than fast,' I replied.

Over the following month, Dick drew up NDAs and contracts, and got me to sign them. Again and again he asked for my bank details, so the big fat advance could be wired into my account. Every time we spoke, which seemed like every two minutes, Dick dropped names... names of people so famous they'd transcended the limits of mortal humanity.

Tapping into the essence of Richard Francis Burton, I scoped out the storyline for a novel, the first in a series – *Hannibal Fogg and the Supreme Secret of Man*. Drawing on my fascination for the so-called 'Antikythera Mechanism', the plot was completely original – a canvas over which I could display my many preoccupations one by one.

Dick promised to get the advance to me before I started writing.

But he didn't.

Rachana quipped that I'd be a fool to write a word before I received payment. My family and friends echoed the same thing.

But, charged with a frantic mania for the project, I signed an addendum to our agreement, by which Dick was permitted to pay whenever he liked. My signing it, he insisted, would enable him to pay me the next week.

Having packed Rachana and the kids off to India for a month, I locked myself away at Dar Khalifa. I filled the freezer with food, asked the guardians not to bother me unless the house was on fire...

Then, and only then, I began to write.

Dick said he needed a clean manuscript in six weeks. That meant if I wrote 3,750 words a day for thirty-two days, it would leave a full ten days for editing.

With a detailed plan of the story positioned beside my left hand, I slipped into the world of Hannibal Fogg. Day after day I travelled a little further along a pair of timelines. With each sentence I wrote, I imagined the fun I'd have spending all the cash. From time to time I deleted a paragraph and chided myself for having flushed money down the drain.

With Dick's promised funding, I was spinning gold.

Within a week I had reached a zombie pattern of life, the kind familiar to most authors who crank out serious wordage. I would get up early, knock back three espressos fast, read through and correct the pages from the previous day, and get down to the coal-face.

My writing system has always been the same.

I map out what needs to be written on a given day, then grind away at it until I'm done. If friends invite me out to lunch, I don't go. If visitors arrive for an impromptu tour of the house, I hide. If I run out of food, I make do with whatever can be found at the back of the fridge. And, until I've done my daily wordage, I never allow myself anywhere near the ultimate danger zone...

The Internet.

By the end of the first week of writing *Hannibal Fogg*,

THE REASON TO WRITE

I had devoured almost everything in the fridge. Cursing the cruelty of fate, I'd resigned myself to go out into the big wide world to buy provisions when I discovered a sack of rice at the back of the storeroom. For the next two weeks, it's all I ate, mushed up in a kind of porridge – the kind I happen to know is provided in Pakistani torture jails.

In the second week I decided that writing in my library interfered with the creative process. Too many books gnawing away at me, begging me to pull them out and procrastinate. So I moved into the dining room – with its serene view all the way through the house and the gardens, past the pool, to the spotless white tent at the end of Dar Khalifa.

Each day I'd do my wordage, and think how I'd spend all the cash Dick was going to pay. I imagined myself in a hand-made suit, at the wheel of a vintage Aston Martin.

And, each night, I would complete the rituals which have kept me on track since the first line of my first book:
- Print out the day's pages and square them with all the others on my desk.
- Write the daily and the total wordage on a list.
- Get the notes ready for the next day.
- Plump up the cushion on my chair, and square my office slippers against the wall.

As I've already said, a key thing with writing books is to get into the Magic Zone. A delightful and ethereal place, it's a realm where everything flows with ease.

Whatever anyone else will tell you, there's no aggro or angst, because the Magic Zone is a land of ultimate harmony.

I often think back to a super-swot at my prep school. He strained to push the boundaries of thought so hard that the veins on his forehead bulged and went purple. Everyone used to crowd around and applaud him – everyone except for me. Even then I saw what no one else did – that the school swot was guilty of the greatest crime known to the inventive mind:

Overthinking.

Fall prey to it, and you pull the shutters down on creativity. Overthinking encompasses all sorts of territory – including making a plot so convoluted you tie yourself in knots, and what's possibly the worst crime of all... questioning your ability.

So fearful am I of tumbling down the overthinking hole, I avoid venturing anywhere near it. In the way that, if there's a spider in the corner of my bedroom, I'll screw my eyes shut as I slink past, pretending it's not there, I refuse to allow the spectre of self-doubt into my world when I write.

On the rare occasions I've doubted my ability, I resort to a remedy which works every time...

At the side of my desk is a clutch of books, each one a bestseller regarded by society as a modern classic – The Shelf of Wretched Reads.

Whenever I question my skill as a writer, I'll pick one

THE REASON TO WRITE

of the books from the shelf, open it, and read a random paragraph. There's no question about the quality of the storytelling in any of these works – I must make that clear. But the standard of the writing is nothing short of toe-curling. In each case the author has achieved the glare of limelight long before they have had a chance to hone their craft.

In my opinion, acute trajectories prevent an author from developing in a well-rounded and methodical way.

By the third week of *Hannibal Fogg*, my back was in such a bad state I found it near impossible to get up from the chair. The only way to do so was to rock from side to side so that I tumbled onto the floor. Then, slip-sliding to the doorway like a war-wounded veteran, I'd pull myself up, cursing and grunting in pain.

So as to save time I'd stripped my life right down.

Anything that wasn't absolutely necessary was expunged – including changing out of pyjamas, shaving, or washing. The only thing which mattered to me was cranking out the wordage – so Dick would reward me with bundles of cash.

One afternoon, while I was doing my best to get vertical after a long day at the keyboard, Dar Khalifa's doorbell sounded long and hard.

Through years of living at the house, a system had been honed by which the guardians would always answer the door. I'd briefed them continually never to let anyone in, no matter who they were, when I was dug down writing.

That evening the guardians were skulking down in the stables, no doubt passed out on the virulent strain of hashish brought by their dealer from the Rif. So, once upright, I staggered to the entrance, the bell echoing through the gardens and the house.

Pulling the front door open, I found a thickset man plugging its frame...

A thickset man who was unmistakably American or, rather, Texan.

Unmistakable, because the Stars and Stripes were embroidered prominently on the front of his shirt, along with a name – *Chip*. The weather-worn face was dominated by a pair of watery blue eyes and a walrus moustache tinged yellow from a life-long love affair with Marlboros.

'Chip Watkins,' he announced.

'Huh?'

'Come for a tour of the Caliph's House.'

I frowned.

'I'm writing,' I answered firmly.

'Well of course you are!' Chip countered, pushing past me into the house. 'That's what writers do, isn't it?'

'What I mean to say is I need privacy. I'm working day and night.'

The words were lost on any ears but my own. Chip was long gone, vanished into the shadows beyond the sitting room. Scurrying after him in my bedroom slippers, I begged him to give me a break.

By the time I caught up with him, he was in my dressing room, taking pictures of my shirts.

'You're smaller than I expected,' he said. 'Smaller and paler.'

'I'm pale because I haven't been out in weeks.'

Turning his back on the wardrobe, Chip frowned.

'You've gotta get out once in a while,' he said, 'or else you'll go crazy. You'll start talking to yourself.'

'I passed that point weeks ago. At least when you only have conversations with yourself, you're sure to win the arguments,' I said.

Chip didn't flinch. He just frowned. The furrows of his brow deepening, he whipped out an iPhone and took my picture.

'Maddie asked for that,' he explained.

'Who's Maddie?'

'My little lady.'

'Oh.'

A moment passed in which Chip took a burst of pictures close up.

'She's your biggest fan,' he explained. 'She read *The Caliph's House* not once but twice!'

'Pleased to hear it,' I replied brightly.

Chip frowned again.

'I was raised to speak the truth.'

'Really? So what's the truth?'

'That it was horseshit from beginning to end.'

'Ouch,' I said, bristling.

Chip's gaze was cold and disapproving, the frown deeper than before. He closed the wardrobe door, flinching as he did so, his line of sight ranging down over my grubby pyjamas.

'If I were you, I'd get help,' he said.

You could chalk it down to extreme Scorpio tendencies, but the way I see it there's almost nothing quite so powerful to harness than anger.

I'm sure non-creatives reading this are rolling their eyes yet again. Possibly quite right in doing so. There can be no doubt wrath was conjured by the universe first and foremost as a survival mechanism. Rather like nuclear fission, you hardly need any raw anger at all for the most spectacular results.

The day Chip arrived uninvited at Dar Khalifa I'd hit a wall in both storytelling and belief in myself. The well-trodden path of reading wretched classics wasn't working as it had done before. I needed a new fuel cell.

Anger... anger at Chip... provided it.

All I had to do was to close my eyes for the briefest moment, imagine I were standing in my dressing room with him towering over me, and my bloodstream was fortified with adrenalin.

Fight or flight.

Or, rather... write, write, write.

For a last frenzied stretch of days I churned out hundreds of pages of the bizarre tale of the inimitable adventurer, Hannibal Fogg. Every inch of the way, Chip was with me. At least his hatred of my work, and my hatred of him, was there.

A long while later I got talking to a psychologist on a train heading due south from Alice Springs. It was one of those rambling dining-car conversations evolving from a volley of probing questions between a pair of jaded travellers. The psychologist asked me what helped me write. Given he was a professional, I told him the truth:

'Rage,' I said. 'Fires me up like nothing else.'

My fellow traveller allowed his gaze to slip from my face, down over the beige armchair on which I was seated, and through the window to the baked red sandscape outside.

'Most people I meet achieve very little in their lives,' he said. 'And there's nothing wrong with that. But the ones who do have gotta have a reason.'

'A reason for their ambition?'

'Yup.'

'And what is it... the commonest reason to reach higher than high?'

'A desperate need to prove everyone else wrong,' the psychologist answered.

Later that afternoon I lay on my bed, the carriage grinding a path southwards, my mind on the traveller's words. He was right. As I've already said, no one ever expected a dyslexic kid living in the shadows of others to amount to anything at all. There were no expectations – the kind which ultimately suffocated those around me.

Whereas I was free from pressure, others were not. They were expected to achieve for the sake of achieving – or at least because they feared letting down the person who held them in awe. As far as anyone was concerned my name, written lightly in pencil on the family tree, would ultimately be erased.

And so, with these conditions, I forged my path through the ego-inflated world of editors, agents, and book launches. I wrote because I yearned to write... because if I didn't write I'd turn to stone. But more often than not the fuel cell that powered me was driven by people like Chip.

Or, rather, it was driven by my dislike of them.

Gone Insane

THE FIRST NOVEL in the series – *Hannibal Fogg and the Supreme Secret of Man* – was delivered to Dick three days before it was due.

I could hardly stand, or see, and my fingertips were raw from typing. On the last day of work, I overheard Zohra, the housekeeper, tell one of the guardians I'd gone '*majnun*' – insane. In an all-knowing manner she'd perfected through a lifetime of telling others what she thought, she explained that I was possessed. In other circumstances I might have protested. But for the first time she was right. I *was* possessed. Possessed like any writer, painter, or musician in human history who'd broken through the pain barrier.

Sometimes on sending a manuscript to an editor I've done it with a sense of trepidation. But when I emailed *Hannibal Fogg* to Dick I was serenely calm. I had no doubt in my work. It was an extraordinary feat of craftsmanship and originality – well worth the massive pay cheque I'd been promised from the start.

The only thing was that Dick didn't pay.

At first I sent polite little reminders, framed in jokey banter. Time and again Dick waxed lyrical about the deal of a century we were about to make with Hollywood.

Months turned into years, and still Dick didn't pay up. My emails and phone calls were met with silence.

I would have simply touted the manuscript around myself, but the addendum I'd signed promised to rain down hellfire and damnation if I were ever to step out of line.

In the end, I was left with no choice but to hire a media lawyer in LA and reclaim the rights in court. Few experiences in my life have been so stressful, unpleasant, or costly. At the end of it, I was the legal owner of my work again.

And I was wiser than before.

Never again would I be sucked in by tall promises, and would instead always keep total control of my own work.

Timbuctoo had taught me the joy of publishing books in a form which was a hundred per cent right. To those who haven't written books it must seem like a weird thing to describe. But to those reading this who have written work which has been dismembered by third-rate editors, you know I mean it, and will sense I'm speaking from the heart.

All I care about is that my books are published as I envisaged them. It's because – after thirty years of writing – I know what I'm doing. But, more importantly, it's because I have a sense of my voice. Again, this is something only real writers can hope to understand. I doubt any agent or editor would ever read this book, although I'm sure that with time they'll rail against it all the same. In any case, nothing worries me so little as offending them, because none of them understand the central pillar of writing:

Voice.

Take your first faltering steps as an author, and the voice is nothing more than a whisper lost on the wind. Hell, it may not even be that. But it'll be there, like the faintest trace of light preceding the dawn.

Believe in it, and in yourself, and keep writing, and the whisper grows in strength. It may take years, or even longer, but with every word laid down, the voice will grow. One day you wake up and the timid little voice is loud and booming, and it's sick of being told what to do and how to do it. At that moment you grasp you're no longer going to be ordered around, but rather you are going to be giving the orders from now on.

What amazes me though is how so many writers, having reached this profound point, continue as before. They're like circus lions who haven't grasped they could tear off the ringmaster's head and swallow it whole. They could so easily be the boy in 'The Emperor's New Clothes', but stay as trembling, paid-up members of the crowd.

And what a shame that is...

Because by being kept down as they are – and having their work shaped by others rather than by themselves – they'll never be the writers destiny wished for them to be.

Over months I jumped through all the hoops you have to jump through to prepare a manuscript and release it as a book. Little by little, *Hannibal Fogg* inched forward, as it was edited and proofed endlessly, laid out, and made ready to glimpse the light of day.

Jinn Hunter

BY THE TIME *Fogg* was launched, I had moved on.

Although my intention is to release further novels in the series when the time is right, as well as Hannibal Fogg's 'lost journals', I found myself obsessing over something quite different...

The Thousand and One Nights.

From the day of my birth I'd been raised on stories, coaxed through the eye of a needle into a fantasy world of folklore. In this twilight zone the only sacred altar was the treasury of stories standing as the ultimate testament to human creativity.

When I was nine years old I remember sitting on the floor at our home, Langton House, with my father holding court. There were all kinds of people clustered around, each one of them hanging on his every word.

My father talked so much and so fast, I sometimes zoned out. But on that particular afternoon I couldn't have been more zoned in. The reason was that he was telling the audience how stories are a lifeblood acting as a secret matrix – a matrix which can empower and teach.

What I remember him saying was that *The Arabian Nights* was known in the West, but misunderstood. It was, he said, regarded as an entertainment for children when it was an encyclopaedia for one and all. But, more importantly, I heard him explain how the treasury was rarely accessed in entirety.

An Argentine hippy asked what he meant. Thrusting his arms up and out to make his point, my father said:

'Think of it like this... each day you are welcomed into a dining room on which a banquet is laid out. There's more food than you've ever seen, and a variety of dishes from every corner of the earth – great platters of roasted meat, tureens filled to the brim with soup, and dishes overflowing with succulent fruits. Your eyes grow wide at such a sight, and you could gorge yourself on anything you like. But instead of piling your plate high with food, you take a single grape.'

Half a lifetime has slipped by since that day, but the point has twisted and turned around in my head ever since. My father's analogy about the West's relationship with *The Arabian Nights* was spot on. The Occidental world delights in sampling almost nothing at all, when a vast cornucopia of a feast is on offer.

For years I'd wrestled with the idea of harnessing *The Arabian Nights*, and using its essence in a new way. And for years I'd failed in coming up with a device to achieve my goal. Every time I read another version of the treasury, I became more stressed at the task, and bewildered as to how I might succeed.

One day, while in India, I invited an old writer pal to lunch in New Delhi. Even before a pair of glasses of chilled, filtered water had been poured, I launched into my rant – how I was a fisherman consumed with terror at landing the great fish – the creature of the deep that was *The Arabian Nights*.

My lunch guest wiped a hand down over his mouth ruminatively.

'Jinn Hunter,' he said.

For the next year I planned and I wrote, and I wrote and I planned.

I re-read *The Nights* six times, like a storm cloud sucking up water from the ocean. The more I read, the more I came to understand how the collection worked. As my father had said, it was the ultimate instruction manual to humanity and the world.

Tapping deep into my own imagination, I created a multiverse, in which every permutation of possibility was not only possible, but certain. The version of me with a dog's head, with a peacock's tail, with fish lips, and every other kind of imaginable variation. Against this backdrop, I crafted a realm in which all the most evil jinn in existence were trapped in a jail, a great inverted pyramid of glass – The Prism.

In this far-fetched dystopia, it fell to a brotherhood of Jinn Hunters to maintain the balance between good and evil by trapping wayward jinn.

I'm not going to drone on about the creative process, at least not here. But I do want to make a point: as writers, we spend our lives trying to find the mother-lode so we can mine it. Most of the time it's staring us right in the face, but we don't know it – just as I didn't know it with Jinn Hunter. But when we recognize the motherlode and beaver away at it, the results are potentially spectacular.

In my experience, the best writing happens when you're in the Magic Zone: fingers typing, brain engaged, creativity firing on all cylinders – not because you're trying to impress anyone, but because you just can't help yourself. Get in that zone, live in it, own it, and you'll be the writer you always dreamt of being.

Writing the first three *Jinn Hunter* books – which I did back to back – rooted me to the Magic Zone in a way I'd not been rooted before. It was as though the lights had all been turned on in my head and I knew exactly what I was doing. It's such a cliché, but the books wrote themselves – all I had to do was to sit down in the chair.

Through the months I was writing the *Jinn Hunter* books, my life was being buffeted by gale-force winds of stress. I was transitioning between phases, and was being pitched up, down, and from side to side as I tried to make sense of it all. Seated day after day in the chair, I'd seek refuge. *Jinn Hunter* was the one place I knew in which I was safe to conjure anything I liked.

The result was a phantasmagorical landscape unlike anything which has ever been described. And it's because of that I'd like to make a point, and make it loud and clear:

Non-writers like nothing more than whooping and hollering about what they think, doing their best to shunt one's creative process from the tracks. I've never understood it, but I've watched it for decades now. Just because someone isn't creative, they rant on and on about how a writer, an artist, a musician, or whatever, has lost the plot.

Nothing could be further from the truth.

The point is that as a creative (as my friends in the advertising business call us), you can only do right. Yes, some things will flop, but you'll learn from them, and so in many ways they're likely to be more useful in the long run than the dead certs.

Again, I beseech you:

BELIEVE IN YOURSELF!

The fact you're reading this book tells me you're a real writer through and through. As such, you have to be comfortable with experimentation – in the same way I experimented with a series of small test novels like *Paris Syndrome* and *Eye Spy*.

Writing is creation.

Just as it's not about pleasing anyone but yourself, it's about exploring what works for you. If you need reinforcement on how amazing you are, don't write books – get a dog instead. But if you're ready to embark on the greatest journey of self-discovery imaginable, tread the path...

...but do it in the knowledge you're walking it for yourself.

Full Circle

HUMANS LEARN FASTER and more accurately from experience than from being told what to do and how to do it.

That may sound obvious, and of course it is. The crazy thing is we spend decades behind desks in schools trying to learn what we will need for life. Much of what is presented is rubbish and is immediately forgotten. Most of the rest isn't provided in a way which allows it to get absorbed.

As with anything else, skill at writing develops by doing – exploring, experimenting, and by making mistakes. It comes through challenging oneself, and reaching for new horizons – the kind you didn't know existed when you set off.

My journey has constantly reminded me that writing isn't about fashioning a series of massive monoliths. No, no, no. Big, awe-inspiring novels are all well and good – and great for stretching yourself – but they're only part of the process. Like a bladesmith fashioning swords, it's important to make daggers, scythes, and fruit knives as well. Crafting a well-rounded miscellany of work ensures everything is kept in balance. Write too many weighty novels and too few stories, and you begin to sag. Or, write too many novellas, and your drive will be lost.

It's for this reason that a few months ago I sat down and wrote *Travels With Nasrudin*.

THE REASON TO WRITE

As you may know, Nasrudin is the wise-fool of Oriental folklore. Celebrated from Morocco in the West to China in the East, he's known by different names and guises. Sometimes he's the king, and other times he's a beggar without a cent to his name. Presented with usual situations, he turns life on its head.

I had never planned to write about Nasrudin, but had been brought up with him – and the four books of his stories my father released. Coaxed from early childhood to take refuge in his wisdom, I took him into my heart as a kind of protector.

One day last spring I was sitting here looking out at the garden, thinking about people I've known and places I've been, and found myself realizing Nasrudin was a focal point for my travels and encounters.

Without wasting a moment, I opened a blank document and started to type. When I think of the book, I think of myself standing on the edge of a lake, peering down at my reflection in the water. The book is me – albeit rippled and distorted – and I am it. At the same time, I'm reminded by a voice in my head that it would have been so much easier not to write *Travels With Nasrudin* – but by doing so I stretched myself, and arrived at a place I haven't ventured to before.

The book came into being spontaneously, which was a joy. But most of the smorgasbord of projects I have in the pipeline at any one time are laid down over years. I usually have more than a dozen books in progress. Some of them may never be completed, but that doesn't matter – because even as follies or foundations they've inspired everything else.

I'm currently working on a series of novellas – twenty-six of them. They're all mapped out, and the first one – *Godman* – is ready to be released. I've planned another four *Hannibal Fogg* novels, too, and six lost journals – created with the help of a wonderfully talented artist friend. Recently released are a series of sixteen anthologies of my work as well, arranged by theme – such as *Danger*, *Hinterland*, *Morocco*, *Jungle*, and *Taboo*. Each of them includes a mass of new material, and has allowed me to experiment with a passion of mine – mixing fiction and non-fiction work.

I have six more *Jinn Hunter* books in the pipeline, as well as a series of children's books, and at least a dozen other volumes about life, the universe, and everything.

Most of the time I keep works in progress to myself.

They're my babies and have been dreamt into existence to amuse me rather than anyone else. I am utterly uninterested in hearing opinions from others – especially people who'll stunt my creative growth. This reminds me to provide a word of advice even more forcefully than before:

Don't ever listen to anyone who holds you back.

Sure, use the anger, as I did with my unwanted guest, Chip – harness it. But don't allow it to drag you down. My advice to anyone is NEVER EVER EVER read reviews of your books online or in print. Granted, some will swell your ego like a helium balloon, but others are sure to knock you to the ground. You've got to ask yourself if you can take the rejection. In my opinion, jibes from the world at large run the risk of knocking you off track.

Starting with *Travels With Nasrudin*, experimented by keeping some book covers plain white – with only the title of the book and my name on the cover. I decided on this after dropping in at a local bookshop and being horrified how every publisher was falling over themselves to get their publications noticed. I have since returned to covers with illustrations, photos, or patterns, but secretly long for the simplicity of plain.

In presenting my work with plain covers, and releasing it myself, I like to think at long last things have come full circle.

I've reached the point where publishing began – when authors would publish their own work, in a form which pleased them rather than anyone else. It's a dominion where writing is about creating and being inspired rather than about selling shedloads of books they didn't want to write.

Most of all, though, it's about real writers writing for themselves...

Because, like J. D. Salinger, if they don't, they'll turn to stone.

PART III

DETAILS

Announcement II

THE ONLY WAY to grasp anything in a meaningful way is through an organic process of zigzag experience, rather than studying it A to Z. As with any creative art, perfecting by doing is the essence of writing.

Over the next pages I will showcase a variety of random points which, when grouped as a collection, constitute the writing craft. It's important there's no order, but that they're taken all together – like individual fragments of mosaic forming an image.

Beginnings

The start of a book is very important to me, but then again it's not very important at all. The way I work is to lay a foundation stone at the beginning of the first page. The stone is a line which blows me away with what I consider to be a gleaming gemstone of letters and words.

As I work on the first chapter, I keep looking back to the initial line, reading it over and over. By enthusing myself with how dazzling it is, I bathe in the warm blush of glory at my self-praise. More often than not the first line gets changed as the book develops. I'll either end up starting the story somewhere else, or axe the first pages and cut to the chase.

But that doesn't matter.

What matters is that the first lines and paragraphs get you into the right mindset – giving you confidence so you're up to the challenge of writing the entire book.

Samples

One of my friends in Morocco is a master carpenter named Mr Reda.

What I like about him most is that when he says he can do something, he does it. There's no boasting or tittle-tattle, but rather a body of work which speaks for itself. I once asked him the secret of his success. He replied:

'When I'm not sure how to complete the job at hand, I make samples. They demonstrate various kinds of carpentry that will be needed. The important thing is they are not executed to demonstrate anything to the client. I don't show them to anyone. Rather, they are done to demonstrate to me I have the skill to undertake the job.'

I always think of Reda's words when I have to write something daunting. And, following his example, I open a fresh page on my computer, or turn to a blank page in my journal, and scribble down samples – proof to myself that I'm worthy of the task at hand.

Fights

I recently had to write a fight scene for a novel and found myself stressing over it for days on end. I was anxious because fights tend to be a wild rumpus of commotion, in which all kinds of action and emotions occur.

In the frenzy it's easy to lose yourself, and the characters, without leading to any clear point of resolution. At times of stress, when I don't know how to handle the thing I have to write, I leave the work desk and go sit in a sagging yellow armchair in the corner of my study. My 'thinking chair', it always helps me come up with a solution in an almost magical way.

Time and again I would get up, go sit in the thinking chair, and turn the fight scene I had conceived over in my head. But each time I did so, the more stressed I became. Then, on the morning I had planned to write the scene, the thinking chair gave me what I needed – the greatest stage fight ever written, from *The Princess Bride*. Anyone who remembers the cliff-top scene will recall how the masked protagonist Westley battles with Inigo Montoya. It's a scene I know incredibly well because I've drooled over it so often – both on the screen and while reading the screenplay. Playing it back to myself in the thinking chair, I broke it down step by step.

Then, I laid the action over my own proposed fight scene. Through some kind of creative osmosis I found the template carried over and gave me what I needed to write a fight of my own.

Dialogue
Writers get worked up about dialogue far more than they should.

When I started writing books, Doris Lessing ordered me to take a tape recorder, get onto the top deck of a London bus, and to record the people behind me. 'Go and listen to what you've recorded,' she said. 'And, if it doesn't help, transcribe the tape.' I did as she suggested, and found myself appreciating that dialogue is the most normal kind of writing of all.

What's important is not to suffocate conversation in masses of direction – who said what and how. The authors whose work I respect most highly – people like Bruce Chatwin and Mark Salzman – handle dialogue as a series of fine-tuned movements in a dance. The lines are elegant, fast, and sensitive, with the writer taking a back seat, allowing the characters to shine.

Look through any of my books and you'll see I use a very standard technique for dialogue. From time to time I try and elaborate it, embarrassed it's so simple. But I almost always rework it to the tried-and-tested template which has done me so well for so long.

Description

Different writers handle description in different ways.

A great many authors go heavy on it, to the point they write poetry in prose form. Preferring to tell the story as simply as possible, I throw in pinches of description along the way, and rarely write description for the sake of description. I dislike pages and pages of gloopy, treacle-like description that bogs the reader down.

The way I regard it, if you're cooking with good quality ingredients there's no need to smother them in sauces. Present them with simplicity and they'll be all the more delicious to those eating the meal.

When describing a character and their arc through a book, I like to build on the layers of observational description as I go. Along with everything else related to writing, the important thing is to keep writing. If you find the text is coming out laden with descriptive prose, then keep going.

Don't stress.

You can always trim it down or tweak it later.

Historical

I'm a believer that all writers should experiment, just as I believe writers who churn out the same novel again and again because they know it'll sell are duping themselves and their readers.

Those are two of the reasons why I tried my hand at writing historical fiction and wrote *Timbuctoo*. Set in 1816, the book tells the true-life story of the first white Christian to visit the African Eldorado and live to tell the tale. Having not written historical fiction before, I agonized over the process far too much, rather than just getting down to it and trying my luck.

As I've already described, I started by writing the story as a screenplay, before jumping through dozens of self-imposed hoops to prepare me for the task. The point I want to make here is that by writing historical fiction you have the chance to time travel in a way few other creative people ever have the opportunity to do.

Like most authors, I slip into the books I am writing, and I dwell there in a hollow deep under the ground. When I think back to the books I've written, *Timbuctoo* was the most intense experience of all because it dragged me through the Sahara as a slave, and into the high-life and low-life worlds of Regency London. Lifting the blinkers on the furthest limits of my creativity, it taught me far more than I'd ever have hoped for when I began.

Inspiration

My advice to anyone who's listening is to allow yourself to be inspired in every imaginable way. I've written about how mentors have helped me on the writing journey, by helping me to think in new ways. Multiple mentors are so incredibly useful, because they all think and act differently.

One example is the traveller and novelist Bruce Chatwin, to whom I owe a great debt. Chatwin was critically important not least because he was utterly original. My favourite book of his is the travelogue *The Songlines*.

Somewhere near the middle of that book is a big section of random material in italics. A collection of miscellaneous notes from his journeys, it's labelled simply, 'From the Notebooks'. I adore it because it stirs the reader up and sets them free – free to imagine, to wonder, and to dream.

Humour

A long time ago I overhead a young man asking his sister how to pick up a girl. The advice offered was this:

'Make her laugh, because if she laughs she'll give you her time, and if you get her time you'll win her heart.'

That sentence has been swimming round my head for decades – not because I ever used it to pick up girls, but rather because I used it to write. From my early days as a would-be author I felt guilt that anyone out there should be expected to read my work, and that by giving it to them I was forcing myself on them.

So, by tapping into the advice I'd caught on the wind, I devised a way of making myself feel better by making others laugh. Without quite realizing how I was doing it, I wove humour into my writing – laying it on thick. As a result I found I could set up ideas and thinking which would have been laborious to do without the magic of humour.

The very finest form of humour I've come across is the kind edged with poignancy, so the reader is left feeling moved. When done perfectly, the effect is so subtle you almost don't realize it's taken place at all.

Harnessing

When I hear writers moaning on and on about how they don't know what to write, I find myself yelling:

'Make a list of random people you've known, and places you've been to!' Stare at the names, pick out four people and four places, then let your imagination take over.

So that I don't come across as a complete phoney, I just tried it myself.

Here are my random people and places:
- Mr Gooderson, my prep-school science teacher who wore a wig and was obsessed with Ordinance Survey maps.
- James Labouchere, the prefect at my boarding

school who built an aeroplane in metalwork and it nosedived during a rugby match.
- Sir Wilfred Thesiger, my great friend and hero, who crossed the Empty Quarter of Arabia twice on foot.
- Helena Edwards, my father's secretary, known by the mystic George Gurdjieff as 'Blonde No. 24'.
- The Royal Bombay Yacht Club, a favourite haunt, where I lived when it was at its most rat-infested and run down.
- The village of Narok, in Kenya's Rift Valley, where I stayed as a student in the mid-eighties.
- Gangtok, capital of Sikkim, in northern India.
- A laundromat in Alice Springs where I once had one of the most interesting conversations of my life.

With the random list at hand, I scribble the names in circles on a fresh sheet of paper, like little islands, and start conjuring a story.

Don't overthink this exercise.

When people start off writing they're constantly overthinking when instead they should be allowing their imagination to run free.

So, doing it super-fast, I see the story set in the thirties of a trailblazing woman with flaxen yellow hair. Irrepressible and adventurous, she criss-crosses the world in search of a secret – a secret which will make sense of a map left to her by an elderly explorer in Sikkim.

Little by little, the layers of the story emerge.

I don't wrestle with the imagination, but rather let the story emerge from the darkness, like air bubbles percolating up through water. Force it, and the well of inspiration will run dry. If nothing comes to mind then go off and run errands, answer emails, or prune the roses. Whether you like it or not the story will keep flashing into your head as your mind works away.

Lists

Much of what I do as a writer is geared so that I don't cool down.

Sometimes I get to my desk and just can't face writing the next chapter of the book I'm working on. So what I do is to do something else – something complementary. My holy grail is to do work I'm in the mood for. And, if I'm not in the mood for writing a heavy chapter, I do something more spontaneous and fun.

And on days when I'm barely functioning at all, I make lists.

Lists of characters for novels I will write.

Lists of places I'd like to visit.

Lists of oddities.

Lists of interesting facts gleaned from Wikipedia.

And even lists of lists.

Then, when I'm a little more engaged, I put meat on the bones of the lists. I'll let you into a secret to show you what I mean. A week ago I couldn't face writing a chapter for this book, so I made a list of dozens of points which concern me as a writer – everything from humour to writing lists.

The list sat on my desktop until this afternoon.

Opening it up, I started writing entries for the various listings, and that's how this section came into being.

Brown Water

I've written elsewhere about getting started, but want to say once again that you have to dive in, have faith in yourself, and keep going. It's very easy to stress over the quality of the first pages. More likely than not they'll be uneven, jumbled, and confused. Of course they will be, and there's absolutely nothing wrong with that. Almost every book I've written has a different beginning to the one appearing in the first draft. The first thirty pages of a double-spaced manuscript tend to be the rusty brown water issuing forth from a tap which has been turned off tight. Open the tap wide, let the water flow, and come back to the start when you've crossed the finish line.

First Sentences

There's little so sacred to me as first sentences.

Even though they may ultimately be tweaked or rewritten, I usually know when I've got them right. Where possible I try to keep them short and sharp, and to ensure they lead on to a bigger point. An exception is the opening of my historical novel, *Timbuctoo*. Following the style of the novels of the time I allowed it the time and space it deserved.

Here's a list of first sentences which made the final cut in a selection of my books:

Godman: The Blackpool Grand had hosted the crème de la crème of entertainment in its time, from vaudeville to full musical extravaganzas, and even pantomime.

Travels With Nasrudin: On the eve of my sixth birthday, my father tucked me into bed. 'Are you excited for tomorrow?' he asked.

Jinn Hunter: Book One – The Prism: The vaults beneath the Bank of England on London's Threadneedle Street were utterly silent, as they were on any other night.

Jinn Hunter: Book Two – The Jinnslayer: As Oliver passed the executioner's hood back to Amalorous, he found himself sitting on a pile of sour old straw in Morrock's room again.

Hannibal Fogg and the Supreme Secret of Man: From the snow-laden crags of the Hindu Kush, the vast army of Alexander, King of the Macedonians and subjugator of the known world, seemed to move in total silence.

Paris Syndrome: On the morning of her fifth birthday, Miki Suzuki sat perched on her grandfather's knee at the edge of the porch in the family home, a short distance from Sendai.

Casablanca Blues: The windowless walls at Acme Telesales were painted slate grey.

Scorpion Soup: When I was young and foolish, but so certain I was wise, I took any work offered.

Eye Spy: The waiting room of Dr Amadeus Kaine's practice was panelled in antique mahogany and smelled of Indian lemongrass.

Timbuctoo: A pair of ornate Queen Anne braziers were crackling at either end of the opulent meeting room, warming the extremities, and leaving the fifty gentlemen seated at the central mahogany table wishing they had worn their woollen underwear instead.

In Arabian Nights: The torture room was ready for use.

The Caliph's House: There was a sadness in the stillness of dusk.

House of the Tiger King: The men had lost their smiles and their cheap grins.

In Search of King Solomon's Mines: An inky hand-drawn map hung on the back wall of Ali Baba's Tourist Emporium.

Trail of Feathers: The trail began at an auction of shrunken heads.

Sorcerer's Apprentice: We failed to realize it was an omen when it came.

Beyond the Devil's Teeth: A maze of passageways stretched in all directions.

Belief
'The Emperor's New Clothes' is a story that has seeped

down deep into the marrow of my bones. The older I get, the more I find myself seeing shadows of the story all around me – it's everywhere.

Our society seems to be constructed on the flawed foundations on which the much-loved tale took place. Just as the emperor was naked, a great many of the people society champions as heroes are vacuous and (in my opinion) third-rate. But no one seems to burst the bubble like the little boy in the crowd did. I used to get very worked up indeed about how droves of untalented people make it to stardom. Then, when I was discussing this with my father one afternoon in the days before his death, he said:

'Forget about all those time-wasters. They live fleeting lives with fleeting impact. Instead, strive to be original – to be someone whose work is on a grand scale and is different. Believe in yourself. Not in a half-hearted way, but with absolute conviction. Never doubt your ability – not for a moment – and there'll be nothing in which you cannot succeed.'

Word Counts

Perhaps it's because I'm rather obsessive by nature, or because I like working towards a goal, I've always found noting down a daily word count to be the sure-fire method of staying on track.

My father used to write between seven and ten thousand words a day, and that was on a manual typewriter. I described how it sounded at the start. It was like interminable machine-gun fire. It's because of him I force myself to write an unreal daily wordage – because what I'd heard throughout my childhood was my 'normal'.

Only now do I realize there was nothing normal about it at all.

I've just had a quick look online and found the daily output of a range of authors. In some cases they're remarkably low. The point is not how much you write, but rather that you write. Do the same small amount each day and it adds up.

According to a range of Internet sites, here's a tally of daily wordage:

Tom Wolfe	35
Ernest Hemingway	500
Graham Greene	500
Philip Pullman	1100
Mark Twain	1500
Charles Dickens	2000
Anthony Trollope	3000
Enid Blyton	6000
Michael Crichton	10,000

When planning a book, I give myself a strict writing schedule to keep to, and do my best to stay on course. I've written about this in the main text, so you'll find more elsewhere. The output I manage depends on the amount of creativity required. On a non-fiction book I strive towards 5000 words a day. On a regular fiction book I should be able to get down 3500 or 4000. And on a fantasy work – like the volumes in my *Jinn Hunter* series – I'll be pleased with 3000 to 3500.

I'm not pretending for a moment writing 5000 words a day isn't a challenge. Of course it is. But do it every day for a week, then a month, and another, and your strength builds, as your narrative voice is itself fortified.

Noting down wordage is the one reliable method I know of moving forward.

But don't overdo it.

As with exercising, it's far too easy to do too much on day one – or in week one – and then get burned out. Burnout is the last thing a writer wants. It can set you back months or even years.

Worst of all, it can make a writer hate the craft.

Backups
We've all lost precious work, and I've probably lost more than anyone I know.

The reason can be chalked down to general carelessness. My advice is to do a daily backup in several ways.

When I have finished for the day, I rename the file I'm using with the day's date or the total wordage. Either is fine. Then, I store the draft on my computer's desktop, on an external hard drive, and (most importantly) I email it to myself.

THE REASON TO WRITE

As with almost everything connected to writing, the secret is to have a routine which is followed without thinking. Don't worry if the work you're backing up isn't edited – what matters is that it's safe and secure.

Momentum

Book writing is founded on momentum.

You don't have to be a super-genius to write books, but you have to keep the pressure up. In my thinking it's like the steam engine heading south to north. There'll be uphill stretches and downhill ones too, frequent and infrequent stops, fair conditions and driving rain.

To write the book you have to pace yourself, and ensure that whatever the conditions thrown at you, you keep going towards the distant horizon. Far too many writers like to drone on about the magical process of writing books. They're numbskulls, because there's relatively little magic needed.

But there is hard work.

Do the work by staying in the groove and the book writes itself. And the tried and tested way to stay in the groove is to maintain the head of steam, page after page, steam that'll get you to the very last line.

Introductions

When I wrote my first travel book – entitled *In Gondwanaland* (subsequently renamed *Beyond the Devil's Teeth*), I put an introduction at the front. It went on and on about my motives to write the book, and what I'd hoped to achieve.

Unable to get it published, I used to carry the manuscript around in a plastic bag and show it to anyone who'd take a look. One evening I was invited to a dinner party at which numerous members of the literati were already installed. An established writer present said he'd heard from the host about my book. As if by magic I pulled it out from under my chair. He took a look, flicking through the lengthy introduction.

'As writers we're in the gemstone business,' he said. 'And chopping out work which gets in the way is like faceting a gem. No one reads introductions in any case. Either call it Chapter One, or delete it – which is what I'd suggest you do.'

And that's exactly what I did.

Appendices

I'm an admirer of appendices because they allow a writer to present work which supports the main text, but which doesn't slow the reader down. Publishers loathe appendices because they often go unread, and because they take extra paper – paper which costs money.

My book *Trail of Feathers* has two appendices – one on flora-based hallucinogens of the Upper Amazon, and another dealing with the Shuar tribe of former head-shrinkers. I had to fight tooth and nail to get the appendices included, and only succeeded because I had started off by demanding the right to produce five of them.

Glossaries

As with appendices, glossaries are fodder for an editor's red pen.

Publishers dislike long explanations and tend to insist they're never read, cost paper, and are time-consuming and therefore expensive to proofread.

My own thinking is to include a glossary if you can stand to write it, because it provides balance to the meal. In my *Jinn Hunter* series the glossaries run to twenty thousand words, and are a central pillar of the story.

Collecting Words

Writers love words. It's as simple as that.

We may not admit it in public, but to us they're delicious, like hand-cut mosaics set lovingly into a decorative frieze. I try to use words that are in regular use, so the reader doesn't have to reach for a dictionary (not that anyone ever bothers to these days). At the same time, I do my best to use a variety of vocabulary so that I don't subject the reader to undue tedium.

In my wider life I collect words that are especially delectable, either for their sound, their meaning, or both. Words, for instance like 'petrichor' – the bewitching smell of first rain. Or 'pettifogging' – being unnecessarily trivial, or 'coddiwomple' – to travel in a purposeful manner towards a distant destination. Most of the words I note down are found in newspapers, books, and spoken on the radio. I heard one this morning and scribbled it into my journal right away – sulphurous. I've heard it before, of course, but have never used it. Can't wait to slip it into something soon.

Kubrick

I've been a lifelong fan of the celebrated film director Stanley Kubrick – not because all his work is amazing, but because he stretched himself and experimented.

Far too many directors go on and on making the same kind of movie, just as too many authors keep on writing the same kind of book. My belief is that to grow you have to stretch yourself, in the way Kubrick did. Look at the movies he made, and you quickly see they span a wide variety of genres. More interested in his own learning curve as a director, he gave little time to making movies the studios, or even the film-going public, wanted.

Kubrick's movies span the following genres:
Horror – *The Shining*
Science Fiction – *2001: A Space Odyssey*
War – *Full Metal Jacket*
Comedy – *Dr Strangelove*
Crime – *A Clockwork Orange*
Mystery – *Eyes Wide Shut*

THE REASON TO WRITE

Romance – *Lolita*
Action – *Spartacus*
Drama – *Fear and Desire*

Taking Notes
Not all writers take notes, but most do. Of those, a great many probably do so to appear erudite or worthy. Pulling out their Moleskine notebooks at a dinner party, twanging back the elasticated band, they strain to seem self-important, or at least interesting.

In my opinion, the only reason to take notes is to register something which could be fitted in at a later date. I'd never share my notes, as they are private and wouldn't make sense to anyone else.

More often than not I scribble down details – such as the cost of something, like a ferry journey across the bay in Cochin, or the waxy complexion of a croupier at a roulette table in Colombo.

As a child I was encouraged by my parents to take concise notes on everything new I experienced. The task became a cornerstone of my enthusiasm for collecting people. Alas, my most precious notebook from that time was confiscated by a brutish monocle-wearing master at my prep school.

I find listing details in bullet points to be an efficient method to get the key facts down. For instance, a note taken last night at a dinner that was loathed by absolutely

everyone invited:
- Sixteen random people all sombre, most self-centred.
- Boy, girl, boy, girl down the table festooned with lemon-scented flowers.
- Man to my right dandruff like first winter snow.
- Glass eye. Scarred right hand. Slight lisp.
- Woman across table trepanned herself in about '66 with a man called Mellen.
- Claimed to have known my grandfather and Timothy Leary in Tangier.
- Meal featured quails and undercooked turnips served whole. Gravy curious shade of powder blue.
- Everyone forced to give a three-minute speech. Talked about shrunken head techniques of the Shuar. Went down like a lead balloon.
- Madame G promised to show me her box of bull bezoars if I visit again next week.

Anthologies

In the last year I have produced sixteen full anthologies of my work, arranged by theme, an idea which came about as a procrastination.

At first I planned to publish a single anthology. But, the more I considered it, the more it seemed right to do a series, and in a way no publisher would ever allow. As with anything I do, it's done because it's of interest to me, and me alone.

Taking selections from my existing corpus of

work, and adding to them dozens of new pieces, was an intensely interesting exercise. I recommend that all writers create anthologies. As with anything else, it's easier not to bother, but hugely worthwhile when complete. Most importantly though, the exercise gives one an opportunity to regard one's work in a new way.

Wikipedia Vortex
The Internet has provided even the most challenged writer with a stream of detail, information, and phantasmagorical delight, to use in any way they wish. When I was new to writing books I used to amass hundreds of pages of neatly typed notes that I'd first made by hand. I did this because I was so fearful that the task of writing the book would confound me.

As the years have gone by, and as I have got increasingly confident, I've done less and less research in advance. Instead, I've mined material online and from books as and when it's needed. If it's being done online – especially on Wikipedia – you have to take care.

Don't get me wrong, I'm Wikipedia's No. 1 fan.

But it's far too easy to be sucked into the Wikipedia Vortex. You start by looking up the currency of Gambia (resist the urge, it's *dalasi*) and, next thing you know, you've slalomed your way through a hundred articles on everything from bluebottles to Blackbeard, and half the writing day's gone.

Editing

As with proofreading, it's essential to get your work edited if you're releasing it yourself. Most professional writers agree that in recent years publishers have shirked on having editorial work done. As with everything else, it's chalked down to cost-cutting. This means books with terrible plot holes get launched, like ships with great gashes down the side. The best-case scenario is to find an editor who you like, and to work with them book by book. They will get to know how you write, and what your strengths and failings are. Most importantly, they'll know to be sensitive with their criticisms, and to polish your work rather than reshaping it.

Correcting

This is important:

If you follow my example and publish work yourself, you MUST be certain there are no typos or obvious mistakes. I can't stress this strongly enough. Typos and errors of any kind will leave you open to attack – whether you care about condemnations or not. So, it's critically important to have work proofed numerous times.

I tend to get a manuscript proofed by four different people before typesetting, and then again by another four afterwards. Even then, a typeset book should be read by as many friends, fans, and family as you can muster. You have to explain to them though what they are being asked to proof for. Even though I try to brief friends what I want and don't want, one or two always give lists of punctuation they regard as inappropriate.

Another key point is that everyone picks up different stuff. There's a professional proofreader I tend to use who is completely challenged at the job. He misses almost everything – even the most glaring errors staring him in the face. But every time I give him a manuscript, he'll find two or three mistakes everyone else has missed.

For that reason his work is worth its weight in gold.

Daily Read
I am a fast writer but a slow reader – notched down to my dyslexia. I abhor reading through work I have written line by line, making sure the grammar's right. I do it nonetheless, and find reading through my day's output before leaving my desk at the end of the day is very useful indeed.

In the same way, reading through and correcting the previous day's pages saves a writer like me hundreds of hours of editing work later. Of course you will have to go through newly written work plenty of times before it's published, but early read-throughs tend to pick up on errors which might later be missed.

Listening
This is especially for all the dyslexics out there:

As I'm such a slow reader, I find the best way to stay focused is to get my computer to read passages of text back to me. My Apple Mac is set up so that if I highlight the text, then press Apple+X, a voice reads aloud. This is especially useful when I am editing work – because I can quickly make small changes as the voice continues reading. I find hearing text allows me to pick up errors I wouldn't otherwise notice – like a missing article or pronoun.

eBooks

Publishers like to try to impress upon authors how, by some far-fetched alchemy, they'll get their work released in eBook form. It's nuts of course, because nothing is simpler than getting your book encoded as an eBook. Most of the time it costs very little indeed. My advice to any author is to retain eBook rights when knocking out the terms of a contract, and get an independent eBook firm to put out your work directly. That way you get to keep all the revenue and, even more important, overall control.

Americanization

There are plenty of firms online which will change the spelling and formatting of your manuscript so you can release it in the United States, or vice versa. From my experience, if you are releasing your book directly, it's well worth having a British and an American edition, with separate ISBN numbers and barcodes. The transfers are not expensive, and they open up an entirely new market. Of course, Americans will read British versions, and Brits will read US editions, but they tend to prefer their own.

Motivation

Procrastination, boredom, despondency, and general self-doubt have surely been the curse of writers since books were written on clay tablets – no surprise in that. After all, we're taking a blank tablet, blackboard, scroll, sheet of paper, computer screen, and are adorning it with a stream of letters and words pulled from the ether. All writers tend to hone methods of mitigating doubt and motivating themselves.

What works for me is to read random passages from The Shelf of Wretched Reads. It's proof in an instant that your work is way better than some of the most celebrated names in the business.

Chair

If you're serious about becoming a writer, go out and invest in the best, most expensive chair you can afford. You'll be sitting there for hundreds of hours, so get one with excellent lumbar support which doesn't creak and grind when you move.

A friend who spends her life straightening out bad backs once gave me a top tip – search on eBay for a refurbished company chair. She said the ones from meeting rooms tend to be the least worn, and that there are lots still available from high-end firms which went bankrupt after the financial crash, as well as in the dark days of Covid-19.

Confidence
I've touched on confidence elsewhere, and quite rightly so.

Fear of failure is something uniting almost all creative people, and is one of the greatest threats we face. Meanwhile, confidence is a Promised Land you only reach by sailing out towards the horizon, rather than going round and round in circles.

Write twenty books and you can't help but acquire a hefty dose of confidence. But beware: stop writing for a prolonged period and the confidence dissipates as though it were never there at all.

When You Know
At the time we were expecting our daughter, Ariane, my wife asked the midwife how to know when she was in labour. The answer given was this:

'If you're wondering whether or not you're in labour, you're *not* in labour.'

The same goes for being a real writer.

If you're not sure whether you are one, then you're not.

Being a real writer is a condition, a state of mania and melancholy, a psycho zone controlling every aspect of your day. It's to be gloriously on the edge, in a place most people hardly even realize exists.

Open Sesame!
Follow your heart, write books, and doors will open that were previously locked, or even invisible.

This is something I witnessed first-hand with my father. Clattering away in his study day after day, he released a stream of original work over decades. With each new book that appeared, more opportunities arrived. Many of them were the kind non-creative people rarely encounter.

I've described the mixture of characters populating my childhood, a time when my father was at his creative height. They had all been lured to Langton House as a result of my father's books. Many were celebrated writers, scientists, and thinkers, but many others were unknown. Those were the ones I found most interesting because they'd lived full-spectrum lives.

In addition to the regulars, new visitors arrived all the time – visitors bearing opportunities.

On one occasion a pair of gold-plated Rolls-Royces slunk up the drive, bearing an entourage from an oil-rich state in the Far East. Having followed my father's work since his youth, the Head of State wanted him to redesign the nation's educational system.

As an author, my life also led to opportunities and encounters I'd have never thought possible. They appear when you least expect them, and are a direct result of churning out material and releasing it into the wild.

My books have taken me to experiences I never expected – from visiting Emperor Haile Selassie's treasure vaults beneath the presidential palace in Addis Ababa, to one-on-one meetings with the Dalai Lama and Mother Teresa, to high-level meetings at top-secret diplomatic missions, Boeing Aviation, and the United Nations.

Obelix Syndrome
Do you remember how, in the *Asterix* books, happy-go-lucky Obelix had fallen into the cauldron of magic potion as a baby? While the other Gauls in the village needed a regular top-up of the potion, he didn't, because he'd consumed so much that he was primed with strength for life.

My take on writing is inspired by Obelix.

If you write masses – and I mean MASSES – then an extraordinary thing happens, an alchemy. It's what Doris told me was 'getting to the higher ground'. Read any of her books – especially the later ones – and you feel Obelix in the fluidity and the strength of her narrative voice. The voice was so fluent, so gloriously warmed up, that there was nothing she couldn't write, reason, discuss, or explain.

As I have said, I am no great linguist, and have always struggled with languages. On the rare occasions I have been steeped in a language, I've managed to run free for minutes, hours, or even days. The sensation is like cycling without training wheels for the first time – as it was for me when Greville taught me to cycle.

Writing fluency is very similar to linguistic fluency.

In order to be absolutely fluent you have to write colossal amounts of text. I'm not talking about a few chapters every so often – or a book every couple of years. I'm talking about four, five, or six books a year. Get in that zone, and stay there – like a speed cyclist streamlined in the peloton – and you'll reach a plateau few writers have ever known.

Please don't tell me with all the tools at our disposal that it's such a huge feat of trial and tribulation to knock out a good-sized chunk of pages in a day. Of course it's not. For the Victorians the prevailing convention was very much one of industry, whereas in our time it's quite the opposite. Writers, and would-be writers, drone on and on about the craft of writing while doing relatively little of it. It's something that's plain wrong and needs correcting.

Literary Identity

With the conventional publishing model – the one I've railed against throughout this book – there's almost no way an author can ever reach Doris Lessing's 'higher ground'. Unless you're a fantasy novelist churning out blockbusters hand over fist, publishers will want a book only every year or two. It's the publishers who created the myth that writers can't produce more than they do. In a way, the myth reminds me of the great misguided belief in sport – how running a four-minute mile was impossible... before it was run by Roger Bannister.

There's no question most writers are capable of writing a lot more. The problem is that the publishing houses are incapable of selling more. And, as I've said over and over, all they care about is making cold hard cash, so they'll never release a book that's not expected to sell in droves.

A great many of my friends are authors. As you'd imagine we are supportive of each other's work, having watched our various careers and projects trundling along.

Until the new model of direct publishing came along, the only way around the clampdown was to create more than one literary identity, whether the publishers realized it or not. My grandfather, who was running like a finely tuned engine throughout the twenties and thirties, knocked out up to half a dozen books a year. It was the only way he could survive from his pen.

Raising a small family, and living on his written work, he had no choice but to write under an ever-increasing stable of pseudonyms. His pen names included: John Grant, Richard Drobutt, Raoul Simac, Rustam Khan-Urf, Syed Iqbal, Sheikh Ahmed Abdullah, Bahloal Dana, Ibn Amjed, and even 'Afghan'.

Doing What Works
Most of what I have to say about writing is based on straightforward thinking, and there's nothing more straightforward than doing what works for you. Although I've described my own personal writing methods, I celebrate those of others who have developed a method and run with it.

A perfect example is the Sicilian novelist Andrea Camilleri, who died in 2019 aged ninety-three. Other than being a talented author of detective fiction, the extraordinary thing about Camilleri was the way he worked on a template. Rarely deviating from it, he produced thirty novels – eight a year – each one with eighteen chapters, and a hundred and eighty pages.

Camilleri is proof, if anyone needs it, that you can come to writing late (he was in his mid-sixties when he became a bestseller), producing a full body of work.

In Character
Thirty years ago Daniel Day-Lewis won a Best Actor Oscar for his portrayal of Christy Brown, the Irish writer and painter who could only move his left foot. Unable to sleep one night, I caught a documentary about the making of the movie *My Left Foot*.

The image that stuck with me was Daniel Day-Lewis on a break between scenes. While all the other cast and crew were happily tucking into their lunch, Day-Lewis was slouched in his chair, limbs seized up as though he actually suffered the cerebral palsy he was portraying so skilfully.

The point I want to make is that, especially when slipping into the world of fiction, it's helped me to remain in character throughout the day. I'm not pretending I become all the characters I write about, but elements of each one root themselves within me. As such, staying in character as I break from the desk enables me to stay in the zone.

Collaborations

I am enthusiastic about collaborating with other creative people – whether it's for an anthology, or a book which observes a particular subject from different angles. In the same way friends exercise together at the gym, having a buddy can make the process of writing far less isolating.

Collaborations are a way of pooling common ideas, building on shared interests, and stretching oneself in directions that may well have been unthinkable before.

For both new and established authors, it can be a way of expanding one's readership. Many writers have an overlap in their audience, but very few share exactly the same set of readers.

The only problem with collaborations is they tend to hit the buffers unless there's one key person charged with keeping the project on track. On occasions when I have been approached about a potential collaboration, I've pitched in only when there's a charitable angle. Part of the reason for this is that the division of royalties between numerous authors is like untangling a bowl of spaghetti.

Ongoing Tweaks

This is a small point but an important one.

When writing books it's good practice to leave as little work for later as you can. Getting a book in shape to be published is a hard slog, and so if you can reduce the number of misspellings and basic corrections you'll save yourself days, possibly weeks of hard grind.

In my experience it's much easier to clean text fast when you're in the moment. Later you'd have to remember the precise sense of a passage. Before ending a day's stint in the chair, try to correct spellings and grammar, and basic facts.

Again, beware you don't find yourself slipping down the rabbit hole into the Wikipedia Wonderland of fact-checking – and for this reason I recommend checking at the end of the day, when you'll be only too keen to get away from your desk.

Originality

If there's one single thing I'd wish for a real writer to get from this book it's the importance of being original.

In many ways nothing else really matters to me.

I have always praised my children, Ariane and Timur, when they thought differently, as my sisters and I were rewarded by our own parents. Thinking different, and doing different, is profoundly important – especially as we live at a time in which everyone seems fixated on aping those around them.

Never be afraid to fall flat on your face from failure. What matters is trying new things.

I say this knowing full well that both writing and reading fraternities can be mercilessly critical of anyone who experiments with fresh approaches. But, equally, they can be welcoming.

After all, human history remembers trailblazers rather than those who simply regurgitate.

Payoffs
As a slow reader, I have always been drawn to books with plenty going on.

Aged about seven I'd lie in bed and read *The Guinness Book of Records* night after night, marvelling at so many wondrous feats all packed into a single book. Those world records were, in a way, payoffs. Read one and you were instantly amazed and satisfied, like a rat rewarded with a food pellet for getting through a maze.

In the same way *Guinness* provided payoffs, I have always done my best to provide them while writing books. It's far easier to succeed in this than you may think, and is achieved in considering material in a new way, turning it around on itself.

The best way to see what I mean and to learn the technique is to study Mark Salzman's *Iron and Silk*, itself a masterclass in payoffs. Through Salzman I learned to give the reader a payoff every page and a half.

Alternation

I'm not sure where I picked up the technique of alternation, but I am certain that I did – rather than invent it myself. By alternation, I mean having two, or even more, timelines or strands running through the book.

This was especially conspicuous in my novel *Hannibal Fogg and the Supreme Secret of Man*. In that book I used two clear timelines – almost a century apart. By alternating from one to the other I could keep the narrative moving along the tracks which satisfied me as the storyteller. I've used it in a lot of other books as well, as I find it allows me to sustain a kind of dynamism that might well be lost by writing in a more linear way.

Descriptive Detail

Writing books is like the growth and anatomy of a tree.

You need a good structure with firm roots, a thick trunk, and strong boughs to hold the maze of telescoping branches and twigs. But you need leaves as well – millions of them. Descriptive detail is like the foliage on a great, sprawling oak tree. Hold a single leaf in your hand and marvel at it in the same way you would do with an individual fragment of description. Stripped of their leaves in winter, trees retain their form but are skeletal.

Out of all the elements of writing, I'd say writing fine description is more challenging than anything else. It's something with which to experiment and master, a skill which repays the time spent on it tenfold.

Peanuts

The last thing I'd ever do would be to tell real writers what to write or how to write it. All I can do is to explain what has worked for me and why. Over time, I have isolated a kind of formula which allows me to write simply and efficiently, while sucking in the material I need to include.

I mentioned Charles Schultz previously. He claimed to have reached a stage at which he could make any point through his celebrated cartoon strip, *Peanuts*. In the same way, I like to think that over time I have learned to express even the most complex ideas through a simple matrix.

The challenge for a writer is to break the material down and to feed it to the reader in a way that's both entertaining and nourishing. For me this means a delicious smoothie of succinct sentences, paragraphs, and chapters. I could just as easily alter the mixture, packing it with unwieldy sentences, mind-numbing themes and painful verbosity, but that would be to freeze the smoothie until it were a block of ice.

I'll leave it to you to decide which is easier for the reader to consume.

Brain Freeze
Sit at a desk for twelve hours and you feel as though your brain's been taken out of your head, frozen solid, whacked repeatedly with a baseball bat, and jammed back inside.

I have to admit I LOVE that feeling.

It's terrible I know, but it's proof I've created on a grand scale. I beg anyone reading this not to follow my example. Writing day after day to the point of brain freeze is tantamount to a suicide mission during a war.

It may get the job done, but it comes at a price.

Unfortunately for me, I'm pretty obsessive, so it means I attack anything which needs doing with a full-on barrage of raw enthusiasm.

After a few hours I get to a point at which I can't think about emails, paying bills, phoning friends, or even rooting about the fridge for something to eat.

At the end of a hard writing day I like to sit in a room lit with candles, and to turn my mind off so as to let it thaw. My kids always laugh at me when I'm in that state because I can't get through the complicated crime dramas they enjoy. Instead, I do what my father did when I myself was a child – I watch reruns of something I know inside out, like *Fawlty Towers*.

Sleep
When writing exceptionally long hours it's essential to

get a solid night's sleep. Anything less than seven hours is likely to lead to second-rate work the next day.

In my experience there's absolutely no point in even trying to write anything if your brain is tired. That's because reworking second-rate text produced by a tired brain is far harder than coming up with first-rate passages later.

Throughout the day I monitor my levels of energy. If I get a sense my brain is fatigued, I stop everything and go and take a siesta. When grinding away at long novels I've found myself taking three or four fifteen-minute siestas in the same day. What works for me is to get into bed, power down, and get to the point at which I've just nodded off. If I can wake up a few minutes after that, I'm completely re-energized.

The other use of sleep – especially siestas – is to glimpse the next phase of my story playing out in my mind's eye. I've used this technique in most of my novels, none more so than the *Jinn Hunter* books. I've found watching events take place on the stage of my mind works like nothing else.

Although I can never manage to remember entire dreams, I grab hold of individual details and fragments of storyline. Best of all, though, I love the way that when drifting into sleep, my mind makes associations. Remembering them as best I can, I weave them into the upcoming pages of my book.

Peaks, Troughs

There's absolutely no point in pushing writing output to the limit, so that what you're creating is coming out as mediocre. This sounds obvious but it's surprisingly easy to try and stay on the damned schedule at all costs. All of a sudden what you're turning out is shoddy because you're tired or drained of inspiration.

What I've found works is driving oneself very hard for a few days, then taking the foot off the production pedal just long enough to coast along for a while, before applying it hard again. As I've said elsewhere, when I start a book I'm relentless with production because it's far too easy to get sidetracked onto something else. You must get to the break-the-back stage before you can really allow yourself to coast – at least, that's what works for me.

The Ordinary

One afternoon I took a long, circuitous walk with a friend through the East End of London, back in the days when I lived there. I was ranting on about how I lived for oddity, and that normality bored me like nothing else. My friend turned to me and said:

'Never be afraid to embrace the ordinary.'

At the time I thought he was off his rocker. But, as the remark sank in and as I've progressed through my writing life, I realized how the comment was profound. The ordinary can be just as extraordinary as anything else. It's a matter of observing it though.

Turn the ordinary gently into the light, and allow it to shine.

In my earlier books I used to feature an ongoing rumpus of spectacular oddness and curiosity. But with time I've learned to slow down, and to observe what appears at first glance to be banal in new and mesmerizing ways.

Dyslexia

I drone on about dyslexia a great deal, probably because so few other writers do.

A stigma against dyslexics still prevails, although things are a whole lot better than when I was being punished at prep school for being so incompetent. I've released editions of my books in Open Dyslexic font (which is uneven, like text typed by a manual typewriter). And I myself use a whole range of homespun tricks to alleviate the effects of being so profoundly dyslexic.

These include getting my computer to read my text aloud, rather than struggling over reading it hour after hour. Another staple of mine is to set the background of the document I'm working on to grey, and to change the shade of it every day or so. I make bullet points in my notes, too, as they hone my focus, and of course I rely on spell correction like nothing else.

I encourage dyslexic writers to structure their work with mini ways to move forward and keep on track. But, most of all, I encourage them to take charge of their power of imagination.

In all likelihood it'll be second to none.

Spell Check

The spell correction on Microsoft Word, the program I write with, makes the life of dyslexic two-finger authors like me a whole lot better than it would be without it.

Even when I type fast, making loads of mistakes, they're underlined in red, or are simply corrected automatically. I have to admit though it drives me crazy when the spell correction doesn't recognize a word – or when it continually forces me to use American spelling (or British spelling if I'm using American variations). From time to time I play around with the settings, and get my computer to learn new words, but it invariably forgets them and resorts to what the Microsoft Mothership regards as right.

Grammar Check

While I favour spell check, grammar correction programs are my nemesis.

They're clearly not designed for anyone writing anything longer than a letter, and are certainly not intended for authors churning out books. I almost never have the grammar correction switched on, and if I do it's merely to laugh at the low quality of current programming.

No doubt over coming years AI will change the

editing landscape entirely... even to the point of getting computers to write novels from scratch.

Perish the thought.

Dry Stone Wall
I was raised in a house where dictionaries were regarded as sacred books. My father would always encourage us children to look a word up if we didn't know its meaning. My love of words came from him, as well as my appreciation for keeping vocabulary simple and sentences succinct.

In my study there's a shelf of excellent dictionaries. I enjoy selecting a specific dictionary for a particular kind of word. I have a couple of pictorial dictionaries, too, in which the names of almost anything you could ever imagine are illustrated. They're especially useful when I need the precise word for a little-known stretch of rigging on a pirate ship, a blacksmith's tool, or something like that. I urge anyone who takes writing seriously to always look words up. It never ceases to surprise me how celebrated writers misuse words, and how their editors don't catch the mistakes.

I regard the text I'm writing as if it were a dry stone wall running along a road.

The words are pieces of stone which have to fit perfectly if the wall's going to exist as long as I'm hoping it will. I take great pleasure in selecting a perfectly shaped word for the space it will occupy, so that it will shine by itself and sit well with the other words around it.

Although I am an admirer of printed dictionaries, I recommend keeping a computer's default dictionary open when writing. The one on my Apple Mac is exceptionally good, and usually provides a line or two of precious etymology as well.

Work in Progress
As I have said elsewhere, I rarely, if ever, show work in progress to anyone. Likewise, I prefer not to read anyone else's half-finished writing. If you're a new writer it's best not to ever send anything to established authors unless you have asked permission. I'm sent masses of work – both completed and in progress – and always find myself wishing people would hold off until the work is pristine and as clean as it can be.

When I was a little boy at Langton House, Greville the storytelling carpenter was eventually replaced by a handyman named Stephen. As I remember it, his father was a bishop who'd questioned his own faith. Stephen was not a storyteller but a mathematician. I'm not sure how he came to be working at Langton House, but as a child I wasn't interested in the route he'd taken so much as the fact he was there.

Round about the time Stephen appeared, I'd been given a huge book of puzzles by my favourite aunt, Amina. I would lie on the lawn on my stomach, doing my best to solve the puzzles. The ones I liked most of all were the mazes – some of which were very intricate indeed. I remember working away at the puzzles one afternoon while Stephen was mowing the lawn. I'd do a few more twists and turns with my pencil, then rush over, get Stephen to turn the mower's engine off, and show him what I'd done.

The first five or six times I bothered him, he was polite. After that point, his patience strained, he cried through gritted teeth:

'Why don't you come back and show me when you've finished?!'

I thought for a moment, and replied with uncharacteristic honesty:

'Because you wouldn't tell me how well I'm doing nearly as much.'

That's how it is when a writer sends out half-finished work. They do it because they want to be patted on the head and told they're marvellous. This may make me sound stern – possibly sterner than I actually am – but I think it illustrates my thinking, thinking which is the essence of this entire book.

Real writers don't write for praise, they do so because they're writing for themselves.

Real Readers
Real authors love real readers, and there's nowhere I've found better readers than the Goodreads site.

THE REASON TO WRITE

As I've said, I regard the job of the writer as being to write for themselves, and that of the publisher as nonsensical in this day and age. Likewise, I think 'real' readers – the kind who follow one's work over years and champion it – have an important role to play.

They are our sounding boards.

And the more of a spectrum of them you can muster, the more useful the sounding board becomes. I've always found that everyone reads in their own way, and that women read quite differently to men. Indeed, much of the time women seem to read more accurately than men. Of all the many thousands of emails and letters I've received over the years, by far the most articulate ones have been from women. They've noticed details and asked questions about themes and sub-themes, whereas the majority of male readers writing to me have asked broad-spectrum questions... questions which seek to elevate them by association.

Publicity Quotes

As with anything else, breaking into the world of writing is partly (or rather largely) about credibility. That means even if your work is amazing, you have to persuade others it is, too. As a species we are communal, and strive to mitigate risk.

What better way to do that than to follow what other survivors are doing? When I started writing books I spent a lot of time networking in order to get publicity quotes from established authors. At one stage my life was dedicated full-time to getting quotes.

Each time I got a choice quote, I'd drop it into the stew served up in letter form to someone else, a little higher up the food chain. A great many of the people I wrote to with gushing letters never responded.

Surprisingly, a lot of them did.

I'm not going to come across well by admitting to this ruse, but please take my honesty into account:

When in the desperate-need-for-publicity-quotes racket, I used to write to elderly authors and wax lyrical about their first published book. Most established authors go on to publish work far more impressive than their initial offering. But in every writer's heart there's a soft spot for the firstborn.

Where possible you're best off striking up a correspondence, rather than asking for a quotation outright in the first message. If you want to get good quotes you have to work up to it – flattery first and requests second. The best plan of action is always to try and get a mixture of quotes, as I did with my first book *Beyond the Devil's Teeth*. I sent the manuscript to everyone I could think of – including the Pope, three ex-US Presidents, twelve Olympians, nine Nobel Laureates, and even a serial killer.

The way I saw it, languishing on death row, he had time on his hands.

Writing Routines

My writing method is all about routines.

I'm going to come across as a nutcase here, but I swore an oath of honesty to myself before starting this book, so here goes:

When I sit down to write a book I like to have a clean run ahead of me, like a well-prepared ski slope – a slope I've never skied before. As with a skier ready to set off, I've studied the map and have planned a route. Despite the preparation, I'm aware there'll be unforeseen twists and turns, and patches where I have to jab my poles in and push really hard.

By nature I'm a creature of habit, and find nothing gets books written better or faster than routine. Some author friends inch forward little by little, taking months or even longer to complete a book. I prefer to rush headlong, so as to keep good continuity and, more importantly, to make sure that the book gets done.

Tricks of my trade include:

1. Have an outline on my desk, whether it's consulted or not.
2. Have a tally of what needs to be written on a particular day and work towards it.
3. Reward myself for a hard day at the grind – even if it's only a takeout burrito with extra-hot sauce.

At the same time I have certain objects on my desk when I'm writing. They change from book to book.

Sometimes they'll be a little pile of red paperclips, or three blue gel pens – which I'll have neatly lined up and will never use.

But the key part of my routine happens at the end of the writing day.

If I've hit my writing target I add the number of words to the overall tally, and hopefully have reason to gloat. Then I straighten everything out for the following morning. Before leaving my workroom, I write the next day's goal on a sticky note and place it squarely beside the keyboard.

Whatever ritual you come up with, use it to get the best out of yourself.

In my opinion, rituals are of no service except to make the ski down the mountain easier and more pleasurable to achieve.

Procrastination
Procrastination is part of the creative process.

However terrible it may seem, it's critically useful – because it's the dream zone proving that we need inspiration in order to create. There's a danger in trying to eliminate procrastination, one that may well lead to far less original and inspired work. My advice is to allow oneself regular structured procrastination breaks. Safe zones, they're when you can turn your phone on, guzzle espresso, stare out the window, and allow your mind to slip away into a faraway realm.

The way I see it, daydreaming and procrastination are the waking forms of nocturnal dreaming. As such, they are the place at which the blurred mind creates wonder by zoning out of focus.

I've written about Wikipedia elsewhere, and will touch on it again here. As I usually research information as I move ahead, I generally resort to checking material online, or in reference books kept to hand. What works for me is to write on a scrap of paper exactly what I need to know before embarking on the online search. Diving aimlessly into the enchanted Wikipedia pool is accompanied by the danger of never emerging intact.

Giving in to procrastination, I give myself a challenge. Setting a timer and an alarm, I try and dredge up ten choice nuggets of information online within fifteen minutes.

Gaps

One of the most pleasing times writing is when you're on a roll. All real writers know the feeling. To return to a skiing analogy again, it's like slaloming serenely down the mountain with the sun warming your face.

It's when you're a star, and everything's going oh-so-great.

But, ultimately, even the most skilled real writer hits a patch of ice.

You have to anticipate the rough ground and take immediate action – like a hospital emergency department with an action plan at the ready.

When in the middle of a book, I can usually ski around the patches of ice. This is because I'm worn in and ready for anything. But, especially in the early stages of a book, I get left high and dry like anyone else. The best thing to do is to leave three blank lines, and to come back to the trouble area later. The worst thing you can do is to drop everything and fall head first into a hole.

The other time to leave a gap is when you need to slot in a small chunk of detail – like the name of a particular pistol your protagonist has just grabbed from an enemy soldier at dusk. In my case, the Wikipedia monster perched on my right shoulder is begging me to allow him two minutes to check out high-end German-made armaments, the kind used by special forces.

I never let the monster go anywhere near the Internet.

We both know that two minutes will inevitably turn into an hour and a half of trawling the Wikipedia Wonderland.

Typing
Most of my close friends are writers and almost all of them are terrible typists.

Like me, the majority hammer out their books with two fingers.

My own excuse is that as a child I was given a pre-War Underwood Noiseless Typewriter to learn on. A great hulk of mechanical mastery, it sounded like a freight train clattering through the night towards the dawn. The noise wasn't the problem though, so much as the fact my young fingers couldn't apply sufficient pressure to get the keys to strike. So I ended up relying on my index fingers – as my father had done.

My grandfather, writer and savant The Sirdar Ikbal Ali Shah, who published seventy-four books, wrote them all by hand. My point is that it doesn't matter at all how you commit your work to paper. There'll always be a faster way to do it. But you are a creative writer not a copy typist. So speed isn't important.

It's true I get worked up with myself from time to time at making so many mistakes. But I'm using a computer, unlike my father's generation, which was clattering away on manual and then electric typewriters. If anything, two-finger typing allows me to stare vacantly at the keyboard, and for my mind to wander as I'm doing so. Although I'm half-looking at the keys, I do so no more than I need to. My focus is tuned in to the creative frequency that's feeding me the upcoming lines of text.

Breaking the Back
Get past the halfway mark of a book and you'll most likely get to the end.

In the books I have written I've always found different stretches vary in their difficulty or ease. The first few chapters are usually the most onerous for me.

Until I have the camber of the road worked out, I try too hard. But as I get into the swing of things, I find myself moving briskly forward. Get through the quicksand at the beginning, then up onto the wide plateau, and you'll probably be assured a good long run that'll take you to the other side of the halfway mark.

Get there in one piece and you will have broken the back of the book.

In my opinion this is the point to celebrate rather than when you write the last line. That's because the ending is a moment of sorrow, whereas the mid-point is proof you're on tip-top form.

Questioning
If there's one golden rule of book writing to nail up above your desk, it is:
NEVER QUESTION YOUR ABILITY!
They say if you want to dance like a pro you should practise as though no one is watching. The same is true for writing. If you want to take the craft to a whole new level, write as though no one will judge you. And remember to write for yourself.

Every time you question your ability, you smother the flame of creativity a little more. Remind yourself over and over you're amazing. If you ever doubt it, read a random page grabbed from your Shelf of Wretched Reads.

Remember this: the more you write, and the more differing projects you work on, the stronger your literary muscles and the greater your skill will be.

Writing is a journey which promises no clear destination.

Rather, it provides a route to beyond the far horizon that will be as magical as it is unexpected.

Experimenting

Writing is about being creative and experimenting, and is not about laying golden eggs all the time. The problem is that the established publishing model is fixated on making money through selling as many books as possible.

As a result, editors and marketing teams will never green-light anything that's unlikely to pay their salaries.

The one thing publishers detest more than anything else is risk.

As far as they're concerned experimenting is **RISK** – in bold capital letters, underlined. They want travel writers to be writing travel, novelists to be writing novels, and everyone else to be working away in their groove. A publisher's best-case scenario is for their stable of enslaved authors to be writing the same book over and over, so as to extract every ounce of gold from the mother-lode.

Writer's Block

Writer's block is a subject I find myself questioning.

I'll explain why.

I was raised in the company of people who wrote professionally. Almost every one of them saw themselves as a basket weaver, a carpenter, or as part of a creative guild. They created to sell their wares in the market, but foremost so as to please themselves.

I once asked Doris for her opinion on writer's block.

She said: 'There's no need to ever get that condition at all. The way to steer clear of it is to think of yourself as a conduit channelling water from the mountains down to the village on the plain. Even though you are the pipe, forget that you are, and concentrate instead on the water flowing through you.'

All Talk

In my opinion writers should write and not talk.

By that I mean they shouldn't be ranting on at dinner parties or to strangers in the Starbucks queue about how they're working on the next big literary thing. By talking, you sap your creative energy and lose the most precious thing of all – literary spontaneity, the magic dust of creativity. Even though you may have planned a book down to the last comma, the joy of writing is going off-piste and delighting yourself with the ride.

First Book

When you haven't written a book before you'll find telling people about it will elicit a frenzy of mostly nonsensical opinions.

Some people will rant on that you're not up to it, or that you'd be better off getting a day job. Others will damn you with faint praise, and sow the seed of doubt. The only way to shut them all up is to finish the book and then write another, and another.

Until you've got to the end of the first book and had it published, it's best to surround yourself with people who share a belief in your skill. I'm not sure why, but general society seems structured towards doubt rather than enthusiasm.

I remember writing the first paragraph of my very first book, thinking to myself:

'It's never again going to be harder than this.'

And it wasn't.

Starting Afresh

As with everything else, starting new projects differs from writer to writer.

The very best time to start writing a new book is the day you finish writing one. Having just typed in the words 'The End', you're probably at the top of your game in terms of enthusiasm and self-confidence. More importantly, the journey through the just-finished book has got you fabulously warmed up.

My advice is to have a new book planned out and ready while you're writing the last third of the current book. There's no question you won't finish the book you're working on, as you've already broken the back of it. Given this, allow yourself a day of change. Use it to work out a new storyline, characters, and nail down a reason to write it – one that'll keep you sucked in over the weeks to come.

Then, in the two or three days before finishing the current project, start making the shift in your head. Obviously, don't make the shift so greatly that you lose the momentum needed to get to the finish line.

Then, on the final day, write the ending of the book at hand.

Congratulate yourself, take a deep breath, and tap out the opening paragraph of the next book...

First footsteps towards the next horizon.

Vocabulary Variety
In writing a book. it's easy to run out of fresh words. It sounds crazy, but it happens.

What I mean is that you find you've used all the obvious adjectives and nouns (the low-hanging literary fruit), and to use them again within a stretch of a few pages would be repetition.

There's nothing wrong with repetition, especially if it means keeping things fast-flowing. And I'm not for a moment suggesting using overly obscure words rather than repeating common ones.

My rule of thumb is that if I've used a word twice on the same page, it's easiest to swap it for something else at the first usage. If a thesaurus can't get you a suitable alternative, you may have to resort to changing the sentence construction.

If you've used the same word three times on a page then try changing the second usage.

Ticking Over
The hardest thing to do in the book-writing business is to get back into the saddle when you haven't been writing for a while. Always remember that however long you've left it, you can get back to where you were.

No question of that.

Have faith in yourself and you should be able to slip back within a few pages. The key thing is not to read those initial 'brown water' pages back and judge yourself on them.

Instead, keep writing.

If at all possible, don't allow yourself to cool down, because warming up takes time and causes anxiety.

A great way to stay primed up is to write regular letters or emails packed with anecdotes to family and friends. What I tend to do (I'm rather embarrassed to admit this) is to write the same anecdote to a dozen people. Each time I write it, I polish it a little more, or turn it into the light in a new way. By doing this I create a kind of sampler, an experimentation.

And, most importantly of all, I get that warm glow of satisfaction, even if it's in a micro way.

The Tingle
The tingle down the spine you get while reading back what you've written is what writers dream of – or at least I do.

When I started out, it was hit and miss, or rather *miss, miss, miss*.

Then, little by little I learned what ingredients to throw together into the stew in order to get the effect I was after.

There's no sure-fire way to elicit the tingle. I find myself comparing the tingle with making wine. Although vintners rely on good soil, water, grapes, and decades of experience, the final product comes down to something bordering more on alchemy than on science.

The other point to note is there are different kinds of tingle.

A good one is when you've just written something and read it back for the first time.

A better one is when you get it on reading the passage typeset.

The best tingle of all is experienced when reading a book you wrote decades ago.

Thinking Big
Something rooted deep inside me has always urged me to think big, or rather bigger than big.

I just can't help myself.

It would be so much easier for me to drift through life beavering away at small projects, but the universe has conspired for me to reach far and high. As a result of this delusional calibration, I have dozens of books in the pipeline at any one time.

It's worth remembering here that I am writing for myself. And, although it will always be published, I have no intention to please readers or publishers – only myself.

The great thing about releasing work directly as I do is that you can design projects from the ground up and grow them in entirety, exactly as you want. In the same way that Andy Warhol had 'The Factory', the writer who releases work directly can experiment on any scale they like, trying their hand at any genre or technique.

By keeping a grip on how you want your body of work to be shaped and released, you have the ability to succeed in doing what few, if any, writers have been able to do for two hundred years.

Reading Aloud

A lot of these notes could easily be passed by, but this one is especially important.

Just as people read books in different ways, the same page can seem quite different depending on how the same person reads it. You may not realize it, but when you read text in your head you're doing so in a third-rate way.

Try reading your work aloud.

It alters the dynamic completely, providing a sense of tempo which silent reading can never even come close to achieving. It will highlight the bumps in the road, pointing out faulty construction and grammar.

Best of all though, reading a work in progress aloud (to yourself rather than to an audience) will remind you that you have what it takes to be the real writer you're dreaming of being.

Dedications

My father rarely if ever dedicated his work, but my grandfather liked nothing more than doing so. The majority of his books are dedicated to those who helped or inspired him.

When it comes to dedications, I go through phases.

Over the years I've dedicated books to members of my family, close friends, and to a handful of others. When I dedicate a work, I don't simply think of a name to type in at the front.

I write that book for the person.

Putting a photograph of them on my desk, I keep it there and turn to it endlessly as I go. As I proceed, I think about that person as much as I do the book's storyline.

Whispering

This is something I've never actually spoken about, and so have no idea whether it's normal or if I'm stark raving mad. As I progress, formulating sentences in my head, ferrying them down to my fingers to type, I whisper them under my breath as I go. If they sound right in the whisper, then they're likely to read right on the page.

Book Launches
Twenty years ago, most writers did book launches.

They were opportunities for self-praise and celebration. I've noticed that, as the fortunes of publishers have nosedived, and as the power of the Internet has soared, fewer and fewer real writers do launches any longer. This may well be due to the fact authors now have fans all over the world, and that virtual launches make more sense.

I haven't done a book launch in almost a decade. The reason isn't that I've become jaded with publishers, but because I prefer to spend my time writing books rather than having to make small talk over mouthwash wine.

Signings
Unlike book launches – which I'm generally down on – book signings fulfil a function.

The bookshop will order in copies of your work and do their best to lure their regular clientele to an event. They usually ask a writer to say a few words, after which your latest offering is piled high for the attendees to buy and for you to sign.

The great thing about books made for sale at events is that they can't be returned to the publisher once they've been signed. While you're at a bookshop for a signing, make sure you sign any copies of your book which went unsold.

Festivals

Although in recent years book launches have waned, literary festivals have gone from strength to strength. The most popular festivals, like the one at Cheltenham, have been franchised, with their subsidiaries spanning the world.

I'm always surprised how even the bestselling authors out there get coerced into doing the festival circuit. I suppose many of them don't have a choice. After all, most are owned lock, stock, and barrel by their publishers.

All that, of course, is changing fast.

Pipeline

I've described how I tend to keep the pipeline of projects well filled.

A packed pipeline is incredibly important to me because it means I stay productive. I'm manic when it comes to feeding the pipeline with book ideas. At any one time I'll have dozens of ideas ready to go. Some of them may never see the light of day, while others will start as one thing and eventually become something else.

The pipeline is something I tend to keep to myself

because I don't want to hear anyone's opinion on what direction I ought to take.

Beating Oneself Up
In other books I've written about how my life is constructed on a bedrock of guilt.

I feel guilt-ridden at raiding the fridge in the middle of the night, at watching daytime TV, at buying as many useless gadgets as I do on Amazon, and at not producing as much work as I should.

This last reason for guilt hangs heavy over me much of the time.

There's a devil on my shoulder cracking a whip, lambasting me for what he insists is such a derisory output. Some days – especially when it's grey outside – I feel shell-shocked and broken. I know it's absurd, but it happens again and again.

Please learn from the way I tear into myself needlessly and see it doesn't serve any productive use at all. If you can manage to be a ship sailing towards a distant horizon over a glassy sea, then you'll succeed no matter what.

Letters
From time to time I've written series of letters between characters (such as in my novel *Timbuctoo*). I've resorted to letters especially when I wasn't quite sure how to add depth to characters. I adore writing letters, and so setting myself the task of conjuring

them in a voice other than my own gives me enormous satisfaction.

Conventional publishers tend to strike a long red diagonal editorial line through letters because they tend to believe the technique breaks up a narrative.

On the contrary, my thinking is that letters complement a text, especially if a correspondence is peppered through an entire book.

Gut-think

Like many authors, I get hundreds of emails a week from people asking for advice.

Most of the time my overriding suggestion is not what new writers want to hear. But I dispense it all the same...

Follow your gut.

Think about it for a moment.

You know what you like, what you want to say, and where you want to go. You can lay it all down for me to see, but I'm still never going to get the same three-dimensional grasp of the situation you have right now. Certainly talk to people, ask them for their thoughts, but only do so once you've really examined how you feel yourself.

Stop being frightened about what an agent or publisher will think.

To hell with them!

What matters is YOU.

The book you're going to write will be in your voice,

and your voice alone, so it should be a book written by following your gut.

Clatter

My childhood was played out to the sound of a typewriter clattering down in my father's study. As I've often said, the noise never stopped, not for a minute. That's the reason my father left millions of words of print, and at least as much again to be released in the decades after his death.

When I once asked him what the tools of a writer were, he held up his index fingers.

'These are my tools,' he said. 'If they stop working, and that machine over there stops clattering, then the books stop getting written.'

I often think of the comment.

And when I am working, I listen to the sound of my fingers typing. Tapping away on a keyboard may be less noisy than on a typewriter, but it's essentially the same thing. There's nothing quite so delicious as seeing letters slipping onto a screen. Forming into words, they're like droplets of mercury fusing together...

Words conjured from the furthest reaches of an author's imagination.

Gunpoint

One of the most pressing questions I have about human society is why, when it comes to creative people, such low expectations prevail. We're reminded endlessly of the household names – the Shakespeares, Hugos, Tolstoys and Goethes – but we're never expected to rival them in the quality or quantity of our own output. It's as if they're in a separate pantheon of their own, and God help anyone who thinks they have even an outside chance at creating anything half as good.

The literary world's dumbing down of anyone trying to break into the world of writing leads to chronically low self-esteem. I've met a great many aspiring authors who don't push themselves because they're just too fearful – of agents, publishers, critics, and readers, too.

Twenty years ago I inherited a box of papers left by my grandfather, The Sirdar Ikbal Ali Shah. Inside I found a treasure trove of material – most of it notes from his travels through Arabia in the 1930s. On a little scrap of paper I found a single line typed out, and saved it – as though it were exceedingly important.

It said:

WRITE AS THOUGH A GUN
IS POINTING TO YOUR HEAD

As chance would have it, my Swedish film crew and I were arrested in Pakistan shortly afterwards. Blindfolded and manacled, we were taken to a torture prison, where we spent sixteen dreadful days and nights. Early during the ordeal I was dragged outside in the middle of the night.

A pistol was pressed against the side of my head, and

THE REASON TO WRITE

I was told the end of my life had come. As it turned out, the execution was a mock one, laid on to destabilize me... which it did.

The reason I mention it here is that, although intensely unpleasant, having a gun at my head did wonders to focus my thoughts.

Last week a writer friend asked me why I feel it necessary to churn out so much work. I replied it was because I pretend there's a gun to my head and that if I don't grind away – as many other writers should or at least could be doing – the trigger will be pulled.

'Yeah, but it's OK for you, isn't it?' my friend snapped.

'In what way?'

'Well, you've got a first-rate sense of imagination, so you can just close your eyes and see it.'

'See what?'

'See the gun at your head.'

'This is one case in which no imagination is necessary,' I replied.

Steenbeck
My friend, the film-maker Leon Flamholc, was trained to edit movies on a flatbed editing machine known as a 'Steenbeck'.

A complex series of spools routed the film in such a way that the editor could splice exactly where wanted. Leon used to describe the process of editing on a Steenbeck. He would say it was so complex he never imagined ever being able to master the machine.

But with time he became an expert.

'I used to look down at my hands working so fast that they were blurred,' he once explained. 'It was as if I was completely detached, as though they weren't my hands at all.'

When I asked Leon for the secret of mastering the Steenbeck, he said:

'The only way to conquer it was to do it without thinking. If I thought too hard then I'd lose concentration and film would fly out everywhere!'

The same goes for writing books.

Do it in the right way and the book gets written. Think about it too much and you'll get sucked down into the vortex, and your precious work will end up on the mountain of books that were never written.

Parking a Project
One of the things I've been good at in my writing career is finishing the books I start.

There's no doubt it's easier to hammer out a book when it's been commissioned, and all the more pleasing when you've been paid a big fat advance.

From time to time I've stopped working on a book and parked it. There's no shame at all in stopping work on a book, even when it's well advanced.

The key thing is to place it into a holding pattern, so that you return to it when you're ready. If you find yourself having to halt, make a clear mental note of why you are stopping and how you got into the predicament you're in.

Before moving on to something else, make a vow to yourself to go back to the parked project when you're ready.

Commitment

One of my friends is an exceptional linguist. He speaks at least ten languages fluently, and sucks up foreign grammar and vocabulary like a sponge. One evening at a dinner I drew attention to his remarkable ability to master new languages. Rather than taking the compliment quietly he barked something that's stayed with me:

'The reason I learn languages as I do,' he said, 'is because I put in twelve hours a day hard grind. People always assume I'm some kind of linguistic miracle-worker, but I'm not. The difference between me and all the others who fail at a new language is commitment, and nothing else!'

The same couldn't be more true for book writing.

Almost everyone I meet tells me they dream of having their name on the cover of a book. The answer is they could easily do it, especially given the new publishing technology, but that most of them will fail because they aren't ready to apply themselves.

Dialogue
Some authors smother their dialogue with scaffolding and supports. I am drawn to conversation which is clear, sharp, and has the strength to stand on its own. My suggestion is to lay it as bare as possible, and to trim away anything preventing the words from being heard.

I remember reading Bruce Chatwin's dialogue for the first time and thinking to myself, 'Hoorah! I can hear the characters rather than the writer!' Chatwin achieved this (and I have copied him in almost all my books) by stripping a conversation down to the bare metal.

What works for me is to use a standard set-up for dialogue that's hopefully so subtle the reader hardly even notices it. The structure is no more than a picture frame holding the picture, and is in itself unimportant.

Learning the Ropes
The main reason authors stress about their work is inexperience. In the same way, the very best method of gaining the experience needed to craft different kinds of work is to experiment.

As I said earlier, I was at one time stressed beyond belief at the thought of writing a fight scene. So what I did was to study the best fight scene I could find. It's from the screenplay of *The Princess Bride*, in which Westley duels with Inigo Montoya.

Studying it, and observing it in an almost clinical way, I worked out why the scene was such a triumph on all levels. I've done the same for every challenge that hits my desk – whether it be for description, dialogue, plot structure, or any other element of the writing process.

Priming

I find the first thousand words of the day are the hardest to get down. It's as though the water pipe has got blocked up in the night, and that every little thing adds to the logjam.

I've isolated two clear ways to get around this, enabling forward movement.

The first is to prime myself by writing something purely pleasurable – like an email or a long descriptive letter to an old friend. I only start this having read the last page of work, so that my mind is grinding away in the background, thinking about the book at hand. Or if I'm working on a novel, I might write a letter from one character to another, even if I don't have any plan to ever use it in the manuscript. After five or six hundred words I'm in my stride, and am ready to get back to the coalface.

The other priming mechanism I use all the time is to finish a day in the writing chair by setting things up well for the next morning. This entails not only getting the desk tidied up, but leaving the coalface prepped. Even though I'll be in my flow at the end of a day, ready to write almost anything with relative ease, I'll stop short.

As though poised at the top of a steep hill, I'll leave it, to ski down first thing in the morning.

Loving Writing
This may sound crazy, but there's only one reason to write:
BECAUSE YOU LOVE IT
If you don't love it – and I mean REALLY love it – then there's no reason to do it. Agreed, a lot of the time an author's lot is a rough one, fraught with uncertainty and doubt. But it's one of the most extraordinarily creative mediums humanity has yet devised.

In the years I've been writing I have at times found myself forced to do work which bores me senseless. This has included many hundreds of magazine pieces, and a guidebook that reduced me to a whimpering lump of despair.

Even though I was kicking and screaming at the time, each challenge taught me something of great value – forcing me to think in new ways. The more material I've written and published, the more I've found myself on a wide sprawling plateau...

The Plateau of Sublime Fulfilment.

Standing in the middle of it I feel happy in a deep-down way, as if writing is a best friend, one who's always with me. Get to that point, think of writing as a saviour rather than a demon to be tamed, and your work changes in a profound and inexplicable way.

THE REASON TO WRITE

Literary Seeds

As real writers we are on the lookout for fragments of inspiration, curiosity, and wonder that can be woven into the pages we write.

When it comes to unearthing intriguing details and information, I've always had a pretty good sense. Whether I like it or not my ears and my eyes are always honed in.

For instance, last night I was reading the news online when a curious photo caught my eye: a well-known river in the south-west of England had turned fluorescent blue. Droves of scientists were doing their best to work out the cause of the change in colour.

At seeing the picture many people might have raised an eyebrow before moving on. But the image rooted itself in my mind – just as the one of prosthetic eyes had done. So I noted it down and worked out how to use it... naturally as a mysterious machination of a rogue jinn.

Contracts

First-time authors are invariably so excited to get a publishing deal, they're ready to sign anything if it means their manuscript is magically transformed into a published book.

Any established writer is likely to dish out the same advice as I'm about to do:

Get a professional to look through the contract and make sure you're protected.

If you have an agent, it's their job to fight your corner.

If you don't have an agent, it's worth joining an association like the Society of Authors, which reviews contracts. The good thing about them is that they tend to be impartial, and are in a position to give advice on how your contract reads compared with others they've seen from the same publisher.

As you can imagine, contracts are all about the terms, and getting the most favourable terms possible.

Advances and royalties are the main meat of the contract business, but there are plenty of smaller clauses you can get amended relatively easily. For example, mainstream publishers tend to offer an author a derisory number of printed books – often as few as six. I've always insisted on getting at least forty copies of every edition. Publishers almost always cave in on author copies as it's something which costs them next to nothing.

Contracts can be a minefield as all kinds of sneaky clauses can be buried deep.

The first key point to beware of is the reversion of rights. This means if your book goes out of print the rights come back to you. Until recently this wasn't an issue, because publishers had to choose to reprint a stock of the title, or not. But now, with print-on-demand (POD), what publishers do is to put their backlists on the POD system – so that technically they'll never go out of print. As a result, well-meaning authors are locked into the contract forever.

Another tricky clause to watch out for relates to territories. If you're a first-time author, especially one without an agent, the publisher is going to want to suck up all the rights in all territories.

If you have an agent, they will probably want to break the rights of your work down and sell them off bit by bit, like slices of pizza. The more foreign and subsidiary rights they dispose of, the more cold hard cash they make.

When signing a contract, my advice is to only part with British, American, or whatever rights apply to the territory in which you live. Try to keep hold of the other rights, and don't be afraid to cross out wording you don't like. Later on, if the book does well, you could stand to make many times your initial advance through selling foreign rights.

Foreign Rights

I was going to say a good literary agent is the person to sell foreign rights. But times are changing, and they're changing fast!

There are plenty of agents who are lousy at selling foreign rights – largely because they are concentrating on fewer books, but bigger ones. If your book falls into a particular genre – such as chick-lit, fantasy, or detective fiction – you'd do well to spend some time online checking the market out.

All over the world there's an abundance of literary festivals and book fairs at which key publishers in specific genres are represented. Even if you don't have time and money to get to one of these gatherings, you will find the names of the participating publishers, agents, and authors online.

Foreign-language publishers can be found at most book fairs and are generally quite happy to deal directly with English-language authors. They're always on the lookout for published books whose foreign rights are available.

Film Rights and Options
Foreign rights can be a nice little earner, just as selling the film option can be a gravy train which runs on and on.

An option is essentially a fee paid to lock down your book for a given length of time while a producer tries to raise the finances to make it into a movie. I know dozens of writers, almost all of whom have sold options time and again. Having said that, in very few cases has the movie actually been produced.

Reviews
There was a time when book reviews were everything, and book reviewers were treated like royalty.

In the old days a book would get a tiny window of attention – in which it had to be hyped, reviewed, and piled high in shops.

As with so much, Amazon rewrote the rule book.

There's no longer the manic need to get media attention for a newly launched book in a single week as there used to be. Reviews are still important for writers (especially if they're favourable), but not necessarily newspaper reviews.

More important these days are websites like Goodreads and others where real readers congregate and share their thinking on new and existing work.

The only reason to want reviews in leading media sources is to extract choice publicity quotes to put on the back of a new edition.

As already noted, print-on-demand platforms make it very easy to update book covers at the drop of a hat with a splash of good publicity.

A last point worth making concerns book reviews themselves.

Although I personally steer clear of reading reviews – whether they're good or bad – even unfavourable reviews sell books.

Dictating

When working on my novel *Hannibal Fogg and the Supreme Secret of Man*, I was writing such long hours I got to a point at which I couldn't get out of the chair.

For my back, and my sanity, I downloaded a dictation program, so I could speak the book onto the screen. Curiously, I found the dictation software could only keep up when the sentences were complicated. When dictating simple sentences, the program got hopelessly confused. Even though my typing is terrible, I eventually got so frustrated with the dictation program that I ditched it and went back to two-finger typing.

Agents

In the days of sky-high book advances, literary agents had a key role to play, and they played it well.

As much showmen as they were anything else, they could conjure the smell of the bacon... or, rather, the scent of a bestseller-to-be.

A handful of years ago publishing had reached a point at which publishers were getting so many submissions that most insisted that authors go through an agent. That was the moment at which agents became gatekeepers, their self-importance mushrooming overnight.

The key point about agents is that they are working for you.

As such, you mustn't be frightened to hire and fire – even though they act as though they're doing you a favour... which they're not.

Unless you've just written the biggest blockbuster fantasy novel in history, an agent will never go into battle for you against a publisher. This is because, while they're trying to sell your masterwork to the editorial and marketing teams, they're also trying to offload dozens of other authors on their books.

The only certainty regarding agents is that in publishing's brave new world there'll be no place for them at all.

Blithering Idiots

Commissioning editors are supposed to edit.

That may sound pretty obvious, but it's not.

Although editors did tend to edit until a few years ago, and were often mini potentates in their own right, they're largely sidelined now from their original role. These days most editors do very little hands-on editing – which is more often than not farmed out to freelancers. The result is that, physically speaking, books have turned from being content-based to container-based. Shaped by marketing teams, they've become blaring bling-bling objects that scream out at you like packets of breakfast cereal, rather than works of literary merit.

Now, in its last days, the marketing departments hold the real power in the existing model. They have the final word on whether to buy a manuscript, the author's advance, how and when the book will be launched, priced, and what it'll look like.

What I'm about to say next isn't going to win me any friends in the publishing world, but I've long since passed the point at which I cared.

So here it is, loud and clear:

For decades, mainstream publishing has given jobs

to people my father used to call 'blithering idiots'. Tens of thousands of them over numerous generations. Nice people, but blithering and idiotic all the same – just like those who were once dispatched to the farthest corners of the empire because they were so incapable.

The existing model – the one that's creaking, straining, and collapsing – sees publishers release tens of thousands of books a year. Almost everything published is destined to fail, with millions of tonnes of newly printed books pulped every year. There's no other line of business I can think of with such a poor return on products.

Publishers may rant that only they have the track record to select books which will be winners. Absolute nonsense, of course. In their desperation to make mountains of cash, they commission work which is as wretched to read as it is badly printed.

In the brave new world where self-released books are the norm, readers will find themselves feasting on the most extraordinary stories available – stories that don't tick any of the boxes existing publishers hold dear...

Stories which are fresh, original, and unlike anything anyone has read before.

Literary Prizes
Near the end of her life, our family friend, the novelist Doris Lessing, won a Nobel Prize for Literature. Although bemused, she wasn't overly impressed – with

the award, the insatiable media attention, or the way the honour recalibrated perceptions of her.

Although I was living in Morocco at the time Doris won the Nobel, I used to drop by and see her whenever I visited England. Her home at 24 Gondar Gardens in London's West Hampstead overflowed with cats, books, and mess.

One afternoon, while sitting at the kitchen table, Doris moaned about the 'damned medal' as though it had brought nothing but trouble. She explained that the prize prevented her from writing, and had allowed the worst kind of people to beat a path to her door.

'The Nobel Prize isn't about me,' she said in an uncharacteristically forlorn voice, 'it's Nobel and nothing else.'

In the years since Doris departed, I've thought about that comment frequently.

She was so incredibly right.

Secret of Writing
When my father had been writing books for thirty years, he said he had something to pass on to me.

I asked what it was.

'The Secret of Writing,' he said.

'What is it?'

'Anecdotes.'

'*Anecdotes*? Is that it?'

'Yes.'

'Why?'

'Because anecdotes are stories and, however hard they try, humans can't resist them. Fill your books with anecdotes and two things will happen. The first is that the books will write themselves. The second is that your readers will devour your work as though it's a delicious sweetmeat.'

Now I'm the one who's been writing books for thirty years, and it's I who've just passed the advice on to my own children – Ariane and Timur.

Cologne

In this book I've included a lot of tricks of the trade I live by. They're very much *my* tricks of the trade though, which I've developed over many years.

This entry is especially close to my heart and is one I swear by. Having said that, it's something I've never told anyone before.

When sitting down to write a new book, I place a bottle of cologne to the right of my computer screen. In most cases it's not my preferred cologne. Indeed, quite often it's a scent I dislike, perhaps a bottle someone gave me for Christmas which got tidied away into a cupboard under the sink.

Before I start working each morning, I dab a few drops of the cologne on the inside of my wrists, breathe the aroma into my lungs, close my eyes, relax, and then begin...

Two or three times through the day I'll open the bottle, dab a few drops, smell it with closed eyes, while I recalibrate.

Like many people I am very sensitive to smells, and find that rooting a project to a particular scent enables me to slip back easily into the writing zone.

I know of writers who play a favourite piece of music before they get down to work, or others who eat a handful of nuts or dates. Whatever the ritual, the effect should return one's mind to the point at which creation begins.

Grammar

I don't remember being drilled in grammar at school – possibly because I was so zoned out. But I'm pretty sure no one ever bothered to teach it in English class, although they did in the endless Latin lessons.

His monocle in place, Major Smith used to bark a sentence in Latin, and we'd have to provide the English translation for fear of being beaten. The result was that I learned English grammar as a kind of by-product of dissecting the Latin grammar, as part of the process of translating into English.

Writing prose is a chance to break the rules they tried to grind into me at school. Knowing the rules allows me to break them all the more effectively. Where possible, I do my best to keep sentence structure straightforward. Of course I vary it so as not to put my readers to sleep, but I find that writers who perform endless grammatical pirouettes risk no one accessing their work in a meaningful way.

Chess
A friend who is an especially gifted chess player once commented to me that 'there's always one move that's right, far more so than any other'. The comment has rooted in my mind, not so much for chess – a game in which I do not excel – but for writing.

Authors sit at their desks creating text from letters, words, and paragraphs.

In the course of a day we are faced with thousands of choices...

Choices of a particular word, grammatical structure, punctuation, or literary techniques by which to deliver the story. As I flick through the various possibilities I find myself remembering the chess player's advice – that there's always a right move.

In most cases, there is.

To unearth it, you have to twist the construction into the light, observing it from different angles.

No Clones
Early in my journey as a writer I discovered something which sounds so obvious no one would ever mention it:

The fact that no two words have the same meaning.

When trawling through a thesaurus for an alternative

way to describe something, I bear it in mind. The joy of the English language is the vast variety of similar words, each one very slightly different from the last.

Value of Words

Although I wasn't taught much grammar at school, I had an English master who was obsessed with précis. He'd get his students to distil great chunks of text down to no more than a handful of lines. At the time it was a task we all loathed, but one which taught me something very useful – the value of words.

The same value was reinforced in my days as a feature writer. If you submitted more than they asked for, editors would go nuts. So I learned the skill of packing as much meat in as possible while trimming away unnecessary fat.

Reading, Writing

People imagine that reading and writing are two parts of the same skill, and that if you're a real writer you are a real reader as well. In my experience I've found reading and writing are completely separate endeavours. Those who read voraciously are not necessarily the same as those who have the skill to write.

This is a matter I dwell on a great deal, particularly as I'm such a slow reader. Everyone expects me to be ploughing my way through dozens of books a week, whereas I simply can't.

Despite my painfully slow reading ability, I'm a fount of creativity, and can easily knock out a blockbuster novel in three weeks.

The point I'd like to make is to forget what others say or think.

You are how you are.

The task before you is to study yourself, see what works and what doesn't work – and use the tools at your disposal to weave literary cloth.

Publishing Runes

As I've said elsewhere, publishers only spend money on publicizing a book if they have shelled out precious funds by way of an advance.

Similarly, they won't dish out an advance of any size until they've consulted with the publishing runes.

Just as everything else in our data-ridden lives, book sales are measured in the most absurdly accurate way. The data collection company, Nielsen, produce a series of statistics known as BookScan, and it's these which are the runes.

In the old days an editor may well have taken a gamble on an unusual book. But publishers ceased their casino ways years ago. Before an editor commissions a book, or buys a finished one in, they'll check the author's previous sales figures. And if the book is on a specific subject, they'll check how other recent titles in the genre have done.

The danger is, of course, that if your previous titles sold modestly, the marketing team are unlikely to sanction a big fat advance.

The one intriguing thing is when a writer has no track record at all. It's rather like *Being There*, the movie in which Peter Sellers stars as Chance the gardener who's lived in isolation his entire life. There's no dirt on him, which means he's the perfect candidate to be president. In the same way, a first-time author is in an extraordinary position.

With no BookScan figures on you, you're a clean sheet.

Tweaking

Although most writers have their own preferred system of writing and editing, the majority rely on some form of tweaking. I get the first draft down so it's there, as if chipped out onto stone. Once it's down no one can take it away from me, and it's then I can start tweaking.

What I've found works best is to go through the first draft in a micro way, beavering at each sentence until it's balanced. After that I usually tend to go through it again, and then a third time, before having an editor make corrections.

During the process, the text changes considerably, as individual words are updated and the structure of the sentences is tweaked.

To give a limited idea of what I mean, I'll write a

couple of sentences below and rework them as I would when editing:

Draft 1
Wilson Marfott was a grim-faced man of fifty, who had no time or interest when it came to dogs. He lived in a lean-to at the edge of the woods, and drank a tumbler of Scotch on the porch each evening as dusk melted into night.

Draft 2
A grim-faced man of fifty, Wilson Marfott had no time or interest for people or for dogs. His home was a shack at the edge of the woods on whose porch he would sit, watch the world, and think. Leaning back on his chair he'd sip from a tumbler of Scotch as afternoon slipped towards dusk, and dusk into night.

Draft 3
A grim-faced man of fifty, Wilson Marfott had no time or interest for people or for dogs. His home was a shack at the edge of the woods. On its porch he would sit, watch the world, and remember his youth. Leaning back on his chair, he'd stare out sipping whiskey, the afternoon slipping towards dusk, dusk into night.

Finishing Up

We've all known would-be writers who rant on and on how they're working on a book.

Most of the time they're in need of attention and have no real plans to write a book at all. And that's fine by me. But I wish they'd do something that would cut to the chase instead and get them the attention they so badly need.

Once in a long while I've started a book but not finished it. The way I see it, crossing the finish line is part of the book-writing arc. By setting out on the adventure of writing a book you're entering into a solemn covenant with yourself. It's true that with the conventional publishing model, the covenant (or rather the contract) is usually with the publisher.

But in my experience there's nothing quite so momentous as making a pact with oneself. As for keeping going, my advice is to make every writing day an adventure, and enjoy every line. If you're not loving the writing process, you're in danger of putting your readers to sleep. And, rather than training your gaze on the finish line, focus on the distant horizon instead. Work towards the far-off destination, and stop thinking about it and how much there is to do.

My overall advice is to know where you want the story to end and to work towards it, even if you're not quite sure of the overall plot. When possible, I like to link the ending back to the beginning, although you can't use that trick every time.

I like to have a delicious final line in my head, or at least a scene which caps everything off. Then again, it's also fun to end at another beginning.

The last pages of a book are an exercise in fitting the final pieces into a jigsaw puzzle.

For days and weeks of the writing process it's been plain sailing. You can slot in random ideas, dialogue, procrastinations and deviations, but suddenly you find yourself on the home straight. That means you have to wake up and move deftly to cover the bases necessary to draw it all together.

As I near the ending of a book I usually come up with a final line – the end equivalent to the foundation stone that started my story. Sometimes I'll print the line out and tape it to my computer monitor, working my way towards it as I go.

There's such satisfaction writing the final page of a book, working your way to the last line which fits as perfectly as the final fragment of a puzzle.

Although I tend to write books quite fast, doing my best to keep up momentum, I like to savour the last page or two – writing the text with extra special care. I never attempt the last strides until my brain is well rested, and I know exactly what I want to say, and how I want to say it.

Any fool can start a book, but it takes real skill to end one.

PART IV

DIRECT PUBLISHING

Promised Land

ALTHOUGH I'VE LEFT this section until now, in some ways it ought perhaps to have come first.

That's because we're living at a time when publishing is changing, and it's changing FAST. If you've read through the rest of this book you'll have a pretty good idea of my strong opinions on publishers and the writing craft.

You will know that – as I see it – writing got shunted off the rails it was happily coasting along, and that it's morphed into the most monstrous machine... a machine which works against real writers like you and me, and promotes containers rather than contents.

This morning, while going against all the advice I've meted out to others, I found myself slaloming through Wikipedia on the trail of a fact that needed checking. Next thing I knew, I was reading a piece on the history of electric cars.

With great interest, I learned how the very first commercial car with an electric motor was produced in Des Moines back in 1891.

I can imagine you're scratching your head, wondering what I'm going on about.

It's this...

In the same way we are only now getting back to electric car technology after the internal combustion engine has destroyed half the known world, the standard publishing model is set for the same full-circle change.

What I care about is that the original books are written, rather than more and more third-rate clones of what's sold before. Beyond that, I care about all the real writers who have been locked out of the system until now.

The original model of book writing – in which authors created work and released it directly to the public – is back. And it's back in a way our author foremothers and forefathers could have only ever dreamt of experiencing.

Even as I write this, new technologies are conspiring to make it easier for creative people to release work in incredible new ways. An overwhelming disdain for publishers appears to have put me at the forefront of the new model.

The model which, as I say, is an old one rather than something new. The technology of the first electric cars is surely almost unrecognizable to modern engineers, but I bet the concept is the same.

In the same way, the new revolution in writing for oneself and releasing work directly runs along age-old lines – but the technologies that bring the model to life are new.

Through coming months and years the spell will be broken, and the monolithic publishers of old will disintegrate as the real writers look on and reclaim control.

Over the last handful of years I've worked to champion the new model – one which will serve me as a writer, and others like me.

Please understand: I am totally uninterested in setting myself up as a publisher. Doing so would go against everything I stand for. After all, my message is all about freeing writers from the bondage of slavery, so that they can have faith in themselves.

The plan is to offer authors a blueprint which will enable them to conceive, write, and then release work on publishing platforms using new technology. In the following pages I'll do my best to explain what I have in mind and map out how I think it will work.

Plenty of my author friends are published by mainstream publishers, and many of these friends are thrilled to bits with the attention they receive from the literary world. Despite this, I have no intention of going back to the broken old model. The only reason I'd do so is if I were written a cheque with so many zeros I'd have to count them twice. I'm not trying to lure anyone to the Promised Land with me, preferring both new and established writers to make the decision for themselves.

As I have said through the pages of this book, I'm interested in the Salinger Brigade – writers who write because they can't *not* write. In the same way, my interest is first and foremost in writing to satisfy myself rather than merely to attract the attention of others.

The business of empowering authors is not so much

about giving them strength, but rather about taking the strength from those who have held the reins of the creative process until now. Like all imaginative people, authors are frequently tortured by self-doubt. Far more damaging than self-doubt is the way the conventional publishing system has conspired to keep all but a handful of writers down, rather than striving to build all worthy writers up.

The lifeblood of real writers are letters, words, and paragraphs.

As such, they must be in the creation zone, the realm in which every author worth their salt ought to reside. Once there, you must stay there. Flounder, and you'll end up in the long grass. Ask yourself repeatedly if you're still in the slipstream and whether there's anything you can do to be more streamlined.

And never, ever take for granted that you're in the writing zone.

Forget about how many copies of your new book you're likely to sell, or what to put on the cover. Forget, too, what the readers are going to think about it when it's released.

For now the process is centred around you, the real writer, doing what you love.

The New Model

WITHOUT FURTHER ADO, I am going to explain the new model with which I work.

In recent years, I set up the publishing arm of a charity that promotes my father's corpus of work.

In that time our team has published more than four hundred editions from my father's corpus – including hardback and paperback volumes, eBooks, audio books, as well as limited and even hand-printed editions, too.

I have used the same model to release my own work – both my backlist and a flood of new projects.

The model we have come up with has served our purposes, but may not serve yours. The beauty of the brave new world is that it allows a fully bespoke service. You'll be able to keep total control over your work, use the format which best suits you, and release it as and where you like.

At the same time, you won't have anyone telling you how or what to write.

Everything you do will link to everything you've done and all you have planned for the future.

As a consequence, you'll be able to conceive a great series of books if it's what you have in mind, without the spectre of it being canned by men in suits or the marketing team.

I am going to describe the process in the following way:
1. Writing the manuscript
2. Editing, proofing, and preparing
3. Publishing
4. Promotion

First Draft

As I've ALREADY written plenty about what's worked for me, I'll keep this section pared down as much as possible.

I'd like to reiterate that following the new model means you can experiment as much as you like. Even when your book has gone on sale, you will be able to re-edit it and release different versions. My suggestion is to sit down at the start and jot down what you want to achieve, and the story you want to tell. Get that rooted firmly in your mind. Write it on a sticky note and position it on the edge of your screen. Look at it all the time during the writing process and ask yourself if you're on course.

Plan the book even if you've written others before. As I've said, I always do a plan if only so I can go off-piste. Plans don't have to be detailed or particularly long, but rather provide a structure. In the same way a portrait painter will sketch the outline and features of a face before picking up a brush, the plan allows you to maintain consistency. I try to make my plans as orderly as I can, with headings, subheadings and so on. During the writing process I add to them by hand, listing anecdotes, information, and details.

I used to make a wordage list, too, and would tape it to the corner of my desk. At the end of each writing day I'd fill in the daily number and tally up the total.

Looking back at these tallies, something strikes me... All is well as long as I write every single day. But the moment I take a break, or don't keep to the daily wordage, I lose precious ground. For this reason I like to rope off three weeks or a month to write a large-sized novel, so there won't be any chance to get sidetracked.

Again, there is no right and wrong when it comes to a daily wordage. And, unlike me, a great many successful writers can knock out a book in fits and starts. When I embark on the journey I have to know where the end point lies – the distant horizon. Or, rather, the not-so-distant horizon. Like a mountaineer standing on a summit, I like to get a fleeting glimpse of where I am going, even if it's blurred. My method is to slog like a maniac to get to it, even if it means I'm crushed by the journey.

Once or twice I've written the last page or so early on and worked my way towards it. At least then you know where you're heading. It worked well and provided me with a fixed end point so that I could stop worrying about it.

With the new models in publishing, no one is going to be telling you how many pages to write. As with everything else, you'll have freedom to decide for yourself. If you haven't written books before, my advice is to talk it through with a writer friend. Or, even better, to find a book you know and like, which resembles what you have in mind, and to use it as a blueprint – like one of those paper patterns people used to buy to make their own clothes.

A tip which has worked well for me is to keep writing when I'm on a roll, and to later divide the book into several parts. It's much easier to do that than to write the first part, then cool down and start on the next instalment.

As you'll see, the new system is set up for you to try out formats, layouts, and writing styles that suit your work – rather than having them foisted upon you by an editor.

Cleaning

ONCE YOU HAVE the first draft, it's time to go through and clean it up. Rather like cleaning up an apartment which has had wild, rampaging students trash it, you need to get a grip on exactly what you're going to do. So, just as you might sweep all the mess onto the floor, straighten the cushions, and then vacuum up, I'd do something like this:
- Read through once and make sure the spellings and basic grammar are right.
- Correct glaring errors and holes in the storyline or plot.
- Check the character descriptions and tidy up clunky passages.
- Go through the manuscript again, balancing every single sentence. If you are unsure what to do, read it out loud line by line. Or, as I've described, use the speech function so the computer reads highlighted text.

When editing your own work, it's easy to get hunkered down when you should be moving briskly ahead, or depressed by passages you think are second rate. If this is the case, set yourself specific goals – like an hour to correct a certain wordage. While it's true you can hide dull passages in a book, it's best not to. In truth, every sentence should earn its right to its spot on the page. If it doesn't add to the story or the overall atmosphere, you should think about deleting it. That may be too hardcore for many writers, but most great writers nail it down.

New writers are impatient. They want their work to see the light of day immediately, and get it into their heads that anyone preventing this stands against them. In reality, a book takes time, and a book which has been rushed is very likely to have fault lines running through it which will be challenging to correct later on. The way I regard it, time spent cleaning and correcting is profoundly valuable, because it gets your work up to the next level. But it's not only about polishing the text so much as it is mastering the craft.

Writing is as much an expertise as cabinet-making or karate. It's something that is learned through application and diligence, perfected through hands-on experience. You can only ever get good at it by doing it, and definitely NOT by talking about it. Yes, there are certain propensities which will make the journey easier, or will make you more of a 'natural', but most of it is hard grind. Along with the grind, a second sense slowly emerges through which you develop an appreciation of what works and what does not.

One of the things I have learnt is to give a work in progress the right gestation period. Not all projects are the same. A novella may only require a couple of days of consideration, while a long series of books could well take years of thought. The point I am trying to make is that books take time. Of course you can rush them, but they'll suffer as a result. Don't get me wrong – I am all for writing fast. It keeps up momentum. But I fully recognize the value of planning and editing as well.

Although I have sometimes been impatient to get a new book out there, I've come to learn the huge value of holding back, waiting, and reworking text after a gap of months, or even years.

In writing this I'm reminded of an elderly Czech violin-maker called Fredic whom I got to know while down and out in my early twenties. I'd go and sit in his workshop at the 'bad' end of London's Portobello Road. I'd watch him and would listen to him. But most of all, I'd gaze at all the half-finished instruments hanging on the walls.

One afternoon I asked Fredic why he never seemed to start on an instrument and finish it in one go. Peering over at me, the craftsman seemed to smile through the corner of his mouth, as though he'd waited years for the question.

'Everything I'm doing in here is thought out,' he told me. 'It may seem like chaos to you, but it's all planned. All these instruments are on an adventure. They know it, and I know it. But neither they nor I quite know where the journey will lead, and that's where the magic lies. The only way to make certain they complete the journey is to be sure they're perfectly prepared. To do that, I give them time, and myself time.'

I asked Fredic what he meant.

Brushing his tabby cat off his armchair, he slumped down onto it.

'Every day I come in here, open the shutters and make some tea,' he said. 'If someone was watching me from out there they might think it was the same day lived over and over. But they'd be wrong. Every day is completely different. That's because I'm different, the weather is different, and the date and time are different. All that means I see and experience things differently.'

For years I turned Fredic's words around in my mind, half-wondering whether I understood them at all. But gradually, over time, I did – and they made perfect sense.

Look at a painting, a page of text, or even a half-finished violin a thousand times. To the untrained eye they may appear pretty much the same. But to the questioning mind, the mind which created them, subtleties will be apparent. The ability to pick up on the subtleties allows you as the creator to shape them from the inside out.

Just as Fredic would hang a work in progress on the wall until he was ready to continue with it, I have learned to do the same with my writing. At any one time I have at least five works in progress sitting on the mantelpiece.

Eventually, I get to a point at which I am ready to pass the manuscript on for a first read. It's not a moment I particularly savour, and giving it to the right person is important.

Editing

I TEND TO pass all new work on to my close Argentine friend, Agustin.

There are many qualities I admire about him – among them his kindness, his patience, and his ability to see detail with one eye and the big picture with the other. But most of all, I value the fact he doesn't judge. Like everyone else I'm sensitive about unveiling new work, and don't like having to do it at all. I've sometimes considered following the lead of J. D. Salinger, who left a storeroom filled with completed novels. But then again he had written *Catcher in the Rye*.

So, I send the manuscript over to Agustin and forget about it.

Actually that's a lie – I don't.

I pace up and down, checking the time incessantly, wondering what's keeping him from getting back to me. It's not that he's slow in reading but rather I'm skittish with nerves. I realize this doesn't tally with my need to write for myself, but I've sworn an oath of honesty.

Agustin usually comes through with two lists of comments. The first are general and relate to structure, and the second are specific points relating to detail, or prose that could be cleaned up. An important point to stress is that I give Agustin my work for two reasons – the first is that I regard his suggestions highly. The second, more important, is that he knows my work and he knows me. He's read all the books I've written and has a clear understanding of how I think.

I usually dread receiving Agustin's notes, because I'm fearful he'll think the book is a waste of space. Thankfully, he's always exceptionally accommodating. If he says a passage could be improved he'll usually make suggestions how it could be done.

That's a big point...

An editor is there to help you tweak your work and hone it. I know next to nothing about bonsai trees, but I like to think of an editor as one of those doting bonsai guys – like Mr Miyagi in *The Karate Kid*. They'll observe the tree intently for what seems like hours and only then will they make a few careful snips – so the bonsai's inner beauty is brought out.

My advice to any writer is to get an editor who will follow them from one book to the next. The key thing is that they get to know you and your work, and that first and foremost they enable it to shine in a way you've wanted.

In the days when I was published by the big-name publishers on either side of the Atlantic, I had a string of editors assigned to me. They were all forgettable, except for Caroline Oakley at Weidenfeld & Nicolson. Her extraordinary skill at honing text equalled Mr Miyagi's expertise with the scissors. Rather than chopping and changing everything (as a great many of them wanted to do), she would make changes at a micro level and somehow achieve the desired result.

I should say that writers are not usually editors. I for one am hopeless at going through text and offering sensible advice, and I dislike being asked by people to evaluate their work. Prodigious readers aren't necessarily good editors either. They tend to get sucked down so deep into the work that they can't see the wood for the trees. The best editors I have known tend to have a kind of split personality, enabling them to evaluate in different ways – in the way Agustin does for me.

Once your editor has gone through the manuscript it's up to you how much to take on board and what changes to make. As I have moved along the arc of the writing process, I've tried to get my books in the shape I want them before even showing them to Agustin. I snip away loose ends, plug holes in the plot, and try to reshape anything I know will get Agustin's attention for the wrong reasons.

At one time I had an overly enthusiastic editor who used to return manuscripts covered in thick red pen. It was like having my homework graded by the teacher from hell, and made me very jumpy indeed. The only way I could make sure anything saw the light of day as I wanted was to use the 'Monkey's Paw' technique.

For anyone who doesn't know it, the story goes that an artist was asked to paint the portrait of a particularly fussy member of the aristocracy. Knowing full well she would criticize every last detail of the finished work, he painted her right hand as a monkey's paw. When the picture was unveiled, the duchess at once seized on the fact that her hand was not a hand at all. Horrified, she went on and on about it. In doing so, she overlooked the other failings of the work.

As a writer who had to jump through hoops laid out by my publishers, the Monkey's Paw was useful for drawing away the fire. With the new model of direct publishing there's no need to devise complex ruses to save oneself.

Another thing I should say is that editing is not proofreading. First-time authors tend to get mixed up with this. An editor is concerned with the structure and form of the work – questioning whether the characters arc in the right way and ensuring that the themes develop as they should.

The fact most mainstream publishers are cutting costs – replacing editors with marketing teams – means that most books no longer get edited well at all. These days most editing is done by freelancers, who tend to get paid by the hour. As budgets are continually being slashed, they're permitted to bill less and less – meaning a great many manuscripts don't get more than the roughest read through.

Proofreading

ONCE YOUR MANUSCRIPT is structurally sound, it's ready to be proofed.

How much work will be involved depends on what kind of a writer you are. I do my best to clean up glaring errors before sending a book to Agustin, but even so there are always plenty of them left.

A key point is that no author writes text devoid of clunking mistakes. The more you write, and read through a text, the more blinkered you become to it.

A good proofreader is worth their weight in gold. In my opinion you're well advised to pay for at least one professional proofing. As with editors, it's advisable to try and use the same people if you think their work's good. I have a team of proofreaders I rely on – a mixture of professionals and friends.

As I noted earlier, different people read in different ways. Some proofreaders are tuned to pick up grammar, while others are especially good at hunting for three different spellings of the same name.

The main proofreaders I use – who will correct this manuscript before it gets to you as the reader – are all excellent at grammar, spelling, and at rooting out all kinds of inconsistencies and errors. What I appreciate about them most is that they all seem to read in a slightly different way. As a result, they each pick up different points for me to note.

Once the book has been proofed by several professionals, I read it through again, twice. The first time slowly, checking the weight and value of the words, and asking myself whether the sentence structure could be improved upon. The second read through is much faster – usually a case of my computer reading aloud to me as I sit in a chair, listening.

Then, when the last corrections have been incorporated, I print out a final version and put it with the other manuscripts to be bound. It's a silly tradition of mine, and one that seems to be dying out.

When I moved to Morocco a decade and a half ago, I found a business card in my grandfather's papers – the business card of a bookbinder in Rabat. Having published seventy-four books during his lifetime, my grandfather would have his manuscripts bound in red morocco, a tradition that my father continued and that I myself have acquired.

For the last decade and a half I've used the same atelier as my grandfather, the son of the son binding batches of my manuscripts each spring.

Typesetting

WITH YOUR MANUSCRIPT ready to be typeset, it's time to dance a jig around and congratulate yourself. You've made it much further than most people, and the pleasure of seeing your work in print is about to begin.

This is the point at which the path of the conventional publishing model and the brave new world go in opposite directions. So say goodbye to all the writers destined to lose control. You won't be seeing them again. From now on you'll be waited on hand and foot in a bespoke tailor shop, with your every wish and whim catered for.

First things first.

You have to get a sense of what you want. The best way to do that is to go to the biggest bookshop you can find, and to browse like you've never browsed before. Look at the books in the genre where you would expect to find your book, and then look at a dozen or so other genres as well.

Try to find editions that excite you in terms of their physical look. Check out the covers and the text on the back of books. Most importantly for now, look at the interior layouts.

There are a few things conventional publishers absolutely loathe.

Now I think of it, there are more than a few – there are masses of things which get on their nerves. I know because I've been at the sharp end of their displeasure time and again. Their many pet peeves include when authors want to:

- Use a particular font or design
- Suggest a cover design
- Give ideas on marketing
- Know what the retail price will be etc., etc.

Almost no author I've ever encountered has ever got involved in the layout. It may be because they don't care, but my thinking is that it's because they've never been asked.

I've always taken an interest in how books look, what kind of paper they're printed on, and even (don't judge me) how they smell. It's because I love paper books. I appreciate eBooks and think they're great – because they get people reading – but at heart I'm a paper man.

The thing which gets me excited like nothing else is a well-printed book with off-white paper, wide margins, and ink that doesn't rub off on your fingers when you read it.

Unless you live on a different planet from me, you would have noticed that a great many paperbacks have slid down a steep slope into the Abyss of Low-Grade Rot. More and more publishers are doing something I regard as sneaky – they're blowing the budget on printing the cover, and wrapping it around a splotchy, fifth-rate mass of paper little better than newsprint.

While browsing you may come across a book you really like and think it might work well as a source of inspiration for physical style. My suggestion would be to buy a copy, or at least take a few photos with your phone. In the feeding frenzy of bookshops – whether they be bricks-and-mortar or online – every title's trying to grab your attention. As a result, they all seem to cancel one another out. Once in a while you'll spot something which sucks you in – more often than not through its pristine simplicity.

When you've done the research, it's time to find yourself a typesetter. This is one of the many areas publishers like to pretend is their preserve, and theirs alone. Just as car mechanics don't like anyone but their own fraternity to have anything to do with engines, publishers disapprove wholeheartedly of writers who want to get involved.

The way I see it, creating a book is about so much more than merely writing the thing. As someone who loves books, and the writing process, I am enthused down to the marrow of my bones by every single detail and stage. For years I was locked out, told it wasn't my place – that I was meddling in something which didn't concern me.

How stupid I was, because for years and years I believed them.

Finding a book designer is just about the easiest thing on earth. As with anything, there's a massive selection of designers – some charging eye-watering amounts for what is (in my opinion anyway) rather basic work.

Most of the book designers I have on my team are based in India. They're efficient, highly skilled, and they follow the template I have asked for.

A top tip that's worked well for me is to get a book designer to scope out the first twenty or thirty pages in the font I like.

I tend to use Bulmer, the font I used for my limited edition novel, *Timbuctoo*. Over the years I have developed a general look which pleases me, involving masses of uncluttered prelim pages and extra space.

There are plenty of typesetting details to indulge yourself with should you feel inclined. Just like having made-to-measure clothing, you can for the first time have any cut or finishing you like.

There are design pet peeves I swear by, which drive everyone else mad. Top of the list is hyphenation. I get the shivers when a word is split needlessly across two lines. Mainstream publishers go for word-splitting because it speeds things up, and typesetters cost money.

Another of my bugbears is widows and orphans – stray words on the first or the last line.

You'll need a checklist of various standard bits and pieces, which include:
- A copyright page – which you can copy from a published book, substituting your own details.
- An ISBN number, which you get online (some POD

platforms charge for them, while others provide them for free).
- An optional name of a publisher and a logo.
- A list of social media links to put at the end, along with an invitation to your readers to write reviews.

Typeset Proofing

ONCE THE BOOK is typeset, the designer will email you a PDF file, and you'll get a first glimpse of your book looking like a book.

It's an exciting moment, one that never ceases to thrill me. Right away you're likely to see mistakes, which is quite normal. The magic of typesetting is that it allows you to see, with fresh eyes, work you have read a hundred times.

An important thing to remember is that changing text which has been typeset isn't like changing words at the manuscript stage. Every change made from now on has a knock-on effect. The best-case scenario is to only make alterations if they're absolutely necessary.

The priority is for typos and glaring errors – like incorrect capitalizations and indention, misaligned headings, and so on. If at all possible try not to rewrite because it'll drive you – and the typesetter – crazy. Make sure to put in the time before sending the manuscript to be laid out, so that the typesetting stage is a final polish.

But, again, there will be corrections – especially when you get others to proofread the typeset book. My advice is to work with a typesetter who is happy to incorporate revisions made over two or three drafts of the typeset version. Go through the laid out pages carefully yourself and mark anything which leaps out at you. When you're done, ask the typesetter to incorporate the changes.

Then, at that point, email the pages to friends and family and, if you can afford it, to a professional proofreader again.

Unless you send paper copies of your typeset book out (which most people don't bother with any longer), it's worth downloading a good PDF viewer which incorporates editing tools, and checking your proofreaders have the same version, too. That way they can mark corrections and use digital sticky notes.

By this stage I usually find it's fine to send the book out to multiple people at the same time, as they're hopefully not going to pick up massive mistakes. Make sure to brief family and friends in particular on what you want – otherwise they'll flag up far too much. It's essential they understand you're only looking for typos and other glaring mistakes.

Covers

MOST AUTHORS WHO have been producing books for a while have a best and worst cover. My best cover was for my travel book *Sorcerer's Apprentice*, and featured an Indian godman. The worst cover (for the same publisher) was for the paperback of *Beyond the Devil's Teeth*. A wretched mishmash of psychedelic confusion, it was so bad I hid under my duvet for three days, moaning like a wounded wildebeest. I would have insisted the publisher change the cover, but I couldn't. The contract said they had the right to come up with anything they wanted, although they had to show it to me in advance.

By the time I delivered my second book, *Sorcerer's Apprentice*, I had written in the right to refusal – a point which made the publisher very jittery indeed. They came up with yet another monstrous cover. Wild with anger, I found the godman image. On the back of it, the book was a success. As with every other detail of the creation process, the brave new world of direct publishing allows you to make all the decisions, and to have covers you love right from the start. If you're planning to write a stream of titles, or at least a series, then it makes sense to have continuity in the book covers.

I myself have used various artists over the years, and have also released my work with a plain white look. The reason is that I don't give a damn if anyone buys my books at all – I wrote them for myself. And as every other title being released is vying for your attention, it's quite pleasing to be the only writer whose cover is understated and low-key.

Print-on-Demand

I'M A HUGE fan of the new print-on-demand (POD) platforms, and have watched them evolve in a handful of years to hold the position they currently do. Things are moving so fast in the print-on-demand industry that I'm not going to try and give a comprehensive breakdown of the entire sector.

What you need to know is that POD platforms take your typeset book and cover files, as well as key bits and pieces of information, put it all together and spew it out as a finished book. There's a wealth of formats available, and every month more and more choices come on stream.

The way POD works is that – as the name suggests – when someone orders a title from Amazon or elsewhere, a copy is printed specifically for them and shipped out. Almost too many to mention, the advantages include the ability to update the files at the drop of a hat, and the fact that the books aren't rotting in a damp warehouse somewhere.

Better still, you can change the covers whenever you like, insert pages of rave reviews at the front, and even print limited editions for a certain period of time.

Pricing

WHEN THE NET Book Agreement ruled, the price of new books used to be set in stone. With its abolition, anyone could sell any book at any price. Supermarkets piled chick-lit and fantasy fiction high and sold them cheap. Publishers wheezed and groaned at getting pennies rather than pounds. Then one morning they were hit with the single word that changed everything: Amazon.

Overnight, the idea of standard prices came to an immediate end. As I understand it (believe me, no one except for Amazon really seems to understand it), the friendly online shop of everything gives different prices according to their algorithms. I have no idea whether this is myth or reality, but what I hear happens is that Amazon will show you a price they believe you'll be tempted by. And if, for instance, you put a book in your online basket and let it stew there for days or even weeks, they'll suddenly drop the price. After all, they'd rather you buy from them at a low cost price than go to anyone else. The blessing of the POD system though is that you get to set the profit margin you're comfortable with.

Someone told me there was a book for sale online entitled *How to Make a Million By Selling a Single Book*, and that it was priced at a million bucks.

Alas, I can't find it.

Perhaps it sold!

Bound Proofs

IN THE OLD days of publishing, there were fixed (if unwritten) rules. These included the principle that reviewers wouldn't go anywhere near a paperback, but rather expected hardbacks. The reason for this – as everyone in the business knows – was that book reviewers are paid next to nothing. I should know – I've done it. They're expected to supplement their derisory earnings by selling the boxes of brand-new books which turn up on their doorsteps day and night.

These days publishers often go straight to a paperback edition, bypassing the hardback incarnation altogether. It's confirmation of how things are changing, and changing fast. Until a few years ago most publishers didn't dare send out finished paperbacks to reviewers – for fear of being laughed out of town. Instead, they'd bind up a quantity of proof copies – a special soft-covered early version... an uncorrected proof.

I've always had a thing about uncorrected proofs. It must be because they're prepared in very limited numbers – sometimes no more than a dozen or two. If you're still being represented by a conventional publisher you know your stock value is high if they'll churn out a good big batch of proofs.

The point I want to make is that with the POD platform you can upload your own proofs, order as many copies as you need, and hand them out privately to family, friends, reviewers, bloggers, inspirers, or anyone you like. Then you simply update the files (removing the words 'Uncorrected Proof') and load them onto the POD platform you've decided to use.

You can also print a few copies with an additional page inserted into the prelims. The page can announce something like, 'For Private Circulation Only. Limited to 50 copies.' By numbering and signing the books you've created an instant special edition.

Crowdfunding

ALTHOUGH I HAVEN'T yet used crowdfunding to bankroll a project, a number of close friends have. In asking their advice, I was provided with a range of tips in response, which I'd like to share.

The one point on which they're all agreed is that there's no such thing as free cash.

As one seasoned crowdfunder told me:

'Crowdfunding can be a useful tool, and even a thing of wonder, but it's damned hard work.'

Below are a variety of pointers accumulated from a number of authors who have used crowdfunding successfully:

- The first thing to remember is your campaign will only be as good as your social media network. Making a database of family, friends, and others is a MUST. Crowdfunding is about engaging them, making them feel a part of what you're setting out to achieve, and taking them along for the ride.
- The second thing to get your head around is what your project is all about. There's no point in launching a half-baked idea – crowdfunding is founded on clear goals, and there's no goal so important as the project description itself. Work hard at it. Study the market, checking what similar books there are in the genre, and how yours will

stand apart. Hone your project brief over time, rounding off the corners, and don't be afraid to return to the drawing board if it simply doesn't pass muster.
- 'Innovation' is a key buzzword in the crowdfunding world. Be innovative in coming up with ways your followers will want to get involved. This includes thinking of lots of rewards they'll fall over each other to lap up.
- Rewards come in all shapes and sizes. A campaign could feature, for example a schedule such as this:
  - Signed copy of the book   £15
  - Signed copy with donor's name
    printed in the back   £20
  - Signed, numbered limited edition with
    illustrations   £40
  - Limited edition with folio of artwork £60
  - Limited edition with invitation to
    private launch   £75
  - Dinner with the author   £150
  - Hand-corrected proof of the
    original manuscript   £1000
- Another thing to get right is the amount of funding you need. A lot of campaigns flounder because they're asking for too much. However hard they try they never quite manage to break across the halfway mark. It's sometimes advisable to lower the bar so progress appears all the more impressive.

The advantage of this is that would-be funders are likely to be wowed by a campaign which is well subscribed.
- Most crowdfunding campaigns have at their heart a video of the author lifting the veil on the project. In some cases, these films are sleek marketing tools worthy of a high-end advertising firm. Most of the time, however, they're passionate, honest explanations of what you are trying to achieve and why.
- Bear in mind you have to factor in the cost of packaging your book up and shipping it out. If it's a big, weighty tome then the mailing costs will eat into the funds raised. Always add a margin to take into account higher costs than expected.
- Every step of the way you must take your supporters with you. This includes posting updates on as many social media platforms as you can stand, championing your progress and, more importantly, giving thanks for all the support.
- Involve funders by asking them which design they think works best, and even which ending they prefer. A rapport with supporters is worth its weight in gold, and will form the foundation of the next campaign.
- Although most authors who turn to crowdfunding do it because they need the cash, some don't. Instead, they mount campaigns because they're

such a sure-fire way of guaranteeing sales once their book is released.
- The final point to make is crowdfunding only hits the high-water mark when the author has put everything they can into the campaign and pulled out all the stops.

Special Editions

SPECIAL EDITIONS AREN'T anything new. Publishers have been using them for centuries, and self-published authors have been releasing their work in special editions for even longer.

In my opinion the person who excelled unlike any other was the Victorian explorer, traveller and polymath, Sir Richard Francis Burton. He's always been a towering giant of inspiration to me, largely because he did whatever he liked irrespective of whether it irked those around him. He fell out with publishers so frequently that he started releasing his work directly. As I mentioned earlier, the other reason for the direct route was the increasingly salacious nature of his corpus.

Burton's genius (or rather, one part of his genius) was to release one limited edition after another, selling them to subscribers. Trawl online book searches or eBay and you'll see what I am talking about. The most famous of all his editions are *The Arabian Nights Entertainments*, published by his Kama Shastra Society. Magnificent objects in their own right, they were designed in a way that an author designs a book rather than a publisher, a bookseller, or anyone else. That's so important to me and I wish others would wake up and understand it.

Writers know about books in a way that no one else can comprehend them. If you're a writer, a *real* writer, I think you may get what I mean. It's that we obsess about books – the words, the paper, the ink, the glue and the thread, the font, the spacing, the endpapers and the thickness of the boards. Our love is shaped by creation and not by cold hard cash.

Over the last decade or so I've released a stream of exceptionally fine and rare editions – predominantly of my own work. Some of them have been hand-printed, or at least printed in small batches. A few – like my books *Timbuctoo* and *Scorpion Soup* – had elaborately folded maps. The thing that sets them apart from anything you see launched by conventional publishers is that they were created not for profit but for love.

A few months ago I began work on a project to hand-print copies of individual stories by my father on a fabulous century-old Heidelberg at the Letterpress Collective in Bristol. The first time I went round there and met the master printer, Nick Hand, I picked up his obsession with printing right away.

As I write this, a handful of copies of each story are being printed, the Heidelberg clattering and flapping like a creature from the Underworld. When they're ready, the sheets will have illustrations tipped in, and will be presented in glorious boxes. If I get my way, they'll never be sold – at least not online anyway.

Some things are too special.

Ultimate Control

THIS IS PROBABLY a good time to reveal that, in truth, I'm a relative lightweight in the brave new world of direct publishing – even though I have grand plans. I admit it because there are others who take the business of retaining control to far greater heights than me.

A case in point is my close writer friend Jason Elliot.

Celebrated for an extraordinary corpus of work that fuses travel and cultural literature together, Jason spent the last five years working on a masterpiece, *The Madhouse*. As he ground away at the story, I watched him descend into a state of self-possessed delirium – the matrix of truest creation. Whenever I'd ask Jason what the book was about, or how it was going, he'd look at me face-on, eyes wide and bloodshot.

'It's impossible to say,' he would tell me.

'Impossible to say what it's about or how it's going?'

'Impossible on both counts.'

When at long last the manuscript was ready, Jason shunned all offers of help – quite rightly. Over drinks in London I recommended a reliable typesetter in India. Clutching the manuscript to his belly as though it were a newborn babe in arms, Jason seemed horrified that I could expect him to farm the typesetting out. Instead, rather like a mother set on making her infant's clothes, Jason taught himself how to typeset *The Madhouse*, and he laid it out himself.

If I weren't so challenged when it comes to design, I may well have followed Jason's example. After all, the book he released into the wild was exactly the book he'd conceived as a seed, planted, and raised. I'm in awe of anyone who produces work which sings to them as the creator. Although I've always been very appreciative of people who read my work, it's ultimately down to me to judge the book I've created.

Now that I've broken free from the monolithic publishing empires of old and am my own form of Andy Warhol with his Factory, I feel like I'm walking on air.

Please don't get me wrong.

As a writer the last thing I ever want to appear is arrogant and self-obsessed. That's not what excites me. The thing which drives me beyond all else is creating in a way that interests me right down to the cellular level.

Bearing that in mind, I'm enthused about experimentation – the kind that teaches you in a micro, inside-out way. Thinking about it now, this form of self-experimenting runs like a vein through my entire life.

Ever since I was a child I'd potter about to see what worked and what didn't work. From the age of four or five I hung around in the workshop with Greville, the eccentric storytelling carpenter who was such a constant presence when I was young. He would let me choose a chunk of wood from the stack and give me a clutch of hooped nails to bang into it.

As I got older, I pushed the boundaries of

experimentation forward.

I used to go into the storeroom where the big metal tubs of paint were kept, and would mix up samples until I'd reach a kind of holy grail of colour... an impossible tone of phosphorescent black.

But wood and paint weren't the only mediums with which I experimented. I was always drawn to paper, too. There was always a huge amount of waste paper coming through the house in the form of newspapers, discarded circulars, and old manuscripts.

At six I made a kite from staves of bamboo, wax, and newspaper. It was the most beautiful thing I'd ever imagined creating. The truth was that Greville did most of the work – but we pretended it was mine because it was so much more fun.

I'm not sure why, but since early childhood I'd tell everyone everything – not in a random or gossipy way, but rather as an announcer. My parents and sisters called me 'The Information Officer'. I just felt that no one else was passing on key pieces of information, so took the role.

Three days before the kite was ready to fly I walked through the grounds of Langton House and then out into the village, announcing through an empty toilet roll that the first flight would take place at a certain time and date. I made posters as well, and even had one put in the window of the local post office by Mrs Knock, the woman who ran it and lived above.

On the morning of the kite's maiden flight I woke up with mumps. Our exceedingly elderly doctor was called. Having made a thorough examination, he ordered me to stay in bed.

'But there's the kite flight today!' I bawled.

'Bed!' growled the doctor.

'Bed!' echoed my mother.

'But I've told everyone, so there'll be a crowd.'

'Someone else can fly the kite,' my father said.

At the appointed hour I watched from my bedroom window as a boy I liked and trusted called Rex read a short statement from a scroll that I had prepared. Written in my illegible hand, it seemed to go down well with the audience, who'd come from all corners of the village.

The scroll was furled up and put away, and the kite was taken out from a sack. Even though it was paper, it seemed to gleam in the early summer light.

I've never been prouder in my life than in that moment.

Obeying my orders, Rex held the kite above his head and ran like the wind. The magnificent kite took flight, soaring up into the air as the crowd of at least thirty watched.

Ten seconds later it had flown straight into the upper branches of an oak tree – impaled and forlorn.

The audience traipsed away, shaking their heads in sadness.

Alone up in my bedroom, I jumped up and down

screaming until my throat was hoarse.

Apologies.

I got off the topic then, but that's what happens to you when you're a writer. Stray memories well up from the recesses of your mind. It's your job to grab them like butterflies caught in a big billowing net and use them in your work.

After the kite fiasco I set about making a series of miniature books, no bigger than matchboxes. I'd heard that the Brontë sisters and their brother Branwell used to make little books filled with plays and stories.

With an interest in very small objects, I did my best to make a series of little books, as they had done. Except my books weren't quite so fabulous as those crafted by the expert hands of the Brontës. The fact my books weren't as sensational didn't really matter.

What did matter was that they were the one and only thing I'd ever created which were made for me, and me alone, and weren't shown to anyone.

Now I think of it, I've never mentioned them to anyone at all, and have certainly never written about them. The fact they were only known to me was utterly intoxicating – as though they were part of my own secret realm. This is something I find challenging to explain, and don't expect most people reading this will understand. But I like to think that out there someone is smiling and feeling warm, because they know exactly what I mean.

As for my little books – which I called collectively

The Griniads – they were eventually eaten by our yellow Labrador.

It was my fault for using so much fish gelatin glue.

Direct Publishing Resources

THE FOLLOWING IS a list of resources and services I have used and recommend.

Websites at which you can find editors, proofreaders, typesetters, book designers, illustrators, and others. When I connect with great people I tend to use their skills over and over.
- Fiverr.com
- Upwork.com
- Behance.com

Print-on-demand Platforms
- Kdp.amazon.com
- Ingramcontent.com
- Lulu.com
- Printondemand-worldwide.com

Resources for Writers
- Societyofauthors.org
- Goodreads.com

Tribal Publishing

IN PLANNING AND writing this book, I've resisted recommending many people or organizations involved with direct publishing. The reason is that what works for one writer may not work for another. I want to be certain my recommendations are a hundred per cent dependable.

For the last eight years I have relied on a couple of extraordinary people – Agustin Gonzalez and Holly Worton. Problem solvers par excellence, they have mapped out from scratch an entirely new way of direct publishing.

Agustin and Holly handle almost everything for me – from arranging my manuscripts to be edited and proofed, to getting finished books uploaded onto the print-on-demand platforms, working on reader and media requests, visibility of my work, and a whole lot more.

As a selfish Scorpio, a devil on my shoulder was whispering for me to not mention them. After all, if they're solving other peoples' problems, they'll have less time for me.

But, having deliberated long and hard, I have decided to provide fellow members of the Salinger Brigade with the details of their small firm, Tribal Publishing.

Based in the UK, their vision is global, and their eye for detail is second-to-none.

The services they offer, in English and Spanish, include:
- Developing a story for publication
- Editorial and proofreading of a completed manuscript
- Typesetting
- eBook coding
- Audiobook recording
- Setting up advertising on Amazon and social media
- Designing publishing strategies
- Translations into Spanish

Tribalpublishing.co.uk

PART V

WRITERS ON WRITING

Announcement III

THE PAGES OF this book are heavy with advice from my own journey as an author. As it's my name on the spine, I'm hoping I can get away with ranting on and on as I have. But, just as I included thinking by a handful of Teaching People along the way, I wanted to feature the thoughts of some others.

First, I'd like to start with some of my writer friends, to whom I am so sincerely grateful. I asked them to send three top tips about writing. Some wrote even more than that.

What I love about their input is that it's all so varied.

Reading these points, I found myself reflecting on who authors are, as much as what's important to them and their work.

Second, I have provided a few of my very favourite quotes.

Third, I'm giving the last word to Doris, who really ought to stand alongside Francis de Sales as the patron saint of writers.

Three Tips

Sir Michael Palin

Writing is one of the best jobs in the world and one of the easiest to resist. Why should something so rewarding be so difficult to get down to?

Here are my top tips:

1. Just get started. Don't be frightened by a blank sheet of paper or an empty screen. The moment you begin to put words together – any words – your journey's begun.
2. Never be frightened to start again. Crossing out is not a weakness, just an acknowledgement that you can do even better.
3. Good writing is not a tap you can turn on or off. Some days it happens. Some days it doesn't. Don't worry about it. Wait for next morning.
4. Don't try and be clever. Be yourself when you write. Find your own voice, not someone else's.
5. When you think you've finished, the hard work has just begun. A good editor can be like a fairy godmother.
6. Writing is about quality not quantity. Cutting might hurt, but it's almost always an improvement.
8. The *Paris Review* series 'Writers At Work' is a fascinating series of glimpses into how the best writers confront all these sorts of problems.

Esther Freud

1. Decide on a start and a stop time, and even if it's going

well, stick to it. You'll be hungry to get to your desk the next day.

2. Include two elements in your book. Something you don't know enough about – enjoy the challenge, and something about which you know a lot – to give yourself a break.

3. Don't research too much. You are the reader as well as the writer of your book. It can be intriguing to find out what's going to happen.

Paul Theroux

1. Writing my first draft in longhand has served me well.

2. Regarding every chapter of a novel as a short story, as well as a continuation, has been my aim.

3. Most of 'writing' is being at a desk, not writing, but thinking hard, doodling – the act of writing is much of the time sitting.

Justin Marozzi

1. Make the time to write. It sounds obvious, it is obvious, but it's the most important thing. You'll never write anything unless you give yourself the time to do it. I've lost count of the number of people who have said to me over the years they were going to write a book and never did. They never made the time.

2. Get into a routine. Why do you think a dog is a man's best friend? It is because we are both craven slaves to routine. Sit in the same seat in the library, start at the

same time in the morning, have a walk in the afternoon, preferably with a slavishly adoring dog, drink wine in the evening, whatever it is. Writing a book is a long haul. I regard it as a war of attrition. Word by word, paragraph by paragraph, page by page. You only get there by refusing to give in. Stick with it and take comfort from the routine – and the progress it helps you make. I always start the writing day by reviewing the work of yesterday and see if it's any good or is so lousy it needs a complete rewrite.

3. A new rule I have found works wonders in our Age of Distraction. No emails, Internet, social media, WhatsApp or ANYTHING DISTRACTING before lunch.

You're writing a book, so write the damn thing!

Barnaby Rogerson

I write because writers are my heroes and I want to join this group who listen so carefully – both to what is being said and to what cannot be spoken about, manage to winnow out all the boring bits, and both capture this passing world and through stories help point it to a better direction.

I sell books, I help make them, I buy them, I publicize them, I review them and I even write them – but the most satisfying thing I ever do with them is read them. I have never met a writer whom I admire who is not an enchanted reader. If I would give any advice to a young writer wanting to establish a good first impression with a publisher, it would be to also reveal yourself as a passionate reader. Conversely I am discouraged if I meet a writer who wants an audience but is not prepared to be one.

I have noticed that there are very real personal problems with being a writer. So often the desire to write is connected with their failure in the real world. Books can often feel like the act of an unhappy loner trying to assert themselves. So historians can reveal themselves as frustrated monarchs, novelists create the love and adventure story that never quite happened to them, diarists remake the world with themselves at the centre, biographers often want to gut an individual of their mysterious charisma. Be careful of your real life, treasure your family, try and make friendships independent of use to your glittering literary career, learn to do something immediately useful with your hands other than writing, like cooking or making useful things like gardens, children, or bookshelves.

As the Lord Apollo taught us: as a child learn manners, as a youth control your passion, be just in middle age, in old age give good advice, and then die without regret.

Dame Marina Warner
1. Carry a pencil, notebook – and a pencil sharpener! – with you and make notes of scraps of conversation,

sounds, scents and thoughts that strike you. A camera can act as a very useful recorder, too, but is limited to the visual and is not verbal.

2. If possible go and see places, buildings, objects that have shaped the setting and surroundings in the story you're writing – scale, position, texture, all the properties of things can be very different in reality (this applies to settings of fantastic literature, too – Dante's hell is mapped out in every detail so richly that you could build it).

3. Read... and read... and read... widely and deeply in our forebears. Listen to their word music, get the rhythms in your muscle memory and the hum of the language in your ear (translations can give us this, too).

Nigel Cawthorne

I am with Dr Johnson, who said: 'No man but a blockhead ever wrote except for money.'

1. Always get the money first. Never write a word until you see their cash. Publishers always like what you have written when you already have their dosh.

2. Get a big mortgage, you never get writer's block.

3. Get a chair with arms. It makes it harder to flee from the keyboard.

Steven Nightingale

1. Work so that love and learning come to be words that mean the same thing.

2. See how everything that is, is enveloped in what it means.
3. Remember that there is only one thing in all the world that will not be taken away from you: what you have given away.

Nigel Hinton
I remember what I like in other people's storytelling, especially the books I read when I was growing up, although films made a big impact on me, too. I remember the excitement of the sudden unexpected plot revelation, the cliffhanger chapter endings, the suspense created, the laughter evoked and the way I was made to be moved by an event. I want – really want – to do that to the reader. I think creativity starts with intensity of intention.

It's a game of 'let's pretend' – let's pretend and let's see intensely. It's about living it in your mind. Rather like the 'zone' sportsmen talk about, I think concentrating to the point of forgetting all else takes you to a place where things happen beyond the vague idea you start with. When that detail of description – the passing shadow of a bird, say, or the way someone tugs a stray strand on a fabric plaster on their finger – gives a scene something unexpected and memorable. The more real it is in your head, the more real it will be in the reader's one – even to the point that if you have seen the scene intensely enough, what you haven't put down in words will be mysteriously carried by the words you have put down.

I read out loud what I have written, especially to hear the rhythm of the sentences. I want simplicity and clarity and directness.

Cut, cut, cut. Often the bits you thought were great while you were writing them are the phoney bits.

Tim Mackintosh-Smith

To paraphrase the famous quotation attributed to Somerset Maugham ('There are three rules for the writing of a novel. Unfortunately, no one knows what they are.'): There are three thousand rules for writing a book. Unfortunately, if you try to learn them you'll never get down to writing it.

That said, plenty of creative writing courses claim to be able to teach you those rules. I don't; but my own top three might be as follows:

Start each writing session with a blank mind. I don't mean an empty head: you obviously have to have the info there, or some idea of where the plot or characters might take you. But some higher stratum of the mind must be utterly free – of social media, shopping lists, spouses, kids, lovers. You don't need to be in an ivory tower. But you must have a sanctum to retreat to, a sort of virtual panic room, even if it's a favourite chair in a corner. Once in it, you can free that higher layer, as you might do when meditating. Then the inspiration can drip in, if it's ever going to; whether from inside or outside I don't know.

THE REASON TO WRITE

Yes, writing *is* ninety per cent perspiration and only ten per cent inspiration, as they say. But the magic, if there is any, will be in that ten per cent.

Pace is crucial. Unless you are compiling a dictionary or writing on the genomes of turnips, you have to keep your readers on their mental toes. Lull them for a bit, by all means, but always wake them up. Writing is performance, conjuring – both hocus-pocus, and the con*juri*ng, in the old shamanic sense, of spirits. It is oratory on paper: you must hear in your head how it sounds. Better still, read it out loud. You are the direct descendant of the fireside storyteller in the cave, and you *must* capture your audience, heart, mind, soul and guts. And if you can make turnips captivating too... what more could you want?

Read lots. Not just what is selling now, but the time-proof writing going back through Golding and Conrad and Goethe to Homer, to Gilgamesh. See yourself as the new-honed cutting edge of an immensely long worldwide tradition, not as a chaser after trends that will be blunted in a season or two. Homer and Conrad got it right: that's why their work has lasted.

Don't do it for publishers – they live off trends, and as often as not are enemies of talent. Don't do it for money: Samuel Johnson was right when he said, 'No man but a blockhead ever wrote except for money' – with a few lucky exceptions, writers are born blockheads. No: do it for posterity ('But what,' you might ask with Lytton Strachey, 'has posterity done for *me*?').

Jane Johnson

1. Because I still work four days a week, I need to be very focused on the three days I have to myself. It's so easy to get distracted away from my task down social media's infinite rabbit holes, so I have to physically take myself away from an internet signal. What I like to do is to find a quiet place away from home – on a day of poor weather, a corner table in a café; on a good day on a rock down by the sea – and write longhand in a notebook. I find – probably because I am a terrible typist who spends as much time correcting her typing errors as creating – that writing by hand frees my mind and stops me worrying at sentence structures and imperfect wording. I can write faster and looser in a notebook and know that I can tighten and hone the text when I type it into the laptop.

2. Finding time to write is difficult for most of us: there are so many pressing issues and people requiring our time; and for those of us still working, free time is always a rarity. Because I only ever have a long weekend in which to write, I have to find a quick route into the book again after days away from it (my job requires long hours of email and editing other writers' work – it's impossible to switch easily between my editorial head and my creative head, so I cannot write during my working week). Two tips I find help are, firstly, leaving my handwritten draft to type up at the weekend, which eases me back into the story, and secondly, a tip given to me by science fiction maestro Robert Silverberg, whose work I used

to publish, I always leave a writing stint mid-scene, and sometimes even mid-sentence, so I am never faced by a standing start when I come back to the book.

3. Reading. Reading, reading, reading. When I'm writing, I can find reading almost anything becomes relevant to what I am writing – it could just be a sentence structure that strikes me, or the use of voice, a turn of phrase, or an entire narrative shape – even if I'm reading non-fiction. You learn so much from other writers. We all face similar problems in wrangling the elusive thoughts in our heads out into hard and fast words on a page; seeing how other people do it is always enlightening. What I will not do, though, is read anything that is too close to what I'm writing. It's not a matter of plagiarism or even influence, but weird unconscious echoes that creep in, ways of approaching the subject – and with historical fiction, ways of interpreting the past. You need your angles and approaches to be your own, but other than that very specific corner of the book world, I regard everything else as a wonderful, nourishing fertilizer for the ideas burgeoning in my brain.

Pico Iyer

The important thing for any writer is to be as focused and precise as possible and to find what you can see in any subject that few others could – and to capture that in words that no more high-tech medium could evoke more powerfully. Your voice, in other words, is nothing more – and nothing less – than the special set of eyes you have, born of passion and experience and upbringing, that the rest of the world might envy.

The longer I've been doing this – and I've been a full-time freelance writer for almost thirty-four years now – the more I find that writing is the best way I know to make a life and one of the worst ways to make a living. By which I mean that writing has taught me how to process experience, to see past my own thoughts, to try to understand others and to look for the larger picture in everything around me; it's enriched my life immeasurably and given every day an intimacy and sense of space it would never have had otherwise. When it comes to paying the bills, however, it more and more resembles a very expensive hobby.

All the joy and adventure of writing comes in the process of being at your desk; publication is the sales tax we have to pay for the privilege of sitting still and taking off into the unknown. I've never found any experience so transporting, so surprising, so endlessly opulent as writing – even when it forces you to look into the dark places in the world (or the self) that you'd much rather overlook or look past. When it goes out into the world, though, you find yourself watching your fourteen-year-old daughter take off on a blind date with a distractible stranger, and even the happy faces and compliments you may receive will seldom be a source of comfort or delight.

Jason Webster
1. In order to write you need to know what you believe, what you know, and what you are. The only way to know these things, though, may be through writing.
2. Writing that feels like writing isn't writing.
3. Get out of your own way.

Simon Singh
1. No such thing as 'writer's block' (is that where the apostrophe goes?). Just write any old rubbish, push ahead and rewrite 'blockages' when you revise the entire draft.
2. Ask for feedback from multiple readers with differing (and trusted) perspectives (agent, partner, expert, target reader). The skill is collating and acting on feedback.
3. You're not making a movie or producing a play, so there is no cost, except your time. And you can write in your spare time, so you don't need to quit your job or take any major risk. So, if you're starting out, there is not much to lose, and in the worst case scenarios (e.g. you don't finish the book, or nobody wants to read it) then, at the very least, you should have stretched your brain in new and interesting ways.

Mark Salzman
Before I reveal my tip, I feel I should put it into context: I am an oddball. I didn't start writing because I wanted to become a writer, or because I loved books, or because

I had stories inside me that simply had to be told. I started writing because telling stories had always come easily to me, and I loved doing it, so I assumed that writing stories would come easily to me and I would love doing that, too. I thought that if writing became my job, I would never hate my work. Who wouldn't want to build a career around an activity he or she enjoys? My father spent his life working at a job he hated, and I saw what it did to him, so I had reason to fear that outcome.

I soon discovered that telling stories and writing them down require different skill sets, and alas, writing did not come easily to me. I built a career around it anyway and ended up hating it for a while, but that's a long story and this isn't the place for it. All you need to know is: the approach to writing that I follow now, and that I will reduce to a single tip in a moment, is not designed to motivate anyone to work harder or aim higher or be more productive. If better results and higher output are what you want, I recommend *The War of Art* by Steven Pressfield, a writer and ex-Marine who all but screams at you through the pages of his book that writing is war, and if you aren't prepared to be miserable while doing it then you should be doing something else. I know people who swear by his approach, so keep it in mind.

But if you're an oddball like me and are hoping that the very act of writing itself – rather than its products, whatever they might be – will help make life seem worth living, then hail-fellow-well-met, and may this tip ease your journey.

My tip: give acceptance a chance.

There it is – that's all I've learned since turning pro in 1985. If art is indeed war, then save yourself a lot of time and trouble and raise the white flag now. You were raised to believe – we all were – that your destiny is in your hands. It is up to you to decide whether to write a novel or story or poem, and it is up to you to decide how hard to work at it and how good to make it. No excuses! If you succeed, credit goes to you; if you fail, you can only blame yourself. This is a way of looking at art and life that is clearly designed to act as a stimulant, and many people claim that it works. But at what cost? And what if it is an illusion to begin with? What if creativity, aspiration, and even determination are as determined by circumstance as eye colour, fast-to-slow-twitch muscle fibre ratio, and the ability to digest lactose? That would mean that the relentless self-scrutiny and self-flagellation we do as artists is gratuitous, and ultimately meaningless. Without all of that destiny-shaping business hanging over your head, what would writing be like for you? What would you write? Would you write at all, or take up something else?

Let me approach this from another angle. I'm a mediocre writer, and I'm pretty sure you are, too. We're all mediocre writers. (Yes, there are a few real geniuses out there, but they are anomalies, we needn't concern ourselves with them.) For us, the main enemy of writing isn't lack of talent or self-discipline or access to MFA programmes – it's discouragement. We feed this enemy with the stories we tell ourselves about how we should be writing better, or more often, or with more enthusiasm or originality or seriousness than we are right now. Or how underappreciated we are, or how stupid or corrupt the publishing industry is, or how unfair life is that we can't devote ourselves full-time to writing yet, etc. We make ourselves sick with all of this blaming and worrying and comparing and browbeating, and who has energy left to write after going fifteen rounds every day with Reality, which doesn't give a shit about us and our dreams? Stop feeding the enemy. Give yourself a target you can't miss, drop the idea of aiming at it, and instead, put all of your attention into what it feels like to release your arrow, or your words, or whatever it is that is coming out of you.

One more angle. Have you been trying to write a story for months, or years, but you're stuck and now it is painful to even think about sitting down and opening that notebook or laptop? Do you feel like a failure because you haven't gotten published yet, or because your second (or third, or fourth) novel was a flop? If so, have a look at this, my favourite quote of all time, from Iris Murdoch:

'Happiness is a matter of one's most ordinary everyday mode of consciousness being busy and lively and unconcerned with self. To be damned is for one's ordinary everyday mode of consciousness to be unremitting, agonizing preoccupation with self.'

If writing hurts, consider the possibility that this is not a writing problem at all. Could it be that you're trying to prove something to yourself or the world, life is not cooperating, and you're upset about it in a way that will do no good at all? You've tried everything positive you can think of and none of it has worked, so now you're punishing yourself with the negative stuff. Is this really the role you want writing to play in your life? Would you want your children to do this to themselves when they grow up? Is this what art is for?

Here's my bottom-line message: when practised in a spirit of acceptance and release, writing allows us to explore conflict (among other things) without the writing becoming an unhealthy source of conflict in itself. It becomes a way of rehearsing trust rather than dissatisfaction. In that sense, it qualifies as an act of faith. It's not hard to write this way, but it is hard to give yourself permission to do so, because it requires that you be willing to view literary success as a by-product, not as something that can be expected or demanded from your work. Good luck to you, fellow writer!

Lisa Alther
1. When I was starting out, I asked an older author for career advice. He said the most important thing is

to keep your overhead low. I've come to recognize the wisdom of this tip: the lower your expenses, the less time you have to spend at outside jobs, or at writing for pay things you aren't interested in – and the more time and energy you have for your own work.

2. Don't write hoping for money or fame because most writers receive very little of either. Write instead for the enjoyment of the writing process, for the discovery of truths about yourself and your world, and for the pleasure of watching yourself improve at your craft.

3. Experiment with the conditions under which you write to find out which work best for you and your situation. Some writers write so many hours per day, or turn out so many words per day. Others (such as I) prefer to sacrifice vacations in order to only write, sleep, and eat for a week or two at a time. I write with a pencil on a legal pad. Others prefer a computer. There is no silver bullet, only what is most possible and productive for each writer.

4. Finally, don't get discouraged by rejection. Almost every writer I know experienced numerous rejections before getting published, as well as after publication. I wrote for fourteen years and collected 250 rejection slips before getting any fiction published. But if you're writing for the rewards of the writing process itself, you can endure these rejections for as long as you have to. It also helps to be a masochist!

Hugh Thomson
1. Know yourself and be totally ruthless about writing when you actually have a fit of inspiration, which in my case is rare. Gabriel García Márquez was taking his entire family on holiday to the coast in Mexico when he had the idea that became *One Hundred Years of Solitude*. He turned round halfway and drove them all back home and refused to go anywhere till he had started the book... I can't claim anything quite as dramatic but do cancel all other engagements or displacement activities if you feel the muse has come calling.
2. Slow and steady is better than short bursts. Graham Greene claimed just to write 500 words every day, which he reviewed the next morning before repeating the process. But he did it every day. Having a couple of days and nights of intense work and then being exhausted for a week is less productive.
3. For reportage and travel writing, get it down as fresh as you can while on the move, even if that means recording as you go. No, you won't remember it that evening back in the hotel. Or at least you will only remember the generic, not the particular.

Robert Twigger
1. Go where the fun and energy is in your writing.
2. Everything that keeps you writing is good, everything that stops you is bad.
3. Always write from the position of a surfeit of material.

If you feel the cupboard is bare, look at the material from a slightly different angle. You may only need a twenty-degree shift in viewpoint. You may want to write a 'serious' book about the history of cheese but maybe you have not enough good material. So change to a 'personal' book which includes all your own cheese-eating experiences etc. Another great way to increase material is to GET CLOSER. So your story of being lost in Waitrose aged six may seem a bit thin – but if you GET CLOSER you will have far more material.

Jason Elliot
American journalist and author Gene Fowler famously wrote, 'Writing is easy. All you do is stare at a blank piece of paper until the drops of blood begin to form on your forehead...'

So the humane thing, really, is to advise others *not* to write, if they can possibly avoid doing so.

But if that doesn't work:

Distinguish, firstly, between wanting and wishing. Many people *want* to write; fewer *wish* it deeply enough to overcome the obstacles that will rise up in every direction once the decision is made. These are both practical as well as psychological, and greater than you might think.

It is tempting to believe that you can improve your writing by attending courses, seminars, or 'practising' journalism. But your writing comes from your life; if you want to improve your writing, improve your life. Not materially, but qualitatively.

Whether you like it or not, you have a particular voice, which represents a set of unique (and possibly painful) limitations. Detach from it, and your writing will be liberated.

Rory MacLean
Be curious, be bold, be humble. That's my advice for writers.

I write in a need to understand. On the road I, like all travel writers, meet people, make observations and collect stories. A parallel journey, equally real, is then made back home at my desk. There, experience and memories are drawn together and distilled in a process that is inevitably partial and impressionistic. The interplay of these parallel journeys – on the road and on the page – creates the opportunity to compose a narrative that combines facts and feelings, a true travel tale that's shaped in part by an instinctive need to infuse the moment with meaning and value. Such creative risk requires courage. But it can bring forth a work that is at once true and full of wonder, both of its time and timeless, enabling readers to step over a border, to imagine another place or time. It can even draw together – on the page at least – our divided worlds, and so engender empathy. And the humility? To me, the writer is a conduit. He or she – especially if a travel writer –

is not saying 'look *at* me' but rather 'look *with* me' at all these things which are so much larger and more important than me. Curiosity. Courage. Humility.

Kevin Crossley-Holland
1. Don't begin to write until you can't help it.
2. Be parsimonious: when I've reached the point at which it's a must to hunker down, I keep my thoughts and feelings and excitements and anxieties to myself.
3. Momentum is the child of discipline.
4. Look, and look again, and see: 'Way to go the same way I went yesterday.'

Beatrix Mannel
About the kiss and the hug
Long before I wrote my first novel, I was crazy about self-help books on writing.

Back then though, it was very difficult to find any. Amazon didn't exist. In Germany, where I live, there wasn't much of a culture on writing as something you can teach or learn. The general idea was that an author was a genius, living in the perfect solitude of an ivory tower, waiting for their muse to arrive. So I begged friends in the United States to send me books about writing.

All those books on writing with their strict rules tended to contradict one another: start with the weather... forget the weather... you must plot... don't plot... but that didn't keep me from reading them. It was as though I was addicted. While learning about writing from them, I yearned for a eureka moment, enabling me to write the story by myself.

Having written forty or so novels in German, with translations in other languages, I have come to realize that there's not one perfect tip for writers. Although I still do pick up useful ideas from books about writing, I've come to see that it's important to pay attention to how writing tips resonate with your body and soul. Every writer is different and has to find his or her own special tools.

First: *Always remember the kiss.*

What does that mean? I'm a tremendous perfectionist and therefore also a huge procrastinator. That's why I tend to improve beginnings endlessly. I polish my sentences, want them to be extraordinarily intelligent, to shine like stars and sound like symphonies. And yes, you can keep doing it until the end of time.

It's absolutely nuts!

It took me several novels to grasp that it's much better for me to sit down and clench my teeth until I've completed even the most faulty first draft. Once I have it, no matter how weak I might imagine it to be, I know exactly what the end's going to be like.

At that point it makes sense to rewrite and interweave, adding material you'd left out of the first draft. Until your beginning kisses the end, you don't have what you need. Even if you're very meticulous with plots and structures, you have to write the whole story. You've got to know in detail what happens to your characters and how the end will link to the start. Now you can polish the beginning, and now the beginning will achieve the underlying sparkle of the kiss.

My second tip has to do with your life as a writer: *Hugs help you to survive.*

From reading all those self-help books on the craft of writing, I came to the conclusion that if I give my very best, the universe will support me. Like Julia Cameron says in one of my favourite books, *The Artist's Way*: 'Jump, and the universe will catch you.'

The truth is, that this is not the truth.

Even if you write like hell, that doesn't mean anything to the universe. There are so many books out there, well-written, interesting books. Even if your book was to be a work of unsurpassed genius, there's no guarantee of success.

This doesn't mean you shouldn't write.

But there's something schizophrenic about writing. Nobody in all these books was talking about it – and that is true even if your book hit the *New York Times* bestseller lists:

On one hand your novel must be the most important thing in the whole world to you. Your heart must bleed for the sake of your story. Nothing in the universe should rival its place in your affections.

On the other hand, you must be able to see your novel only as the game it really is. You've got to grasp that it's the most unimportant thing in the world. There are plenty of things way more pivotal and essential – like your family, friends, and your health.

Thirdly, you've got to recognize that you're much more than your novel. Your self-respect and self-worth should not depend on the book you're writing. It sounds crazy, and in many ways it is. But you have to remember this: you have to live in the real world to have something to write about. You have to hug the world, not only with your words, but with your heart.

And you need someone who 'hugs' you and your writing. During all those dry periods while you're working hard through your first draft (just because of this important kiss), it will make your writing life much easier if you have someone, who's interested in your writing, who's asking how the story is coming along, and who gives honest helpful feedback. That can be a friend, a writing colleague or a writers' group. In order not to go utterly nuts while writing, you need and deserve that support.

John-Paul Flintoff
1. I write to understand what I think. I let it reveal itself, just as Michelangelo discovered what was inside lumps of rock as he bashed at them. Keep putting things down, ask myself if it's right, and eventually get it close (or,

close enough).

2. I have rediscovered the pleasure of writing with a pen. At the start of this year, while researching and writing a book very fast, I hand-wrote about 60,000 words in a pair of notebooks. There's something about writing by hand that connects me to myself in a way that a keyboard just doesn't, quite.

3. Sometimes I hate words. I get too much 'in my head', and have to draw or make music (or hum, or whistle) instead to reconnect to my heart, for want of a better word.

Dr James Lovelock
What, for example, is the meaning of the word 'alive'?

I know that we both are very much alive but is a tree, bursting with green leaves and blossom, alive? A giant conifer tree, a hundred metres tall, of the kind that live in California seems to me to be very much alive yet only one per cent of it is living tissue. The rest of it that forms the massive trunk is deadwood and so is much of the bark that surrounds and protects the growing part of the tree. We do not object when someone says, 'The redwood tree is alive.'

So why do most object when I claim that the Earth is alive? It is true that, like the tree, the bulk of the Earth is dead. It is made of primeval rock or molten iron; these were never active components of a living system. So how can I say, as I sometimes do, the Earth is alive and her name is Gaia? I say that it may be alive because unlike all the other planets it has regulated its climate and other physical conditions, such as the salinity of the ocean and the composition of the atmosphere, so as to be for at least two billion years habitable by the various forms of life.

Now there is a wonderful subject to debate.

Tony Hiss

The main job as a writer is to get out of the way. If you're a fiction writer, it's the characters who tell the story. If you're a non-fiction writer, it's the subject – the place, the event, the people. Writers make this possible by what they do beforehand – creating and getting to know every last detail about their characters and subjects. Drinking in a place's sights and sounds and long history – listening to a place or a moment until you can hear it calling out to you. This is the part of writing that's real work and may take time. The other tip comes from my writing mentor, E. M. Frimbo, who, when I was getting started and having trouble with the wording of a piece, told me that in fifty years of editing he found that 'There's always a way.' Words are there, waiting for you.

The Great and the Good

'The first draft is just you telling yourself the story.'
Terry Pratchett

'You can always edit a bad page. You can't edit a blank page.'
Jodi Picoult

'And by the way, everything in life is writable about if you have the outgoing guts to do it, and the imagination to improvise. The worst enemy to creativity is self-doubt.'
Sylvia Plath

'Don't tell me the moon is shining; show me the glint of light on broken glass.'
Anton Chekhov

'Don't bend; don't water it down; don't try to make it logical; don't edit your own soul according to the fashion. Rather, follow your most intense obsessions mercilessly.'
Franz Kafka

'A professional writer is an amateur who didn't quit.'
Richard Bach

'There is something delicious about writing the first words of a story. You never quite know where they'll take you.'

Beatrix Potter

'I hate writing, I love having written.'

Dorothy Parker

'Easy reading is damn hard writing.'

Nathaniel Hawthorne

'Writing a book is a horrible, exhausting struggle, like a long bout with some painful illness. One would never undertake such a thing if one were not driven on by some demon whom one can neither resist nor understand.'

George Orwell

'A good writer possesses not only his own spirit but also the spirit of his friends.'

Friedrich Nietzsche

'My aim is to put down on paper what I see and what I feel in the best and simplest way.'

Ernest Hemingway

'I write for the same reason I breathe – because if I didn't, I would die.'

Isaac Asimov

THE REASON TO WRITE

'A person is a fool to become a writer. His only compensation is absolute freedom. He has no master except his own soul, and that, I am sure, is why he does it.'
Roald Dahl

'My books are like water; those of the great geniuses are wine. Everybody drinks water.'
Mark Twain

'Concentrate on what you want to say to yourself and your friends. Follow your inner moonlight; don't hide the madness. You say what you want to say when you don't care who's listening.'
Allen Ginsberg

'The best time for planning a book is while you're doing the dishes.'
Agatha Christie

'To write well, express yourself like the common people, but think like a wise man.'
Aristotle

'In old days books were written by men of letters and read by the public. Nowadays books are written by the public and read by nobody.'
Oscar Wilde

'I finished my first book seventy-six years ago. I offered it to every publisher on the English-speaking earth I had ever heard of. Their refusals were unanimous: and it did not get into print until, fifty years later, publishers would publish anything that had my name on it.'

George Bernard Shaw

'Publishers are notoriously slothful about numbers, unless they're attached to dollar signs – unlike journalists, quarterbacks, and felony criminal defendants who tend to be keenly aware of numbers at all times.'

Hunter S. Thompson

'*Publicamos para no pasarnos la vida corrigiendo los borradores, para librarnos de un texto.*'

Jorge Luis Borges

'It is bound to be a failure, every book is a failure, but I do know with some clarity what kind of book I want to write.'

George Orwell

'An author who gives a manager or publisher any rights in his work except those immediately and specifically required for its publication or performance is for business purposes an imbecile.'

George Bernard Shaw

Source: *Goodreads*

A Doris Lessing Afterword

'A writer is the conscience of the world.'

'I don't know much about creative writing programs. But they're not telling the truth if they don't teach, one, that writing is hard work, and, two, that you have to give up a great deal of life, your personal life, to be a writer.'

'It's amazing what you find out about yourself when you write in the first person about someone very different from you.'

'I write because I've always written, can't stop. I am a writing animal. The way a silk worm is a silk-producing animal.'

'If you read, you can learn to think for yourself.'

'Remember that the book which bores you when you are twenty or thirty will open doors for you when you are forty or fifty – and vice versa. Don't read a book out of its right time for you.'

Doris Lessing

IN THE TIMES I've got to know famous people, I've found it difficult to square their public persona with the way they really are.

When I was young at Langton House, Doris Lessing was one of so many who turned up at weekends. She liked to work in the herb garden most of all, and was often found there making potpourri.

Doris didn't stick out in any way at all.

She dressed in an understated way, drove a battered old Volkswagen, and conversed quietly. Her favourite subjects were gardening, Africa, storytelling, and cats. She always struck me as someone who relished life at Langton House because when there she could be herself.

I liked spending time with Doris because she was sensible. Not in an obvious way, but in a way that might be called 'profound'.

When Doris told you something, you knew full well it had been uttered after careful thought. More often than not, I got the sense that her mind was always grinding away, and that in conversation she tossed in handfuls of ideas and conclusions prepared earlier. Never once can I remember Doris saying something on which she hadn't mused long and hard.

As I grew older, I discovered Doris had a life outside Langton House. Of course she did. The mind of a child makes sense of what it sees and knows, and that's what mine strained to do. Gaps in what I knew were simply filled in with invention – which is why the way children think is the default setting of us all.

In my teens, I would often get a lift up to London with Doris, when she was on her way back to West Hampstead. We would talk about Africa, and travelling, about stories, and Nasrudin.

On one journey, as we jolted forward through nose-to-tail traffic in south London, Doris ended a long silence with the words:

'You know, I was at your naming ceremony.'

'Where was it?'

'At Coombe Springs, a few months before your parents moved to Langton House. I remember the date. It was 21st March 1967 – when Safia and you were four months old.'

'On *Nauruz*, Afghan New Year?'

'Yes, that's right.'

'Who else was there?'

'A long list of luminaries,' Doris replied, her eyes widening at the memory. 'Russell Page and Robert Graves, and dozens of others – all of them quite extraordinary in their own right.'

'Do you remember anything from the ceremony?'

Doris fell silent, her mind scrolling back through more than twenty years.

'Yes, I do,' she said. 'Your father wore a magnificent robe over his shoulders, presented to him by King Ibn Saud. He quoted passages from the *Rubaiyat* of Omar Khayyam, and from Rumi's *Masnavi*. Prayers were spoken, and thanks for your life were given. You were both named, and then something remarkable happened.'

'What?'

'Your father touched a hand to your forehead and announced you would be protected throughout your life by your sense of humour – the kind contained in the wisdom of Mulla Nasrudin.'

'My suit of armour,' I mumbled. 'The one he said would always shield me from danger and injustice.'

Like me, Doris savoured conversation, following the thread of an idea, teasing it out, and seeing where it led.

A voracious reader, she had a vast knowledge ready and waiting to be harnessed. An inspiration in a deep-down way, she expected others to work as hard as she herself did.

'The secret of success is applying oneself,' she once told me. 'Not in a mediocre way, but as though your life depended upon it. Most people fear hard work, or are too lazy for it. I feel for them, because they have no idea of the joy it brings.'

From time to time, we'd meet somewhere unexpectedly, and take up right away where we had left off.

On a handful of occasions I saw Doris out in the bear-pit of superstardom. At best it was uncomfortable to witness, and at worst it was like having one's teeth pulled. I watched as the quiet woman I knew and loved was overwhelmed by seething, frenzied crowds of fans.

One memory springs to mind.

We happened to be in San Francisco at the same time. I was on my way to Tokyo, and she was speaking at a literary event.

Many hundreds of people from the Bay Area and far beyond had packed into the huge auditorium. Most were clutching well-thumbed copies of their favourite Lessing novels. Some wore T-shirts that blared:

I LOVE DORIS EVEN
MORE THAN YOU!

I was bustled into the green room, where Doris was sitting alone with a cup of tea. As soon as she saw me, her eyes lit up.

'Take me somewhere with you,' she said.

'You mean, outside, to a café – somewhere like that?'

'No time.'

'So where?'

'Let's go somewhere in our imagination,' she said.

So we did.

We chatted about the scent of the first rain on African soil, and how people in Harare dress up to go to Sunday church. We laughed about the foolishness of publishers, and how the same object or idea can seem different along the journey of one's life.

Then, sipping her tea, Doris said:

'You will be a great writer, but only if you remember not to be like them.'

'*Them?*'
'The others.'
'Which others?'
'The ones who write for the wrong reasons.'
'What reasons?'
'For publicity and fame, for attention and glory.'
'Why do *you* write?' I asked.
'Because I can't stop. It's a fountain inside me, a fountain that can't be turned off. Or at least, I haven't yet found a way to control it. So it gushes and gushes. Like something out of *The Arabian Nights*, I summon it, and have shaped it over time. If I stopped writing, the fountain's water would get higher and higher, and would drown me.'
'But would you ever want to stop writing?'
'Don't think so. You see, it gives me great pleasure.'
'How?'
'By allowing me to take a lump of clay and shape it. I do it out of curiosity as much as anything else. Taking a handful of characters, I put them into a situation, and watch how they react.'
I fluttered a hand towards the auditorium.
'What about all that?'
Doris huffed in boredom.
'I write for myself,' she answered. 'I don't do it for anyone else. I suggest you grasp the bull by the horns and dive in. Keep writing, even when you're down. Don't wait for people to praise you. Hone your style,

and observe yourself from above as you move ahead. Experiment with ideas, and in the way you present them. Of course, use an audience as your sounding board, but remember who you're writing for.'

'For myself?'

'Yes! That's it. For you, and no one else. Just as your father and grandfather did. To keep on track you have to write, write, write – and not listen to anyone who holds you back. Put out work the way you want it to be, and not because you're getting a big fat advance for it. Advances are all well and good for paying the gas bill, but they're blood money – blood money paid by the Imbecile Order.'

'*Imbecile Order...?*'

'The Imbecile Order of Publishers!'

Again, Doris huffed.

'They can all go to hell!' she growled. 'Find me any other vocation in which the so-called "professionals" are as incapable as they are in the publishing business. Most of them don't have a clue. They're all Bertie Wooster!'

'Maybe they're secretly Nasrudin,' I chipped in.

Doris balked.

'I wish it were so,' she replied. 'At least then they'd be wise fools.'

From: *Travels With Nasrudin*

PART VI

SAMPLES

Announcement IV

ON THE PAGES that follow I am presenting samples drawn from my corpus of both fiction and non-fiction work. The intention is to showcase a variety of situations and techniques that I hope explain some of the points I have made.

The Entrance

GETTING STARTED ON a book is the hardest thing of all, but it doesn't need to be...

I once got talking to an expert on carnivorous plants. Lovingly, he showed me a specimen of pitcher plant, explaining how the tubular structure was irresistible to flies, moths, and other small insects. Awed by this wonder of nature, he revealed how it lured the quarry by being apparently simple in form. Unsuspecting flies would land on the outer edge and, before they knew it, they were progressing inside... a realm with no escape.

Construct an entrance into your book that is seductive and seemingly simple, and the reader will find it impossible to resist venturing on.

A series of beginnings follows from a variety of my books. I am not claiming that they are all as succulent as they might be, but I think you'll get the point.

Langton House, 1972
On the eve of my sixth birthday, my father tucked me into bed.
'Are you excited for tomorrow?' he asked.
'No,' I whispered.
'Why not?'
'Because I'm frightened.'
'Frightened of what?'
'Of the monsters under my bed.'
Stooping down, he peered into the darkness.
'Nothing there.'
'That's because they're invisible monsters.'

'If you don't think about them, they'll go away.'
'But they'll just hide under someone else's bed, and that doesn't seem fair,' I said. 'You see, that's how they came to my bedroom in the first place.'

Perching on the edge of my bed, my father smoothed the blanket with his hand, and said:

'I'll tell you something... something that will protect you throughout your life.'

'From monsters?'

'Yes. And all kinds of other things... things that frighten you, or that you don't understand.'

'What is it, Baba?'

'A suit of armour.'

'Like the one down in the hallway?'

'A little bit like that, but different as well.'

'Will I wear it?'

'Yes you will.'

'Can I see it?'

Leaning back, my father grinned, the kind of magical grin that preceded something special.

'This suit of armour isn't like others that you've seen before. It's different because it's not made of metal.'

'Then it won't stop the arrows and the swords.'

'Ah, but it will... in its own way.'

'How?'

'By protecting you from the inside out.'

I didn't understand. All my friends had fathers who said things simply, while mine spoke in riddles.

'What's it made of, then?'

'Of stories.'

'What kind of stories?'

'Stories about the bravest and most amazing fool who ever lived.'

'What's his name?'
Dark eyes reflecting the lamplight, my father replied:
'His name is Nasrudin.'

From: *Travels With Nasrudin*

30th March 327 BC
From the snow-laden crags of the Hindu Kush, the vast army of Alexander, King of the Macedonians and subjugator of the known world, seemed to move in total silence.

The battle cortège comprised more than a hundred thousand men, marching eastwards toward the Khyber Pass, gateway to India.

The cavalry led the way.

Among them was Alexander himself, his burnished bronze armour glinting in the early spring light.

Behind the horsemen followed snaking lines of archers and miles of infantry, camp followers and equipment, animals and supplies.

The men had endured the bitter winter months of Bactria, and the crossroads of Central Asia, by rubbing sesame oil into their frozen skin. Battle-hardened and exhausted, they were far from home.

Alexander's campaign had lasted more than a decade – a conquest in which he had taken the Balkans and Asia Minor, sacked the mighty Persian Empire of Darius, and finally brought his men to the gentle waters of the Indus.

Few had ever imagined their great leader would triumph for so long, and without a single defeat.

It seemed like a miracle.

But the young Macedonian king had a secret.

A secret that had rendered his army invincible and allowed him to cleave a path from West to East in what had been the greatest military campaign in human history.

Far behind the lines of cavalry, the archers and endless legions of foot soldiers, the camel corps booming like thunder with their giant timpani, was a huge canvas tent perched on a wooden platform. Like everything and everyone, it too was moving forward. A cohort of battle elephants was dragging it, their riders armed with lances tipped with blades of tempered steel.

Filling the tent was an object so precious that it was guarded day and night by soldiers hailing from Alexander's own elite Macedonian brigade. So great was the level of secrecy surrounding it that none of them had ever been permitted to see inside.

Had they done so and pushed through the six concentric curtains of sewn canvas, they would have set eyes on a truly astonishing sight: a mechanical machine of magnificent proportions, fashioned from silver, brass and gold. Pendulums and cantilevers swung on their axes, gears clattering as they engaged row upon row of interlinking cogs.

There were flywheels blurred by frantic spinning, pistons mounted on diamond bearings racing back and forth, and dials – hundreds and hundreds of dials. A system of conduits united the individual parts, running with liquid mercury like an infernal flow of supernatural blood.

Once across the Indus, Alexander spent an evening alone in the canvas tent. Those who saw him exit in the light of the full moon said he was trembling, his eyes touched with fear.

The next morning, he doubled the guard on the secret machine. Then, having rallied his weary legions one last time, Alexander led them into the mother of all battles against Porus, the Indian giant-king.

Although exhausted, his legions engaged the foe with a ferocity, brilliance and ease that have amazed scholars ever since.

Despite the overwhelming odds facing Alexander's army, the

victory was his...

...Yet again.

From: *Hannibal Fogg and the Supreme Secret of Man*

There was a sadness in the stillness of dusk. The café was packed with long-faced men in robes sipping black coffee, smoking dark tobacco. A waiter weaved between the tables, tray balanced on upturned fingertips, glass balanced on tray. In that moment, day became night. The sitters drew deeply on their cigarettes, coughed and stared out at the street. Some were worrying, others dreaming, or just sitting in silence. The same ritual is played out each evening across Morocco, the desert kingdom in Africa's north-west, nudged up against the Atlantic shore. As the last strains of sunlight dissipated, the chatter began again, the hum of calm voices breaking gently over the traffic.

The backstreet café in Casablanca was for me a place of mystery, a place with a soul, a place with danger. There was a sense that the safety nets had been cut away, that each citizen walked upon the high-wire of this, the real world. I longed not merely to travel through it, but to live in such a city.

My wife, Rachana, who was pregnant, had reservations from the start. These were fuelled all the more when I ranted on about the need for uncertainty and for danger. She said that our little daughter required a secure home, that her childhood could do without an exotic backdrop. I raised the stakes, promising a cook, a maid, an army of nannies, and sunshine – unending, glorious sunshine.

Since moving from India eight years before, Rachana had hardly ever glimpsed the sun in the drab London sky. She had almost forgotten how it looked. I reminded her of what we were missing – the dazzle of yellow morning light breaking through bedroom curtains, the drone of bumblebees in honeysuckle, of rich aromas wafting through narrow streets, where market stalls are a blaze of colour, heaped with spices – paprika and turmeric, cinnamon, cumin and fenugreek. All this in a land where the family is still the core of life, where traditions die hard, and where children can grow up knowing the meaning of honour, pride and respect.

I was tired of our meagre existence and the paltry size of our flat, where the warring couple next door plagued us through paper-thin walls. I wanted to escape to a house of serious dimensions, a fantasy inspired by the pages of the *Arabian Nights*, with arches and colonnades, towering doors fashioned from aromatic cedar, courtyards with gardens hidden inside, stables and fountains, orchards of fruit trees, and dozens and dozens of rooms.

Anyone who has ever tried to make a break from the damp English shores has needed a long list of reasons. I have often wondered how the pilgrims on the *Mayflower* ever managed to get away at all. Friends and family regard would-be escapees as crazed. Mine were no exception. At first they scoffed at my plan to move abroad and, when they realized I wasn't interested in the usual bolt-holes – southern France or Spain – they weighed in with fighting talk. They branded me as irresponsible, unfit to be a parent, a dreamer destined for failure.

The pressure to abandon my dream mounted. It became so great that I did almost back down. Then, one dreary winter morning, I passed a crowd of people on a central London street. An elderly man at the middle of the group was being wrestled to the ground by two police officers. He was dressed in business attire – pressed white shirt, silk tie, three-piece suit and a plump red carnation pinned to his lapel. In a bizarre display of eccentricity, he had taken off his trousers and was wearing his underpants on his head. The police, who were not amused, were busy cuffing the man's hands behind his back. A young woman nearby was screaming, begging the authorities to lock 'the madman' up.

As the man was bundled into an armoured police van, he turned and shouted: 'Don't waste your life following others! Be individual! Live your dreams!'

The steel doors slammed, the vehicle sped away and the crowd dispersed – all except for me. I stood there thinking over what I had seen and what the supposed madman had said. He was right. Ours is a society of followers, trapped by an island mentality. I made a promise to myself right then. I would not be subdued by others' expectations. I would risk everything and leave the island, dragging my family with me. Together we would search for freedom and for a land where we could be ourselves.

Casablanca's evening rush of traffic rivals any in its ferocity. But it has never been so wild as it was on the late spring day that I took possession of the Caliph's House. I had sat in the café all afternoon, waiting for the rendezvous with the lawyer. He had told me to come to his office at eight p.m. At seven fifty-five I pressed a coin to the tabletop, left the café and crossed the street. I passed a glass-fronted hotel flanked by proud date palms. An empty tour bus stood outside it, a pair of donkey-carts beside, each piled high with overripe fruit. A moment later I was climbing up the curved stairwell of a dilapidated art deco building. I rapped at an oak door on the third floor. The lawyer opened it, greeted me stiffly and led the way into his office.

There was an official-looking Arabic document on the desk. The lawyer ordered me to read it through.

'I don't know Arabic,' I said.

'Then you'd better just sign it,' he replied, glancing at a gold Rolex on his wrist.

He handed me a Mont Blanc. I signed the paper as instructed. The lawyer stood up and slid a hefty iron key across the desk.

'You are a very brave man,' he said.

THE REASON TO WRITE

I paused for a moment to look him in the eye. He didn't flinch. I lifted the key. As I did so, I was knocked to the floor by the force of a violent explosion. The windows blew inwards, shattering with spectacular energy, sending a hailstorm of glass through the office. Deafened, covered in broken glass and confused, I struggled to my feet. My legs were shaking so badly that I had trouble standing. The impeccably dressed legal man was crouched beneath his desk, as if he had previous experience of some kind. He rose silently, dusted the glass from his shoulders, straightened his silk tie and opened the door for me to leave.

Out on the street people were screaming, running in all directions; fire alarms were shrieking, police sirens wailing. There was blood, too. Lots of it, strewn across faces and over slashed clothing. I was too shaken to be of any use to the injured, who were now streaming from the glass-fronted hotel. As I observed them in slow motion, a small red taxi pulled up fast.

The driver was calling desperately from the passenger window: '*Étranger! Monsieur étranger!*' he yelled. 'Come quickly, it's dangerous for the foreigners!'

I clambered in and he swung the wheel, hurling us into the slipstream of traffic.

'It's bombers, suicide bombers,' he said. 'They're going off across Casablanca!'

From: *The Caliph's House*

An ornate Queen Anne brazier was crackling with coals at either end of the opulent meeting room.

The heat warmed the extremities, and left the fifty gentlemen seated at the central mahogany table wishing they had worn their woollen underwear instead.

Long portraits of the Committee's founders obscured the dim silk-covered walls, absorbing the light from a great

Bohemian chandelier, suspended from the panelled ceiling above.

There was a tension in the room, as if each of the frock-coated gentlemen was well aware of his good fortune at being invited to attend.

The dark waxed table was strewn with papers, ledgers, and with maps of Africa, most of them little more than outlines – hinting at the vast unexplored regions and of the riches awaiting the foolhardy and the brave.

At the far end of it was seated Sir Geoffrey Caldecott.

A fleshy red-faced bulldog of a man of fifty-six, he lurched up from his chair, swept out the forked tails of his coat, and thumped the polished surface with his palm. His breathing was excitable and asthmatic, his manner aggressive.

'Gentlemen!' he boomed, raising his hand. 'Gentlemen, I call this session of the Royal African Committee to order!'

The hum of conversation subsided, and the prosperous-looking men seated turned their attentions to the chairman.

'Since the earliest glimpses of history,' Caldecott called out, 'chroniclers have documented its treasures. Ibn Battutah and Leo the African among them – all have recorded its astounding wealth. Never before has a land so abundant with bullion been known!'

William DeWitt, a meagre figure with small calculating eyes, seated to the left of the chairman, stood up. He coughed to gain the attention of the room. DeWitt was a merchant whose immense private fortune had been constructed on the misfortune of others.

He coughed again, more forcefully.

'Gentlemen,' he announced, 'I coax you to conjure your imagination. Picture an African El Dorado where the only known metal is gold! Storehouses overflow with it, and coffers are brimming with it. Roof tiles and cobblestones, cups and plates, buckets and bedsteads, all are fashioned from that most intoxicating yellow ore!'

'The purest gold,' Caldecott broke in, 'all of it awaiting any gentleman who subscribes to this sound project. Our own Major Peddie will be the first Christian, the first Caucasian gentleman, to journey to the golden land and back. And with him will come the entire bounty of that sacked metropolis! But we *must* hurry!'

'Just this morning a messenger has brought news of the French expeditionary force,' DeWitt added urgently, 'departed three nights ago from Marseilles. Their feet already tramp south across African sands.'

Caldecott nudged a finger at the wiry, hunched man to his right. Liveried in a flamboyant lilac frock coat with oversized cuffs, a froth of cream silk wound tight around his neck, Simon Cochran held the title of Committee secretary, although he spent most of his time carrying out duties well below his position.

He did not stand, but instead held up a crisp white sheet of laid paper and a goose-feather quill.

'Pledge your savings now, gentlemen,' Caldecott urged, 'and tomorrow you will be prosperous beyond all imagination!'

With the long-bearded founders peering down in witness from their gilded frames, the investors sprang to their feet. They huddled around the secretary, each one eager to sign the paper, headed with a single word in copperplate script –
TIMBUCTOO.

From: *Timbuctoo*

The windowless walls at Acme Telesales were painted slate grey.

A sea of uniform desks filled the central hall, each one the same drab shade. The chairs were grey as well, and the telephonic headsets, and the complexions of the sales staff who wore them, and even the plastic plants.

The only splash of colour in the entire place was the baseball cap pulled down tight over Blaine Williams' blond mop of hair.

It was fire engine red, and had the word 'CASABLANCA' written in large letters across the front.

'Good morning to you, ma'am,' said Blaine into the headset microphone. 'No, no, I didn't call last week. No, not even the week before. Why am I calling? Well, ma'am, I've got an offer... an offer for the silver generation...'

Click.

Blaine dialled again.

'Hello, ma'am. Let me be blunt: Do you have trouble with your drains?'

Click.

'Good morning to you, sir! Could I interest you in a case of Drain-O-Sure?'

Click.

A miniature buzzer mounted on the left of Blaine's desk, number 52, emitted a muffled warning sound. Beside it was a black and white studio shot of Humphrey Bogart – with signature cigarette, fedora, and sullen stare. And next to it was an empty mug, Bogart and Bergman's cheeks pressed together on the side.

In a well-practised movement, Blaine slipped off his headset, leaned back in his chair and closed his eyes.

'For Christ's sake! Beam me up to the mothership!' he bellowed.

From: *Casablanca Blues*

Examples

THE FOLLOWING SECTION is comprised of passages to illustrate how I have handled specific kinds of writing.

Desperation

THIS EXTRACT FROM my *Paris Syndrome* follows, which pleased me for the way it dragged the protagonist of the sorry story, Miki Suzuki, down through layers of torment to the bedrock of absolute anguish.

Miki might have been terrified, but Alexa was there to comfort her.
'Keep going, Francine,' she said, over and over, 'and you *will* reach the light.'
'But my leg is hurting, dearest Alexa,' Miki whimpered, 'and I am so anxious that I'll drop you.'
The little grain of grit seemed to laugh.
'If you lose me then just pick me up again,' she said.
'But I'll never find you!'
Again, Alexa laughed, a little squeaky, snickery laugh.
'I am every speck of dirt under your feet,' she said.
So, for three hours, Miki stumbled and fumbled, whimpered and moaned. Sometimes she screamed, and at other times she wept. But still she kept moving. Banging from side to side, she felt her way down the walls of skulls.
She was about to give up when she heard something.
A galumphing sound. Like the marching of feet...
'What shall I do?' she said fretfully, without speaking.
'Quickly, go to the feet and you will be saved!' Alexa replied.
And so Miki scurried forwards towards the thumping, her hands jostling fast over the skulls.
All of a sudden she made out another faint glow of light, a glow that became a pinprick, and a pinprick that melded into a dazzling shaft of luminescence.
Squinting, cowering, hiding her face, she got down on all fours.

THE REASON TO WRITE

The light became so bright that Miki screamed. The next thing she knew, she was being dragged back down the tunnel by her hair.

On either side of the passageway, the lines of skulls seemed to watch, stacked neat and orderly like spectators in a grandstand.

'I've got a little surprise for you,' said Remus, a cigarette held in his teeth. 'Something a friend of mine knocked up. Something a little special.'

Again, Miki screamed. Not because she was frightened, nor from pain. But because she had dropped Alexa.

'I need to stop!' she wailed. 'I must stop to get my friend!'

The Romanian grabbed the collar of Miki's dress and dragged her back into the ossuary. Her outburst silenced, she furled up into the foetal position. Her muscles had gone stiff, as though she was in rigor mortis.

Remus plunged a hand down inside his jacket and pulled something out. The size of a large hardback book, it had coloured wires and four straps, and seemed to smell of marzipan. On the bottom edge there was what looked like a cheap mobile phone, hard-wired into the contraption.

Jerking Miki upright, he slapped her hard on the face. And then, with uncharacteristic care, he strapped the device onto Miki's body.

She didn't flinch.

'I can hear you asking me what I am doing,' the Romanian said, with all the gusto of a James Bond villain. 'Well, it's a way of coaxing the people up there on the surface to be a little more generous.'

Once the explosive belt was fitted, Remus whipped out his camera and took another shot, drenching the ossuary in platinum light.

He chuckled, then grinned.

'Don't move a muscle,' he said. 'Because if you do...' the Romanian chuckled again... 'there'll be a big *KABOOM!*'

From: *Paris Syndrome*

A Meeting

THIS EXTRACT SHOWCASES a meeting in the first person, between me and an elderly gentleman. Written as a short self-contained story, it gave me the chance to describe a character I adored, and to give a sense of him through a short interaction.

On the scale of immaculate soft-spoken gentlemen, Hugh Carless was in a league of his own.

As a young diplomat, he'd been sent as Third Secretary to the British Embassy in Kabul, in 1951, and then as First Secretary to Tehran. It was there he received a telegram from his friend, would-be writer and rag-trade virtuoso, Eric Newby. The message suggested they make the first ascent of Mir Samir in the Hindu Kush together.

The journey resulted in Newby's hilarious book *A Short Walk in the Hindu Kush*. The travelogue ends with the desperately pathetic Carless-Newby party crossing paths with Thesiger, who was hard as nails.

Having spent years in the Foreign Office's Central Asian Service, Carless was dispatched to Latin America – where he was later promoted to ambassador. It seemed an odd placement, after all he was an expert in Asia and knew next to nothing about South America.

He explained the thinking to me years later.

'The men in grey suits always have the same worry,' he said.

'What is it?'

'That the chaps in the field will go native!'

The week after my friend first suggested the introduction, I received a letter from Carless, inviting me to his flat for tea.

Unsure what to expect, I made my way to the splendid building on Bryanston Square, a stone's throw from Marble Arch – a long way from the retired diplomat's former stomping grounds of Central Asia.

Having learned everything I knew about him from Newby's travel book, and from a pithy entry in *Who's Who*, the moment we came face to face was one of pronounced expectation.

Carless was standing at the top of the stairs, as though waiting to receive a visiting dignitary. Although not tall, there was something utterly superlative about him.

The first thing I noticed was his posture.

A thing of wonder, it was well beyond ramrod-straight, and must have been achieved through years of self-discipline and sacrifice. After the posture, I took in the shoes: jet-black Oxfords with a parade-ground shine.

Ascending the stairs in what seemed like slow motion, my line of vision ranged upwards: over grey flannel trousers with a razor-sharp crease, up higher over a Savile Row blazer, a cravat, and finally onto the face.

Eyes deep pools of blue, his cheeks were clean-shaven, and his elongated forehead led down to a perfect short-back-and-sides. But it wasn't the features that I noticed, so much as the way that, in collaboration with one another, they conjured a sense of utter tranquillity.

Again, my subconscious pondered whether such a lack of fear and worry was natural or learned.

I've heard it said that to get elected as president, a candidate must greet voters one-on-one as though they're meeting the most singular person on Earth... a combination of eye contact, sincerity, and sedateness. That's how Hugh Carless greeted me – not only the first time we met, but always.

THE REASON TO WRITE

As we entered the drawing room, my eyes picked out objects and textures I knew from my travels. I couldn't help but give voice to the delight, as I roamed from damascened brass dish to Oriental tapestry, and from Mughal miniature to lacquered Kajar screen.

'I've lived with all this bric-à-brac for so long, I hardly see it,' Carless said in his soft trademark voice, ushering me to a low, leather armchair.

'But I'm sure you love it all,' I said.

'I do... but not the part of the object you see.'

'How do you mean?'

Carless smiled, the slow, meandering smile of a man who had gained wisdom through travel.

'Everything has two parts,' he replied. 'The first is the part I suspect you see – the thing visitors tend to marvel at or admire.'

'What's the other part?'

'That which is formed from an object's own secret history, and from the story connecting it to what came before.'

Afternoon tea was brought in, and the elaborate ritual of politeness began for which it was invented to display.

We talked about Central Asia, Africa, and the Americas, telling stories and sharing points of etiquette. Taking turns, we described destinations we had both known and loved, realizing our lives had overlapped.

When telling a story, Carless would pause expertly before delivering the punchline, censuring himself in the name of modesty. A diplomat to the core, his entire performance was designed to elevate his guest by lowering his own sense of worth. As the afternoon progressed, I wondered how I would ever be able to bear conversing with anyone out in the real world again.

After a second cup of orange pekoe, my eyes scanned the room for the twentieth time. Without thinking, I asked if there was an object for which he reserved a special fondness.

'Indeed,' Carless said, his deep blue eyes staring into space.

'May I ask what it is?'

Standing, he drifted in silence to the far side of the room. And, hovering there for a moment, he held a hand towards a metal object, as one might do when introducing two strangers.

I observed it with care.

Two foot high, it was a simple model of a peacock fashioned in steel, the display at the back intricately etched with a pattern and what looked like the sun.

'This is the most precious object I have ever had the pleasure of knowing,' he said.

'Where's it from?'

'From the Yezidi culture of Iraq.'

'The People of the Peacock Angel?'

'That's right,' Carless countered. 'They were once thought to be devil worshippers, but that was nonsense of course. Theirs is a fine and quite remarkable society.'

'If this is the object, what is its story?'

Carless seemed pleased to have been asked.

'Well,' he said, pondering on how to shape his answer, 'diplomats are taught about the country to which they are being sent, or at least they were when I was a young man. While informative, what they learn is from the outside in, and not from the inside out.

'When I was sent to Tehran in the 'fifties, I looked for ways of knowing Iran in another way. I read its literature, appreciated its marvels in architecture and cuisine, but most of all, I liked to visit the Grand Bazaar.

'It was like something out of the pages of *A Thousand and One Nights*. Caverns packed floor to ceiling with treasure – the kind of things that had been crafted as empires rose, and carried away by the hordes when they fell.'

Hugh Carless fell silent, as though seduced by the memory of a particular day.

'Rustam Ali Mansur was rumoured by some to be king of the smugglers, and by others to be second in wealth only to the Shah,' he went on, turning slightly to face the light. 'I never discovered what was true and what was not. Like everyone else with an interest in knowing Iran in a less than obvious way, I became a customer of the inimitable Rustam Ali Mansur.

'You will need to take advantage of your own imagination to picture the scene of the emporium,' Carless expressed. 'Winged lions sculpted from tremendous blocks of stone in ancient Babylonia. Solid silver bedsteads made for emperors and kings. Venetian chandeliers, grand pianos, grandfather clocks made for Louis XIV.

'Whenever I visited, I would wear my roughest old hiking clothes. I'd pretend I was a writer on my travels, and that my budget was next to nothing. Many of the other dealers might have shooed me away, but Rustam Ali Mansur had a skill they did not possess. From the moment you entered the emporium, eyes wide at the wonders contained inside, he would – as my American friends say – be "sizing you up".

'In his mind he would have picked out an object for you to buy, without letting on what it was. Like a stage magician executing the perfect illusion, he'd lead you to it in an almost telepathic way.

'One afternoon I slipped out from the embassy, went home to change into my hiking clothes, and took a taxi down to the Grand Bazaar. Weaving through miles of passages, I made my way to Ali Mansur's shop, where I found the dealer waiting for me.

'My visit coincided with a government crackdown on tax. Antiques had been subjected to additional duty, which had caused great problems for many of the *bazaaris*. However, the ingenious Rustam Ali Mansur didn't think like the others.'

'How did he think?' I asked.

'Like a fox.'

Turning back to the peacock, Carless allowed the side of his hand to brush against it, as though transporting him back to Tehran's Grand Bazaar.

'If an object was presented as a gift, no tax was due,' he said. 'And so, seeing me intrigued by our friend here, the old fox called out to me, "Everything this afternoon is free!"

'Although delighted at the information, I was naturally suspicious. So I asked for clarification. "It's simple," Rustam Ali Mansur said, "take anything you wish – including that peacock – for nothing. However, you should know that connected to every object is a story. A story that is as much the object as it is itself. Being a treasure in its own right, the story does have a nominal price."

'I asked what the story attached to the peacock cost. Rustam Ali Mansur shook his head. "Better to ask first what the story is," he responded, "rather than the price. After all, you may not wish to buy it."

'"But it's actually the peacock I am interested in,"' I said, '"rather than its story." The dealer shook his head again. "With one comes the other," he explained. "They are inseparable." Weary of Oriental logic, I asked for the story.

'This is what he told me:

'"Once upon a time, Nasrudin put all his savings into a pen of cut-rate peacocks, or rather into peacock chicks. Every day, he fed them with grain, greedily waiting for the time when he could sell them for their feathers. As you know, peacocks are intelligent birds. They soon worked out the fate destined for them. So, just before reaching maturity, they stopped growing. Nasrudin couldn't understand it. He asked another peacock farmer, then a vet, and after him an astrologer, but none had an answer why the adolescent creatures had not grown, with magnificent plumage. At

THE REASON TO WRITE

his wit's end, Nasrudin went to the pen where the birds were kept. Waving his fists at them, he screamed: 'You think I've been raising you for your adult feathers, don't you?! Well, it may interest you to know that it's not the case. I've been raising you for lovely soft down with which to fill my pillow... the kind young peacocks like you possess. So, unless you get moving to the next phase of your development, you'll be cuddling my head as I dream tonight!'"

Hugh Carless passed away in 2011, robbing me of the last soft-spoken gentleman I have had the good fortune to know.

Days before he died, he sent me a typed memoir of his life. Though a wonderful surprise, it was not the last that I received from my impeccable, straight-backed friend.

For, a few weeks after his funeral, the porter at my London club said a large cardboard box had come for me.

A large box filled with polystyrene chips.

Delving both hands in, my fingers touched a metal object. Even before my eyes had seen it, I knew what it was.

The Yezidi Peacock: as much a wonderful story as it was itself.

From: *Travels With Nasrudin*

Light vs Dark

As I HAVE learned the writing craft, the techniques I work with have improved. Looking back at work from earlier in my career I tend to think that I was trying too hard, whereas now I've mastered the ability to set a scene with light brush strokes.

Two passages follow.

The first, from *Travels With Nasrudin*, was written relatively recently, and in my opinion is a text that's nimble on its feet. The second piece, from *Trail of Feathers*, is much more laborious. The second piece strikes me almost like a piece of half-finished sculpture in stone.

Passage 1
When hiring the porters back in the village where the river was wide, a puny young man called Giovanni had stepped forward.

All the other men were built like trees, and so Giovanni didn't seem like an obvious choice. With two tons of food and equipment to be hauled upriver, we needed brawn.

I was about to turn Giovanni away, when one of the men yelled out that he could tell stories like no man alive.

As soon as I heard that, I hired him right away.

Through the dark windswept nights of many weeks, Giovanni told a tale that went on and on. It was a tale of demons and cannibal tribes, of magical kingdoms, buried treasure, and mermaid princesses whose hair was plaited from strands of pure gold.

Each night, once the men had eaten, and had dried and bandaged their feet, the tale would begin where it had left off

THE REASON TO WRITE

the night before.

Like a master storyteller recounting the next installment of *A Thousand and One Nights*, Giovanni would tailor the evening's episode to the conditions in which we found ourselves.

On nights with especially ferocious weather, or when we had hauled the rubber boats and rafts up rapids, the story would be filled with even more action and dreamlike description than usual.

Giovanni had the ability to gauge what his audience needed – like a doctor devising the perfect treatment. A rare and quite astonishing faculty, it's one I've never forgotten.

Of all the magic in his long twisting saga, one element has stuck in my mind more than any other: the way he breathed an emotional quality into the tale.

Like a gold thread woven into a tapestry, it gave an intoxicating value – appealing to something primeval in all who received it.

As in the tale that Giovanni spun in the jungle each night – the emotional paradigm seeped in through the listener's ears and into their soul. The tale became part of them. Or, rather, the poignant connection became part of them.

The porters came to rely on the prospect of Giovanni's storytelling as a way to get through the hardship of the day. While hauling the Zodiacs and the homemade rafts upriver, their thoughts dwelt not on their aching muscles, or injured feet, but on the next instalment of Giovanni's tale.

In the twelfth week we reached a kind of plateau – not in the geography of the jungle, but in our ability to go on. Utterly exhausted, the men were like a military corps unable to continue. They were on the verge of mutiny, and I didn't know what to do.

At dusk one night, I took Giovanni aside and said to him:

'We both know I'm a terrible leader and that the men hate me... but they *love* you. You're the one person who can rally their spirits. Is there anything you can do to get them moving again?'

Giovanni sighed, as though I were asking for a miracle.

'They want to kill you,' he said. 'They're talking about it openly.'

'I know! I can see it on their faces.'

'This is a dangerous situation,' the storyteller said.

'I'm begging you to help me!'

'There is something,' Giovanni said.

'What?'

'Something that may help.'

'Yes?'

'*Sí*.'

'Please don't suggest more food – we can't spare any more rations.'

'Not food.'

'Then...?'

'Something more delicious than food.'

'What?'

'A story.'

'But you tell stories every night.'

'There's another story – a special one.'

'A better one?'

'A story I've been keeping.'

'Keeping for what?'

'For an emergency.'

As someone who's searched for treasure, lost cities, and even for King Solomon's mines, there are moments in which I feel jaded by it all. In my adventures, every possible excuse, fragment of advice, stray idea, and spoken observation, has reached my ears.

But I'd never once heard of a story being kept for an emergency. It was like breaking the glass to reach a hammer with which to smash a train window in the event of a crash. I asked Giovanni what tale could save us from the jungle, and ourselves.

'The Story of Henrique de Cabarone.'

THE REASON TO WRITE

'*Henrique de...?*'
'Cabarone.'
'Who's he?'
Giovanni the storyteller bit his lower lip anxiously.
'You are Henrique de Cabarone, señor.'
'*Me?*'
'*Sí* señor.'
'How could a tale about me – or Henrique de Cabarone – save the expedition from impending disaster?'
The storyteller rolled his eyes.
'By making the men laugh,' Giovanni said.

Passage 2

The round bar at Hotel Gran Bolivar was once known as the 'Snake Pit', because every socialite tongue could be found there, hissing gossip. These days it's hardly patronized at all. Bartenders are positioned at strategic points around the salon, waiting for the bustle of clientele which never comes. Their bow-ties are tight, their hair groomed back with brilliantine, and their eyes alert. Each evening, the small dance floor at the centre of the room is swept and polished with beeswax. But years have passed since feet last swanned over its parquet.

Despite my friend's fretting, I survived the night at Gran Bolivar. I'd seen no ghosts, but had woken with an excruciating headache. It felt as if I'd been clubbed with a baseball bat, but the woman with the cleaver had left me alone.

After breakfast, I set out into the river of honking traffic in search of Professor Cabieses. The street corners were jam-packed with moneychangers, clutching rolls of dollar bills. They vied for space with a swarm of hawkers, selling potted plastic flowers and hurricane lamps, frying pans, Zippos and chicks dyed pink. One man ran into the road with his stock of squirming puppies.

Anywhere else motorists might be uninterested in snapping up a dog. But in Lima, where there's a deep mistrust of retail stores, the street is the only place to shop.

The Peruvian capital gets a bad rap from tourists. They say it's rundown and dangerous, that the sewers stink and that everyone you meet is out to either rob or kill you. It is partly true. I've never known another city where a waiter chains your bag to the table, or where the knifings are more common.

At its height, Lima was one of the grandest cities on the continent.

It was rated as more beautiful than Paris, as refined as Rome. Stroll in the backstreets off Plaza de Armas and the flamboyant baroque doorways, heavy with crests and friezes glare down. Like the enclosed balconies of the *palacios*, the palaces, they signify the opulence of a colonial power with a point to prove. But the high life came to an abrupt end in 1746 when a great earthquake struck. Most of the resplendent villas and colonnades, the plazas and the *palacios*, were reduced to dust.

In the century which followed, the wars of independence slashed the capital's population, as Limeos were sent to the front lines. With time, their city was rebuilt, but it never regained its majesty.

A few telephone calls tracked Cabieses to a large teaching hospital near Miraflores. An elite suburb, the area is reserved for those who have made it. In Miraflores rich women walk in Italian shoes. With their hair swirled up like candyfloss, they prowl the pavements, flashing off their jewels. The streets are free of *vendedores ambulantes*. There's no one touting moss-green lizards or surgical gloves, and the only smell is of espresso brewing on spotless stalls.

Professor Cabieses' secretary mumbled that he had gone to a neurosurgical conference and would be back in a week. I said that

THE REASON TO WRITE

I'd thought the doctor was an authority on drugs. In a secretive voice, the assistant replied that Dr Cabieses was an expert in many things.

Again my journey had been becalmed. With a full week to kill, I cursed myself for conducting a search where any answers proved soon to be further questions. What began as a trail of feathers, was becoming a trial of unfulfilled hope. I went to the concierge of Hotel Gran Bolivar for words of comfort. He pushed me towards a taxi. Museo del Oro, the Gold Museum, was the only thing worth seeing in Lima, he said.

No one was quite certain when Miguel Mujica Gallo founded his remarkable museum, which nestles in the suburb of Monterrico. I cannot think of a greater shrine to the art of collecting. A treasure trove, it's brimming with loot. Even before I'd got into the main body of the building, I found myself wading through Gallo's less important collection – several hundred thousand weapons. He had bought up just about everything one might care to look at, from General Custer's revolver to a set of rare Persian helmets.

The scope of Gallo's museum was impressive, but the size of the collection was almost irrelevant; it was his collecting spirit that mattered. That spirit, I reflected, had kindled my current journey. Everyone ought to be working on a collection of some kind. I would count myself as a collector of *tsantsas*, shrunken heads, even though I have yet to afford one. When I was nine my aunt explained to me that a man without a collection was like a house without a roof. She presented me with a triple-edged Malayan dagger-cane, and advised me to collect sword-sticks, which I have done ever since.

Most of Museo del Oro was devoted to artefacts from pre-Incan Peru. There were textiles of Birdmen and funerary dolls, macaw-feather cloaks, Chancay ceramics, ritualistic daggers, mummies, and a dazzling accumulation of gold ornaments. But, for my money, all the rest was eclipsed by four understated objects. Two of them were skulls adorned with yellow and blue feathers. The other two were figurines. About two feet high, they were covered in bright feathers as well, and had crude jeering faces. In their hands were trophy heads.

From: *Trail of Feathers*

Interleaving

As I HAVE highlighted, one of my very favourite writing techniques is to have two or more interleaving threads. I tend to write short chapters, and flit between one thread and the other.

This is an example:

Seven
1888
Hidden away at his study in Balliol, Hannibal Fogg cleared the oak desk of books, placing a heavy iron retort at one end.

The journey back from the Greek Islands had been painfully slow, and had filled him with anxiety, as though an ancient way of life was about to collide headlong with a grand new order.

During days and nights at sea he had found himself imagining what breakthroughs the future might hold, and how they might shape the life of his descendants.

One day, he felt sure that man would travel the open skies in powered gliders, travelling faster than the speed of sound. He conceived a time in which people would communicate through miniature contrivances, sending messages anywhere in the blink of an eye. A time in which electrical machinery would usher in an age of unimagined possibility. A glorious future inspired by the genius of the ancients. The same genius that had created the device from Antikythera Island.

Hannibal's study was cramped, with a single window high on the east wall. At least a third of the space was packed with boxes of equipment, with discarded scientific experiments, anatomical samples, and notebooks tied up with coarse brown string.

In one corner, a home-made cooling system had been rigged

up – coiled tubes, conical flasks, and jars half-filled with ammonia.

At eleven minutes past nine, Hannibal placed his silver pocket chronometer on the bench, heaved the salvaged device onto the retort, and began the examination.

Beside his left hand were fifty sheets of fine white foolscap paper and half a dozen sharpened pencils.

By lunchtime, twenty sheets had been filled with mathematical calculations, equations, sketches, scribbled details, and pages and pages of notes.

Hannibal linked the device up to a series of coloured wires leading to a home-made electrical generating machine. Taking off his jacket, he rolled up his shirt-sleeves, his thoughts lost in concentration.

There was a knock at the door.

'Fogg, are you there?'

Before he could reply, a slender figure with aristocratic Arab features swept in.

'Good news my dear friend! I've received the funds for the new prototype. My father must be in a good mood! He was unusually generous this time. Shall we call it Prototype-B? If we get moving, we'll have it built by the solstice.'

Hannibal was so engrossed in the gears that he didn't look up.

'Fogg...?'

The visitor clapped his hands.

'Did you hear me, Fogg?'

'Hmm? Oh, Osman, hello... How are you? Look at this!'

'What is it?'

'The very most extraordinary object in existence!'

'What?'

'Proof of the genius of the ancients!'

'It looks like a clock.'

'It is! It is! But it's so much more than that!'

THE REASON TO WRITE

As Osman stepped closer his shadow fell over the device. As best friend and confidant, he was permitted rare and privileged access into Hannibal's world.

'Is that a gear?' he asked, taking in the concentric rings.

'Yes, but not just one gear. There are dozens of them!'

Straightening his necktie, Hannibal took in his friend, his cheeks flushed with anticipation.

'It's an elliptical gear transfer system, created a thousand years before the great Arab inventors!'

Osman shrugged.

'Did you ever doubt the expertise of my people?'

'Of course not.'

'So what is it for?'

Hannibal caressed a hand over the device.

'Once we have discovered its secret,' he said, 'the world will never be the same again!'

Eight

That afternoon, as he strolled down to the mailroom, all Will could think of was Britney, and how stupid he must have sounded to her. Kicking himself, he made a plan to ask Todd for girl advice.

The clerk handed over a letter, a heavy envelope bearing English postage stamps. Will recognized the profile of Queen Elizabeth right away, as he did the lack of a country name. Every philatelist knows that British stamps are not required to feature a nationality – reward for inventing prepaid postage in the first place.

The envelope was filthy, as if it had passed through dozens of hands and destinations.

Tearing it open, Will took out the letter.

Inside was a single sheet of cream writing paper crowned with an ornate embossed letterhead. Beneath a few lines of impeccable manual type was a flamboyant signature in maroon-coloured ink.

The letter was apparently from a British legal firm, Messrs Penshaw, Willis, Smink & Company, founded in 1678.

Will's eyes scanned the typed text:

16th January 2017

Dear Mr Fogg,

We write to you as Executors acting for the Estate of your great-great-grandfather, Hannibal Garrett Fogg.

On 29th April of this year, having reached maturity, you will be confirmed as sole inheritor to the Fogg Estate. Upon the precise orders of Hannibal Fogg himself, the full complement of the Estate shall pass to you, and to you alone.

In order for our firm to administer to you the inheritance which is due, we require that you be present for the formal reading of the Will, at 16.00 hours precisely on Tuesday 2nd May 2017 at our offices in London.

We are, sir, your obedient servants,

Basil Penshaw

Messrs Penshaw, Willis, Smink & Co.

When Will had finished reading the letter, he let out a groan, and took a closer look at the postage stamps. Junk mail might be rarer than it was, but the quality was certainly improving... improvements no doubt a result of the data gathering centres Will had read about in the Far East. After all, how could anyone have known he had an ancestor named Hannibal?

He had only heard the name once himself – even then it had been uttered in anger. Great-Aunt Edith had provided it as sole reason for the family's dire financial state.

Slipping the letter back in its envelope, Will stuffed it in his pocket, and ambled back to his dorm.

Inside, Todd was lying on his bed, hungover and bleary.
'Where is she?' he mumbled, confused.
'Who?'
'That little blonde. The one who came over last night.'
'Guess she had classes.'
'No chance of that.'
'Why not?'
'Cos I picked her up at the diner.'
Will unlaced his Converse All Stars, took them off, and slid them neatly under his bed.
'You're not the only one who got lucky,' he said.
'Huh? You telling me you got some action?'
'Yeah, well, almost. I'll be getting some soon.'
'Who's the lucky lady?'
'An angel up in C21.'
'Slick!'
Will grinned.
'What if I was fabulously rich... and English?'
'*English?*'
'Yeah.'
'Oh sure. That'd help. Chicas love an accent.'
Reaching for his pocket, Will pulled out the letter.
'Have a look at that.'
Todd strained on the lines of type.
'An inheritance?'
'Yeah, well, kinda. Would be if it wasn't junk.'
Holding the letter to the light, Todd rubbed the paper between his fingers.
'Watermarked full bond,' he said. 'And the heading's been die-stamped. We're talking hand printed on a Heidelberg, or something with real punch. And look at that signature. Hand-signed in Indian ink. This isn't junk, Will.'

'Then what is it?'
'It's a frigging work of art!'

Nine

1888

An impenetrable green smog had swept silently down the Thames and laid siege to the genteel district of Bloomsbury.

One by one, the residents in the buildings running up towards Camden Town had shut their windows and turned up their gas lamps.

The faint aroma of roasting chestnuts hung on the breeze along with muffled strains of music.

Beyond the front gates of the British Museum an organ grinder was standing at his usual pitch, his right hand wheeling a crank handle slow and hard.

On the right side of the organ, lost in smog, lay the grinder's cap, as invisible as it was empty.

From time to time, the wail of a policeman's whistle cut through the fog, urging anyone left outside to quicken their step, for fear of thievery.

A minute before one, the outline of a gentleman hurried past the organ grinder from the direction of Great Russell Street. Navigating through the pea-souper effortlessly, as if by echolocation, he bounded up the museum's steps. He took them two at a time, the soles of his hand-made Lobbs hardly touched the stone.

The figure raced into the grand circular Reading Room, a twill gabardine overcoat thrown over his arm. Without wasting a moment, he made a beeline for the rows of green index files, poised in the middle of the room.

Finding the author catalogue labelled TWI-UTA, he opened it, drawing a fingertip down tight columns of titles.

Soon his shadow was roaming the bookshelves, his feet running furiously over the parquet, as the hunt began.

Scanning the uppermost row of leather-bound books, then down at ankle height, he lurched left and right.

Tossing his overcoat to the floor, he stopped in his tracks.

There it was...

A slim volume bound in cherry-red morocco, gold embossed lettering down the spine.

The Secret Life of Alexander the Great.

Slumping in a reader's chair, Hannibal opened the book, thumbing his way quickly towards the back. His face streaming with perspiration, he flicked forwards, and back.

Then, turning a page, he breathed in sharply like a man in fear of drowning.

'My God!' he exclaimed. 'I cannot believe it!'

Placing the volume on one of the desk's turquoise leather surfaces, Hannibal swept out from the Reading Room.

His pace gathered speed again.

By the time he was in the museum foyer, he was running full tilt.

Down the long stone corridor.

Through the Assyrian Gallery, past the massive winged lions of Mesopotamia.

Around a corner.

Towards the spiral stairs.

Down, down, down into the belly of Bloomsbury, beneath the great treasure house itself.

More corridors, far narrower than those on the surface.

A series of doors, each dustier and more forgotten than the one before.

As he reached the last, Room 64B, Hannibal caught a flash of his childhood.

A memory of cool lemonade on a winter afternoon, a field freckled in buttercups, a meandering river pungent with wild garlic.

Knocking, the joint of his middle finger stung from the force.

'Open up at once!' he cried. 'I know it... I know it! The Secret! The Supreme Secret of Man!'

Ten

Great-Aunts Edith and Helen were reclining on a pair of matching red velvet chairs set at right angles to one another in the living-room of their modest Oakland home.

They were so old they could remember a time when people were proud to live in the apartment block, back in an age when the walls had been white – free from gang graffiti and grime.

On a good day, their balcony was a pleasant place to sit and soak up the sun. Strain one's nostrils and you could just smell the honeysuckle growing in flowerpots on a balcony opposite.

On a not-so-good day, one had to cover the mouth and nose from the stench of rotting garbage festering in the unemptied bins down below.

Aunt Helen had made cherry flan, a family recipe her mother had passed on two-thirds of a lifetime before. She had placed it on the low coffee table to cool. Neat beside it were three Wedgwood side plates rimmed in royal blue. Next to them, silver cake forks lined up, hallmarks on the handles.

Great-Aunts Edith and Helen had always lived together. Neither had ever married, although Edith had once fallen in love with a Latvian sailor who had eventually run off with her best friend. Never well off, they had always struggled to make ends meet.

Both harboured dreams of winning the lottery, which they played in secret each week. Neither ever told the other – not even when they won.

Part of the reason was the sense of shame.

Over the years the winnings had gone from scarce to almost non-existent. Indeed, they rarely even won the small-fry ten or twenty bucks that kept diehard players hooked.

Dead centre in the middle of the table was a gift.

Wrapped in Little Bo Peep paper, it was tied up with yellow string.

'I hope he won't be late,' said Aunt Edith testily.

'Hush. He's got a long way to come,' replied her sister. 'We should feel fortunate he bothers with us at all.'

'The flan will get cold.'

'The cherries are better at room temperature in any case.'

'I thought gooseberry is what he likes.'

Aunt Helen looked up.

'No, no,' she said firmly. 'Everyone knows, cherry is William's favourite.'

Edith pretended not to listen. She looked out of the window, her nose catching the scent of honeysuckle.

Footsteps.

The doorbell.

A familiar voice.

Before he had even made it through the hall, Will was crushed to Great-Aunt Helen's abundant chest.

'Thank you for coming darling,' she said, tears welling in her eyes.

'Of course I came.'

'She's made a flan,' said Aunt Edith, plopping her knitting down on the chair.

'I'll cut you a piece.'

While Aunt Helen reached for the knife, her sister pointed to Little Bo Peep.

'Aren't you going to open it, William?'

'Can't wait to.'

Will slipped off the string and the paper fell away, as if the gift were unwrapping itself. He stared at a tattered old album, bound between beige canvas boards. On the cover the name of a previous owner had been crossed out in magic marker.

Flicking through the pages, Will's gaze took in the rows of unusual and colourful postage stamps.

'I absolutely love it. Thank you!'

'We are so pleased,' said Aunt Helen, speaking for them both.

'Where did you get it?'

'At a thrift store,' Aunt Edith said icily.

The cherry flan was cut and served.

Moist in the middle as it was supposed to be, its pastry crumbled at the touch of silver prongs.

Silence followed.

A silence in which the pair of great-aunts waited for their grandnephew to praise the flan.

'More delicious than ever,' he said, dusting crumbs from his shirt.

Aunt Helen smiled wickedly.

'I'll pass on the recipe to your wife one day.'

'That'll be no time soon.'

'What, a handsome boy like you still without a girl?'

Will felt awkward discussing dating, especially with his great-aunts. Struggling to change the conversation, he exclaimed:

'Guess what? I got a letter from a lawyer in London. Apparently I'm the inheritor of an Estate.'

'An Estate?'

'What Estate?'

'The Estate of Hannibal Fogg.'

The great-aunts looked up, their cake forks hitting the bone china at the exact same moment.

'They want me to go to London to claim what they say is mine.'

'*Hannibal?*' gasped Great-Aunt Helen.

'Curse that man! Curse his memory!' Great-Aunt Edith spat caustically. Pressing a hand to the mother-of-pearl cameo pinned neatly over the top button of her blouse, she seemed short of breath.

Will took the letter out from his pocket and unfolded it.

As soon as the cream bond paper was in the light, Aunt Edith's birdlike talons snatched it and ripped it into shreds.

'Hannibal Fogg was evil personified!' she growled. 'He was a traitor to the English Crown! He was a spy in the employ of the Nazis – shamed and discredited by one and all!'

Aunt Helen placed her plate on the coffee table, her customary smile gone.

'He disowned his only son,' she said. 'Our father, your grandfather.'

'May he rot in hell,' Aunt Edith grunted. 'The black sheep of the family, he was the reason we emigrated to America.'

'Why?'

'To avoid the shame.'

'When was that?'

'In the 'thirties... After the Purge.'

'What Purge?'

Great-Aunt Helen let out a pained sigh, but did not look up. Her eyes were locked into the pattern of the faux Persian rug.

'All the books he'd written were gathered up from libraries and bookshops alike and were destroyed. Anyone found owning one of Hannibal Fogg's works was fined, or threatened with imprisonment. A special commission was established by the English government. It hunted down all memory of the man... and burned it all.'

Standing, Will stepped over to the window and looked out at the honeysuckle on the balcony opposite.

'Who exactly was Hannibal Fogg?' he asked.

'I've told you, William,' snapped Aunt Edith, 'he was a spy!'

'He was a soldier,' Aunt Helen corrected, 'an explorer, a genius in his own peculiar way.'

Great-Aunt Edith regarded her sister with a poisonous glance.

'He was no genius!' she countered. 'He's the reason we've lived in poverty our entire lives. If I were you, I would forget you ever heard his name.'

'What became of him?'

'He fled to North Africa,' said Aunt Helen.

'Did he die there?'

Aunt Helen looked up, and found herself staring into her grandnephew's eyes.

'He disappeared,' she said. 'No one really knows what happened. He was last seen in Manchuria.'

'When?'

'On Christmas Day, 1939.'

From: *Hannibal Fogg and the Supreme Secret of Man*

Listing

IN MY EARLY travel books I would often be working direct from my journals. The form of the prose was definitely affected by this fact. When taking notes on places visited, I tend to make lists of details. Sights, sounds, smells – they're the blend of rawest magic that leap out from a scene viewed through fresh senses. I've always enjoyed travel literature that conjures a place through masses and masses of detail. In my first travel books I would do what I call 'listing': essentially rewriting bullet points as prose. It's a device I've largely dispensed with in later books. Despite this, rereading the short passages below I can see it has a place in a certain kind of prose.

Seething forward in a savage whirlwind race to the finish line, the maelstrom was thick and furious. There were bullock carts loaded with towers of sugar cane, buses with passengers swinging from the windows; Ashok Leyland trucks piled high with baskets of rotting fish, cows with nowhere else to go; petrol tankers steered by chain-smoking drivers; taxis and rickshaws, steamrollers and articulated lorries; a full traveling circus, complete with a wagon of clowns, a convoy of elephants, a cohort of cyclists with their families riding pillion; and a man on crutches trying to keep up. At the eye of the tornado's vortex, helpless amid the intense black fog of diesel fumes and blaring klaxon horns, was the Express bus.

From: *Sorcerer's Apprentice*

A young Quechuan woman was crouched in the shade, a scarlet blanket spread before her like a toreador's cape. Spread upon it was a pile of dried coca leaves. She adjusted the torn brow of her hat, stroked a hand across her cheek, and waited. All around the island of her shawl, feet were criss-crossing: porters' dusty lace-ups, backpackers' thongs, an official's brogues, a contingent of matching Japanese Reeboks. With an abrupt jolt the train was alive. It came again, jerking me forward and back, as the wheels gnawed into the tracks.

We rolled through the shanty-towns at walking pace. A line of women were selling guinea-pigs, carrots and fruit; their husbands gambling at cards, their children running slipshod through the dirt, like lambs before the dogs. A barber was clipping at a mestizo's proud moustache; beside him, a tarot reader was deciding someone's future. An army of peddlers offered pink plastic combs, dusters and brooms. A pair of fighting cocks lurched at each other in the dust, and a class of school children stood to attention, singing.

From: *Trail of Feathers*

The back streets of the old city were crowded. Old men sat playing draughts with upturned bottle caps, reclining on charpoys or sipping glasses of mint tea. Lines of women in traditional Harari pantaloons loitered outside the many mosques, hoping for alms. There were children too, tottering along with great bundles on their heads, savage dogs snapping at their heels. And everywhere there were donkeys and goats, tattered chickens and underfed dairy cows. Doorways led from the narrow streets into courtyards shaded by sprawling acacia trees. Barbers ran cut-throat razors over cheeks, then rubbed kerosene into the skin. Mothers washed clothes in tubs. The faithful prayed in silence, and in every doorway sat bearded men, their mouths stuffed with qat, their eyes

THE REASON TO WRITE

glazed like those of the Lotus-Eaters. By early afternoon, most of Harar's men were in a trance.

From: *In Search of King Solomon's Mines*

Short, Sharp

WHILE I HAVE dropped the technique of listing, I've delighted in peppering my prose with ultra-short, sharp sentences. Designed to nail a point down, I find they work admirably, and are a cornerstone in my appreciation for writing with short paragraphs. A number of random examples follow to illustrate what I mean.

As children we were obsessed with chocolate.
It's all we thought about, talked about, and wished for. Whenever guests came to the house to visit my parents we would rate them on their generosity in bearing chocolate gifts.

From: *Travels With Nasrudin*

Retracing the route back through the books, parcels, and cats, I went home, leaving Doris to read *In Gondwanaland*.
Two days later, a letter arrived – small, spidery writing on the front.
I sat on my bed, the envelope in my hands. Gripped with fear and anticipation, I knew it would be make-or-break.
Doris Lessing may have been a genius, but she had no halfway setting – she either loved or despised.
Tearing the envelope open, I read the contents.
Right from the start I could tell it wasn't the kind of letter I was used to getting from Doris. Gone was the lyrical description of life at home with the cats, or of her childhood in Africa. Gone, too, was the seductive frivolity of one traveller writing to another. In their place was the brutal yet dazzling advice from an author at the top of her game, to a wannabe nobody...

From: *The Reason to Write*

THE REASON TO WRITE

Kaine was a long lean man, standing six foot two and a half. His shoulders were broad, his hands impressively wide, the nails expertly manicured. He was fifty-three, but could have passed for a man a decade younger, his bottle-green eyes bright and mischievous, and his slender face capable of conjuring expressions of extreme gravity.

The buzzer sounded a second time.

Kaine blinked. Resting the Limoges cup on the desk's walnut veneer, he thought of that evening's meeting. The first Tuesday of the month meant it was the rendezvous of the Obscure Cuisine Dining Club, of which he was a proud member.

It was his night to host.

His ears having picked up the faint sound of a brass door handle turning, he smiled.

From: *Eye Spy*

The Unexpected

THIS IS AN example of surprise, which I have included as it worked to enliven a rather heavy section of my historical novel, *Timbuctoo*:

Shortly after Caldecott left Hampstead, a fog descended over the village. It seeped down from the Heath, along Church Row and through the cemetery at the end of the lane. Percy Waitley would have headed home, but the coins had triggered his greed, which had been compounded by two points of detail.

The first was that the caskets were of the lowest quality, damp pine, the sides uneven and the lids hardly fitting at all. The second, more important, point was that the mourners had provided no names for the deceased.

Working fast, Percy exhumed the second casket, the thickening mist concealing his work. The soil came away easily. Within a few minutes he had reached the coffin.

While drinking in a tavern at Chalk Farm the week before, he had found himself in conversation with Billy Crane. Over many jars of ale, he was coaxed into an arrangement on which he was eager to capitalise.

As any sexton knew, removing a casket from a grave was far more cumbersome than placing it there. In the twenty years he had been digging plots at St. John's, he had never had cause to make an exhumation. Pulling the coffin out alone was not an option. The answer was to prise off the lid and remove the cadaver first.

Jabbing the side of the shovel into a gap where the box's sides fell short of the lid, Percy jemmied it hard. To his surprise the nails popped up with no effort at all. Hurling the shovel out of the hole, he wiped his face again. As he did so, the lid of the casket was flung backwards.

Gasping for air, his body twisted from shock, Robert Adams leered forward from the box.

From: *Timbuctoo*

Grandeur

THE FOLLOWING SCENE from *Timbuctoo* describes a key encounter between the protagonist, an illiterate American sailor Robert Adams, and the English aristocracy. I worked hard to get the historical detail right, and to engineer the scene in such a way that it demonstrated the arrogance of the upper classes.

The great chef Antonin Carême had been at work in the kitchens since five that morning, overseeing the legions of staff. The subjugation of Napoleon had been a triumph in every way. But it was the Regent who had celebrated most of all, for it had enabled him to poach Carême from the emperor's foreign minister, Charles Maurice de Talleyrand.

An architect as much as he was a gourmet, the chef was celebrated for adorning banquet tables with *pièces montées*, elaborate sculptures crafted from spun sugar, pastry and marzipan. As for his cuisine, he blended delicate flavours and colours, concocting menus the likes of which even the gastronome Regent had never imagined, let alone ever seen.

Before quitting London for the coast, Carême was advised by Hastings of Adams' invitation, and instructed to create a special dessert. The budget was set at £100, for a pudding that was to be more elaborate than anything he had created before.

When it came to his guests, the Regent liked to feign forgetfulness, but in reality there was not a detail that slipped his shrewd attention. And few things gave him as much joy as to fashion a spectacle that would be admired by all.

The Pavilion kitchens were cavernous, as large as the banqueting hall itself, and were regarded as the most advanced of their kind ever constructed. There were mechanically operated roasting-spits, huge tent-like copper awnings to waft away the heat, special sash vents in the roof and, in the middle of the room, a thirteen-foot steam-heated preparation table.

Bronze pots and pans covered the walls, hung by their handles, the burnished undersides reflecting the lamplight. An army of sous chefs was darting about, obeying their orders. As for Antonin Carême, he himself was huddled over a sheet of paper in a back room, sketching out a design with which to surprise the Prince.

Dinner was normally served at seven, but having overindulged at luncheon, the Regent instructed for it to be delayed until eight. Waving a hand in the direction of the filly, he ordered her back to the stables, and excused himself to dress for dinner.

Adams found himself alone with Cochran and Lord Salisbury.

'You would do well to be sensible to our host,' said the peer curtly.

'Indeed, Robert,' added Cochran, 'it is not prudent to condemn the notions of the Prince.'

Adams took a step backwards.

'Are you telling me to bite my lip?'

'Indeed we are,' said Salisbury. 'He is the Regent, after all.'

'Well maybe it's time for you English to get rid of your royal family,' said Adams, rising to the bait. 'You'd be better off without them. The French seem quite improved, and I can tell you that across the Atlantic we certainly haven't missed the royal touch. Look around! Look at the fortune that's been lavished on this place! A child of ten would have had more sense than to waste so much.'

Cochran patted a hand to the air in front of him.

'I would caution you, Mr Adams,' said Salisbury, stiffening his neck. 'For such a seditious attack on the ruler of the realm is a foolhardy pursuit.'

'If speaking out is going to get me locked up in the Tower, that's fine. You have all forgotten how the people you're suppressing live. Sometime, when you're not parading around like peacocks, I suggest you take a look out there.'

Hastings hurried in.

He was followed by Frosch and by a team of porters. They had been instructed to remove the entire Collection to the music room, where the orchestra was preparing something a little unusual for the Prince's American guest.

Frosch pointed his baton at the bull elephant.

'Start with that,' he said, 'and then the others. Move them in order of size. And take care of the wheels.'

The sound of the great pachyderm rolling forward mingled with the grunts of the porters. When the beast was gone, Hastings invited the three gentlemen to join the other guests in the south drawing room.

Entering, Adams prepared himself for war.

Thirty of the most self-infatuated members of English society glanced to the doorway making sure it was not the Prince himself, who was expected at any moment. A string quartet was playing Handel's oratorio *La Resurrezione* near to the window, the lichen-green curtains forming a pleasing backdrop. Most of the gentlemen were standing, the ladies seated primly on chairs made specially by Hervé, and upholstered in striped yellow silk.

Cochran and Adams were introduced by Hastings to an elderly gentleman poised ponderously beside the fire. He was staring into the flames, reminiscing of a time when his bones did not ache and his eyes were not misted by cataracts.

'Sir Frederick, I should like to present to you Mr Adams and Mr Cochran, both of whom are associated with the Royal African Committee.'

The old soldier drew his gaze from the flames and moved it up and over to Adams.

'I have heard of your narration, sir,' he said. 'I should not say it but my granddaughter seems quite smitten with you. Your name is the only word on her lips.'

'Has she attended the narration herself?' asked Cochran.

'Indeed. She has hardly missed a moment. And quite a trouble it is, for she is chaperoned by my cousin, the former Ambassador to Berlin. It appears that your journey has excited much animation.'

'I don't know why so much attention is being devoted to me,' Adams replied.

Sir Frederick stared back at the fire.

'The reason seems very obvious,' he said. 'Your intentions are well-meaning of course, but you have stumbled into a contest and seem remarkably naïve as to its rules.'

'To which contest do you refer, Sir Frederick?'

'The contest of Timbuctoo, of course. It is after all far more than the name of a distant destination. It's a symbol of the unreachable, a legend, the reality of which can never be attained. And of course, my dear Mr Adams, our faulty society has no conception of it. For it is only when a man nears blindness that he can see with clarity.'

'Are you saying that you have not sunk all your money in the Committee's expedition?' said the American with a grin.

'Hah, no!' replied Sir Frederick. 'I would be more likely to place every penny I have at my disposal on whether a lame dog could juggle apples.'

The room fell silent and all eyes moved quickly to the doorway, where the Regent was standing, his equerry at one side.

'Salutations, my dear friends!' exclaimed the Prince, who had bathed in rose water and was wearing a red dress top, adorned with medals, his chest bisected diagonally with a sash. 'I am most honoured that you should have ventured here to my little retreat, most honoured indeed.'

The Prince stepped into the drawing room and mingled with his guests.

'He is not the man his father is,' mumbled Sir Frederick.

'You mean that his father *was*?' corrected Cochran.

'His Majesty may be of unsound mind, trussed up like a common convict at Windsor but, believe me, he stands tall over *that*.'

Sir Frederick cocked his head towards the Regent, who was lumbering across to them.

'Gentlemen, a good evening to one and all,' said the Prince. 'What a pity the weather is a little dismal, for a perambulation of the grounds makes for a pleasurable diversion.'

Hastings stepped forward and whispered in the direction of the Regent's ear.

'Ah, excellent!' said the Prince. 'Gentlemen, shall we lead the way to dinner?'

The banquet hall was panelled in silk friezes depicting successive generations of Chinese court life, illuminated by freestanding lamps. The ceiling was domed, edged in gilt, painted with banana leaves, and hung with a chandelier of colossal proportions, a fire-spitting dragon leering from its base.

Beneath the fixture, a long oval dining table was arranged down the centre of the room. It was laid for forty-one, with a silver service completed by Rundell and Bridge only seven days before.

As the guests entered, they were shown to their seats and attended to by a bevy of waiting staff.

The Prince Regent took his place at the head of the table, seating himself on a chair upholstered in crimson calfskin. Before changing for dinner, he had given the seating plan to Hastings, who had been required to commit it to memory.

On the Prince's right was his mistress, the Marchioness of Hertford and, on his left, Robert Adams. A connoisseur of the unusual, the Regent regarded his American guest as by far the most interesting guest of all. Cochran had been placed at the other end of the table, opposite Sir Frederick Ponsonby, and across from Lady Poole.

The tablecloth, starched Egyptian cotton, was blindingly white, and laid with a vast array of silverware. Each setting had a dozen forks and spoons of varying sizes – ranging from diminutive to very large, and as many knives, some sharp, others blunt or curiously shaped. There were a dozen glasses for each guest, again in a range of sizes, all of them lead crystal from Tutbury. As for the service, it was royal blue, rimmed in gold, crafted by Spode at their factory in Stoke-on-Trent.

No sooner had the guests been seated than the stewards poured the first wine, a Muscadet, chilled to the point of crispness. The Regent took a gulp and called for the sommelier. The man appeared within the blink of an eye, a tastevin hanging like a pendant around his neck.

'What do you call that filthy liquid?'

The sommelier stooped, then stepped backwards so that he could stoop all the more.

'The Muscadet de Sèvre, from La Chapelle-Basse-Mer, Your Highness.'

'Is it now? Well I wouldn't feed it to pigs. Get it out of here at once!'

'Of course, Your Highness.'

Fresh glasses were laid and the offending Muscadet was hurried away and poured into the drains.

The Prince jabbed a hand at the menu card, which was covered in an ornate black script.

'I do hope you find the menu satisfactory, Mr Adams,' he said.

'Thank you, I am sure I do. But I cannot read, sir.'

'Have trouble with your eyes, do you?'

'No, Your Highness. I have never learned to read.'

The Regent held up the card.

'We shall begin with a selection of twenty entrées – *Les profitralles de volaille à la moderne, Le sante de poulardes à la d'Artois* and *Les côtelettes de lapereaux en lorgnette*. After that there will be *Les bécasses bardées Les sarcelles au citron, Les gelinottes, Le dindonneau*, and after that, some pudding!'

Wide-eyed, Adams leant forward and reached for the glass of Château Lafite a steward had just poured.

He picked it up.

The room went silent, all eyes pinned on his fingers fastened around the crystal stem. To his left, Lord Alvanley coughed, grunted, and nodded his head at the glass.

'You do not drink before the Prince has done so!' he hissed.

The Regent applauded.

'Excellent, excellent! Mr Adams is the first man I have encountered in twenty years who's ready to show a little gall.'

The guests sat in silence, quite uncertain of whether the Regent was fuming or amused.

'I should like to make a toast!' he cried. 'A toast to my American friend, Mr Adams of Timbuctoo!'

Reluctantly the guests picked up their glasses and took a sip of the Médoc.

'Now,' said the Regent, leaning back in his chair. 'Please inform me, sir, what are the fashions in Timbuctoo?'

'The fashions?'

'Indeed, sir, pray tell, how is the hair being worn? Are they still in powdered wigs?'

'Wigs?'

'Yes, sir,' said the Regent attentively. 'For I am sure that all of us are united in our desire for such valuable information.'

Adams took a sip of wine. He glanced to his right where the

Regent was lounging back, glass in hand, and then to his left down the table of assembled aristocracy.

He wiped his mouth with his hand.

'Observing the fashion was not my priority, Your Highness.'

'Oh dear,' said the Prince. 'I had so hoped for a little information.'

The Marchioness of Hertford stroked her hand over the cream-coloured terrier on her lap.

'Do tell us, Mr Adams, what *was* your priority while at Timbuctoo?'

'Escape, madam. It was escape.'

Alvanley cleared his throat.

'Would you be so good as to inform us, sir,' he said slowly, 'how you prevailed when our renowned Mr Park fell short in reaching Timbuctoo? What was your method, sir?'

'My method?'

'Yes, sir, your method.'

Again, Adams thought before replying. Then, looking Alvanley in the eye, he replied:

'My method was slavery.'

'Slavery?' echoed Lady Asquith, seated to Alvanley's right. 'How very quaint!'

'*Quaint?*'

Lord Exeter raised his glass.

'To slavery!'

'The abolition of the practice was a veritable crime!' said Lord Greville, at Exeter's right, a man whose family prided itself on not working for six generations.

'A crime indeed!' echoed Alvanley rowdily.

'Good honest work,' added Lady Asquith with a grin.

Adams stared down the table in disbelief.

'Slavery is an unspeakable trade!' he said coldly, rising to his feet. 'Your ignorance is surely a comedy!'

The guests looked at the American, then at the Regent, waiting for him to say something. But he remained silent, and so the table turned their attention back to Adams. There was a clatter of bowls as the stewards moved nimbly around the table serving soup, *potage de mouton à l'Anglaise*, garnished with fresh chives.

Still standing, Adams ran a hand back through his hair.

'Only a man whose wrists have felt the shackles of bondage, who has been starved, beaten and bartered like a common runt, can understand the meaning of the word "slave".'

Lord Alvanley began to say something, a tight grin on his face, but Adams cut him off:

'Seated here in grandeur, dining on fine food, and pampered like lapdogs, *you* cannot begin to understand... to understand the fear, the torment of real suffering. To watch as your friends are beheaded for no crime at all, to sever the veins on your arm to quench the kind of thirst none of you will ever know!

'You mock the notion of Christian slavery – the "white" variety, and certainly it is a misdemeanour that we universally decry. But the other form – heathen natives dragged from their African huts, shackled and shipped to a distant land... taming the savage as you see it. Black, white, yellow – the colour of the skin is irrelevant.'

Unable to resist, Lord Exeter poked a hand at Adams.

'What is the negro for, sir, if not for a source of labour?'

Adams sniffed as if disgusted by the company.

'The senses, the sinew, the mind,' he said, his vocal cords straining, 'they have no colour. A man is a man. It doesn't matter what his clothes are like, how he holds himself, the tone of his speech, his ambition. What matters is the essence inside.

'I may be an American, and an illiterate one at that, uncertain which fork is which, ignorant of your etiquette and your customs. You can ridicule me and despise my country, but don't demean yourselves by speaking with sincerity in support of slavery!'

'I say,' quipped Lord Rothermere from across the table. 'Steady on, sir! I caution you to keep in mind the company in which you find yourself.'

'That is exactly what I am doing!'

The Regent took a sip of his wine, put down the glass and began to clap.

'Bravo!' he called once and then a second time. 'Bravo to Mr Adams! Now please sir, seat yourself and take advantage of the epicurean delights that await us.'

From: Timbuctoo

Stories Within Stories

ONE OF MY favourite literary devices is stories within stories. It's something I first found mastered in *The Arabian Nights*, and has long been an obsession of mine. This sequence comes from my small book *Scorpion Soup*, in which each story leads into the next.

The Fisherman
When I was young and foolish, but so certain I was wise, I took any work offered.

Sometimes I toiled days at a stretch without ever sleeping – cleaning fish, bailing water from flimsy craft, scrubbing filth from the decks. And at other times I would lose myself in strange lands, listen to the tales that sailors so like to tell, and would think of the love I had left a world away at home.

The years passed.

Look at my hands and you will see I tell you the truth. My palms are coarse and calloused, tattooed with adventure and with the trials of fate.

Frequently, I promised myself to quit the life of roaming, to settle down in Haifa, where my family was from. But each time I reached my own port, I was talked into embarking on yet one more journey.

And another.

Then, one night in the month of August, my fishing vessel was wrecked during a violent summer gale off the coast of North Africa. The only survivor, I was captured and taken prisoner by a band of Barbary pirates.

Nothing pleased them more than gaining another seaman for nothing, a lost soul to barter in the slave market at Oran.

They had in their party thirty others already. Each one a rough sea dog scraped up from Barbary shores; each just enough alive to coax a ransom.

Day after day after day we marched, dawn until dusk.

One foot after the other, as the dreaded destination of Oran inched closer. And, each day, we appreciated a little more the freedom we had once known, but hadn't realized that we possessed.

Weeks passed, and the wretched captives descended towards Hell. It came one night in the shape of the cells at the infamous Oran death camp. No description however wanton could do justice to that place.

We were trussed up in a long stone barrack in the dark. Emaciated bundles of sinew and bone, we were chained together in rows of a dozen and a half. The dead were left where they had expired. Only when their putrefied flesh was quite rotten, were they removed, their bones pulled from the manacles like a roasted chicken.

I languished there for months, quite certain I would never see the light of day again. I prayed for God to take me, to release me.

And I gave up all hope.

But, one night, the captive beside me murmured a mouthful of words.

I dared not reply or greet him. For if the jailer heard so much as a whisper coming from the cells, he had a habit of severing the windpipes of innocent men.

In no more than the faintest mumble, he recounted a tale.

And it was by that tale's sustenance that I survived:

Idyll
The heat more terrible than I can describe, we sailed into a small cove far to the south, a cove nestled on the coastline of far-off Senegal.

We went ashore, slung hammocks in the trees, built a fire on the beach, and cooked up some langoustines.

I can taste their meat now: all juicy and tender, a hint of coconut and spice.

That cove was idyllic, a paradise known only to one who has courted the sea. Close my eyes and I see the shadows thrown by the palm fronds in late afternoon, and I hear the sound of the birds chirruping in the heat.

As the evening approached, we sat round and shared stories, stories of our travels and of our lives.

I remember it, clear as I am here with you now.

The man beside me was a Spaniard. His name was Alfonso, and he had one of those faces you could never forget: hollow features and an expression baked through from ordeal and tribulation.

Drawing a little on his pipe, he stooped forwards to stoke the fire for a moment, his eyes lost in memory.

'I will tell you a tale,' he said softly. 'A tale of another time, a time when I was not a sailor, but an apprentice to a master bookbinder, in Toledo. The bookbinder was the greatest craftsman of his age, from a family of ancestral binders to royalty no less. Clients would arrive at his workshop from across Spain. Sometimes they even came from France, and beyond. And it was a Frenchman, a famous writer from Troyes, with whom this tale is concerned...'

Capilongo

One day the French writer made a special journey to Toledo to meet the master bookbinder. He arrived by appointment as he always did. For days before his arrival, the apprentices polished and cleaned the workshop, and laid out the finest leathers and samples of the very best work.

On the morning that the writer was due to come, there was a great sense of expectation. We put on our best clothes, polished our shoes until they shone like silver, and greased back our hair with lavender pomade.

At a little after ten, a lacquered carriage pulled up in front of the workshop. The bookbinder, whose name was Fernandez, swept up to the door and opened it wide. Greeting the author with deep respect, he invited him in.

Under the Frenchman's arm was a handwritten manuscript.

It was not so big, about the size of a prayer book, but was printed on very fine paper. Each folio was watermarked with the author's crest, and had an uneven deckle edge.

The writer explained to Señor Fernandez that the manuscript was very important indeed. It was his masterwork, and was to be a gift destined for the Pope. Accordingly, the volume was to be bound in the very best leather, the title embossed with the most expensive gold leaf.

For an hour or more the author went over the details, the exact method of binding that was to be used. He said that price and time were no object. The most superlative materials were to be sought out and used, and only the master craftsman himself was to work on the binding itself.

When Señor Fernandez enquired how long he would be given to complete the task, the writer shrugged.

'Take all the time you require,' he said. 'But remember that I am expecting the best work of your life!'

With that, the French author opened a briefcase and removed a purse filled with gold coins. After he had poured them onto the bookbinder's palm, the two men shook hands.

A moment later, the writer was gone.

As soon as he had left, my master collapsed onto a chair and thrust his head into his hands.

'Where will I get a piece of leather worthy of this manuscript?' he asked, over and over.

I motioned at the swatches on display.

'None of them will do, you fool!' the bookbinder cried. 'Don't offer me coal when I am in need of a diamond!'

A few days passed, and then weeks, and months.

Señor Fernandez slipped into a terrible depression. He began to drink heavily, and we feared he had forgotten about the French author's commission altogether. Whenever any of the apprentices mentioned it, the craftsman would fly into a rage and bawl at us. Without the right leather, he declared that he could never begin.

Then, one morning in September, Señor Fernandez was reading a letter from a correspondent at his desk when, suddenly, he leapt to his feet. Waving the paper in the air, his face gripped with mania, he yelled:

'*This* is the answer! *This* is the answer!'

The apprentices gathered round.

I took the paper and read aloud from the bottom of the page:

'A new species of mammal has been seen for the first time in the Spice Islands. It has been named the "Capilongo", and it is a cross between a boar and a bird, with the hands of a monkey, and with the intelligence of a human child. No one has yet managed to catch the Capilongo alive.'

The old bookbinder instructed his apprentices to line up and to clear their minds. We did so, and he then asked for a volunteer – for a man sufficiently brave or foolhardy to go and capture the Capilongo. Only the creature's leather would do, he insisted, for the manuscript destined for the Pope.

No one volunteered.

One by one, the apprentices stepped back in fear. After all, they were bookbinders, not explorers. Unsure quite why, I leant forward, no more than an inch or two, but it was enough.

'I will do it,' I said in less than a whisper. 'I will go and capture the jungle beast and bring back its hide.'

THE REASON TO WRITE

The next day I set off.

I travelled first to Constantinople, and from there by sailing ship, dhow and hollowed-out canoe, until I reached the pristine waters of the Spice Islands. Never has an adventurer embarked on a journey with less preparation or know-how than I.

Until then, I was a raw page waiting for a story of its own.

All I knew was that the Capilongo was out there, somewhere, and that if I could hunt it, capture it, and take its hide, then there would be a smile on the lips of an old bookbinder, a writer, and possibly the Pope as well.

The voyage was uncomfortable in the extreme.

But, in my untested condition, I hardly knew the meaning of the word – *discomfort*. Had I any inkling of what was to come, I would have savoured the weeks I spent upon turbulent seas.

The one meeting of interest was with a missionary who was drunk from one dawn to the next. He was accompanying a shipment of bibles, printed in Cintra. He told me that they were destined for tattooed savages.

'Where are they, the savages?' I asked.

'Deep in the jungle,' came the reply.

After a great many deviations, the vessel docked at a ramshackle port. I descended the gangplank onto the quay, the name of a mythical creature filling my head and my mouth. With no idea how to proceed, I followed the bales of bibles destined for savages.

There is no feeling quite so contrary as arriving in a foreign land, with no grasp of language or etiquette. The heat was the first thing that hit me, dead straight between the eyes.

The bales of bibles were unloaded by sweat-drenched stevedores and hauled in fits and starts towards that terrible seething undergrowth.

And I followed them.

The missionary bought a bottle of home-made liquor, quaffed

it down, and thanked God for protecting him.

'Pray to the Lord so that you, too, might be blessed,' he said caustically. 'Neglect the Saviour, and the Angel of Death will be your shadow.'

Draining the bottle, he reeled about.

'The jungle...' he said after a long pause, rolling the word off his tongue as if it were a bitter olive, 'it will swallow you whole, devour you, crush your bones to dust.'

We progressed on wagons and on mule carts, on hollowed-out logs, and skiffs, until at last the precious cargo was unloaded on the banks of a great russet-brown river. It was all murky and warm like bathwater left through a long sultry afternoon, and it stank of both life and of death.

The missionary drank another bottle of liquor.

Then another... and declared that the Word of the Lord would be the salvation of the savages.

I asked him again where they were, the savage peoples of whom he spoke so often and with such trepidation. Raising a fist out before him, he pointed at the trees.

'They live on the Mountains of Medusa,' he said.

With no other plan having presented itself, I tagged along, in the hope that the savages would in turn lead me to the elusive Capilongo.

A team of porters were hired.

The bibles and supplies having been laden onto their backs, we set out from the river and into the canopy.

After a few minutes of staggering under loads, we found ourselves in a fearful realm of nature. The towering trees reminded us of our frailty. The creepers and the vines tripped us, the chorus of unfamiliar sounds haunting each step.

The missionary kept the porters content with a ration of dates in honey. But it soon ran out. When it did so, he resorted to a whip.

THE REASON TO WRITE

Any man who refused to pull his weight was lashed to the bone.

Each night we slung hammocks, squeezed water from oversized tubular flowers, and we prayed.

The missionary prayed that the bibles would reach the savages, and I prayed that I would find the Capilongo, smite it, and return to my master with its skin.

The porters had never ventured into the undergrowth before. They spent their lives down at the river and said that only a madman would wish to trek towards the hinterland. When I asked them about the Mountains of Medusa, they seemed to shake with fear. Then, one morning, the missionary and I awoke to find ourselves alone.

The porters had absconded, and they had taken the supplies with them. The only thing they left was the bibles. We called out, our voices lost in the trees.

'We can try and retrace our steps to the river,' I said limply.

The missionary spat at the idea. He opened one of the boxes and removed half a dozen of the bibles. They were well bound in indigo buckram with silver lettering down the spine.

'The savages need the Word of the Lord,' he said firmly, 'and so I will go on.'

'You will die,' I replied.

The missionary smiled at my remark, smoothed a hand down over his grey beard and said,

'The Lord is my protector and my guide.'

With that, he turned on his heel and moved boisterously into the undergrowth, clutching an armful of the holy books.

I stood there in silence for a long time, unsure of what to do. There would have been safety in numbers, but the missionary was hell-bent on suicide. Without food or equipment, he had no hope of survival, with or without the Word of the Lord.

Standing there, the jungle encroaching around me, I was

suddenly overcome with a vision. In my mind's eye I glimpsed a great and unwieldy creature with the snout of a pig and the feathers of a bird. Poised erect on two feet, taller than a man, it appeared to have a very singular presence. As I watched the hallucination, the creature, what I supposed to be the Capilongo, opened a leather bag, removed a book, and began to read.

I blinked, and the vision was gone.

For seven days and nights I waited there at the same spot, the emerald canopy pressing ever closer, hunger gnawing at my ribs. I survived by squeezing water from the tubular flowers, and by eating the berries of the low shrubs that were common on the forest floor. I might have retraced my steps down to the river, but I had no idea in which direction it lay.

Something inside me was telling me to wait.

So I did.

And then, on the seventh night, the vision came again.

This time, the Capilongo was not reading, but smoking a pipe, staring into the embers of a dying fire. As I watched, he narrowed his eyes, and he whispered:

'Dear apprentice, I know you are watching me. And I am waiting for you.'

Then, as if answering my unspoken question, he added:

'Follow the golden bird.'

At dawn next day, I was woken by the shrill sound of a tiny bird, no bigger than a hummingbird. It was hovering beside my face, as if it were hoping to gain my attention. Rubbing my eyes, I saw that it wished for me to follow it. I jumped up and, before I knew it, was running through the jungle in pursuit of the golden bird.

I chased and chased, the tangle of vines and twisted branches hampering each footstep. The little bird seemed to understand that I was an unfamiliar visitor to its jungle. Floundering about clumsily, I wished for wings to take to the air as he. From time to time, he would hover beside me, allowing me to catch my breath, before hurrying on.

By the night of the first day I reached a glade of empty ground. Pinned out in the centre of it was the headless body of a man. Even before I had drawn near, I had guessed its identity. For all around it were torn pages, the Word of the Lord.

I buried the missionary under a pile of flat-sided stones, and read a passage from Genesis over him. I ought to have had fear, because his head was missing – chopped off I imagined by savages.

But, for the first time since my departure from Toledo, I had hope.

Through three more days I chased the golden bird, until the air became cool and free from the insects that plagued my waking hours. I crouched on the banks of a little stream, chewed a handful of berries, and fell back with surprise.

Standing over me was the Capilongo.

'Excuse me for startling you,' he said in a polite voice.

I breathed in hard, choking in surprise.

The Capilongo reached down and offered me his hand. It was soft, covered in chocolate-brown feathers.

'I saw you in a dream,' I said.

'And I saw you,' the Capilongo replied, 'and I know why you have come.'

Glancing at the ground, I mumbled the word 'duty'.

'Before you kill me,' said the Capilongo, 'please do me the honour of dining with me. You see, I have very little chance to make intelligent conversation.'

I agreed readily. After all, it was the least I could do.

The creature led me to a cave behind the stream. It was gigantic, carpeted in scented moss, and illuminated by shafts of natural light. Arranged down the middle was a long banquet table, at which two places had been laid at one end.

Welcoming me to his home, the Capilongo ushered me to the head of the table, and clapped his hands.

Nothing happened, not for a moment at least.

Then, slowly, an army of sloths slipped from the shadows, their long, curved arms laden with dishes and plates.

We dined on wild fruits, the seeds of which looked like cut diamonds, on slivers of raw blue meat, and on a kind of jelly that smelled of frogs. The sloth servants ferried one dish after another to the table.

I asked if there were savages living near. The Capilongo looked up sharply.

'There is a tribe up in the mountains,' he said, reaching for a segment of fruit. 'They live on the brains of their vanquished foes. The skulls are stored beneath the ground in vats, pickled for months in the juice from the lowreeh tree.'

'Do they hunt Capilongos?' I asked.

My host sniffed.

'I am pleased to report that they do not,' he said.

Before I could reply, the Capilongo reached down and picked up a knife. An assassin's dagger of sorts, it had a sharp point and a long, straight shaft. He turned it carefully so that the blade was held in his fingers, the hilt pointing towards my chest.

'Capilongos have two traditions,' he said in a kindly tone. 'The first is always to assist a guest in anything he might require. The second is to entertain an assassin before he carries out his duty. This knife is sharp enough to stab me easily in the heart, or to slit my throat, whichever you prefer. But, before you dispatch me,' said the Capilongo earnestly, 'I would ask that you permit me a small indulgence.'

Wondering what it was, I nodded.

'Of course.'

THE REASON TO WRITE

'Would you mind me regaling you with a story? Think of it as an entertainment, a parting gift.'

I could hardly believe what I was hearing. But, delighted at having arrived at my quarry so easily, I accepted.

The Capilongo clapped his hands and the sloth servants cleared the plates.

When the serving dishes were gone, an elderly sloth glided over to the table. Between his upturned hands was held a salver, a bottle of aged jungle brandy upon it. When two glasses of the tawny liquid had been poured, the Capilongo lit his pipe and his tale began...

From: *Scorpion Soup*

Descriptions

I STARTED OFF as a travel writer, hammering out books on adventures and journeys in mysterious corners of the world. Coming to writing from that discipline, I learned to add plenty of descriptive passages to the soup I was making. Several examples follow – of an illegal gold mine in Ethiopia, then the Upper Amazon, Calcutta, and Tangier.

The crater almost was the size of a football pitch and about a hundred and fifty feet deep at its lowest point. It had been carved out of the rocky African dirt, a fragment at a time. A thousand shades of golden brown reflected in the bright sunlight. The miners were covered in mud. I hardly noticed them at first, but as my eyes adjusted, what I saw took my breath away.

Thousands of men, women and children were digging with their hands. A few had basic implements, shovels or iron pikes. All were barefoot, dressed in ragged wet clothes, their skin glistening with sweat, and all were labouring desperately to dig out the earth and haul it to the surface. It was a sight out of the Old Testament, and at that moment the notion of Solomon's mines fell sharply into focus. For the first time I understood what I was searching for.

In the village I'd been the cause of great interest, but at the mine itself the workers were too busy to look up. Each had a role to play. If one person paused in his work the system would begin to break up, then production would slacken and money would be lost.

At the bottom of the pit were the diggers. Many of them were women and children. They'd chiselled their way further and further down, through layers of clay, rock and earth. You could see the gold seam clearly. It was a honey-yellow strata, which started about thirty feet down. The upper layers of soil had been piled in a bulwark around the edge of the crater, and the precious vein was being chipped away and carried to the panning pools. Moving such an enormous quantity of earth called for brutish manpower. Hundreds of men, perched on fragile ledges, tossed the pans of soil from one to the next in a giant relay. Their biceps were savagely over-developed, enabling them to transfer a forty-pound pan from the bottom of the crater to the surface in thirty seconds flat.

Once at ground level, the gold ore began another relay, to the panning pools. A great deal of water is necessary for panning, which is the usual way to extract specks of gold from an alluvial lode. The river had been dammed, creating a large pond edged with rushes and water hyacinth. A series of sluices had been built to filter out rocks and to allow a constant stream of fresh water into the pool. In fact, the system hasn't changed much since it was invented by the ancient Egyptians five thousand years ago.

Most of the panning was done by women and children, using round, wooden pans about three feet wide. A gentle sluicing movement removes unwanted dirt and, if you're lucky, leaves a fine crescent of gold dust at the bottom of the pan.

The ancient Egyptians turned panning into an art form, and it was from them that Solomon's kingdom learnt the technique. In the late nineteenth century, gold tailings in the Egyptian desert were discovered and processed by archaeologists. They found that almost no gold had been left by the miners working five millennia before. But the cost was high. The Nubian Desert is littered with human bones, no doubt those of slaves who succumbed to the heat and the toil. The main difference between Solomon's mines and the illegal ones in Ethiopia is slavery, or rather the lack of it. The Ethiopian miners were working for themselves. There was no need for whips and threats of death. Greed was their master, goading them to work from before sunrise to dusk.

Noah led the way from the main crater to another area, where many hundreds more were working in a labyrinth of tunnels. The openings were like well-shafts, dozens of them stretching out over a distance of about three hundred feet. Etching out smaller, individual seams, the lone workers labour in an underworld where cave-ins are a constant threat. Samson said that every year the narrow tunnels entomb many young men. But for the men without fear the rewards are high. If they find a nugget, they swallow it or stuff it up their rectum, for retrieval later. In the mining camps, trust doesn't exist.

When I asked how much precious metal had been found, I was always greeted with anxious looks. No one would admit to finding any gold at all, even when everyone knew they had. Although the gold was supposed to be shared out equally in a loose cooperative, everyone lied, cheated and stole from their neighbours. The only people who'd boast were the younger men. They did so to impress the whores, whom they hoped would give them a free servicing. But, as the girls knew very well, anyone boasting about what they'd found, hadn't found anything at all.

From: *In Search of King Solomon's Mines*

The jungles of Latin America have a power, a darkness, one that's almost impossible to accurately describe in ink. I first travelled through the Amazon as a student, and remember coming to the conclusion that I was moving through the heart of the Earth.

There was a sense that I was a part of something colossal, and that I was connected in the rawest way. Since then, I have returned time and again to the jungle, and have been touched by the harmony of the natural world. It sounds like an empty cliché, but it's not. The jungle is perfectly in balance, perfectly choreographed. And, the people who reside there are part of the harmony, never taking

THE REASON TO WRITE

more than they need.

During the journey up river on the *Pradera*, I gleaned for the first time the astonishing value of shamanistic knowledge. In the West, we base almost all our pharmacological remedies on a handful of plants, whereas there are tens of thousands of flora that have never been tested – a great many of them located in the Upper Amazon.

From: *Trail of Feathers*

Like extras in a film the first characters saunter on to the set shortly after first light.

Well rested, they're ready for another day of furious activity. Some scrape out the gutters, or scrub down the cobblestones, like studio janitors making ready for the arrival of the cast. Others set out dog-eared copies of *Time* and *National Geographic* on makeshift wooden stalls.

Nearby, beggars hobble into position, bracing themselves for the crowds. Street-side astrologers prop up their hand-painted boards depicting the constellations. Perfume-sellers dust down their carved glass bottles; toothpick vendors arrange their stock. Pickpockets step stealthily into doorways. Fruit-sellers divide sour green oranges into clusters of six. Traffic policemen tighten their white steel helmets and climb up on to their rostra.

Then – and only then – as if an invisible director has cried *ACTION!*, Calcutta is switched on.

Within moments, the streets are choked with vehicles. The air boils with exhaust fumes. And the pavements are packed with shoals of people, jammed shoulder to shoulder like lambs in a wagon.

Nothing in Calcutta is so important as the pavement.

Far more than mere conduits for pedestrians, the walkways are dormitories, typing bureaus, markets, cafes, doctors' surgeries and umbrella repair shops, rolled into an endless profusion of activity.

Calcutta's pavements are wider than in most other cities, constructed by the British for a grand imperial capital. Twenty yards of Calcutta pavement has more on offer than entire countries. Plastic combs and squashy toys, showers caps in camellia pink, hard-boiled eggs in trays, reconditioned engine-blocks, Bakelite telephones, mothballs in sackcloth pouches, beetroot and jackfruit, dental floss and wooden legs, Zimmer frames and pogo sticks, Turbines and theodolites.

From: *Sorcerer's Apprentice*

Poised at the edge of the old medina, the Grand Socco is a cross-section of East and West. There are market stalls erupting with produce, cafés packed with gritty no-nonsense men, fountains, benches and a great mosque. There is a gate, too, leading into the shadowed passages of the medina.

Burton had passed through it into the square during the winter of 1885. He had come to seek fresh air, while working on his epic translation. Part of the reason for his visit to Morocco was to scout the country out. It had long been his dream to become the British ambassador and the signs were good that his appointment was imminent. With twenty-five years of experience in the Consular Service, Burton had never been promoted, despite regarding the Prime Minister himself as a personal friend. He put his stalled diplomatic career down to a report he had written four decades earlier, while in the employ of Sir Charles Napier, on a Karachi male brothel touting a wide range of eunuchs and young boys.

The first volume of *Arabian Nights* had appeared with much media attention in the second week of September, three months before Burton docked at Tangier. Each month or two another volume was completed, then printed, and mailed directly to subscribers. The early reviews had been mostly encouraging and no subscribers had demanded their money back. Despite the good

THE REASON TO WRITE

reception, Burton must have been seething from an article in the well-respected *Edinburgh Review*. Its correspondent Harry Reeve had written: 'Probably no European has ever gathered such an appalling collection of degrading customs and statistics of vice. It is a work which no decent gentleman will long permit to stand upon his shelves... Galland is for the nursery, Lane for the study, and Burton for the sewers.'

Tangier's damp winter climate had brought on Burton's gout. He didn't much appreciate the town, so it was perhaps just as well that he was passed over for the position of ambassador. He wrote to John Payne, a fellow translator of the *Arabian Nights*: 'Tangier is beastly, but not bad for work.' His description of the Grand Socco is recorded in the tenth volume. He said that the coffee-houses were all closed after a murder had occurred in one of them. The usual clientele had been forced to drink their refreshments and take their *kif* out on the street, despite the miserable conditions.

It was there he found a storyteller plying his trade. Characteristically harsh in his judgement, Burton was scathing of the square, just as he was of the town in which it was found. He wrote: 'It is a foul slope; now slippery with viscous mud, then powdery with foetid dust, dotted with graves and decaying tombs, unclean booths, gargottes and tattered tents, and frequented by women, mere bundles of unclean rags.'

Of the storyteller, he was a little more approving: 'he speaks slowly with emphasis, varying the diction with breaks of animation, abundant action and the most comical grimace: he advances, retires and wheels about, illustrating every point with pantomime; and his features, voice and gestures are so expressive that even Europeans who cannot understand a word of Arabic divine the meaning of his tale. The audience stands breathless and motionless surprising strangers by the ingeniousness and freshness of feeling under their hard and savage exterior.'

Alas, there were no storytellers in evidence any longer. I scanned the square, taking in the detail, wondering how the atmosphere had changed in the century and more since Burton had stood there. One significant alteration was the fabulous Cinema Rif.

Now restored to its former glory, the Rif is an Art Deco jewel, a reminder of the years when the kingdom was a French Protectorate. I sat on a bench opposite, closed my eyes and let my mind slip into the past. I could see the high-society limousines rolling up, mink coats and scarlet lipstick, greased-back hair, and flashbulbs popping on opening night.

The sound of young voices stirred me back to the present.

Five boys were sitting at the far end of the bench. They were dressed in weatherworn clothes, all caked in mud. Their leader said something fast. The others groped through their pockets and pooled their funds: six marbles, four bottle tops, a painted twig, a blunt penknife and a few coins. The money was separated out. Three of the boys started arguing, shouting at one another. Their argument broke into a scrap. One of the older boys suddenly turned on the smallest. They fell into the dirt, punches flying. The leader pulled them apart. He handed all the coins to the youngest boy, whose shirt had been ripped in the fight, and sent him off towards the cinema.

The others began playing marbles.

I asked why only one of them was going to the cinema. The leader glanced up, his sienna eyes catching the light.

'We have the money for only one to see the matinee, monsieur,' he said. 'So we send Ahmed. We always send Ahmed.'

'Why him?'

The leader flicked a marble into the dirt.

'Because Ahmed has the best memory,' he said.

From: *In Arabian Nights*

Letters

A LITERARY DEVICE I have always enjoyed using is letters embedded into the text. The reason I love them is because as a child I was a deeply enthusiastic letter-writer. I've used letters in several books, but especially liked crafting the ones in *Timbuctoo*.

16, Fleet Street, London
17th October 1815

Dearest Beattie,

Salutations, my little cousin, from a colder London day than I can recall. To think it is only October! I have stoked the fire since before dawn, but was frozen to the bone half the night. So cold was I, that I pulled on my breeches while under the covers. Imagine that! What suffering! This night I will sleep in three pairs of stockings and the maroon felt nightcap you so sweetly presented me with two Christmases ago.

The Committee's chairman, Sir Geoffrey, has been whipped into a maniacal state these past days. There is much talk of the French expedition. The very mention of it, and Sir G flies into a rage. Indeed, the mention of anything French drives him wild with rage. He refuses even the finest glass of claret – remarkable for a man with such an unquenchable thirst. But then, Waterloo is so recent in all our minds.

I have heard tell that the French contingent, under the command of General Dumas, has packed a hundred gallons of eau de cologne in which they intend to bathe the natives when they arrive. The chocolate shops of Mayfair resound to talk of how King Louis insists his monogram be nailed on the palace walls of far-off Timbuctoo.

Our only advantage is that Bonaparte is impotent at last, en route as I write this to his incarceration at St. Helena. Thank God for that, and for our victory last summer.

Major Peddie will set sail a week tomorrow from Plymouth, and plans to make landfall at Tangiers, leading the largest and best prepared expedition that has ever sought out that glorious desert emporium. The investors appear to have covered the costs for the mission many times over, much to the delight of Sir G.

There is no doubt that Major Peddie marches into history, holding high the colours of the Committee, of Britannia, and the King.

Yours affectionately, my dearest Beattie,
Simon

Palazzo Carignano, Turin
7th March 1816

My dearest Simon,

I have dipped the quill six times and sat here staring into space, wondering quite how to begin. I do not know who else to turn to, or indeed what to say. You have known me since childhood, since the carefree days of summer at Chavenage. And you know me well enough to grasp that my marriage was one constructed upon obligation rather than affection.

Mr Wittershall and I reached Turin a day or so ago. We travelled by way of Paris and Geneva, before making the arduous Alpine crossing. The horror of the journey was erased at being welcomed here at the splendid Palazzo Carignano.

My dearest Simon, my tears smudge the ink as I write

this. I am at a loss for words, and forlorn in my awareness of your gentle sensitivity. Yet I feel I have no choice but to speak directly.

During the journey thus far my husband declined to complete the duty expected of him before the eyes of the Lord.

This afternoon, while strolling through the Palazzo with my servant, I heard a raucous clamour from a nearby room. Without a moment's thought, I turned the handle and thrust open the door. Inside, in the most depraved and abominable state imaginable, was my husband in carnal union with another gentleman.

He, Mr Thomas Wittershall, was much alarmed by my intrusion. After pretending that the act was a customary tradition in the region, he came to his senses and admitted that the fairer gender is of no interest to his eyes.

Expecting me to be enamoured by the prospect of a spouse so inclined, he insisted that it would permit me to take certain liberties. But I am not enamoured, not in the least. I have wept for half a day, and feel myself desiccated from the tears.

At dawn tomorrow I shall leave here and return by ship to London and, if the grace of God has respect for my wishes, I shall never set eyes on Mr Wittershall again.

I am,
Your affectionate cousin and dearest friend,
Beattie

From: *Timbuctoo*

Dialogue

OVER THE YEARS I've tried to develop a simple use of dialogue – inspired largely by the work of Bruce Chatwin and Mark Salzman. I do my best to remove as many of the 'he said', 'she mused', 'they pondered' and so on. If the dialogue is well constructed you'll find it should be able to stand on its own with very little extra structure.

This text is from *Paris Syndrome* when, as a little girl, Miki is talking to her grandfather.

On the morning of her fifth birthday, Miki Suzuki sat perched on her grandfather's knee, at the edge of the porch in the family home, a short distance from Sendai.

Giggling and grinning, and tugging at his scraggly beard, she pleaded for her birthday gift.

Narrowing his eyes until they were little more than creases in a wrinkled face, the old man said:

'I am going to give you something very special my little plum. A gift that you can never lose – one that will be with you every minute of the day, forever.'

Squirming up closer to her grandfather's face, Miki kissed him gently on the cheek.

'What is it, Ojiichan?'

'It is a story,' he said.

And, before the little girl could utter another word, her grandfather began:

'Once upon a time,' he whispered softly, 'there was a city that was Paradise on Earth. All the women were beautiful and were dressed in the finest gowns, their skin scented with delicate perfumes. And all the men were handsome, like movie stars. The streets were wide and graceful, and were lined with trees abundant with blossom all year round. The sun never stopped shining, and the warm air was filled with butterflies and birdsong.'

Miki tugged at the long hairs of her grandfather's chin, and she laughed.

'I want to go there, Ojiichan!' she cried. 'Will you take me there, please, please, please?!'

The retired old salaryman smoothed a wizened hand over his little granddaughter's cheek.

'One day we will go there together,' he said, 'and will walk the length of the great boulevard hand in hand.'

'But, *when*, Ojiichan? When will you take me?'

Miki's grandfather looked deep into the little girl's eyes.

'When you are a little older, my little plum.'

'Tomorrow? I will be older tomorrow.'

'Well, maybe a little after that.'

'Next week?'

'Perhaps.'

Miki stood up on her grandfather's lap, and wrapped her short arms around his neck.

'Do you promise?'

'Of course I do.'

'Ojiichan?'

'Yes, Miki-chan?'

'Will you tell me one last thing?'

'Yes, what is it, Miki-chan?'

'What's the name of the city – the one in the story?'

The retired old salaryman hugged his granddaughter, and pressed his lips to her ear.

'It is called Paris,' he said.

From: *Paris Syndrome*

Depth

WHEN I READ novels in which the protagonist is lacklustre and two-dimensional I feel short-changed, as though I'm not getting my money's worth.

Although passing characters may not get the full treatment, I very much like working on the protagonist as much as possible. Even if I have no reason to include a detailed summary of the central character, I usually write one all the same. What follows is a description of Hannibal Fogg, the lead character in *Hannibal Fogg and the Supreme Secret of Man*. I'd written it in my notes, adding more and more as the research stage progressed. Only when writing the novel did I decide to incorporate it into the story.

What is presented here is Hannibal's fictitious Wikipedia page:

HANNIBAL GARRETT FOGG (Born in Edinburgh, 26th December 1868 – disappeared Manchuria 25th December 1939). Eldest son of Sir Uriah Fogg and Baroness Esmeralda Lascelles. Diplomat, explorer, soldier, author, spy, Fogg was born into a wealthy landowning family, with estates in Perthshire and Somerset, and extensive property in central London.
Education: Educated at Wellington School and at Balliol College, Oxford, from where he was sent down.
Career: Through family contacts, Fogg secured a commission with the Royal Engineers. In addition to a military career, he was for a time private tutor to the children of Tsar Alexander III. Throughout his life Fogg undertook numerous explorations – both

THE REASON TO WRITE

on his own behalf and for foreign dignitaries and governments. The precise details of these missions are unknown – having been expunged from recorded history during the Great Foggian Purge.
Marriage: While on an expedition up the Volga River in 1902, Fogg attended a slave auction near Samara, where he bought an enslaved princess, Alina Pasternak. The couple were married and enjoyed numerous adventures together until Alina was poisoned in 1925.
Children: Alina Fogg bore a single son, Wilfred Fogg (1904–1951), who emigrated to the United States and died in poverty.
Awards: Fogg was awarded numerous honours, including the *Most Exalted Order of the White Elephant of Siam*, the *Imperial Order of the Lion and the Sun of Persia*, and the *Order of the Tower and the Sword of Portugal*.
Interests: Fogg was regarded as an authority on ethnography, the Classics, swordsmanship, clockwork mechanisms, cartography and on rare postage stamps. He was an accomplished linguist, speaking more than twenty languages with fluency – including Albanian, Russian, Japanese, Mandarin, Serbo-Croat, Maori, Hindustani, Arabic and Esperanto. As well as being a proficient swordsman and martial artist, Fogg was a renowned pianist, and the inventor of numerous mechanical machines. Of these, the most celebrated were a series of mechanical animals which he referred to as 'Viventem Machinis'.
Memberships: Fogg was a member of the Athenaeum Club in London, and the Cercle de l'Union Interalliée in Paris – until the time of his disgrace. He was known to have dabbled in Freemasonry, having belonged to Lodge 349 in Calcutta. As a young man in Damascus, he was initiated into the Order of the Peacock Angel through his mentor Sir Richard Burton, a fraternity to which he was faithful his entire adult life. It is for his association with the Order of the Golden Phi that he is best known, although he never

spoke publicly about membership, and little of it is known. He was also a member of the Worshipful Company of Clockmakers, the Ancient Order of Odd Fellows, the Ancient and Mystical Order of Rosae Crucis, the Brotherhood of Lost Souls, and the Order of Sanctified Hope.

Associations: Fogg was acquainted with a number of famous and infamous characters of the time, including Freud, Zamenhof, Crowley, Conan Doyle, Hemmingway, Graves, Einstein, Shackleton, Tolstoy, Hitler and Blavatsky.

Disgrace & Purge: In November 1928 Hannibal Fogg was arrested and imprisoned in the Tower of London for treason to the Crown. The following month, on 2nd December 1928, a bonfire of Fogg's collected work was set alight on the Victoria Embankment. A Royal Commission headed by Lord Rothermere subsequently found that Fogg had been engaged as a spy for the Third Reich, having received orders from Hitler himself.

Exile: Upon a request from Sultan Abdelhafid of Morocco, Fogg was exiled to North Africa. Little is known of his years in exile, except that he undertook a series of missions concerned with exploration, necromancy and mechanical machines.

Lost journals: Fogg is known to have kept a journal through his life, as well as a set of encoded expedition journals which, it is believed, contained the locations of five treasures. As with much information surrounding of Fogg's life and work, it is not certain whether such material ever existed at all.

Publications: Hannibal Fogg was the author of numerous books and academic monographs. Precise details on many of his works were lost during the Great Purge and in the years that followed it. Despite exile Fogg continued to publish privately, although in almost all cases the editions were seized and destroyed. Fogg's published works are thought to have included *Lost Years* (1890), *The Pain of Silence* (1891), *Twixt Hell and Marshland* (1892),

THE REASON TO WRITE

Ballads of Hope and Anguish (1894), *Perfidious Albion* (1895), *Advanced Techniques in Swordsmanship* (1896), *Experiments in Metallurgy* (1897), *A Poem of Love* (1898), *Considerations on the Subject of Desert Fauna* (1899), *Short-blade Weaponry* (1899), *Warfare in the Tribal Context* (1899), *Elementary Mechanics* (1900), *Electro-Mechanics Made Easy* (1901), *An Evaluation of the Nile and Its Sources* (1902), *Joy on the Volga* (1903), *Lichen Growth and Its Unique Specification* (1904), *Flight in Ancient Times* (1904), *Destinations Unknown* (1918), *Methods and Mysteries of Shrinking Heads* (1912), *Siamese Bronzes* (1913), *Philatelic Irregularities* (1914), *Sexual Dysfunction Among the Hema Tribe of the Belgian Congo* (1914), *Letters to Satan* (1914), *Why?!* (1915), *Philately of Empire* (1915), *A New Approach to Mechanics* (1916), *In Search of Hidden Animals* (1916), *The Orisha Stone and Its Role In Cultural Ethnography With Reference to the Human Leopard Society of Sierra Leone* (1916), *Perfidious Albion* (1917), *Advanced Maori Etymology* (1918), *Accelerated Learning Techniques* (1919), *Common Misconceptions in the Study of Oriental Folklore* (1920), *Forty Truths Regarding Advanced Palaeontology* (1921), *Cartographic Conundrums* (1922), *Manx Birdlife* (1923), *Ancient Egyptian Necromancy* (1924), *Encoded Mnemonics* (1924), *Further Ancient Egyptian Necromancy* (1925), *Cyclonic Ciphers* (1925), *A Short Treatise on the Study of Mechanical Instrumentation* (1926), *Unexpected Phobias* (1927), *Collected Poetry* (1928), *Mathematic Brevity* (1928), *Finite Infinity* (1929), *Studies in Assyrian Masonry* (1930), *Eleven Poems* (1931), *A Bibliographic Appraisal of the Dark Arts* (1931), *Travels in Disguise* (1931), *An Eye to the Future* (1932), *An Investigation into the Nocturnal Practices of Three-toed Sloths* (1933), *Palaeontology For Beginners* (1934), *Berber Love Magic* (1935), *Spells of the African Hinterland* (1934), *Myths and Legends of Central Africa* (1934), *Ceremonies in Black Magic* (1935), *Advanced Philatelic*

Considerations (1936), *Carpology and Its Uses* (1936), *Astronomy and Related Cartography* (1937), *Social Rethinking* (1938), *Forced Ineptitude* (1938).

Legacy: Fogg's life and achievements continue to be celebrated by a number of groups throughout the world, including the Hannibal Fogg Society of London, and the Association for the Study of Foggian Adventure in New York. On the rare occasions that items thought to have been owned by Fogg are sold at auction, they command high prices. Foggian afficionados believe that with time the truth about Hannibal Fogg will come to light and, along with it, the body of lost work leading in turn to treasure. Perhaps the most intriguing aspect of the interest in matters 'Foggian' is a series of novels and encoded notebooks written by Tahir Shah, a British author, based on the life and adventures of Hannibal Fogg.

From: *Hannibal Fogg and the Supreme Secret of Man*

Reusing Material

READ THE BOOKS of any author who's released a large body of work and they almost always reuse choice pieces of material. As a reader I love unpicking a favourite writer's work, and watching how elements are used over and over. I have enjoyed using material gathered as a travel writer again in my fictional books.

An example of this, which has cropped up three times, is concerned with the bizarre subject of so-called 'human hibernation'. The first time I mentioned it was in *Sorcerer's Apprentice*. Next, I wrote about it in *Hannibal Fogg and the Supreme Secret of Man* and, most recently, in my novella *Godman*.

The detective motioned for me to step closer to the holy man.
'What's he here for? What's going to happen?'
'Just watch.'
The ascetic continued to sit cross-legged in meditation. A few minutes later another man appeared, dug a shallow hole in the earth with his hands, and left. We continued to wait. A modest crowd, about fifteen people, turned up and circled around the Aghori. They appeared to know exactly what was going on. The godman stirred from his trance and rose to his feet. Then, having wrapped a rag shirt around his head, he leant over and pushed it into the hole. Sand was carefully filled in around the head, with the *sadhu* now balancing upside down.
'Vatson, what's happening?'
'The Aghori is going into hibernation,' said the sleuth.
'Why?'

'Why not?' said Vatson.

'Human hibernation... I've heard about this... it's all an illusion!' I shouted.

Vatson gave me a stern look.

'I know it's illusion,' he whispered, 'but be quiet.'

An hour passed. The crowd watched the *pandit's* upturned body with great concentration. Another hour went by. A pye dog was warded away with a stick when it made a run for the Aghori's drinking skull.

After another hour of waiting I was mad with boredom. At last Vatson turned to me.

'Did you notice that very fine, dry sand was being filled in around the Aghori's face?'

'Yes, I did, it was different from the earth around it.'

'Exactly: look closely, and you'll see that the ground here is clay. The hole was filled with dry sand. The *sadhu* can breathe through it.'

Four hours after his hibernation had begun, the Aghori suddenly pulled his head from its sand-filled hole. He unwound the cloth from his face and took a sip of water from the skull. Vatson and I might not have been persuaded, but the crowd was visibly moved by the feat.

As Vatson Private Eye led me away, I told him about the most famous of all human hibernations, which I had once heard about.

In the 1830s, fabulous tales of hibernation came from a remote mountain community near Jammu. They told of a slight, dainty man with calculating eyes, named Haridas, and this soon reached the ears of the Maharajah of Lahore.

The Maharajah, who was a sceptic, sent for Haridas, requesting that he perform his feat under controlled test conditions. Haridas arrived, and the experiment began.

Various distinguished English physicians and soldiers were

present at the Maharajah's palace. At the initial examination, one of the doctors noticed that Haridas had cut away the muscles beneath his tongue, allowing him to push it backwards, sealing his throat. In the days preceding the burial, Haridas took hot baths up to his armpits, flushed out his bowels, and consumed only milk and yoghurt.

The day before the burial, he swallowed a piece of linen, thirty yards long. Officials and courtiers looked on in stupefaction as, before their eyes; Haridas withdrew the bandage, dislodging any remaining material from his digestive tract.

At last, preparing himself for hibernation, Haridas sat in the lotus position, sealed up his nostrils and ears with dainty wax plugs, closed up his throat with his flipped-back tongue, and folded his arms.

His pulse was no longer traceable, and the European physicians were already at a loss for words. Haridas was placed in a great chest, fastened with a padlock embossed with the Maharajah's own seal.

The trunk was carried out ceremoniously into the palace gardens, a cavity was dug, the box was lowered down, and the hole was filled with earth. As a further precaution, a crop of barley was planted above where the hibernating *sadhu* lay. A towering wall was constructed around the entire area. Palace sentries guarded the spot day and night.

Forty days passed. The court was rife with anticipation. With the courtiers unable to stand the suspense any longer, the Maharajah gave the order for the wall, the barley and the soil to be removed. The chest was hauled from the hole, and the padlock was smashed away. Hesitantly, the box's lid was opened. To everyone's amazement, the godman was alive, sitting in the same position as when buried more than a month before.

A doctor removed the nostril and ear plugs, pulled the ascetic's tongue forward into position, and breathed air into his lungs. Within an hour he was as fit as ever before.

Haridas was lauded by the Maharajah, who presented him with a handful of diamonds. The people of Lahore rejoiced in the streets and followed the *sadhu* wherever he went. Further public hibernations took place in cities across India. Haridas became a celebrity, shunning his simple clothes for more resplendent attire.

Wined and dined, and courted by high society, Haridas forgot his humble birth. When complaints accumulated that the godman had seduced a number of high-ranking ladies, it was too much for the government. Haridas was sent back to his mountain village, and was never heard from again.

I asked Vatson for his impressions.

He thought hard for a few seconds. Then, looking me in the eye, and screwing up his face, he barked:

'Poppycock!'

From: *Sorcerer's Apprentice*

1881

A *sadhu* was squatting on platform fashioned from packing crates, an audience watching. Comprised of Indian gentry and a smattering of foreigners, they were standing in a circle around him.

The holy man had a long white beard, tiny maniacal eyes, and almost no body fat at all. His waist was furled in a grubby loincloth, and his head wound in a turban made from a length of jute.

The only person not on their feet was a European woman, seated on a low wicker chair, her arms by her sides. She was fifty, with dark eyes set in a plain face, the kind that would be lost in a crowd.

When the audience could wait no longer, a child of about nine or ten began beating a drum, slow and rhythmic: *Tack! Tack! Tack!*

As the strikes grew harder and louder, the *sadhu* took a meat skewer, forcing the sharp end into his cheek. Oblivious to any pain, he threaded it through to his mouth and out through the other cheek.

After that, he walked across a pit laid with burning embers and, then, swallowed a box of glass marbles, gulping them down as if they were boiled sweets.

In the interval, Professor Maa made the introductions.

'Madame Blavatsky, I should be delighted for you to be acquainted with Mr Hannibal Fogg.'

The European woman held out a hand so that it might be kissed.

'My pleasure,' she said in a severe Russian accent.

Hannibal bowed, pressing his lips delicately to the bleached white skin.

'The pleasure, Madame, is all mine.'

With the interval over, the godman ripped a long strand of jute from his turban, the width of a household bandage. With due care, he began to swallow it.

Having heard of the routine, Hannibal looked on with interest.

'What's he doing?' one of the spectators asked.

'He is cleaning his digestive tract,' answered another.

'Whatever for?'

'Wait and see,' whispered Professor Maa.

The *sadhu* withdrew the cloth, and again squatted in the lotus position on the dais. Breathing heavily, he closed his eyes, palms upturned on his knees.

A yard or two away, Hannibal made out the god-man wheezing. He wondered if the feat, which had made him famous, would kill him this time.

After ten minutes of forced breathing, the holy man stood up, flipped his ears inside out, and clambered into a sturdy wooden box.

The audience chattering among themselves, posing questions and craning their necks for a better view.

Three assistants strode up. One of them fastened the box's lid, securing it with a Chubb padlock.

'Now they will bury him,' said Maa.

'Where?'

'In the hole they have dug. Look, it's six feet deep.'

The box was lowered into the grave, the mound of earth beside it used to fill in the hole. One of the assistants sprinkled a handful of grain, splashing water over it from a bucket.

'What now?' asked Hannibal, raising an eyebrow.

'Now,' Madame Blavatsky replied, 'we return in a month, when the barley has grown.'

A full calendar month after the burial, the same audience reconvened on the banks of the Hoogli. As before, Madame Blavatsky was seated and, once again, Hannibal Fogg and Professor Maa stood nearby.

The barley had been tended by the *sadhu's* grandson, the boy with the drum. With sunshine and plenty of water, it had grown quite high.

'Now for the moment we have been awaiting,' said Maa.

'I bet he's dead,' heckled an Englishman at the back.

Hannibal's weight fell onto the front of his boots.

The assistants exhumed the box with their shovels.

Although a little dirtier, it looked much the same as it had done a month previously.

The lock was unfastened, the lid furled back.

Inside, lying quite motionless in the box was the holy man.

'Dead,' intoned Maa with disappointment, 'I knew it.'

Hannibal Fogg cocked his head to the left.

The *sadhu* opened an eye.

THE REASON TO WRITE

'He's alive, by George!' burst out the man who had doubted it.
'Of course he is,' sniffed Hannibal, as the god-man was heaved up onto the grass.
'Why do you say that?' asked the professor.
'Because almost anything is possible with a little self-discipline,' Hannibal replied.

From: *Hannibal Fogg and the Supreme Secret of Man*

On the fifth night Sri Omo-ji performed his greatest miracle.

An hour before it was to take place, Karnaka announced through the public address system that everyone was to sit on the floor wherever they were and pray for the soul of His Celestial Highness. They were to chant '*Mamana!*' over and over, and think of a turquoise river wending its way through valleys down to the sea.

At the appointed moment, Karnaka revealed that the miracle wasn't going to take place in the Hall of Unconditional Love, but outside in the gardens.

Ten minutes after that, every single devotee arrived in the orchard, between the main ashram buildings and the orderly rows of log cabins. Milling about, they wondered aloud what the miracle might be.

After a short delay, Marney stepped forwards and called for three volunteers. Everyone put their hands up and begged to be chosen.

Selecting three burly Russians who'd arrived the week before, Marney gave them each a spade and asked them to dig a grave beneath the apple trees.

At hearing the instruction, and at seeing the grave take shape, a sense of panic swept through the devotees. Dozens fell on the grass and began wailing, tearing out their hair and lamenting that their beloved Omo-ji had gone.

Once the grave was six feet deep, a stream of *poonyas* came forward, wooden buckets of turquoise rose petals their hands. As their fellow disciples watched, they gently scattered handfuls of petals into the grave, until the hole was uniformly blanketed in turquoise.

Then, and only then, a casket was borne forward, carried by the six Swedes from the inner circle, Marek at the front. Crafted from polished teak, the coffin was placed on the ground, and surrounded in yet more rose petals.

Chip and the other trusted Americans pushed their way to the front and solemnly kissed the casket. As soon as they had done so, the other devotees lined up to do the same – assuming it was part of a ritual.

From the comfort of the staff room, the Maharaja and the godman watched, the screen filled with the view of the grave.

'Looks like they're ready for me,' Harry said.

'I've got a bad feeling about this,' Bitu riposted. 'Let's call it off.'

'I've longed to do a human hibernation since I was a kid. Thackur said a *sadhu* called Haridas had performed it in the 1830s and survived.'

Bitu grunted in protest.

'That's all well and good, but did he have a bandwagon like this to keep going while he was six feet under?'

Harry didn't answer.

Taking a turquoise turban from the back of the chair, he wound the full length around his head, looked at himself in the mirror, pulled a face, and glided out into the orchard.

Setting eyes on him, the devotees' spirits were buoyed.

A clutch of *poonyas* from Rio de Janeiro spontaneously prostrated themselves on the grass. A minute later, everyone was doing the same, as if the Latinos had upstaged them. His forehead beading in sweat, Sri Omo-ji whispered a final instruction to

Marney. Then, in silence he stepped into the coffin and lay down.

The atmosphere was electrified, as though something tremendously significant was about to take place. The Brazilians, who'd started the craze of prostrating themselves to His Celestial Highness, lurched forwards and begged to be buried in the godman's place.

Marney asked them to step back, which they did. Then, just as he'd been told to do, he knelt down, and held Sri Omo-ji's wrist.

Fearfully, he turned to the devotees.

'There is no pulse,' he said.

The Brazilians, Russians, Swedes, and at least half the Koreans, wept uncontrollably. The Americans were more sanguine. Chip covered his face with his hands and gave blessings for the short but extraordinary Seventeenth Incarnation.

Once the lid was screwed into place, the casket was lowered down into the grave. The *poonyas* took handfuls of turquoise petals and scattered them down onto the coffin, muttering prayers of their own.

Little by little the hole was filled in.

The topsoil was raked flat, and a crop of carrot seeds were planted, and watered. A pair of copper timpani was carried to the side of the grave, and two of the Bulgarian disciples began striking them in a slow rhythmic beat.

Hundreds of the devotees stayed at the graveside until the middle of the night. The thought of Sri Omo-ji being buried was too much to bear for many.

Night and day, the kettle drums were struck, reminding the *poonyas* that His Celestial Highness was six feet under. As they kept retelling each other, he was performing an act of selfless love and peace for them, and for the unloved children.

A week passed and the drumming didn't stop for a moment. Proving themselves to be first-rate drummers, the Bulgarians shared the task between them, taking it in shifts to mark the passage of time.

During the day the devotees would pause from their classes or their duties and drift out to sit beside the grave in silence. A few of them slept out in the garden, and refused to leave.

Within a few days the first shoots pushed through and, by the second week, they had turned into luxuriant tufts of green. The inner circle Americans took charge of watering the crop, measuring out the exact amount of purified water necessary – the liquid having been blessed each morning at the Great Stone.

Six weeks after the burial had taken place, the carrot tops were leafy and lush, and were tended as lovingly as ever by the inner circle Americans.

At the graveside the Bulgarians were still drumming, as they had done night and day since the godman had been interred. The sound of the drums was hard-wired into everyone's heads, so no one heard it.

That's not to say anyone had forgotten His Celestial Highness. On the contrary, he was in the thoughts of many thousands of *poonyas* in Varanasi and around the world.

During the final week of the so-called 'hibernation', a wave of mania tore through the ashram. It was different from the usual frenzied high spirits, and was characterized by something Marney described as 'Divine Turmoil'.

The first evidence of it appeared in the form of 'sewing'. Unable to bear the trauma of Sri Omo-ji's absence, some devotees sewed the wrists of their turquoise robes together, forcing them to go around in pairs or clusters of three. The practice developed when a couple of *poonyas* had the idea of linking their nose rings together by a short chain. Within days, hundreds of devotees were chained together in little groups.

THE REASON TO WRITE

A second example of Divine Turmoil was the practice of what became known as 'scarring'. A devotee would take a sharpened stick and chisel a large 'O' deep into the back of another. If performed correctly, the scars developed in little lumps over the individual chisel hole.

But without doubt the oddest manifestation of emotional agitation was when a devotee from Albania grabbed a knife in the dining hall. Yelling, 'In the name of Omo-ji!' he cut off the outer part of his left ear.

Within a day, a hundred and fifty devotees had copied the act. By the middle of the week, more than a thousand *poonyas* were missing either one or both their ears.

Alarmed at the manifestations of Divine Turmoil, Bitu begged his friend to end the pointless hibernation before someone was killed. Heavily bearded, Harry was virtually unrecognizable from the godman who'd stepped into the casket seven weeks before. So much so that he was able to do what he'd joked of doing. A chartered Gulfstream took him to the French Riviera for a few days on the beach. Dressed in a T-shirt and shorts like everyone else, he looked like any other hipster rather than a godman on holiday.

On the fiftieth day since Sri Omo-ji's burial, an announcement was made over the ashram's speaker system: 'Time for the carrots to be picked.'

The *poonyas* streamed to the orchard from the Great Stone, the lines of log cabins, and the main buildings, whooping as they came. The inner circle stood at the graveside, several of them holding baskets, the timpani still marking the passing of time. As the full complement of devotees watched, the carrots were eased out of the soil ceremoniously one by one. Having being doted over for many weeks, they were magnificent. The carrots were cut up into little pieces and passed around, as a dozen devotees excavated the casket.

Digging fast, the timpani striking hard, they slowed in fear and anticipation as they sensed the coffin was near. Many of the disciples – especially those who had sacrificed ears – threw themselves onto the ground and began writhing about.

All of a sudden one of the shovels struck wood.

Carefully, the diggers quarried the last buckets earth, and the casket itself was raised, then placed on the grass, amid chanting, more whooping, and the ear-splitting drumming from the timpani.

As if every second counted, half a dozen *poonyas* raced forwards, brandishing electric screwdrivers.

A minute later, the coffin's lid was lifted away.

Seven thousand disciples held their breath and watched.

All over the world, tens of thousands more did the same – glued to smart phones and computer screens.

Bearded, Omo-ji was lying outstretched and lifeless.

Lurching urgently forwards, Chip felt for a pulse.

There wasn't one.

The drummers ceased.

Falling back, the American broke down inconsolably, and all around him the *poonyas* did the same.

Sequestered away in the former staff room, Bitu watched the video feed – the only person alive to have shared in the godman's secret.

Very slowly, the fingers on Sri Omo-ji's right hand began to tremble ever so slightly. Radiating out, the faint movement progressed up his arm, and into his chest.

Marney clasped his cheeks and screamed:

'He's alive! Sri Omo-ji is alive!'

From: *Godman*

Endings

As I HAVE described in the main text, it's worth keeping an eye on the ending of a book – where and how it will be. The danger is that you'll just keep going. I don't see that as a problem, because you can always divide the book into volumes. I am presenting here a sample of endings I have enjoyed writing, and I think have stood the test of time. Each one of them was planned and considered with some care long before I reached the final pages of the book.

Ramón's chanting hadn't waned. The rustling of his *chacapa* and the low platform of his voice dispersed. I took my place again, cross-legged on the hard bamboo floor. Soon after, a second bout of purging overcame me. Scurrying fitfully across the floor, down the ladder and through the mud, I found sanctuary back with the frogs. I glanced up at the stars, drunk and off-balance, questioning how they could allow such a predicament.

Back on the bamboo floor, as Ramón's smoke enveloped me, I sensed the *ayahuasca* moving on to the next phase. The hallucinations had begun. I leaned back, my eyes closed, my lungs breathing the dastardly *mapacho* smoke. It began with my arms sensing warmth, as the base of my spine had done. I questioned how anyone could take *ayahuasca* for pleasure. As I lay there, wondering, my body changed.

My shoulder sockets were growing warmer, as my arms evolved. They transformed from being feeble, feckless limbs. The bones altered first. I could see them. I watched astounded, as they grew more delicate, shedding themselves of my sunburnt skin. After the bones, came the muscles – colossal ones, like those of a body builder. Only then, when my arms were fleshed with tremendous arteries and veins, did the final covering emerge – feathers. White, fluffy feathers.

I might have panicked, but the shaman's chanting gave a framework to the experience. His song was mournful, like the dirge at a funeral. Appropriate, for I was dead. I could not distinguish the words, the individual sounds. But, despite this, they made perfect sense. The incantations were beyond a language. They were protecting me... comforting, teaching. I breathed in the sound, inhaling it until my diaphragm was taut.

The song was speaking to me in a language without a voice. It was ordering me to thrust my wings outwards, to soar up, high into the air. I called back that I did not know how to fly. The sound of the *chacapa* touched my wings and dragged them up on a cushion of air. I laughed maniacally. I was flying. My wings moved with unequalled ease. There was none of the frantic, feverish motion of a man emulating a bird in flight.

This flight was natural, an obvious sensation. Glancing down, I saw the desert far below. I saw *el colibrí*, the hummingbird. I was at Nazca. Circling round the symbols on that plain I understood the stupidity of the Western mind. *Ayahuasca* was the key which decoded the etchings, just as *datura* explained the witches' flight. Without one, the other had no meaning.

I flew on, guided by the *chacapa*'s sound, soothed by a spray of saliva from the shaman's lips. The colours were bright – purples and blues, yellows and pinks. I was on the far side of a magnificent wall, flying in a no man's land of illusion. I felt the rush of air on my face, and learned to control my wings by tilting their edges up and down. Ramón was with me. He said this was no illusion, but was the real world. We had died and come to life. I was alive for the first time. I was meant to fly, to be a part of the air. I sensed the shaman's

THE REASON TO WRITE

energy, the force of his knowledge. I could not see him, but I knew he was there. I was Icarus and he Daedalus. But our wings were not made of wax and feathers. They were living. We were birds, yet we were men, we were men, but birds.

*

We flew for many hours.

I do not remember when the journey ended, or the moment I awoke. Sunlight streamed through the morning rain. I strained to open my eyes, retched and rolled onto my back. The *maloca*'s chonta palm floor was as hard as quartz. At my sides, my arms ached, as if they had been flayed with a whip. I roused the fingers of my left hand. They were grasping something. Still lying on my back, I raised the hand to my face. In its grip was a long feather. Three triangular notches were missing from the leading edge.

It had been dipped in blood.

From: *Trail of Feathers*

The sun slipped down behind a screen of poplars, its outline broken by the naked branches. Two women were sitting alone in the house they had inherited when their father died suddenly four years before.

One of the women was reading *The Vicar of Wakefield*. She had never married, although she hoped one day a man would arrive and ask for her hand. The other, a little younger, had once been wed down at the church on Union Street. But on the night of her marriage, her husband had disappeared.

Two summers had passed before she had discovered the truth, that her father had disposed of him. She vowed to wait, until the end of her life if need be, for her love, a man named Robert, to return.

Unsure where he had been sent, or what had become of him, she felt in the bottom of her heart that he loved her more deeply than any other thing – that he was alive and was desperately working to cover the distance that separated them.

Lighting a candle, she placed it on the window ledge, as she did each evening at about the same time. Then, she put on her coat, tied back her hair, and stepped outside to listen to the birds as they roosted in the chestnut trees.

Choosing her route over the damp ground, she walked to the field of ripe winter barley and stared at the sun as it inched down through the branches. She closed her eyes, felt the last touch of warmth on her face, and she prayed.

A cart had pulled up at the farm, halting just long enough to allow a traveller to jump down. A moment later it was gone, the wheels leaving no mark at all on the baked mud ruts.

The traveller placed his cases on the ground. As if lost in a dream, he walked very slowly out into the field. There, he saw the woman's figure standing tall, the fingers of her right hand extended, stroking the stems of barley.

Without a sound, he walked towards her.

In his hand was a fragment of lace, so black with dirt that it was hardly recognizable as cloth.

He touched it to his lips one last time.

The woman turned.

She frowned, stretched out her arms, and held him tight.

From: *Timbuctoo*

Book Proposals

ELABORATE BOOK PROPOSALS were only important when an author was trying to get an agent to sell the sizzle of a work that was merely a glint in the eye. Advances are largely a shadow of their former glory, and so proposals are less important than before.

I have written dozens of book proposals in my time – some of which led to eye-watering advances, and others which never actually led to a sale.

I am presenting here the proposal for my book *The Caliph's House*, which became something of a sensation, running into dozens of editions all over the world.

Reading through it now, what strikes me is that I managed to create a kind of literary meringue. At the time that I wrote the proposal I had only spent a few days actually living at Dar Khalifa, and knew very little about Morocco. Despite the severe lack of information at hand I did my best to tell little anecdotes, as my father had instructed me to do – and to create a patchwork cloak of them, to seduce the publishers into opening their coffers...

A ploy that worked.

THE CALIPH'S HOUSE

Look into the eyes of a *jinn* and you
Stare into the depths of your own soul.
Moroccan proverb

A Book Proposal

By Tahir Shah

THE REASON TO WRITE

The Attack

Casablanca's rush hour traffic rivals any in its ferocity. But never has it been so wild as it was on the morning that I took possession of The Caliph's House. After signing at the bottom of a long official Arabic document, the lawyer slid a hefty iron key across his desk.

'You are a very brave man,' he said coldly.

I paused for a moment to look him in the eye. He didn't flinch. I lifted the key. As I did so, I was knocked to the ground by the force of a violent explosion. The windows blew inwards, shattering with spectacular energy, sending a hailstorm of glass through the office. Deafened, covered in glass and confused, I struggled to my feet. My legs were shaking so badly that I had trouble standing. The impeccably dressed legal man was crouched beneath the desk, as if he had previous experience of some kind. He rose silently, dusted the glass from his shoulders, straightened his tie, and opened the door for me to leave.

Out on the street people were screaming, running in all directions, fire alarms shrieking, police sirens wailing. There was blood, too. Lots of it, strewn across faces and over slashed clothing. I was too unsteady to be of use to the injured, now streaming from a nearby hotel. As I observed the slow motion, a small red taxi pulled up. The driver was calling desperately out from the passenger window:

'*Etranger! Monsieur étranger!*' he yelled. 'Come quickly, it's dangerous for the foreigners!' I clambered in and he swung the wheel, hurling us into the slipstream of traffic. 'It's bombers, suicide bombers,' he said, 'they're going off across Casablanca!'

The red Peugeot slalomed westwards, out of the centre of town. But my mind was not on the traffic, the bombs, or the blood. Rather, it was on my wife, at home in London. From the very start she had been sceptical of my ambition: to buy a wonderful rundown old Moroccan house, and escape rip-off Britain. I could see the newsflash tearing over the TV screen, and her clutching our toddler to her very pregnant belly. I felt sure she would now be in no mood to embrace the new culture. She was fearful of Morocco's Islamic society, especially in the light of Al-Qaeda and September 11th. But it was too late to turn back; the money had been paid, the documents signed and stamped and stamped again.

In my hands was the key, a symbol of the future or, perhaps, of a deranged purchase. I stared down at it, taking in the ancient iron notches. At that moment, the driver slammed on the brakes.

'*Nous sommes arrivées à la Maison du Caliphe!*' he announced. 'We have arrived at The Caliph's House.'

Deserting Britain

Anyone who has ever tried to make the break from the damp English shores has needed a long list of reasons. I have often wondered how the immigrants on the *Mayflower* ever managed to get away. Friends and family regard would-be escapees from England as crazed individuals. Mine were no exception. At first they scoffed at my idea of living abroad and, when they realized that I wasn't interested in the usual suspects – southern France or the east coast of Spain – they weighed in with fighting talk. My mother said I would soon come running back 'with my tail between my legs'; and a friend of my wife accosted me at the fish counter in Safeway, barking '*What?!* Spain's not good enough for you then?!'

The reasons for Morocco were many. They were endless. Of course, I wanted to be rid of British overpricing, the terrible food, under-service, and the frenetic pace of life. But my reasons ran far deeper. I had grown sick of our society's climate of political correctness, the junk food, the complacency, a cultural landscape stripped of its depth. Like so many dreamers, I yearned to live in a place with bright sunshine and warmth, where exotic aromas waft through streets, and where the market stalls are a blaze of colour: a place where traditions still die hard, and where children can run free.

I longed to have a house of serious dimensions, not a cramped two-up, two-down, but a mansion with gardens and staff. I craved an affordable fantasy, inspired by *the Arabian Nights*: with arches and towering doors fashioned from cedar, and courtyards with gardens hidden inside, and an orchard of orange trees, and stables and fountains, and dozens of rooms.

The Kingdom

Morocco sits in the north-western corner of the African continent. It is bordered by the Atlantic Ocean on the west, by the Mediterranean to the north, and by the relentless sands of the Sahara on the south and the east. It is a land of fierce contrasts, where tribal people from the desert interior mingle with the native Berbers of the High Atlas Mountains, and they in turn overlap with the mysterious bastions of Islam, the great medieval cities of Fez, Marrakech and Meknes.

The country takes pride that it lies at the furthest western point of Islam, and is ruled by the Hashemite kings, who are descended directly from the Prophet Muhammed. Their ancestors swept across North Africa with the Islamic Faith; within fifty in the years after the Prophet's death, they head reached the Atlantic Ocean, and stood at the gates of Europe. These Moroccans, known to Europeans as 'Moors', crossed the narrow Straits of Gibraltar and conquered much of medieval Spain.

But long before the Arab conquest, Morocco was visited by other would-be conquerors, including the Phoenicians, the Romans, and by Africans from the Saharan interior.

These days Morocco is as much a land of contrasts as ever. Tourists jet in to experience a weekend taste of the 'exotic East', businessmen export products to Africa, the Arab world and beyond; and the royal family strive to stress the moderate face of Islam to the outside world. For, while being Islamic, Morocco has a large Christian and Jewish heritage. It is a land where you can easily buy alcohol, visit nightclubs, and where women need not veil.

Casablanca

The city was made famous for the Hollywood film that wasn't even shot there. When you mention Casablanca to people outside Morocco, you immediately get a sense of them thinking of Bogart lounging around at Rick's Café Americain in his tuxedo. It may seem unlikely, but the best place to get away from the film is to venture to the city. No one in Casablanca ever mentions the movie. It's not that they are embarrassed by it, rather, it's as if they don't know of its existence.

Casablanca may date back to the fifteenth century, when it was conquered by the Portuguese, but its real boom came five hundred years later with the French. They began a massive building project, constructing avenues of Art Deco apartments, theatres and shops. These days the Deco core of the city is very run down. You walk around it, marvelling at how wonderful it must have been, or how it could be again. Despite the dilapidated buildings, the bustle of Casablanca doesn't stop for a moment. The city is by far the largest in Morocco, a home to five million people, and one of the most cosmopolitan centres in the Arab or African worlds. There is a large expatriate community, made up mostly of Americans and Europeans. Many international companies have located their African headquarters in the city, companies such as Coca-Cola and Procter and Gamble. As a result, there are two American High Schools, which teach the US curriculum.

THE REASON TO WRITE

Moroccan Memory
My own connections with Morocco began long ago. Throughout my childhood my father, who was an Afghan, had wanted to take us to his homeland. But the nation's enduring wars prevented us from ever venturing to the lofty mountain passes of Afghanistan. So, from the time we could walk, my sisters and I were frequently bustled into the back of the family station-wagon, vinyl cases laden high on the roof. Our gardener would drive from the serene, dull lanes of the English countryside, through France and Spain, and up into Morocco's High Atlas Mountains.

For my father it was a chance to reveal to his children a hint of his own homeland. And, for my mother, it was an opportunity to snap up all manner of bargains, and to order the delirious heaps of hippies home to their own mothers far away.

We would spend weeks at a time trundling though the mountains, or driving down to the northern edge of the Sahara, where the 'blue men' traipsed in from the desert, their dark skin dyed by their indigo robes. There would be regular breaks to throw up in the bushes, to gorge ourselves on cactus fruit, and to trade our pocket money for fragments of amethyst at the quarries in the hills.

My earliest memories are of the great vaulted bazaar in Fez. Cobbled, dark, bewitching, it's stalls sold anything you could ever wish to buy. There were mountains of spices and fresh cut herbs, cinnamon and cilantro, turmeric and fenugreek; and small cedar boxes inset with camel bone, fragrant leather sandals, and rough Berber rugs, gold kaftans, amulets and talismans.

But by far my favourite corner of the *souq* was where the black magicians went to buy ingredients for their spells. The walls of those shops were hung with cages. In them were chameleons, cobras, salamanders and guinea pigs. There were cabinets, too, made from battered Burma teak, their drawers brimming with the hair of dead men and other such things, or so I was told.

There was a second reason for Morocco... my father's father. In the last years of his life he lived in a small Art Nouveau apartment on the seafront in Tangier. When his beloved wife died before him, aged just fifty-nine, he was crushed. Unable to bear the memories, he moved to Morocco, because it was the only country he could think of in which they had not travelled together. One morning while walking his usual route, from Café France back to the flat, he was hit by a Coca-Cola truck. He died instantly. I was too small then to even remember him, but I feel a sadness all the same. While residing in Morocco, I hoped to learn more of his last days and of his death, to visit his home and to track down the faithful servant of whom he wrote so often in his journal.

Morocco had brought colour to my sanitized English childhood, cloaked in itchy grey flannel shirts and matching corduroy shorts. The astonishing intensity of the experience has enthralled me ever since. With a young family of my own, I regarded it as my duty to pass on the same gift, a gift of cultural colour.

The Search
But the gulf between talking and doing is a wide one.

We searched Morocco for a year or more, desperate to find a house where my delusions of grandeur could run wild. It seems as if everyone I meet these days is heading to Marrakech. They hire *riads* in the medina, houses built around an inner courtyard, filled with exotic plants. Instead of renting, the more adventurous buy such sanctuaries as *maisons secondaires*, secondary homes, a fashion that has sent the city's house prices soaring. The only consolation is that the rapid influx of Europeans – keen to renovate their own corners of the mysterious East – has sparked a revival of traditional crafts: among them *zelij* mosaics, *bejjmat* tiles, and the dazzling polished Marrakchi plasterwork prepared with marble dust, called *tadellakt*.

THE REASON TO WRITE

The Europeans' eagerness to buy *riads* is matched only by the Moroccans' willingness to sell them. In the medina of Marrakech everyone shares the same dream. They all long to trade their crumbling family home for a vast profit, and relocate to a prefab apartment block in the new city. We yearn for rustic detail and old world charm, while they ache for vinyl wallpaper, fitted carpets and all mod cons.

After looking at more than seventy unaffordable houses in Marrakech, we turned to Morocco's greatest treasure, the medieval city of Fez. It's the closest the Arab world can come to replicating the ambience of the *Arabian Nights*. The Old City is mesmerizing in its size and breadth of life. Famous for its Islamic heritage and Brotherhood of Sufi mystics, its architecture is superior to that of Marrakech. Fez was a centre of Arab trade for a thousand years, and its houses reflect an ancient wealth. The greatest artisans of Islamic style still hail from the labyrinth of narrow streets that make up the medina, where the finest mosaics and tiles, textiles and ceramics, are still crafted today.

By chance I was taken to a large merchant's house on the northern edge of the old city. It had been constructed in the grand *Fasi* style, and dated back four hundred years or more. There were six cavernous salons clustered around a central courtyard, each one adorned with mosaic friezes, the floors laid with marble slabs, hewn from the Atlas Mountains. In the middle of the main courtyard stood a lotus-shaped fountain, and high on an adjacent wall was a window covered by a filigree screen, a veiled aperture to what was once the harem.

I began negotiating for the property at once. The problem was that it was owned by seven brothers, each greedier than the last. Unlike in the West, where a house is either for sale or it is not, in Morocco it can be in the property twilight zone: possibly for sale, possibly not. Before even getting to the price you often have to coax the owners to sell. This 'coaxing' phase is an Oriental feature, perhaps brought by the Arabs as they swept westward through North Africa fourteen centuries ago. As you sit over mint tea, coaxing madly, the vendors look you up and down, inspecting the craftsmanship of your clothing, the stitching of your shoes. The better the quality of your attire, the higher the price of the house.

I must have been too well dressed on the morning of my meeting with the seven brothers. In the event their untamed avarice forced me out of the equation, and I slunk back to Britain, depressed beyond belief.

Dar Khalifa

At that moment, as the worst facets of Western life consumed me, the telephone rang. On the line was the mother of an old school friend. We talked pleasantries, while I wondered why she could be calling. Then she came to the point: she had heard on the grapevine that I wanted to buy a Moroccan house. She owned a place in Casablanca and was eager to sell. The lady was too discreet to mention the price, and I was too nervous to ask it. All she said was that it was an 'important' house and was in need of someone who would love it very much. Then she added in a whisper, 'It is going to need a strong man to take it on.' I swallowed anxiously, and arranged to go and have a look at *Dar Khalifa*, 'The Caliph's House'.

The history is complicated and sometimes uncertain, but it seems that *Dar Khalifa* was once the summer residence of the Caliph of Casablanca. A local man told me that the building had been used by high level American diplomats during the Anfa Summit of 1943, when Roosevelt and Churchill met to smoke fat cigars and discuss wartime strategy. Someone else said that the house had been a brothel, reserved for French officers in the early years of the Occupation. The site may well date back to ancient

THE REASON TO WRITE

times, for the Phoenicians built a port a few hundred metres away, at the luxurious suburb of Anfa.

The day after the telephone conversation, I landed in Casablanca after a three-hour flight from London. An hour later, I found myself in a taxi rattling through a sprawling shantytown, donkey-carts and camels blocking the way. It was late afternoon, and the *muezzin's* call to prayer, was raining down from a modest whitewashed mosque. A group of boys were kicking a homemade football about in the dusty streets which ran between the breeze-block shacks. Three haggard men huddled nearby in the shade, wrapped in *jalaba*, traditional robes; beside them stood a set of haphazard market stalls and, opposite that, a woman selling chicks dyed pink.

At the far end of the shanty, the taxi halted at a low doorway set in an impressive stone wall. Before paying the driver, I made sure of the address. He nodded, then pointed, before nodding again. I rapped at the door. A moment passed, then, very slowly the door opened inwards.

Inside lay a fantasy worthy of a far wealthier man than I:

There were courtyards overflowing with date palms and fragrant hibiscus flowers, fountains erupting into symmetrical pools, mature gardens planted with all manner of trees, an orange orchard, and beyond it, were stables.

The guardian welcomed me, kissed my hand, and led me down a long galleried corridor into the main house. A maze of rooms stretched out. Entering the house for the first time was like entering a dream. There were arched doorways, with cedar wood doors, octagonal windows filled with fragments of coloured glass, mosaic friezes, secluded courtyards, and so many rooms: salons and kitchens, a library, staff quarters and storage halls, and endless bed chambers.

But The Caliph's House had been empty for a decade. Its

walls were discoloured with algae, its tiled floors were grimy and in need of repair. Alarming damp patches had taken hold on every surface, and a number of ceilings had fallen in. Cobwebs hung across doorways, birds were nesting in the lamps, and termites had burrowed into the great wooden doors. A burst water pipe had transformed one bedroom into a lake, and most of the shutters were hanging rotten on their hinges. As for the gardens, they were like a jungle, plagued with savage dogs seeking refuge from the dust of the shantytown.

Three months after first setting eyes on *Dar Khalifa*, it was ours. My wife had been apprehensive beyond belief, but had come round seduced by the prospect of living in such luxurious surroundings. Fortunately, the English owner had needed no coaxing. She had taken into account that the bank balance of a struggling author was pathetically dry. She had been well aware, too, that any Moroccan paying the market price would have torn the house down and built monstrous apartment blocks on the land.

The Jinn
So it was that on the morning of the multiple suicide attacks, I first crossed the threshold as the owner of *Dar Khalifa*, The Caliph's House. Inside, the four guardians were standing to attention, awaiting my orders. As if by some medieval right of sale, they came with the property. There was Muhammed, a round-shouldered brute of a man, with a week's growth of stubble, and a nervous twitch. The others called him The Bear. Beside him was Mehdi, younger, with a smile which never left his lips, and a cool, collected disposition. Next was Abdallah. Older than the others, he had a natural grey tonsure of clipped hair, and said he had worked at the house since he was a boy. Finally, there was Layachi, their leader, tall and respectful; like the others, he pressed his hand into mine,

before placing it squarely on his heart. He whispered a prayer of welcome, beseeching God to prolong my life.

I quizzed them, asking whether they had heard about the suicide bombers. They shook their heads. There were other more pressing problems, they said.

'What could be more serious than multiple suicide attacks?'

'Jinns', came the reply.

'*Jinns?*'

The three guardians nodded in unison.

'Yes, the house, it's full of them.'

When you buy a house abroad, you have to prepare yourself for the unexpected, but nothing had readied me for an unseen army of metaphysical spirits. I asked the men for advice on dealing with the problem. Layachi spoke for the others:

'Kill sheep,' he said softly, 'you will have to kill some sheep.'

'*Some?* How many?'

'One in every room,' explained the Bear.

I did a quick calculation.

'There must be thirty rooms, at least... that's an entire flock. It would be a bloodbath!'

The guardians blinked in the sunlight. Then they nodded again. They knew the traditions, and in Morocco traditions are taken very seriously. An empty house in the West may attract squatters, but in the Islamic world everyone knows that a boarded up mansion fills with jinns.

Never have I come across a land whose people are so preoccupied with forces of the Underworld. All Moroccans, rich or poor, will eagerly converse until late in the night about the supernatural. The guardians of the house were even more obsessed than most. Every morning they advised me to sprinkle salt in the corners of the rooms. 'It keeps the jinns happy,' they would say. At night I was obliged to leave platters of fruit and ceramic bowls of meat and couscous out for the spirits. By morning the plates had been invariably licked clean. It seemed totally ridiculous, but the guardians insisted that if the food was not left, my family would not be safe. It was a form of blackmail, for they quite obviously scoffed the food as soon as my back was turned.

Layachi made talismans from conch shells. He presented them to my little daughter, my wife and to me, exclaiming that they had been blessed by a living saint and they would protect us from the dark forces.

Each evening he would beg me for scraps of leftover meat. I would find him tossing it into the well. Moroccans believe that jinns live in the walls of a house, or in wells, where they lurk just beneath the surface. When the well water turned into a mild poison everyone seemed surprised. I asked Layachi what to do, expecting him to advise a chemical treatment. He said the only remedy was to toss a kilo of brown sugar into the water. The jinn would taste the sweetness and be content again.

One of the first things I did was to get costly fire insurance for the building. When Mehdi found me moaning about the price of the policy, he howled with laughter.

'Everyone knows that fire insurance doesn't work,' he said.

'What do you mean, *it doesn't work*?'

'The only way to keep the fire away,' Mehdi maintained, 'is to hang a dried, salted frog outside the front door. But if the house does catch fire, you take it down and put it in your pocket. Then you can enter the burning building without being harmed.'

The Move
We had arrived in Morocco frazzled by the society we had left. Like all our peers, we were paranoid, unhealthy and overworked. I was unable to cease worrying about our two-year-old daughter, but could never appreciate her, as she was shut up in a nursery all

day while I worked to pay for it. The expected baby just added to the stress, levels of which ascended sharply in the days before the move. For weeks on end, my daughter's bedtime stories had been passages read from a book entitled *Morocco: Culture Shock!* I had a basic grasp of the country, yet my mind was whipped up into a frenzy of anticipation. The more I strived to prepare, the more pressured our family became.

Then at long last, we touched down in Casablanca. This time it felt different though: we had not come as tourists, but had come to live. We had six suitcases, strollers, car seats and safety gates, along with a toddler in tow. Two containers of furniture and books had been sent by sea.

A Moroccan friend advised me to hire an assistant as soon as I could. He suggested a good rule of thumb was to ask applicants to bring their family tree to the interview. The idea was to employ the person with the most impressive lineage, for such an applicant was sure to have useful contacts. I took the friend's advice, and hired a young woman, named Zohra, whose recorded genealogy stretched back seventeen generations.

Teething
The first night we spent at Dar Khalifa was a rite of passage. The guardians had pleaded with us not to stay in the house until the wayward jinns had been dispatched. I protested vehemently. It seemed like madness to stay in a hotel when we had our own property with grounds. So the guardians suggested we all sleep in the same room; they said it would allow the spirits to get used to us. At eight o'clock sharp, Layachi, Abdullah, Mehdi and Muhammed knocked at the door of the room. They had come, they said, to wish us luck. It was as if we were about to endure a feat of extreme discomfort. Mehdi threw a handful of salt into each of the four corners, and Abdullah recited a prayer from the

Qur'an.

At first the night passed easily enough, donkeys braying continuously from all sides of the shantytown. But then, at 3.50 a.m. the chorus of donkeys were drowned out by the sound of the Call to Prayer. It came at full volume, roared by a fanatical *muezzin* from the top of the minaret. The next morning Ariane asked me why a man had been singing nursery rhymes in the night.

As we began to settle in, and I started to understand that acquiring *Dar Khalifa* was not like buying a place in France or Spain. Morocco is geographically so close to Europe, but it's a universe apart. The people may think like Orientals, but they also think like Africans, and they depend on native superstitions, and folklore of the Berbers.

Take a stroll through Casablanca and, at first sight, it may seem like the epitome of European life and design. Most people dress in western clothes, and many of the buildings are constructed in the Art Deco style. But beneath the façade lies an indomitable layer, a hybrid of Arab and African belief. Try to get anything done and it greets you. Try to avoid it, pretend it's not there, and it will get the better of you. Instead, you have to learn to co-exist, to appreciate it, and to navigate through what can be treacherous waters. Slowly, you learn to operate, by asking yourself how a Moroccan would confront a problem. This involved shunning the most obvious solution at all costs.

I learned this lesson early on, when I needed a car. The natural thing to do was to go to Hertz. Instead, I hired a car on the cheap from a butcher who lived near the house. Had I made a beeline for a large rental agent, the guardians, their families and friends, would have never be able to live down the shame... the shame of not getting involved. Nothing fired them up so furiously as when I arranged something myself or, worse still, when I paid the going rate.

The butcher never drove his car so, as the guardians told me, it made perfect sense for me to take it on. What made less sense was the fact that the vehicle had been used for twenty years to ferry sheep carcasses from the slaughterhouse, to the fly-smothered butcher's stall.

Like every other vehicle in Casablanca, the wretched car was dented on every side and falling to bits, but I valued it for the veil of authentic camouflage it provided. When out driving, no one would take me as a foreigner, or so I thought. But the moment I crept timidly into the ferocious stream of traffic, retching from the smell of rotting blood, I stood out like a pacifist in a battle zone. Moroccan traffic isn't like normal traffic. It's armed combat, a war of wills, in which only the very bravest have a chance to survive.

My wife's greatest fear was finding a trustworthy nanny for our daughter. We hadn't been in Morocco two minutes, and everyone we encountered was already lecturing on whom to choose. Some said that girls from the mountains were the only people to be trusted with children, others that only a desert woman would do, or one from Fez, Meknes or Marrakech. Finding someone for your children is always a disquieting prospect, and in Morocco it was daunting. The society adores children, in the same way that Italians do. As soon as you have a vacancy in your staff, everyone you know tries to fill it with relatives of their employees, as if it were a peculiar game. Before we knew it, women – young, old and ancient – were arriving at the door. As word spread, they came from farther and farther afield, until at last I could stand it no longer.

I asked Zohra to solve the problem.

'I was waiting for you to ask me,' she said with characteristic efficiency. 'I have already found a girl. She is from the desert, but grew up in the mountains, and she has lived these last years in Marrakech.'

Her name was Leila, and her eyes were the colour of cobalt, her smile delicate and warm. Ariane fell in love with her instantly and whimpered whenever they were parted.

The next hurdle was to find a kindergarten. Casablanca has an abounding selection of schools, embracing many systems: Moroccan and French, American and Spanish. I had heard that the American school allowed the children the greatest freedom, and encouraged the arts. But then, after the suicide bombing, my instinct taught me to stay away from obvious signs of American culture, just as I sat well inside McDonalds (the thinking is that a suicide bomber would lose his cool and detonate near the door).

Ariane took one look at a small French-run nursery and refused to leave. She made friends immediately and developed a passion for tortoises.

Her best friend was called Mary Ann, the daughter of an American anthropologist. As so often happens, we became friends with her parents, Burt and Alice, a fun-loving couple from San Francisco. Burt had gone brick-red in the sun, except for his forehead which was always covered in a baseball cap. He was a bear of a man, with oversized shoulders and plate-sized hands. Cryptic blue lines were tattooed over both his arms.

'Got them in New Guinea,' he said, one evening over a cool beer, 'I was out there with the headhunters a few years ago. They said the lines symbolize the spirit of the trees.'

As always with expatriate conversations, talk turned to matters of security. I asked Burt if he was worried about Islamic fanatics, and the suicide bombs.

'Not at all,' he said quickly. 'I've lived in dangerous places and this isn't one of them. You've got to remember something: Islam is about six hundred years younger than Christianity, and six centuries ago the Christians were just as fanatical. The Church was omnipotent. Witches were being burned at the stake, and when Galileo said the Earth was flat, he had to retract it on the order of the Pope.' Burt paused to take a long sip of his beer.

'The fanatics will burn themselves out,' he said confidently, 'it'll happen soon because ordinary Muslims are sick of these people who pretend they are the *real* face of Islam.'

Fortunately, the battle of selling Morocco to my wife, Rachana, who is from India, had been won by of her love of *Dar Khalifa*, even though the multiple suicide attack was still fresh in all our minds. At first I was constantly apologizing for the minor irritations of Moroccan life: the blazing heat, the fact that nothing runs on time, that you have to spend hours bargaining for the smallest thing. To my surprise, she smiled blissfully. 'It's wonderful,' she said, 'it's just like India'.

The bargaining culture was, for me, the greatest hurdle. In the Arab world daily shopping is seen as far more than a means to an end. It's a social activity, to be enjoyed by both buyer and seller. As such, you are expected to make every effort to chat to the stall-keeper in the *souq*, to take miniature glasses of mint tea, and to haggle like Hell. Failure to bargain and you're greeted with stern looks, as if you have robbed the shopkeeper of an unspoken privilege of some kind.

The loss of privacy was another matter that had to be endured. As an Indian, Rachana was delighted for strangers to traipse through the house from morning till night. There was always a melange of street hawkers, distant neighbours who'd come to poke around, artisans, and knife-sharpening men. Rachana would constantly exclaim how pleased she was to have a hustle and bustle at home. I found myself wishing that the high wall around the property would keep strangers out.

Another point I found hard to grasp at first was the concept of employment. Just as the guardians had worked there for years, serving previous owners, they were part of an ancient system. One of the unwritten rules of that system states that as an employer, you are expected to take care of the people who work for you, whatever the cost. In return they will uphold your honour, protect you, and won't rip you off more than they have to. Their difficulty stemmed from the fact that, as employed people, a vast cast of characters lived off them. In the East the practice is known as 'living off Abdul's job'. As soon as someone gets a job, everyone else gives up their jobs to live off the employed person. The result is a situation whereby normal salaries are never enough to live on. The longer you are employed, the more money you need, merely to support all the hangers-on. So all employed Moroccans need extra cash.

When it came to asking for money, the guardians were diffident and shy. They were always reluctant to ask for an advance on their wages, or for a loan. Instead, they would turn on their Oriental charm and request help in a roundabout way. 'My wife is nagging me again,' Layachi would sometimes say, 'she wants a new dress because her friend (Mehdi's wife) has a new dress. I have told her to be quiet, but the nagging, oh how it's wearing me down!' Such money became known as 'nagging money', and developed into a kind of infrequent handout to all the men.

Ariane was still very small, but begged me for a tortoise. She wanted one like the tortoise at school. I fended off the request, as all my energy was taken up exorcizing the jinns. She begged and begged, until I could stand it no more. I asked Zohra to find out where the best tortoises came from. Two days later, she advised me that you could buy very nice ones from Tan-Tan.

'But that's way down south, in the Sahara desert!' I exclaimed.

'Of course,' said Zohra.

I was sick of Casablanca, of talk and tortoises and the jinns, and so I packed everyone into the car, loaded suitcases on the roof, and headed south, in search of tortoises. We hadn't left the city limits of Casablanca, when Ariane threw up all over her lap.

The road ran along the coast as far as Agadir. Beyond that, we were in the desert. The only thing to take our minds off the sand and the dust were the boys with squirrels. There were just one or two at first, standing on the side of the road. As soon as they saw a car, they'd whip their arms up, whirling a string around their heads like a lasso. At the end of the string was a terrified squirrel. I slammed on the breaks, cursed the boys, bought the squirrel from them, and released it a few miles on... in time to meet another boy with another squirrel. The more damn squirrels I rescued, the more there were being tortured waiting for a stupid foreigner to save.

After two days of driving, we arrived at Tan-Tan exhausted, still shaking from the road. It was a dusty encampment of a town, built of breeze blocks and sand. I vowed I would never drive anywhere again. Ariane was still moaning about her tortoises. I rolled up to the market and quizzed the first man I saw, a butcher. He had blood splattered down the front of his shirt, and a big toothy grin.

'*Tortue?*' he said lovingly, before motioning to a man at the far end of the bazaar. That man pointed to a box. Inside was a frail young tortoise. He said it had been savaged by a dog. I told him we would buy it at any price, and my daughter would nurse it back to health.

'It is a gift,' the man said thoughtfully, 'because nothing is so sweet as to make a child happy inside.'

Such gentle consideration is a feature that is so typical of Morocco. It is a kind of honour, a characteristic that forms the foundation of the society. I remember so vividly being a child with my own parents, in Fez. We were in the bazaar and my father noticed a beggar approach a fruit stall. The man was dressed quite well and, to my father's surprise, the shopkeeper spent time selecting the very best apple, orange and melon. He gave them to the beggar with his blessings. My father was surprised.

'Who do you give your very best fruit to a beggar?' he asked.

The shopkeeper replied:

'Do you think that just because someone is a beggar they should be given items of inferior quality? We are not like that here in Fez.'

Ariane quickly made friends with the children from the shantytown. Her friendships helped us to realize that the barriers of class are so often invented and meaningless. We like to draw well-defined lines between certain layers of society, and we are short-sighted when it comes to breaking down such barriers. Our guardians, who lived in the shantytown, were invaluable in spreading the word of our respectability. For in a country of fast traditions, like Morocco, nothing is so important for you to be seen as respectable. Layachi and the others introduced us to the key players in the world of the shantytown. There was the baker, Abdul-Malik (meaning 'the Servant of God'), and the fruit-seller, Yusuf; and an aged blind man called Rafiq, who told folk-tales in the shade of a high whitewashed wall, and there was Hussein, a softspoken man with a bad back who could make you an amulet to ward away the jinns.

On some days it seemed as if the house was collapsing around us; and on others I would have sworn it was perfect in every way. There were always obscure things to be mended or replaced, things I barely knew existed. A major problem we faced early on was with the sewers. Most Moroccan houses had squat toilets until recently, if they had any toilets at all. The municipal sewers were laid when there were fewer people living in an area, and when residents didn't use toilet paper. This luxury, brought by the French, has caused havoc across the kingdom. As any Moroccan sewer clearer (a miserable job if ever there was one) will tell you, people use far too much loo paper and it jams up the narrow clay pipes which run under the ground.

Layachi constantly took it upon himself to warn us of the

problem. Whenever my wife or I were happily doing our business in the bathroom, Layachi would run up and pound at the door.

'Not more than ten centimetres!' he would cry. 'Please, I beg you, more paper than that and the pipes will get plugged up!'

I learned to put up with his protestations, but several of our early visitors were more alarmed than I can say.

Post 9/11

After the September 11th 2001 attacks, life changed for everyone in Morocco. It is as if the country is trying to make sense of Al-Qaeda and its violence, while at the same time reassessing its own Islamic belief. But life for no one has changed so drastically as it has for the ex-pats. They continue to live comfortably, with servants and sprawling villas; but many now employ security men to guard their children and their homes. After the multiple suicide bombs, Americans in particular have tried their best not to stand out. Gone are the Stars and Stripes from the fronts of buildings, the bumper stickers of US baseball teams, and other visible signs of American culture.

I found many Americans calling themselves Canadians, especially during the recent Gulf conflict. At a café on Casablanca's seafront, I met a young American student on the day the Coalition forces invaded Iraq. He was called Wayne and was from Idaho, having come to the Kingdom to study Arabic. I noticed a copy of *Le Monde*, a French national newspaper, on the table, and that he was wearing a T-shirt with writing in Dutch.

'I'm just hoping to blend in,' he said earnestly. 'I'm giving off un-American signals. Being an American in Morocco right now is crazy, but I'm going to stick it out. My dad's worried sick. He keeps calling me, begging me to come home.'

Wayne gave me his number and I called him the next week, but he had acceded to his father's wishes and flown back home.

My own father had taught us from early childhood the unwritten rules and regulations of the Islamic world. I found them invaluable in Morocco, and would so often explain them to my wife and our little daughter.

For example, charity is very important in the Islam, and is one of the Five Pillars of the Faith. If you see a beggar, my father would tell us as small children, it's good to give something, however small. And, if in doubt in a situation, follow the example of the Prophet. When he died, Muhammed's disciples collected many thousands of real examples of his behaviour, known as the Hadith. To Muslims, these illustrations are second only to the Qur'an in their importance. For example, when the Prophet passed a crust of bread on the ground, he stooped, picked it up and left it on a wall, ready for a needy person.

We had been brought up with the moderate face of Islam. My father taught my sisters and I to be wary of the fanatics. 'They are not real Muslims,' he would say. 'They are like boiling milk frothing out from a pan: out of control, a great deal of commotion, but no substance.'

Zohra, who was from a respectable Muslim family, knew better than most the discrepancy between traditional Islam and its newer radical face. She wore makeup and did not veil, although many young Moroccan women do, and she warned of the danger.

'It's for all Moroccans to understand,' she would say often, 'that these radicals are hijacking the Islamic faith. They are nothing to do with Islam, they are not believers, but they pretend to the outside world that they speak for us all!'

Whenever we passed through the shantytown together, Zohra would wave her finger at the mosque.

'They're fanatics!' she would shout, 'they are not real Muslims. The *imam* at the mosque here is a strict one. You must take care.'

'How can you tell?'

THE REASON TO WRITE

'Look at the men around here,' she said, 'they shave their heads and wear long beards! It's all the proof you need.'

One plus point was my family background. It helped to unfasten some of the locks which surround various aspects of Moroccan life. As a Muslim, I was welcomed in mosques, at religious gatherings, and into peoples' homes. Locals would constantly exclaim:

'Tahir is a Moroccan name! You are Moroccan; you are my brother!'

My family, originally from Afghanistan as it is, is descended through the Hashemite branch of The Prophet Muhammed's line, the same lineage as the ruling family of the kingdom.

Exorcizing The Jinn

As the weeks wore on, I grew sick of putting out platters of food for the jinns, sprinkling salt to placate them, and shouting out my name as I entered a room, to warn the spirits that I was coming. I was tired, too, of the locals from the shantytown giving me evil glances as I passed. They all knew of *Dar Khalifa's* supernatural residents. As far as they were concerned the house was uninhabitable, fit only for a sorcerer or, perhaps, a foreigner.

So, one morning, I assembled Layachi and the other guardians, and told them that it was time to bring the co-existence with the jinns to an end. We would have to ask them politely to leave.

There is only one way to rid your house of supernatural forces. You have to employ the *Ganoua*, the so-called 'Devil Dancers'. Like every other foreigner with an interest in Morocco, I had read about them. I had heard the wild tales, the tales of the blood-soaked ceremonies, and I had been told of the terrible things that can happen if the rituals go wrong. Their exorcisms, famous throughout North Africa, involve tumultuous drumming, trances, and frenzied dancing, during which the jinns are sucked from the walls. To find the *Ganoua*, I would have to venture far from

Casablanca, into the High Atlas Mountains, which hang like a snow-capped curtain above Marrakech.

Renovation

At the same time as tackling the jinns, there was the very real problem of renovations, and the making good the paperwork associated with the house.

Zohra explained that Moroccan craftsmen are regarded with the kind of reverence they once were in Europe. As respected people, you have to be very kind and never shout at them or lose your temper, she said, even when the work has gone way over budget and over deadline. Craftsmen, she told me, were divided into a hierarchy, with the stone masons at the top. Their ancestors supposedly built the European cathedrals, and brought Freemasonry to the continent. Even now they are said to guard a secret knowledge, the same that is sacred to Freemasons.

When I told Zohra that I was going to have the spirits exorcized, she seemed pleased.

'Craftsmen are very superstitious around here,' she said, 'and none of them are going to want to work in a house with jinns.'

'Do you believe in jinns?'

Zohra was surprised at the question.

'Of course I do,' she replied, 'everyone does... I have a woman jinn living on my shoulder. She speaks to me in the night.'

One of the first problems to attend to was finding master craftsmen. Locating them can take weeks, and once you have tracked them down, they need extended bouts of coaxing to take on the job. We needed experts in restoring and laying *zelij*, traditional geometric mosaics, as well as others to lay *bejjmat*, terracotta tiles, and someone to treat the walls with *tadellakt*, the marble-dust plaster from Marrakech.

There can be nowhere on earth with such an extraordinary

array of traditional crafts with which to decorate a house, as Morocco. Royal patronage, and the recent boom in tourist homes, have ensured that the ancient systems of apprenticeship endure. Visit any atelier and you find small boys, no older than eleven or twelve, learning techniques which have developed over a thousand years. Each region of the country has its own distinct skills, whether it be in carpet-making, tanning or leatherwork.

The Moroccan Godfather
At the same time as finding the craftsmen and expelling the jinns, I had to solve a land dispute. The well-groomed lawyer had explained there was a 'trivial' legal dispute with a neighbour. When I had signed the papers and paid over the funds, I learned the truth. The disagreement was with two neighbours, both of whom were encroaching on my land. One of the men had already stolen a thousand square metres of what should have been my garden. The hostilities had endured for almost twenty years, and things were now so hostile that, as the lawyer put it:
'The only way to solve the situation is for a little blood to be spilt.'
I asked whose blood that would be.
'The blood of the weakest man,' he sniffed.
With time, the details of the dispute unfolded. A friend of the first neighbour summed him up as 'the Devil incarnate'. I shuddered to think how his detractors described him. I then learned that he was married into the royal family and with such connections he was untouchable. The other neighbour turned out to be godfather of Casablanca's prime gangster family. He had terrorized the city for decades. The guardians were always telling me tales of his adversaries who can now be found all over Casablanca buried in shallow graves. Talk of mafia ruthlessness worried me, but even more worrisome was a scrawled note that

came in the mail one morning. It was a tip-off, which said that my lawyer was also employed by the gangster. The one man whom I had to trust was working for the enemy.

Going Native

Some weeks after our arrival, I found myself taking the chief guardian's advice. He had led me aside and made clear a key point: In Morocco just as you use exorcists to remove troublesome jinns, you are expected to employ the services of a witch to deal with difficult neighbours. In the West I would have been shocked at the idea of using black magic to sort out a troublesome neighbour, but now we were living on Moroccan soil, nothing seemed more sensible. Congratulating myself at having made a full cultural transition, I ventured into the dusty alleys of the shantytown in search of a sorcerer, whose magic could conjure up the wickedest curse in the land.

Moving to Morocco with a small child and another one on the way had been a tremendous gamble. We had invested what little money we had to buy *Dar Khalifa*, and had borrowed thousands of dollars to do the renovations. But the greatest gamble was the emotional one. I'd promised my wife a new future, one filled with justice, freedom and high ideals. Until we arrived to live in Casablanca, I had no idea whether it would work or not. At the same time, our friends and families regarded us as mad, taking a toddler into what some regarded as a terrorist's den.

Like so many parents in Europe and North America, I was willing to gamble, and prepared to anger those close to me, if it meant that my children would be raised in a land, steeped in a rich blend of history, culture and romance.

The Caliph's House

The Caliph's House will chart a year in the life of a writer, seeking to

THE REASON TO WRITE

escape the injustices of rip-off Britain, while renovating a sprawling Moroccan mansion, and freeing it from its evil neighbours and accursed jinns. The book will explore the Art Deco charms of Casablanca, a city trapped by the memory of the Hollywood film, while revealing the underbelly of Moroccan society, with its obsession for the supernatural. The narrative will also chart the trail to the artisans and their traditional crafts, delving into the cultural heartland of Morocco.

Although *The Caliph's House* will not be a travel book as such, there will be travel. While searching for crafts, artisans and the array of other people and things needed to put the house in order, I will venture to the different corners of the Kingdom, among them:

Tangier
If any city surpasses Casablanca in reputation, then it is Tangier. Staring out across the Straits of Gibraltar, it has harboured generations of spies and smugglers, exiles and eccentrics. In the twentieth century, the city became a pleasure dome for the European gay set, welcoming a long list of homosexuals, including Oscar Wilde and Joe Orton and Truman Capote. It was, too, where my grandfather lived out his days, in a small villa on Rue de la Plage.

Fez
The Islamic heart of Morocco, the walled city of Fez is the closest we have to a medieval *Arabian Nights*. Founded in the ninth century as the capital of the Idrisids, it is an overpowering blend of Islamic design and culture, set against a backdrop of labyrinthine passageways, vibrant bazaars, and artisans' workshops. In the backstreets of the medina craftsmen continue to produce the finest quality glazed tiles and metalwork, textiles and leatherwork. For anyone renovating an old Moroccan house, the city is an emporium of craftsmanship and goods.

Marrakech
If Fez is the Islamic heart of Morocco, then Marrakech is its African heart. Lying in the lee of the High Atlas Mountains, nestled on a desert plane, the city's famous central square called *Jema'a al Fna* 'The Place of Death', abounds with water-sellers and storytellers, snake charmers and local medicine men. Marrakech has become a playground for rich Europeans seeking the exotic East, and as a result a revival has taken place in traditional architecture and design. While the finest materials may still be found in Fez, the best craftsmen live in the maze of streets that make up the old city.

The High Atlas Mountains
A jagged line of snow-capped mountains to the south of Marrakech, the High Atlas resemble a desert mirage of some kind. Standing in the furnace-like heat of Marrakech, with the tarmac melting around your feet, you find yourself entranced by the clean cold sweep of peaks. The High Atlas is the highest mountain range in Africa, surpassed in height only by the freestanding Kilimanjaro. They are home to the ancient Berber people, long despised by the Arabs for their pagan traditions, but these days appreciated for their unique crafts, their language and traditions.

The Sahara
The dunes of the Sahara make us realize how feeble we are. The Arabs, who have long-crossed this, the world's greatest desert, regard it as a giant ocean, an ocean of shifting sands. When I first moved to Morocco, a friend told me that I had no hope of ever understanding the place, or the people, if I did not first understand the Sahara. I didn't know what he meant until I had begun to learn of the staunch traditions of the 'blue men' who

THE REASON TO WRITE

cross in dunes with their camels, and have evolved a culture to endure the heat. But, with time, I began to comprehend that these people and their traditions are a bedrock upon which the Kingdom is forged.

Ends

Notes

A selection of notes follows that I wrote for *Hannibal Fogg and the Supreme Secret of Man*.

They were designed to be on hand and to be woven in as and when necessary, as well as to give structure to the story. I stuck with the plot more in *Hannibal Fogg* than in many recent books because there was such a danger I would tie myself in knots. As you will see, the notes are rough and are not designed to be shown to the world as I am doing now.

THE REASON TO WRITE

HANNIBAL FOGG AND THE SUPREME
SECRET OF MAN

FOGG NOVEL NOTES

THE SEVEN QUESTS

The seven components taken from the Alexander Mechanism, and hidden within religions by the Brethren of the Order of Zoraster.

- Christianity   Jacob's Ladder   (Ethiopia)
- Vandal   Hands Of God   (Madras, India)
- Inca (Shuar)   Tumi Dagger   (Amazon, Peru)
- Santeria (Yoruba) Stone Orisha   (Miami, Usa)
- Buddhism   Prayer Wheel   (Miao Keng, China)
- Aboriginal   Blue Diamond   Gem/Heist
                                    (London, UK)
- Taoism   Jade Dragon Mask (Buru, Pacific)

The components themselves have specific powers.
- JACOB'S LADDER: the power to have superhuman hearing
- THE HANDS OF GOD: the power to know what someone is thinking
- TUMI DAGGER: the power to withstand unimaginable pain
- ORISHA STONE: the power to have no fear
- BUDDHIST PRAYER WHEEL: the power of extraordinary dexterity
- THE BLUE DIAMOND: the power to see into the future
- JADE DRAGON MASK: the power to be brought back to life

CHRISTIANITY JACOB'S LADDER
- The ladder that links the Earth and Heaven was symbolic within Christianity. A symbolic ladder was created by the guardians of the Mechanism and hidden in Ethiopia, in the monastery Debra Damo. This is the monastery where you have to be pulled up a sheering cliff face on a leather rope. William has to go to the Septuagint, the earliest form of the Bible, and make the journey there. The ladder, utterly symbolic, is not as one would imagine.
- The component gives the power to have superhuman hearing

VANDAL HANDS OF GOD
- The Hands of God were a Vandal faith object, kept in a special box lined in a rare metal. They had been passed down through centuries and were responsible for the Vandal success in defeating ancient Rome. This Vandal supremacy gives us the term vandalism. And the Vandals were linked to the Aryans of Central Asia. During the 19th century however, the Vandal hands of god were acquired by Madame Blavatsky and were taken to her Theosophical centre in Madras, where they are kept to this day. (Hitler was influenced by the Theosophical Foundation. Fogg had met Hitler of course and warned against him).
- The component gives the power to know what someone is thinking

INCA (SHUAR) TUMI DAGGER
- The sacred ceremonial dagger of the Inca himself. When the Spanish Conquistadores attacked the Incas, they fled into the Madre de Dios jungle to the city of Paititi, and they were eventually attacked by the Shuar, the tribe of headshrinkers. William has to go to the land of the Shuar and take Ayahuasca

THE REASON TO WRITE

with a shaman before the dagger is presented to him.
• The component gives the power to withstand unimaginable pain

SANTERIA (YORUBA)   STONE ORISHA
• The sacred Stone of Orisha had been housed in the Yoruba community in what is Nigeria, for centuries, possibly since the dawn of man. It was the key object in the temple that bore its name. But then in the 1700s, the community was enslaved and taken to the New World. Before they were enslaved, the stone was carefully packed up and taken by the slaves on board, and became a focal point of the new 'Santeria' faith. It was originally taken to the Caribbean, before being transported to a temple in Miami, where it lies today. The guards are aware of the myth that one day a man will come for it. Their rites, blood, sacrifice etc.
• The component gives the power to have no fear

BUDDHISM   PRAYER WHEEL
• The Wheel was captured by the Chinese and hurled into the Miao Keng cave system during the Boxer Rebellion. Hannibal had been in China then and had been unable to retrieve the Wheel. He had studied the Miao Keng, and had mapped the caves, as well as developed a system of equipment to descend into it.
• The component gives the power of extraordinary dexterity

ABORIGINAL   DREAMTIME, GEM/HEIST
• The Aboriginals of the Great Australian Desert had believed that a clear blue diamond was the balance of the world, their world of Dreamtime. They did not regard the stone as valuable as the west does, but valuable for its sacred power.

An Afghan cameleer stole the gem and it was eventually sold to a Maharajah in India. The stone went up for sale at Sotheby's Paris, and was bought by a Russian billionaire, who keeps it at his home in Kensington Palace Gardens. The new owner would never part with it to satisfy William's need. SO William has to steal it. The heist.
- The component gives the power to see into the future

TAOISM   JADE YIN-YANG DRAGON MASK
- Under the ocean in a ruined city. The mask was actually worn by priests in Taoist rites, and were supposed to have magical powers, and allow the wearer to have supernatural powers.
- Can only be accessed when a tsunami strikes. William has just X minutes to run forward as the waters are receding, and then he has to locate the mask and escape before the tsunami strikes full force. Possibly into airship of Foggian invention.
- The component gives the power to be brought back to life

FOGG LINEAGE
- HENRY OF FAUGUS (died 922)
- BENEDICT OF FAUGG (1137-1191)
- HORATIO FOGG (1561-1616)
- ARCHIBAL FOGG (1779-1815) Hannibal's great grandfather, William's great great great great great grandfather
- JOSIAH FOGG (1800-1848) Hannibal's grandfather, William's great great great great grandfather
- URIAH FOGG (1831-1891) Hannibal's father, William's great great great grandfather
- HANNIBAL FOGG (1861-1937 disappeared, presumed dead), William's great great grandfather
- WILFRED FOGG (1888-1940) Hannibal's son, William's great grandfather

THE REASON TO WRITE

- ALEC FOGG (1910-1944) Hannibal's grandson, William's grandfather
- HARRY FOGG (1940-2001) Hannibal's great grandson, William's father
- WILLIAM FOGG (1990-) Hannibal's great great grandson

WILLIAM H. FOGG
BACKGROUND
- William is 20 years old, and a bit of a geek. He lives in San Francisco and has a girlfriend called Emma, who longs for adventure. William himself is quite satisfied to spend his free hours with his postage stamps. And his idea of a good time is rooting through the bins at the local Stamp shop, hoping to find one cent guinea magenta stamp. William has never travelled, or has ever really ever wanted to, but he has experienced the world to postage stamps. And seems to know its history and geography through stamps.
- Money is always a worry, and William is on student loans. He's taking a university degree in European History.
- Emma constantly rattles him questioning why he doesn't go out into the world and experience it, and why he is quite happy just to spend his time peering at his tiny insignificant objects.
- William doesn't realize it at the beginning, but embedded within him at the seeds of greatness. There have been placed there by Hannibal Fogg, who knew William would exist... for Hannibal had seen the future.
- William inside him many of Foggs qualities, a specially with regard to the ideals and values. He gets very worked up with the idea of injustice, is selfless as a person, and is always mindful of charity.

TRAINING
- The Senses: Must learn to heighten his senses, for instance develop echolocation so that he can move in the dark.
- Endure Pain
- Memory: must learn to develop a memory for extreme detail, after seeing a face, or a room for even the shortest moment.
- Training according to French Foreign Legion methods. Fogg had served in the legion after being disgraced. After which he moved to Morocco. The training takes place in Marrakesh.
- Ready for attack day or night.
- Breathing control. It's all about breathing, the most basic function of life.
- Discomfort all the time.

HANNIBAL FOGG
FOGG'S DATES
- Born Tunbridge Wells 2nd January 1861
- Disappeared in Manchuria 16th November 1937

FOGG FIRST HAND CHAPTERS
- We have the Fogg blast chapter, and he ends up holding an object, the thing or the clue that was part of his quest. This links in the next chapter to William holding that object to the same clue, in Hannibal's hand.
- There are chapters of Fogg in place, for example in the Trenches (where Fogg led from the front having assuming a former military position despite his age), or as a tutor to the Tsar's children. We realize later because of a note he's left, or something William finds out, that Fogg was only there in that position to get information which would enable him to locate specific components. These chapters are written as if they are happening right then. There are also notes left by Fogg to

THE REASON TO WRITE

William in particular books etc.
- Hannibal's childhood
- As a private tutor to the Tsar's children
- At Corpus Christi College, Oxford
- At Kitty Hawk with the Wrights
- Duelling with Samurai swords
- Hannibal and the siege of Khartoum
- Hannibal in Damascus with Burton and Jane Digby
- Hannibal and freemasonry, Calcutta
- Hannibal and Aleister Crowley
- Hannibal search for the lost city of Paititi
- Hannibal as a designer, campaign furniture etc
- Hannibal in the trenches
- Hannibal's disgrace
- Hannibal and Greek Magical Papyri
- Hannibal and the Secret Service
- Hannibal and the Order of the White Elephant
- Hannibal and the French Foreign Legion
- Hannibal as a designer of machines
- Hannibal and his curiosities
- Hannibal in the Boxer Rebellion
- Hannibal in India
- Hannibal's quest for the Gold Mines of King Solomon
- Hannibal's quest for the lost treasure of Ahmed Shah Durrani
- Hannibal and his quest for Gilgamesh
- Hannibal's journey in disguise across Central Asia

FOGG AND POSTAGE STAMPS
- In the early days of the Marrakech house, William remembers the story when the Nazis were storming into a Jewish house (remember which movie). The Jewish family frantically searched for a place to hide their money and valuables. Then

one of them has the bright idea of hiding it on the dining table under a newspaper in plain view. i.e. it is the one place that is so obvious that no one will search. And when the house is searched, it goes unnoticed. William looks of the room again. In plain view there is a selection of postage stamps in the frame. They are nothing very special, and William had hardly noticed them before. Suddenly he realizes "he's speaking to me through the stamps". The stamps are a sentence, a set of directions. These lead to another clue, and then another. Hannibal Fogg had made sure that William was passionate about postage stamps. And he uses William's obsession for philately as a tool, a device.

- The weird thing is that in no album that William finds later a house, there is one Stanton was printed long after Hannibal Fogg's disappearance. William imagined that the postage stamp just got mixed in later but now realizes that it was supposed to be there.
- With stamps, Williams sees much more than most of us: taking in the perforation the way the stamp is printed, the ink, and the Post Office cancelling of the stamp. With only a handful of stamps in it, the stamp album William finds is of great interest will stop. It is later found to have a secret pouch, with a letter hidden inside info.
- Through encouraging William to collect postage stamps, without him even realizing it, William has learnt and attention to detail.
- One letter is held in a post restante for William. It's from Hannibal.

FOGG CONTINUITY
- The sense that Hannibal Fogg and his ancestors realized that this great mission could only be accomplished over

generations, themselves divided by centuries. It is part of the selfless notion of striving something for the common good of man rather than the simple personal praise. Hannibal knew that a single lifetime was not long enough to complete the mission, and that it would rely on William to finish the job.

FOGG CURIOSITIES
- During his lifetime Hannibal Fogg collected a vast array of extraordinary objets. These included the severed skull of Leon Trotsky, with the hole in the back with the ice pick went in, and George Washington's rhino-ivory teeth.
- Other oddities:
- A Hand of Glory (a dried and cured hanged man's hand). See Wikipedia
- Shuar shrunken heads and Naga heads with the buffalo horns
- Birdmen textiles
- Ainu religious objects
- Other stuff to mention:
- The Antioch Chalice
- The book of Kells
- The blood of Saint Januarius
- The Cantino Planisphere map
- The Code of Hammurabi

FOGG DISGRACE
- A huge public disgrace. Stripped of his awards and expelled from his clubs. His own family disowned him. His son never spoke to him again. We realize later that it was Fogg himself who engineered the disgrace. It was quite necessary despite being painful in family and professional terms, because it allowed him to devote all his time unnoticed in tracking down the components of the mechanism.

- He was lauded before being disgraced, and then came to learn that by being disgraced, he could concentrate on his life work. It was at this point that he came to live in Morocco in secret.
- During the disgraced Fogg was disowned by his own son, William's great grandfather. The family never mentioned his name except to curse him.
- Collected the boots and shoes of hanged men.
- Following Hannibal Fogg's public disgrace, there was a great purge of his work. During this time, all Foggs writings were hunted down by special commission, and destroyed. This explains why there are no copies of his works at the British Library and the Library of Congress.

THE MIND OF FOGG
- The novel introduces us into the mind of Hannibal Fogg, the pure genius of the man. It's paid out a little at a time, with set ups early on... for example, his investigations into flight and technologies we now have in our world. Fogg had pioneered work in secret in his labs, with no intention of making these breakthroughs public.
- Fogg was not the kind of man who cared about being recognized. So to this end he preferred that others take the credit and that the scientific breakthrough get out there. It's partly for these self-effacing tendencies that Fogg has largely been forgotten. And he allowed himself to be pilloried (and indeed he encouraged it) so that he could work in private, without distraction.
- Fogg's Riad tells us a great deal about Fogg, his obsessions, areas of genius, and the way he worked. As with Hannibal himself, we only get to see the Riad a bit at a time. It's all interlinked, and is very hard to get an idea of the entire

THE REASON TO WRITE

picture. Unlike a western home you can't see the entire structure at one, and that's just as Fogg was.
- Fogg is part Hakim Feroze. A dazzling mind and he's always five steps ahead of everyone else. Sometimes he seems foolish, but like Nasrudin, he's way ahead. He excels in everything he does, always pushes the envelope and NEVER gives a damn what anyone thinks about him. Beyond all else he's selfless.
- Language: Hannibal spoke numerous languages. He had learnt a method of doing so from his friend Richard Francis Burton. Burton taught him how to take a text that one knows very very well, such as the book of the new Testament, and to translate word by word until one has "broken the back of the language". Hannibal knew the founder of Esperanto, and was one of the first people to have mastered it. Hannibal believed that language holds secrets about societies, and that by mastering a language one gains a key to that society.
- Fogg believes that even William must learn and be prepared before he can complete the family quest – to reunite the components for the Alexander mechanism. Preparation, as far as Fogg is concerned, is the foundation of all success.
- Fogg served in the Trenches in Somme, where he knew Wilfred Owen and Graves. He hated war, and after the Great war, he was ever more resolute than ever on the importance of completing the mechanism and turning it to peace.

FOGG AND FRIENDSHIP
- Nothing was so important to Fogg as friendship. He claimed that the bond of friendship was almost sacred.

FOGG AND THE SECRET SERVICE
- Fogg been sent to Germany to set up a network of spies for SIS, reporting directly to C, Smith-Cunningham, because of

his fluent German and knowledge of the country.

FRIENDS OR ACQUAINTENCES OF HANNIBAL FOGG
- Hannibal Fogg had close personal friendships to a lot of notable late Victorian and Edwardian characters. Some of them were:
- Charles Darwin (died 1882)
- Francis Galton (died 1911)
- Aleister Crowley
- Davenport Brothers
- Madame Blavatsky
- Wright Brothers
- Harry Houdini
- Freud
- Roald Amundsen
- T E Lawrence

FOGG DOCUMENTS
- Fogg has left a series of ancient documents, written in old Anglo-Saxon or Latin, which were actually penned by a previous Fogg, centuries before. Members of the Fogg family have through history collected the knowledge of where to find the components. They have documented exactly where each component lies, and have benefitted from the power imbued within each component: example the power of invisibility and so forth. Through time components have in some cases been moved, such as with the Orisha stone.

FOGG FURNITURE
- Campaign furniture made to Fogg's spec on Old Bond Street. Nothing was so important to Fogg as having equipment that could be packed and dismantled at a moment's notice.

THE REASON TO WRITE

- His travelling furniture including a mess carriage, based on Napoleon's field carriage, which was destroyed by fire in 1912 at Madame Tussaud's.
- Fogg loved secret drawers and compartments, and had them built into his tables and desks, along with complete systems of operation.

FOGG INVENTIONS
- Fogg's home is filled with inventions which resemble Heath Robinson creations. From these, William sees Hannibal's genius.
- Fogg invents equipment using contemporary technology. But as discussed, he also made breakthroughs in his lifetime but handed them to others for them to reveal them to the world and to take the credit. For Fogg what was important was the good of humanity, and not the benefit of the individual. He was lauded before being disgraced, and then came to learn that by being disgraced, he could concentrate on his life work. It was at this point that he came to live in Morocco in secret.
- Fogg has developed a primitive form of GPS. Some of the objects are concealed using this strange system. When William learns to use it, he starts finding the objects.
- Aqua-lung, long before Cousteau's system.
- Spy equipment.
- Nerve agent.
- Gun silencer
- A gyroscopically controlled retro Segway.
- Body armour made from spider silk.
- A tea pot with built in thermometer
- A travelling trunk, that has secret compartments, and ways to keep the clothes and other items in perfect shape.
- A steam powered motorbike (did exist in 1904)

FOGG INVESTIGATION
- Richard Matheson a reporter with the London Times newspaper stumbles across the Wikipedia entry for Hannibal Fogg. Intrigued, he starts researching about Fogg the next time he happens to be at the National archives in Kew. He's amazed what he finds. Fogg is a character who was utterly lampooned by society, having been very decorated during his lifetime. Matheson finds that the trail goes cold, the cause key archives are missing. Others are marked classified for centuries, all with no date of declassification. Matheson feels that there was some cover-up within the system, and that Fogg was publicly shamed by the government at the time, possibly as a way of lay hands on his private wealth. Matheson makes a private investigation, which zigzags through the book. Eventually he comes face-to-face with William and fills him in with what he has found. Suddenly, it seems as if Williams does have right to Hannibal's immense private fortune, which has been impounded by the British crown.
- Introduction to Matheson and his finding Hannibal on the Internet
- Matheson noticing Hannibal Fogg's pith helmet on sale at Sotheby's and his renewed interest in Fogg. He was so famous, and then so hated, and has now been all but forgotten.
- Matheson researching about Fogg in the Kew archives
- Matheson finding a mention of Fogg at the Imperial War Museum
- Matheson searching for Hannibal's Equerry
- Matterson finding Hannibal's equerry and the story he tells. The Equerry tells Matheson about the Alexander mechanism and seven components.

654

THE REASON TO WRITE

- More of the equerry's story and the cover-up, the plan to discredit Fogg.
- Matheson tracked down the Marrakech house, and meets William. He gives William a piece of information from the equerry... which allows William to solve the problem of the dragon mask.
- As Matheson leaves the Equerry for the last time, the Equerry is killed.
- Matheson eventually becomes part of the story and saves William's life.

THE ALEXANDER MECHANISM

THE COMPONENTS
- Hannibal Fogg had worked out that the Jade mask could only be retrieved in this tsunami which would fall on a particular day. The timing of the executors contacting Fogg was hinged around this. Hannibal knew that William would have to retrieve the components in order, which would allow him to benefit from their inherent powers. The only way for him to get his hands on the Jade mask would be to use all the powers contained within the other components.
- Fogg specifies that William must keep any of the objects ultra safe because they are powerful in their own right, and he will be hunted for them. But as William goes along he uses the objects' powers to get other objects and to ward away the enemy.
- The specific components each had a special power, whether it be to see into the future, to withstand pain etc. etc.
- Fogg made clear that the objects had travelled over the centuries, and that while some were still to be found in their original place, others had been absorbed into other

655

- faiths. For example, the hands of God were now part of the Theosophical tradition, and to be located in Madras.
- Legend says that when asked in the name of the mechanism, the guardians of the objects readily hand it over. William hardly believes it. The guardians say that they were told that one day, perhaps centuries forward, someone would come and ask for the object.
- As the objects are located, they are left in situ. This is the safest place for them. William somehow knows that he must gather the objects and leave none in their special original place. For it falls to him to gather all seven objects. Hannibal had only managed together the first six, building on the work for previous generations.

POWERS OF THE COMPONENTS
- The power to have superhuman hearing
- The power to know what someone is thinking
- The power to withstand unimaginable pain
- The power to have no fear
- The power of extraordinary dexterity
- The power to be brought back to life
- The power to see into the future

FOGG AND THE MECHANISM
- Just as the mechanism can be used for war, so too can it be used for peace. It's the Fogg family's plan to get the machine working and then use it towards world peace.

THE ENEMY
- Those dedicated to war, to dealing in weapons, and to the letting of blood. Like the Thuggee (devoted to Kali), the enemy are prepared to dig in for years or even generations

to get into a position whereby they can gain power, or information about the components. Like sleeping spies, they are everywhere, embedded. No one can be trusted.
- They kill without any emotion. Children, babies, the old, crippled, anyone. (Kill a child to make a point).
- They all bear a mark a blue birthmark.
- They kill using specific methods. Strangulation with a cheese wire preferred or under the armpit. They are experts. Efficient beyond imagination.
- They have waited for centuries, their sole ambition to gain control of the working mechanism.
- They are everywhere, embedded, ready. No one can be trusted.
- [Suggestion: there are actually two groups of enemy. The first group is trying to get its hands on any of the components, the power imbued within those components. The second group realizes that the Alexander mechanism can only be used once all the components have been found. And they need William arrived to find them... because he and only he can find them, using his family's ancestral knowledge.]
- They are part of an ancestral Order, father and son, going back generations... and they are everywhere. Waiting. Ready. They have been sleeping, poised to gain the Mechanism since the beginning of time. And they will use the mechanism to gain world control, the likes of which humanity has never seen.
- When they kill, the drain the blood of the victim.
- They are William's shadow.
- They kill the manservant and drain his blood

- Quite late on, William realizes that the Grimoire are not trying to kill him. They need him alive, because only he can locate the components. But they are trying to kill people in which he came into contact for another reason. They kill everyone he speaks to, and by communicating with others William knows (realizes later) that he's sentencing them to death).

MISCELLANEOUS SUBJECTS

PLATOMETER
- A device designed the measuring the size and shape of the human skull. Use either Germanen order to ensure that members conforms to the order is Nordic racial ideal. It was also used by the Nazis. Germanen order was powerful between 1912 and about 1922, after which it seemed to disappear or go underground. Johann Albrecht, the grand duke of Mecklenburg was a one-time grandmaster of the order.

VATICAN SECRET ARCHIVES
- The archives located in the Vatican (wiki) were removed from the Vatican Library by Pope Paul V in 1758, and kept closed until the late 19th century, when Pope Leo XIII opened them. (FOGG was the first outsider to gain access)
- 52 miles of shelving. 35,000 volumes in the selective catalogue. The oldest surviving document dates back to the eighth century. The archive includes letters from Michelangelo and King Henry VIII of England's request for a marriage annulment.
- Documents tend to be made public after 75 years.
- An even more secret archive is kept at the apostolic penitentiary also within the Vatican.. This material is never made public and no one is allowed access it.

THE REASON TO WRITE

- Full details of the archive and access are found on wiki.

PHILATELY
- Philately as the study of postage stamps, as opposed to the collection of postage stamps but the sake of collecting. It is possible to be philatelist Without actually owning a single stamp.

INVISIBILITY
- Before sunrise on a Wednesday, take seven black beans and the head of the dead man. Put one bean in the head's mouth, two in its ears and two in the eyes. Probably putting the last two in the nostrils. Mark a symbol only known to yourself on the forehead. Then bury their head in the ground in the face turned up to nine days. Each day before Sunrise, water the head with brandy. On the eighth morning spirit will come and ask if he can do the watering for you. Ask him what symbol you have inscribed on the head. If he knows, then it is the real spirit of the head, and is into deceiving spirit. On the ninth morning you will find that the beans have ripened. Take one at a time and put it in your mouth. Look in a mirror. If the spell has worked you will be invisible. When you want to become visible again remove the bean from your mouth. Don't swallow them.

> From: *Grimoire Verum*

INFANTICIDE
- In India newborn female babies are traditionally drowned in a cauldron of warm milk. Erukum sap can be mixed in with the milk.

WEAPONS

- Nunchaku (twin truncheons connected with a chain)
- The same weapon is never used twice (Mossad technique). Because repetition reduces the act of surprise.
- Fogg had a Nagant M1895 Russian revolver which he had played with tsarist officers in 1900. Russian Roulette for details on this weapon and why it was used.

BUNGEE JUMPING

- Pentacost Island, where vines are used in the Naghol festival... vines tied to the ankles. There is greater danger if the feat is done in the dry season when the vines are drier and therefore less elastic. People jump from tall towers in the hope of having a good yam harvest.

KILLING

- Only strike when you can see the whites of their eyes.
- Never kill with rage because you will miss. Channel the energy of your soul.
- Choose your moment well.
- Keep morale high.
- Breathe right. It's all about the breathing.

POSTAGE STAMP INFORMATION

- The stamp album is a map. The clue is the stamp in the series which is missing.
- Penny Black stamp is came into circulation in 1840, and with the first adhesive postage stamps in existence. More than 68 million stamps were printed, and they are not tremendously rare at the moment. They tended to survive, because envelopes were not used so often as they are now, which meant that the stamp with glued onto the reverse of

the letter, and so of the letters survived, the postage stamp would have survived as well.
- The rarest postage stamp is regarded as the British Guiana one cent magenta. Only one example is that exist. See the Wikipedia entry. Wiki entry on the 1 c Magenta: 'It was discovered in 1873, by 12-year-old Scottish schoolboy Vernon Vaughan in the Guyanese town of Demerara, amongst his uncle's letters. There was no record of it in his stamp catalogue, so he sold it some weeks later for a few shillings to a local dealer, N.R. McKinnon. After that, the price escalated. It was bought by a succession of collectors before being bought by Philippe la Rénotière von Ferrary in the 1880s for US$750. His massive stamp collection was willed to a Berlin museum. Following Ferrary's death in 1917, the entire collection was taken by France as war reparations following the end of World War I. Arthur Hind bought it during the series of fourteen auctions in 1922 for over US$36,000 (reportedly outbidding three kings, including King George V), and it was sold by his widow for US$40,000 to a Florida engineer. In 1970, a syndicate of Pennsylvanian investors, headed by Irwin Weinberg, purchased the stamp for $280,000 and spent much of the decade exhibiting the stamp in a worldwide tour. John E. du Pont bought it for $935,000 in 1980. Today it is believed to be locked away in a bank vault, while its owner serves a 30-year sentence for murder.'
- Hannibal Fogg was a leading member of the Royal Philatelic Society in London, established in 1869. Hannibal had been awarded the Tapling Medal by the society.

ANTIKYTHERA MECHANISM
- Recovered in 1901 by sponge divers. Thought to date to 150-

100 BC. Similar mechanisms are not known to have been created for at least another thousand years. The mechanism is in advanced form of analogue computer. It uses as many as 72 gears and display faces, and was thought to work out information such as solar eclipses and when the Olympic Games must be held.
- 1978 Jacques Cousteau dived the site but found no more remains. Meanwhile, X-ray equipment has been used to study the internal structure of the mechanism.

ANCIENT BATTERY
- The so-called Baghdad battery was discovered in 1936 in Mesopotamia. They consist of terracotta jars 5 inches high containing a copper cylinder and an iron rod. The batteries are regarded as an early kind of galvanic cell, which would be fuelled with acid, perhaps lemon juice. The batteries pre-date Alessandro Volta 1800 invention of the electrochemical cell by more than 1000 years.

BARBIER, NIGHT WRITING
- Charles Barbier, a captain under Napoleon, devised a method of writing that could be read in darkness, known as Night Writing. It was devised for soldiers to pass secret messages from one to another in total darkness in battle. The system of Braille was heavily in influenced by Night Writing. Louis Braille had learned it from Barbier and went on to simply and refine it. Braille himself had stabbed himself in the eye each three years old, with an awl, in one of his father's tools. His other eye went blind through sympathetic ophthalmia.

RED SWASTIKA SOCIETY
- Founded in 1922 as a charitable Association based on

THE REASON TO WRITE

Buddhist values. The swastika of course is a Buddhist symbol and a Hindu one. It supposedly had about 10 million members by 1937. The society's goals with philanthropy, poor houses, soup kitchens, and general social relief.
- After the Nanking massacre, the society stepped in to help with burials. At its height the society had offices in London and Paris and Tokyo, and its professors spoke Esperanto.
- The red swastika society continues today, with schools in Singapore, Taiwan, and other parts of the world where there is a Chinese diaspora.
- The swastika it is used to represent the eternal existence of Tao.
- Link the society to finding the jade mask.

ESPERANTO
- Created in 1887 by Doktoro Esperanto, the pseudonym for L L Zamenhof. Esperanto means "one who hopes". The founders main idea was to create an international language which could promote peace and understanding between cultures. For over a century between 100,000 and 2 million people spoke Esperanto, although there has never been a country that has adopted it as its native language. Google offers an Esperanto version, and Wikipedia has an archive in Esperanto as well. It appears that Esperanto is a good medium through which one can learn other languages. Hitler had clamped down on Esperanto, which he says was used by the international Jewish community to spread evil. Esperanto speakers targeted especially in the Holocaust. And after initially welcoming the language, Jozef Stalin exiled or murdered speakers of the language.
- There is one university in the world which offers instruction in Esperanto: the Akademio Internacia de la Sciencoj in San

Marino, Founded in 1988. (See Wikipedia).

VANITAS PAINTINGS
- A painting which includes great symbolism, usually a form of still life, very popular in the 16th and 17th centuries especially in Holland.
- Paintings in the style meant to remind us of the meaningless of life. They tend to include skulls, which remind us that life comes to an end, or rotting fruit. Hannibal uses these pictures to instruct William about symbolism.

SECRET SERVICE
- SIS: Secret Intelligence service, Known within the service as BOX 850, i.e. from old post office box number.
- From Wiki, William Melville: 'In 1901 he worked with Gustav Steinhauer of the German Secret Service to thwart a plot against the Kaiser during the state funeral of Queen Victoria. In June 1900 Melville met future stage magician Harry Houdini when he came to Scotland Yard to showcase his abilities as an escapologist. When Houdini released himself easily from the police handcuffs, Melville befriended him and reputedly learned lock picking.'
- Check out the elusive G-SECTION

LITTLE AMERICA (Cold War)
- Located near the town of Winnitz, in the Ukraine. Exact replica of an American city complete with drugstores and department stores, were the only language spoken is English. US dollars of the currency and US newspapers. KGB spies spent up to five years there before training graduates were sent to the United States.

THE REASON TO WRITE

MENELIK II
- The Emperor of Abyssinia try to preserve his health by regularly consuming chapters of the Bible. In 1913 having had a stroke he ate the book of Kings of a heavy Egyptian Bible. He dropped dead soon after bowel obstruction. Menelik had heard of the electrocution method in use in the United States. In 1880 Auburn State Prison, New York, used an electric chair for the first time. Menelik wanted one. He ordered three electric chairs from the United States. He didn't want Abyssinia to be left behind. The only problem was that Abyssinia did not have an electrical supply. He only realized when the chairs have been unpacked. Legend has it that Menelik, unfazed, turned electric chairs into thrones.

MATA HARI
- Really called Magaretha Zelle, The daughter of a Dutch shopkeeper. Taken to India soon after marriage to Randolph MacLeod. She became a dancing woman supposedly never exposed her breasts during dancing, possibly because they had been bitten off by MacLeod in a fit of jealousy. They had met through blind matrimonial advertisement.

PYKRETE
- Eccentric British inventor Geoffrey Pyke was made director of programmes under Mountbatten. He developed a new compound from ice and wood-pulp, when frozen and is 12 times stronger than concrete and very hard to melt. Very little energy had to be used to keep it frozen, as the woodpulp formed an insulator. Named Pykrete, after Pyke. Churchill and Mountbatten loved the idea of creating a massive 2000 foot long Pykrete battleship, weighing as much as 2,000,000 tonnes. Thought it would be unsinkable against torpedo. It

665

would be kept frozen by inserting a pipe through the hole. It was an idea to use such battleships to attack enemy ports spraying them with simple cold water, shrouding them in ice. Plans went ahead very far. Whole strategies using the ships were devised. 1000 ton unit tested in Canada worked extremely well. But suddenly and strangely the plans were shelved.
- Suggest: the idea was originally invented by Fogg.

MUMMY MEDICINE
- After the fall of the Egyptian empire, the Christians soon dominated along with the Arabs. Most mummies that were collected by the Arabs were used as pagan symbols, while the Christians cast aside the bodies. The Arabs, who learned of Ancient Egyptian enchantment, saw the mummies as tools of magic and medicinal purposes. Used as medicine, the mummy powder or mummy oil was to be applied externally or taken internally. These false superstitions led to many thousands of mummies to be destroyed. The Europeans imported mummies by the ton, and collected oils from boiled mummy bodies. This oil, which was skimmed off the top of the water, was used to stop bruising and was used to cure a variety of disorders. Many of the monarchs relied upon it. Although used as medicinal purposes by Europeans and Arabs, the Americans used the linen for paper -- the material used in wrapping the mummy. The cholera epidemic broke our soon after and it was seemingly reported that the paper was the cause. Production was halted.

KRIS
- Krisses were worn every day and at special ceremonies, with heirloom blades being handed down through successive

generations. Yearly cleanings, required as part of the spirituality and mythology around the weapon, often left ancient blades worn and thin. In everyday life and at events, a man usually only wore one kris. In many parts of Malaysia and Indonesia, the kris was the choice weapon for execution. The specialized kris, called an executioner's kris, had a long, straight, slender blade. The condemned knelt before the executioner, who placed a wad of cotton or similar material on the subject's shoulder/clavicle area. The blade was thrust through the padding, piercing the subclavian artery and the heart. Upon withdrawal, the cotton wiped the blade clean.

SHOE LASTS
- The Worshipful Company of Cordwainers... one of the livery companies of the city of London, which were given the right to trade in 1272, and received a royal charter in 1439. Lasts are made from very hard wood, which does not expand when wet leather is placed on them.

DEATH BY A THOUSAND CUTS
- Slow slicing, or death by/of a thousand cuts, was a form of execution used in China from roughly 900 AD to its abolition in 1905. According to apocryphal lore, língchí began when the torturer, wielding an extremely sharp knife, began by putting out the eyes, rendering the condemned incapable of seeing the remainder of the torture and, presumably, adding considerably to the psychological terror of the procedure. Successive rather minor cuts chopped off ears, nose, tongue, fingers, toes, and such before proceeding to grosser cuts that removed large collops of flesh from more sizable parts, e.g. thighs and shoulders. The entire process was said to last three days, and to total 3,600 cuts. The heavily carved

bodies of the deceased were then put on a parade for a show in the public.

CARGO CULTS
1. New Hebridean islands, where Fogg did bungee jumping with vines wrapped around his ankles.
2. From MMM: 'Cargo cults are generally thought to have started sometime around the 1880s in Fiji, and since then the pattern has remained roughly the same. Out of nowhere as it were Prophet appears predicts imminent salvation, which may take the form of the islanders' ancestor is returning on a ship... a ship that is also loaded with consumer goods like refrigerators and radio sets, desks and furniture and he orders various kinds of ritual observances including such activities is building a warehouse or a jetty to receive the goods.

MISCELLANEOUS SUBJECTS
- Sedlec Ossuary, Czech Republic
- Poison Arrow Frogs
- Skeleton dealers of Calcutta
- Godmen's tricks (sewing lemons, levitation, hibernation, eating glass)
- Harmonograph
- The Golden Section
- Sacred geometry
- Homunculus (created man), Arabic: Takwin
- Elixir of Life
- Madame Blavatsky
- Penis sheathes
- Opium pipes
- Theosophy
- Flying Ointment (datura)

THE REASON TO WRITE

- Cap of Invisibility
- Tree of Life
- Borojoa, Amazonian aphrodisiac
- Cannibalism
- Harlequin
- Spink
- Order of the White Elephant
- St. Francis of Assisi
- Cryptography
- Shape shifting
- Steganography
- Concealment device (e.g. hollowed out book)
- Lacquerware
- Black Ops (CIA)
- CIA SPECIAL ACTIVITIES DIVISION (SAD)
- CIA MEMORIAL WALL at Langley
- Evil Eye
- Taboo
- North American Ghost dance
- Kris
- Talismans
- Circumcision
- Medusa
- Sin Eater
- Snake Handlers, Appalatia
- Shaman's Drum
- Dwarfs
- Whirling Dervishes, ecstasy
- Fogg's patented metronome
- Eclipse
- Pitt-Rivers
- Naga Headhunting

- ESP
- Visual Memory
- Fakirs (hardships)
- Salamander (living in fire)
- Skoptsy (Russian sect 18th century)
- Judgement Day
- Jacob's Ladder
- Thuggee
- Trance
- Immortality
- Initiation
- Cicatrization
- Suttee
- Mana (Polynesia)
- Mandrake
- Automatic writing
- Davenport brothers
- Dead Sea Scrolls
- Hell Fire Club
- Death Masks
- Phrenology
- Jinn
- Death Mask
- Greek Magical Papyri
- Hunterian Museum
- Secret Service Bureau
- Comte de St. Germain
- Count Cagliostro
- 1908 Summer Olympics, London
- 1912 Titanic
- 1888 Jack the Ripper

THE REASON TO WRITE

MORE MISCELANEOUS

CODE IN THE NOVEL
- Entire random pages of the novel are taken up with numbers and letters. There is a secret encoded into the novel, an upper level. In the same way that Dan Brown had replaced at least one page number in Da Vinci Code with XX or something... I'm thinking of having at least one code hidden in the novel. Maybe on one page all the letter 'e's are replaced by a 4... something like that.

PLOT TWISTS
- Ethiopia
  - Fogg's secret base in Addis Ababa. Descend down through an ultra-narrow passage in the middle of the city. Met by Fogg's friend, now very elderly.
  - Ethiopia: The Afar's Danakil tribe chase William because they all want a set of white testicles to hang round their neck. It's the ultimate object of magical power for them.
  - Mines at Shakiso, William sees ladders, but it's a red herring. His guide is killed and his blood drained.
  - William and Emma flee, for Lalibela.
  - Attacked at Lalibela by albino warriors. William realizes that they are not trying to kill him – but Emma. He tells her to go back to the US. But then realizes it's far too dangerous. The genii's out of the bottle. The only safe place for her is to stay by his side.
  - Civil war in Ethiopia and the stakes are raised yet again.

- India
  - Battle elephants charging forwards, with burning torches tied to their backs.

- At the poste restant there's a letter for William, from Hannibal Fogg.
- Playing chess for his life, William stands in for the white king. As the pieces are taken, an executioner steps forward to behead them. Board drenched in blood.
- Under Madras there is another city. An underground civilization existed there 4000 years ago. William uses the GPS to get the entry point. It's in the KFC downtown. Fogg has left a package for him there.

- Peru
  - Rome: William had instructions to go to the Crypt of the Popes, in the Catacomb of Callixtus. He stumbles into a torch-lit ceremony. In the catacomb he sees an image of the Alexander Mechanism. It's what Fogg had lured him there for.
  - Emma poisoned. William has to get the antidote.
  - William is taken by the Shuar as their Messiah, when he asks for the Tumi dagger. They won't let him leave.
  - William has to undergo a wild feast, including live snakes, tarantula, masato, and a meal of insects, and poison arrow frogs.
  - Antiquity thieves try to get their hands on the Tumi. They switch it with a fake and William has to get the original back.

- USA
  - William cashes a hoard of gold bullion that's been left by Fogg in a drop. He asks for cash, fifties, but the clerk calls the manager. They encourage him to open an account. It turns out that the gold is worth $2 million. It's all spent however. Fogg knew that gold would always appreciate.

THE REASON TO WRITE

When William cashes the bullion (which is marked with a strange symbol), a faceless clerk crosses the street and calls a CIA number from a payphone.
- William swaps the original Orisha stone with a fake... he's had it prepared specially. No one ever notices as they're all too tranced out.

- China
  - Something has been entrusted in a pawn shop for William.
  - Emma stays behind and a beautiful woman seduces William.
  - Opium den: Fogg's opium pipe that's a blowpipe.
  - William plays Russian Roulette.
  - William parachutes down into the Miao Keng cave system. The canopy of the parachute is hexagonal, Fogg's own design. It's weird, and William's concerned at the strange shape. But he realizes a hexagon on purpose, to fit through the hexagonal aperture of the cave bottom.
  - When jumping with the parachute, William pulls the right toggle by mistake. The canopy collapses. He ends up on a ledge, and has to rearrange it, and jump again, narrowly escaping death. As he descends, the canopy drops its own flares to light the path below.
  - William has been given instructions to use the Fogg canoe, and jump into the river. What river? He sees it... it comes in a raging pulse every 26 minutes. It flows at 200 mph. But there are fresh water crocodiles in it, and reptiles clinging to the top of the cave. He illuminates the way, and comes out 1000 miles away.

- London
  - William notices an early microdot on one of the stamps.

- William gets Birdie, a dodgy pal of his in San Francisco to tell him how to rob a safe. The pal has been set up earlier on. He explains what gear to get from a DIY store, and how to do the heist.
- William takes the Z-Grill Franklin stamp to London where he plans to sell it to Stanley Gibbons. But he loses it. Turns out that it's put on an envelope and mailed or something.
- William has to access a package left for me at the now disused British Museum tube stop in London.
- William goes to Lobb, the bootmaker, and is given Hannibal Fogg's shoe lasts. They are packaged and waiting for him. He asks when they were made ready. 'In 1924, Sir'. They had been made for Fogg by the Worshipful Company of Cordwainers.
- The heist: William and Emma pretend to be guests to the billionaire's party. It's a fundraiser and William is in with the cause. He breaks into the bedroom, and opens the special safe using Fogg's safe-cracking device. The diamond isn't there. Just then he realizes that the mistress of the billionaire is wearing it around her neck. He has to seduce her using a potion that Fogg had brought back from the jungle.

- Pacific
  - William has been told to stand at a certain grid location and wait at a certain time. He does so, can't understand what Hannibal had meant. Then, all of a sudden, the tide sweeps back. A fisherman says it's weird because it is time for high tide. William uses Fogg's buggy (hover-machine) to zoom forward, towards where the city lies.
  - Suddenly he hears the roar of the ocean approaching.

THE REASON TO WRITE

The Fogg machine warns him how many seconds he has before the water will strike. He's never going to make it. But saved by a Foggian survival bubble, which blasts to the surface and FLIES.

- Empty Quarter
  - The components are heisted from William
  - Traps in the system that leads to the chamber deep under the sands. Once William gets in there, he's buried alive. No route out.
  - They put the components into the mechanism, but it doesn't work. Then, wham!
  - The mechanism has another mechanism to protect it. Pull the wrong lever and all hell breaks lose.

EQUIPMENT
- A cigarette lighter what has a cheese wire and other tools (William shuns it at first as he doesn't smoke).
- Special light weight body armour made from a spider's aciniform silk.
- Only one piece of Fogg's equipment has a brand name. William Googles it and to his surprise it has a website. And it appears to be waiting for him, even though the internet was devised decades after Fogg's disappearance.
- Enigma machine that Fogg's created.
- Hermetically sealed chamber
- X-ray camera
- Clockwork GPS device
- Steam-powered Segway hovercraft/jetski

Godman

TWELVE YEARS AGO I had an idea for a novella about a British stage magician of Indian descent whose life collapses in on itself, starting off when a magic trick goes spectacularly wrong.

The notion for the story came about through my own training as an apprentice to an Indian magician, which I published as a travel book, *Sorcerer's Apprentice*. During the twists and turns of that period of my life, I got to know more about the feats of stage magic performed by so-called godmen than almost anyone else. One day, while on a long bus journey through Argentina, I mapped out the basis for the novella. For eleven years the synopsis sat in a file, as so many of my ideas currently lie – waiting to be taken out and turned into a book.

I've long wanted to create a series of novellas looking at certain ideas and themes – stories that would range from about twenty to forty thousand words. A few months ago, when I'd finished writing *Travels With Nasrudin*, I dug out the plan for *Godman* and got down to work.

Getting the start point in my head as firmly as possible is always very important to me, and that's what I did with *Godman*. I imagined my protagonist, Harry Singh, in great detail, so much so that I could hear him, see him, even smell him. I knew what his family was like, the trials and tribulations of his life, and what dreams filled his head.

THE REASON TO WRITE

Once I had him sketched out in a way that worked for me, as the person who was entrusted to tell his tale, I scoped out his sidekick.

Placing the synopsis on my desk, I closed my eyes, imagined I was at the cinema, and that the opening titles for *Godman* had just come and gone, leaving me in the Blackpool Grand Theatre, where Harry Singh, AKA The Great Maharaja Malipasse, had just strode onto the stage.

Godman is forty thousand words, and took ten days of writing. In that time I deviated monstrously from the original storyline. But the fact I didn't keep to my original plan didn't matter to me at all. What did matter was that the storyline got the blood rushing through me as though I was on a wild rollercoaster of absolute and unadulterated fun.

What follows here is the original plan for *Godman*, and the opening pages – all of it in an uncorrected and unedited state. I'm presenting them to show how the original story was mapped out, and how I got started. As you'll see if you eventually read the finished book, the final version changed completely from what I originally had in mind.

GODMAN

Original Plot Structure

- Harry Singh is a weak, weedy stage magician, who does tricks at children's parties in Blackpool. Although proud of his technique, and enthusiastic as a magician, he is the laughing stock of his family, who are all entrepreneurs. They're all much more successful than him, all of them entrepreneurs, with cash and carry's, car dealerships, and mini cab firms.
- Harry gets more and more pressure from his family to settle down and to join the family firm – Singh Bros. They are horrified that he likes English girls, and they want him to go to India to get set up with a wife. A list of candidates is shown to him. They're all dreadful. Most of all though Harry doesn't want to settle down. He wants to be the next big thing as a magician, an Asian Paul Daniels. He's always getting new tricks and trying to perfect them, and do them on his relatives and friends.
- One day his family trick him into coming to India, to Delhi, to a wedding. It's his first time in India. He knows the culture and the language but doesn't know the place. It's all amazing to him. He realizes soon that it's actually his wedding he's coming to. The bride is his cousin, a gross girl who's the size of a bus. 'Keep the blood in the family,' they all say. Harry hadn't understood why everyone was congratulating him and being so nice. The night before the wedding, he escapes. He doesn't know what to do.
- He sees a man on a street corner in Connaught Place doing magic tricks. He's a beggar and no one's giving him any cash, despite the fact that he's really good. Harry is amazed by modern India, confused but amazed – especially by the levels of life. He meets a backpacker called Marek and they

discuss India. Harry is Indian but doesn't feel at home there. The backpacker is Swiss but he's gone totally native. They get on really well. Marek has heard about the Kumbh Mela, and talks Harry into going with him.
- They take a train to Varanasi, where they see the burning Ghats, and then to Allahabad, where millions of people are arriving. We get the story of the Kumbh Mela and what it means to people, and we see them, all many of people.
- Marek bathes in the Ganges and is totally taken in by the mysticism of it all. As he bathes and clears his sins, Harry goes around the Juna Akhara. He meets an American Baba there, and sees the various Nagas. Then, suddenly, he sees the equivalent of the Sai Mass sect. He learns about them, and she sees Sai Maa do a magic trick – one that he can perform in his sleep.
- Later, Harry's showing Marek a magic trick, because they have seen a Kali godman with burning camphor on his tongue. Harry lies down on the ground and does an amazing trick. A crowd immediately gathers (Harry's eyes are closed), and when he opens them, there's a pile of money. He can't believe it, exclaiming to Marek that it's more money than he ever made as a magician in Blackpool.
- Harry can't stop about the trick he did the day before. Chatting it over with Marek, he decides to have another go, so as to earn some quick cash for lunch. He does some tricks and the crowd gets very excited. They cover him in marigold necklaces and give loads of money. But then, laughing it off, he shows them how the tricks are done. The crowd gets angry and demand their money back. He can't understand why. Someone explains: It's because they thought you were a real god'. He later watches the kali godman doing his tricks and he's given respect, veneration and cold hard cash.

- The next day, Harry went back to watch the Sai Maa equivalent, with her droves of foreigners, and she spots a man in a side room doing a magic trick – materializing objects. The person he's with is in shadow. Later, he watches Sai Maa do the same materialization in front of a thousand people. He puts two and two together, realizing that the man was a magician. The next day he sees the magician again and strikes up a conversation. It emerges that he, Mr Vakil, teaches simple stage magic and theatrics to godmen. He's quite open about it. Vakil invites Harry to come to his magic camp.
- Leaving Marek, and the Kumbh Mela, Harry travels to the magic camp, taking a train through India. The camp is in Jaipur, Rajasthan. Harry's amazed and wowed by it all. He arrives at the magic camp and is imitated as an apprentice. Vakil sets out what he will learn, and how he will learn it. He will learn the tricks and the knowhow to set himself up as a godmen. He explains that he only came to just have a look, but Vakil talks him into signing on. He's told he has amazing skills already and that for him the sky's the limit.
- Harry meets the other pupils, and begins his apprenticeship with menial chores. After that, he progresses with rudimentary tricks and with learning to observe. Vakil is very firm, but reveals all kinds of bits of information that can be used. Meanwhile we get the stories of the other initiates, with whom he is bonded by a solemn vow of fraternity.
- Before he can graduate from the camp, Harry has to set himself up as a small-time godman in and get various things from the disciples – adoration, money etc. The initiates are sent to all corners of the country to begin this phase of their studies. Harry travels to Bombay and gets a cheap guest house room. He gets the idea of renting a golden costume for

himself, and quickly sets about by getting a small-time name for himself by using a small repertoire of tricks and Vakil's advice.
- Harry goes from having no devotees to having a hundred or so. He gets a call from Vakil, telling him to come for graduation from magic camp, but he refuses, saying that he doesn't need the camp or Vakil any more. He meets an Indian guy who regards him totally as a deity, and this guy – M K Thackur – helps Harry in every way, as his lackey.
- Harry goes from strength to strength and he gets his first couple of foreigners and gets some media attention for a particularly amazing trick, e.g. Levitation. We get more of Harry Houdini here, and Harry develops his tricks, by studying illusions done by David Blaine and others.
- Then one day Marek is brought to the ashram that Harry has just established. He can't believe it and they have a poignant exchange. Marek knows that it's all just illusion and he castigates Harry for passing it off as real magic of a deity. The big point is that Harry is showing himself to the world, even to his close disciples, as a deity. Marek gets heated and is going to expose Harry, but then Harry shows him the stash of cash. He's onboard as Harry's number one devotee.
- The step it up a gear and the ashram gets a whole lot more organized. It starts Facebook and Twitter pages, gets on Wikipedia and other online pages. Journalists start to interview Harry and Marek explains that the last thing he wants is to be so accessible. The important thing is to say that Harry is meditating or in a trance. They develop all kinds of special phrases for their fraternity, and neither Harry nor Marek can be replaced.
- And at the same time, they develop much more of a structure for daily activities. They include dharshans and prayer

sessions, breathing, laughter and humour. Marek starts having a sleazy time with the girls and so does Harry. They can't help themselves.
- One day the Rationalists turn up. We have seen them before, but now they have trained their sights on Harry. They expose his tricks, but he manages to out-trick them, performing one that they can't explain.
- All his spare time, Harry is practicing tricks and learning prayers and other nonsense to spout. He gets his first bit of international publicity when a celebrity from Hollywood who's visiting India unexpectedly comes to pray before him. Suddenly he gets massive more attention and this is the beginning of the next stage.
- Harry goes from having a few hundred followers to thousands. They begin to lavish him with gifts – cars, jewellery, and bequests of land. They offer him all manner of things and in return he cures them. Sometimes Harry has pangs of guilt but they soon melt away when he realizes the kind of wealth they're talking about. He opens a Swiss bank account and Marek is still very much in control, and the two are good friends.
- Gradually the cult begins to snowball, and grows exponentially. As more high-powered people find the Harry cult, more and more climb aboard. They include A-list Hollywood and Bollywood actors, politicians etc. The latter are eager for Harry to endorse their campaigns, and help him siphon cash out of the country without being investigated. Marek is the only person other than Harry who knows it's all a sham. Vakil arrives but is taken off the premises. He prophesies that it'll all end badly for Harry. Even Harry's family are kept at an arm's distance when they start arriving, and try to cash in.
- Harry, Marek and a handful of others are invited to stay

THE REASON TO WRITE

with the A-list devotee in Hollywood. It assures them huge attention and an appearance on CNN. Something happens to Harry which makes him actually think that he is divine. (He's almost hit by a car but escapes injury). To his devotees it's further proof that he's a living god.

- Harry has a love-in in a New York public place and during the event he's bequeathed a huge ranch in Wyoming. Marek talks him into forgetting about India for now, and concentrating on the American following.
- The wealth keeps coming in massive amounts, with the cult really establishing itself firmly as the leading Free Love Cult. People are handing over vast amounts of money, which is being laundered in a variety of ways – including buying cruise ships (because they're off-shore). There are TV-rantings and online messages, and Paypal and Marek's even are selling his bedsheets on eBay.
- A plot to kidnap Harry is thwarted and it's found to be none other than his own family behind it. At the same time the Rationalists come back with the vengeance and publish masses of dirt on Harry, but most of it slides off. During the various phases, Harry changes the colour of his clothing – blue, red, violet etc. By now, the power has gone firmly to his head, Harry starts to criticize Marek, which causes the start of the fault lines.
- There's an assassination attempt, and Thackur is killed in the attempt. The shooting terrifies harry and brings him and Marek back together. All the while there are behind the scenes plans to buy timeshare homes and endless chunks of the Brazilian jungle (either as a cult base or because it'll soon be urban landscape). And Marek starts using the Mafia to sell the vast amounts of stuff that is given to Harry.
- After the assassination attempt they move into an ultra-high-

end building, with stun gas, blast capability and computer screens which zip up out of the floor. It's like NASA Ground Control. Techie guys are brought in to run the whole thing, although they are devotees in awe of Harry like everyone else.
- The cult gets expelled from the United States and are forced to leave everything behind. Harry can't bear to just walk away, but Marek reminds him that it's what the real deity would do. They are refused entry back into India (Harry can't believe that India would ever refuse anyone). And no other countries will take them. They fly from country to country in their 10 Boeing 747s, but no one will take them (or even allow them to land). Finally they are offered sanctuary in Namibia, if they deposit $100 million in cash and keep the funds in the country indefinitely.
- In Namibia, the entire cult begins to unravel. Marek and Harry are at each other's throats and Harry accuses Marek for embezzling masses of funds. They start fighting hand to hand. The fight is seen by the devotees, which take Marek away. They're about to kill him, when Marek saves himself by doubting Harry's real deity status to the guy entrusted to kill him.

Finis

A REQUEST

If you enjoyed this book, please review it on your favourite online retailer or review website.

Reviews are an author's best friend.

To stay in touch with Tahir Shah, and to hear about his upcoming releases before anyone else, please sign up for his mailing list:

✉ http://tahirshah.com/newsletter

And to follow him on social media, please go to any of the following links:

🐦 http://www.twitter.com/humanstew

📷 @tahirshah999

f http://www.facebook.com/TahirShahAuthor

▶ http://www.youtube.com/user/tahirshah999

Ⓟ http://www.pinterest.com/tahirshah

g https://www.goodreads.com/tahirshahauthor

http://www.tahirshah.com

www.ingramcontent.com/pod-product-compliance
Lightning Source LLC
Chambersburg PA
CBHW032055230426
43662CB00035B/305